*f***P**

The Influentials

Ed Keller and Jon Berry

THE FREE PRESS

New York   London   Toronto   Sydney   Singapore

THE FREE PRESS
A Division of Simon & Schuster Inc.
1230 Avenue of the Americas
New York, NY 10020

A Lark Production

For information about special discounts for bulk purchases,
please contact Simon & Schuster Special Sales:
1-800-456-6798 or business@simonandschuster.com

Manufactured in the United States of America

10   9   8   7   6   5   4   3   2   1

Library of Congress Cataloging-in-Publication Data
Keller, Edward B., 1955–
   The influentials / Ed Keller and Jon Berry.
      p. cm.
   Includes index.
   ISBN 0-7432-2729-8 (hc) — ISBN 0-7432-2730-1 (pbk.)
      1. Social action—United States. 2. Leadership—United States. 3. Social influence.
4. Social participation—United States. 5. Civic leaders—United States.
I. Berry, Jonathan L. II. Title.
HN65 .K43 2003
303.3'4—dc21   2002034671

ISBN 0-7432-2729-8

To Karen, Isabel, and Meredith
—Ed Keller

To my parents, Norma and Gene Berry
—Jon Berry

The Influentials

T HIS IS A BOOK ABOUT influence in America. More specifically, it's about people in America who exercise influence. It's not about the first names that might come to mind when you think about the people with influence in this country—the leaders of government, the CEOs of large corporations, or the wealthy. Rather, it's about millions of people who come from every city and town and who shape the opinions and trends in our country.

RoperASW, the marketing research and consulting firm at which we work, has dubbed these people the Influential Americans®. Roughly 1 in 10 of the adult population of the United States, the Influential Americans are the people who make the society, culture, and marketplace run. The most socially and politically active Americans—we screen them from the general population on the basis of their involvement in local affairs—the Influentials are active in their communities. They are highly engaged in the workplace and in their personal lives as well. They are interested in many subjects and are connected to many groups. They know how to express themselves and do so. And, because of their position in the community, workplace, and society, their opinions are heard by many people and influence decisions in others' lives.

Almost certainly you know one of them. There may be an Influential on your block, in your workplace, or in your family. You probably talk with at least one in the course of a week. Chances are you seek out an Influential when you have an important decision to make. Influentials are the kind of people you turn to when you need help. They often know the answer to the question you have. If they don't, they know someone who does. They get your attention. They have people's respect.

At RoperASW, which has been helping companies to "manage and master change" since our founding in 1923, we use the Influentials every day in our work. We have come to see them as the thought leaders, trendsetters, and bellwethers for America. They are at the leading edge of what Americans are thinking, doing, and buying. If we want to gauge the prospects for a new product, service, legislative initiative, or idea to go on to mainstream success, we look at how it is regarded by Influentials. When we test trends, a core function of our business, we look at how they play out with Influentials. They are the canaries in the mine shaft for looming political issues. They point the way to the future. On many levels, the Influentials prove the axiom laid out by our founder, Elmo Roper: "In America, the few act for the many."

At the same time, the Influentials are testimony to the democratic notion that more than a handful of people control the levers of change in America. At 1 in 10 of the population, they are a large group: 10 of every 100 Americans 18 years old or older, 5,000 in every city with 50,000 people 18 or older, and, on a national level, 21 million people.

Who *are* the people who are leading trends in America? How can I better understand them? What makes them stand apart? Are there certain demographic markers? What makes them tick? Do they have a different mind-set from other people? How do they spread influence? What are they saying today? Where are they pointing the society tomorrow? How can I apply their insights and ideas to my company, nonprofit organization, or political campaign? Can I persuade them to spread the word for my product, service, organization, or idea? We are commonly asked these questions by our clients, who as leaders in industry and public policy in fields ranging from advertising, marketing, and media to automotive, technology, telecommunications, packaged goods, restaurants, hotels, airlines, and federal departments and agencies, need to know what's on the minds of the nation's opinion leaders. For decades we've been able to give them answers that come from our continuous monitoring of Influentials. Our clients have used the ideas and insights distilled from our research on Influentials to guide strategic planning, product development, and marketing and to see what's on the horizon.

For example, in early 2002, the Influentials signaled an early alert that Americans would be traveling more for vacations and personal reasons in the coming months. They were putting the "post-9/11" fear of flying behind them and were ready to take to the air again. Good news for the airlines and destinations that rely on them as travelers and time to crank up marketing budgets and cut back a bit on the rock-bottom incentives to travel. We also saw, however, that Influentials were adamant that security be tightened substantially—and that otherwise a large number of Influentials would take to the road for driving vacations instead of flying (and through their actions and words influencing friends, families, and others to do the same).

Years before most people had heard of digital still cameras, Influentials were aware of them. By March 1997, two in three had heard of them, 1½ times the response of the public as a whole. They were well into the adoption curve. By early 2001, one in six Influentials owned a digital camera (double the rate of the public as a whole), and a comparable proportion were planning to buy one in the next year or two (more than double the public as a whole). Three in ten had viewed personal photos over a computer in the past month, about triple the rate of the total public. The net effect pointed to an increasingly digital future for photography. Good news for companies selling digital cameras and software to help people archive, edit, transmit, and tinker with their digital photo collections. Good news for product possibilities: "Like how you look in one picture of the Eiffel Tower, but prefer the backdrop of another? Use *Photo Pro for the Home.*" Problematic, however, for traditional silver emulsion film photography.

Companies and public policy clients use Influentials as a gauge of their image in the "vital center" of public opinion. When the percentage of Influentials with a moderately or highly favorable opinion of the Internal Revenue Service rose by 17 percentage points to 61% between 1999 and 2001, one of the largest gains of any group, it was a good sign for the IRS; the agency's efforts to be more consumer friendly were being noticed. Research on Influentials showed that despite the turmoil in technology stocks after the dot-com bubble burst in 2000–2001, some companies retained a strong public image. More than seven in ten Influentials, a large number, held a favorable opinion of Microsoft. The finding suggested that the software giant was weathering the government antitrust investigations against it and the turbulence in the technology industry and had a strong reserve of goodwill in the marketplace, a favorable position from a consumer standpoint for introducing new products (as we see in more detail as we go forward, a good many Influentials were *waiting* for the next leap forward in technology).

With this book, we take key lessons we have gained from decades of studying Influentials and bring them to a larger audience. The result is our most comprehensive overview to date of who the Influential Americans are, what they think, where they are leading the country, and how you can become part of their conversation. We think the time is right to open the vault and share our research and insights with a wider audience. Word of mouth, the medium in which Influentials traffic, is increasingly appreciated as an important channel of communications for both public discourse and the consumer marketplace. The recognition is overdue.

The American public has long known the value of word-of-mouth recommendations. According to Roper research, Americans today are far more likely to turn to friends, family, and other personal experts than to use traditional media for ideas and information on a range of topics. We know because, on a regular basis for 25 years, we've been asking people which of a variety of sources—TV programs, TV commercials, newspaper stories, newspaper ads, magazine stories, magazine ads, online or Internet sources, friends, family, or other people—give them the best ideas and information on different decisions. More than eight in ten people tell us that their personal network of friends, family, and others is among the two or three best sources for ideas and information about restaurants to try, a response almost 50 points higher than the net response for all advertising sources, a substantial difference as Figure I-1 shows. Similarly, seven in ten say friends, family, and other people are one of the best sources on new meals and dishes, places to go on vacation, and prescription drugs—again, substantially more than the net response for advertising, with differences of 38–50 points. About six in ten rate friends, family, and other people among the best sources on hotels to stay in, how to improve personal health, which

Figure I-1. The Importance of Word of Mouth

Net percentage of Americans 18 years old and older saying "people" (friends, family, or other people) are among the two or three "best" sources of ideas and information, and net percentage saying "advertising" is source of best ideas and information, with point difference

	"People"	"Advertising"	Point difference
Restaurants to try	83%	35%	48 points
New meals, dishes to try	73%	24%	49 points
Places to go on visit	71%	33%	38 points
Prescription drugs to try	71%	21%	50 points
Hotels to stay in	63%	27%	36 points
Ways to improve your health	61%	19%	42 points
Movies to see	61%	67%	-6 points
Which brands are best	60%	33%	27 points
Videos to rent or buy	59%	45%	14 points
Retirement planning	58%	9%	49 points
Merits of cars	58%	36%	22 points
Saving and investing money	57%	12%	45 points
Finding the best buys	54%	47%	7 points
Appearance of home	50%	28%	22 points
Clothes to buy	50%	59%	-9 points
Finding a new job	47%	54%	-7 points
Computer equipment	40%	18%	22 points
Web sites to visit	37%	12%	25 points

Source: Roper Reports

movies to see, which brands are the "best," videos to rent or buy, how to plan for retirement, the merits of one car versus another, and how to save and invest money. As the figure shows, Americans generally are twice as likely to cite word of mouth as the best source of ideas and information in these and other areas as they are to cite advertising. There are a few areas in which advertising outperforms word of mouth. For as many Americans citing people as the best sources for tips on movies to go to, for example, slightly more cite advertising. For most decisions, however, word of mouth rules.

Moreover, the person-to-person channel of word of mouth, particularly among friends and family, has grown in importance in recent decades. Drilling deeper into this question shows that, since 1977, the percentage of Americans citing the word of mouth of friends as one of the best sources of ideas for what movies to see has risen by 14 percentage points to 46%, a major increase. There have been significant increases in the importance of word-of-mouth recommendations of friends in a number of other decisions as well, such as where to find the best buys (up 8 points to 37%), analyzing the merits of particular cars (up 7 points to 35%), what clothes to buy (up 7 points to 32%), and which computer equipment to buy (up 7 points to 24%). Family members' value as word-of-mouth sources, although generally not as important as friends', has gone up even more since 1977 than friends', doubling in many areas, with particularly large increases in decisions about restaurants (up 25 points to 49%), meals or dishes (up 23 points to 47%), movies (up 21 points to 33%), places to visit (up 19 points to 42%), improving the appearance of the home (up 14 points to 30%), clothes (up 12 points to 23%), and cars (up 11 points to 28%).

More Americans are bringing in "other people" as well when they make decisions, including colleagues, acquaintances, neighbors, and professional experts, such as doctors, pharmacists, financial planners, and other kinds of consultants. Among the areas in which they're turning more to others beyond their immediate circle of family and friends are health issues (up 17 points to 36% since 1977), saving and investing (up 9 points to 27%), home improvement (up 6 points to 16%), and cars (up 5 points to 22%).

This is the bottom line: when Americans make decisions today, it's a conversation. Before Americans buy, they talk. And they listen. The first step in the buying process is to ask a friend, family member, or other expert close at hand what *they* think. When Americans have an idea, they'll often go back to the friend and family member for input. Depending on the importance of the decision, they'll test their ideas out again as they go along. Flummoxed? Ask a friend. Use your Lifeline, as they say in "Who Wants to Be a Millionaire?" Magazines, newspapers, and television are still important. Today, people get ideas from more sources, one of the side products of

A NOTE ON STATISTICS: In this book, we use research in basically three ways: as a measure of the importance of an item, as a gauge of the differences between groups, and as an indicator of directionality, that is, the trend. Statistical significance can vary according to such factors as the size of the response and the size of the group. In our surveys of the total public, which are based on personal interviews of 2,000 Americans 18 and older, chosen as statistically representative of the population, and with a different sample of respondents each time, a difference of plus or minus 3 points is generally considered "significant." For Influentials, a subset of about 10% of the total public, we generally focus on differences of 7 points or more. The greater the difference, of course, the more significant. We report many differences of 20 points or more between the Influentials and the public as a whole: these are *very* significant. At the same time, we show patterns of change over time, because steady trend increases that in one study are not statistically significant when registered over time can add up to very significant changes.

a more educated society. In turn, the role of media has changed, more toward supporting the conversation ("Here's exactly why we think you should buy our product" or "Call or e-mail or visit our Web site if you want to learn more") than directing people to a decision ("Buy Brand X").

The Internet has broadened the conversation, allowing people to research purchases, post questions to companies and to other consumers, e-mail their friends, forward Web links, and develop bulletin board relationships with people with similar interests. That the Internet is increasingly important is, at this point, commonly accepted. Our research also shows, though, that the change is more profound than is usually acknowledged. Our research about the sources of the best ideas on decisions shows that, in only a few years, the Internet has become as significant in a number of purchase decisions as traditional media. Americans rate online and Internet sources the fourth best sources of ideas on places to travel (15%, up 12 from 1997, a large increase), behind only friends (50%), family (42%), magazine articles (26%), and TV commercials (17%) and on a par with or ahead of newspaper articles (14%), TV programs (13%), newspaper ads (12%), and magazine ads (10%). For ideas on computer equipment, the Internet ranks second (22%, up 15 from 1997), behind only friends (24%). The Internet is the third most important source for ideas on finding a new job (26%, trailing only newspaper ads and friends), the third for hotels (19%, up 15 from 1997), the fourth for finding the best buys (19%, up 16 from 1997), the sixth for judging cars (17%, up 14), the fourth for ideas on saving and investing (16%, up 12), the sixth for discerning which brands are best (15%, up 12), the sixth-rated source for retirement planning (14%, up 10), and eighth in personal health (10%, up 9). In all these areas, the Internet is competitive with at least some traditional media.

In addition, more Americans are becoming active participants in the word-of-mouth conversation by sharing their experience and expertise with others. Other research shows us that large numbers of Americans make recommendations to others when they find something they like. Six in ten Americans, for example, tell us that they have recommended a restaurant to someone else in the past year. About half have passed along a recommendation on a movie. Four in ten have recommended a television show, one in four a vacation destination, and one in five a retail store, car, or clothing. One in seven have told others about Web sites they like. And the numbers increased substantially in the past decade: up 13 percentage points for movies, 11 points for restaurants, 9 points for TV shows, 7 points for vacation destinations, and 6 points for retail stores. (We report the Influential Americans' responses on this question, as well as where they turn for ideas, in subsequent chapters.)

Young people also place a high value on word of mouth. According to the 2002 Roper Youth Poll, when Americans 8–17 years were asked what most influences their decisions, they placed their parents first in most areas: whether they drink alcohol (71%), what they think they will be when they grow up (53%), which videos they watch (51%), what they buy with their spending money (46%), which TV programs they view (43%), what books and magazines they buy and read (37%), and what Web sites they go to (37%). Best friends, meanwhile, exert the most influence on the kinds of music kids listen to (64%) and their choices of clothing (47%). Kids rate parents and friends about equally on what movies they go to see (45 and

44%, respectively). TV and advertising are rated as lesser influences. On average, only 20% of young people rate TV the most important influence in the ten areas, only 11% say so of advertising, and both are substantially less than the average responses for parents (45%) and friends (34%).

Increasingly, we see Americans talking more about community affairs as well, from schools, development, traffic, and other close-to-home issues, to far-reaching issues, such as the quality of life in the community and the legacy they are creating for the next generation. The tragedy of the September 11 attacks on New York and Washington seems to have become the type of "galvanizing crisis" that Harvard Professor Robert Putnam in his book *Bowling Alone* said could reverse the long-term decline in Americans' sense of connectedness.

Even before September 11, we saw evidence of this change toward more involvement by Americans, with growing numbers placing more emphasis on community. The events of recent months, however, seem to have made the change "palpable," to borrow a word from Professor Putnam. Even allowing for the predictable letdown as people return to the normal rhythms of their lives, large numbers of Americans began reevaluating their priorities and trying to rebalance their lives with their values—planning in the coming months to spend more time on family and friends (35% of Americans), go to religious services more often (22%), or do more volunteer and charity work (19%).

This rising tide of conversation about life, the direction of communities and the nation, and everyday decisions about what to read, watch, and buy is creating a major ripple effect in business, government, and other entities. As Americans are talking more among themselves, and are more confident about what they hear from their friends, family, and personal experts, they are growing more selective about when and where they listen to the "official" voices of the society. Tuning out advertising has become part of daily life. Four in ten Americans tell us they "often" switch the channel whenever a commercial comes on, almost triple the level of 1985. Another half flip to another channel at least occasionally. More viewers hit the mute button to turn off the sound of commercials whenever ads come on, one in four doing so often and another four in ten at least occasionally, both double the levels of 1985. Little wonder growing numbers of Americans regard the TV

Figure I-2. Tuning Out Commercials

Percentage of Americans who say they do activity "often" when they're watching television and commercials come on, with point difference from 1985

	Point difference from 1985
Are annoyed about the number of commercials on at one time	
50%	-4
Get up and do something else before the show comes back on	
46%	-5
Switch to another channel	
36%	+22
Talk to other people in the room without paying attention to the commercials	
36%	-9
Fast forward through the commercials when watching programs on a VCR	
35%	*
Are amused by funny or clever commercials	
27%	*
Turn the sound down on the TV or mute it	
23%	+14
Sit and watch the commercials	
21%	-12
Talk to other people in the room about the commercials	
15%	-1

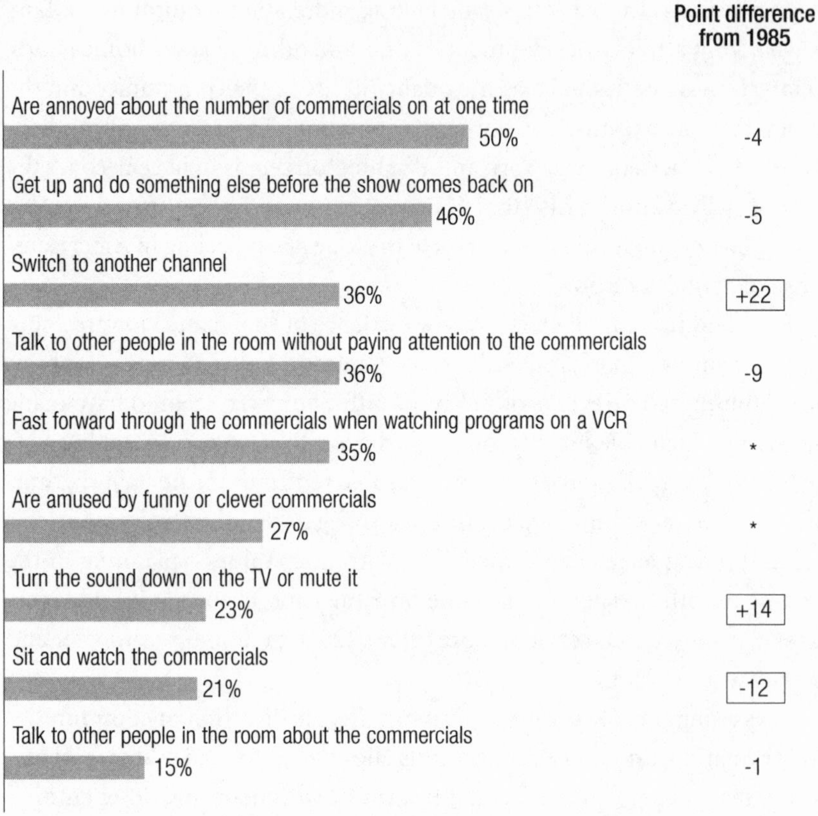

Source: Roper Reports

*Not asked.

remote control as a "necessity" they can't do without (44%, up 21 percentage points from 1992).

Only one in five Americans say they often just sit and watch the commercials, down from one in three in 1985, with half saying they watch the ads only "occasionally." Three in ten say they "almost never" watch commercials (up from two in ten in 1985).

Marketers who have tried to fight their way through the remote control firewall by loading more advertising into the traditional media or placing ads in new venues seem to have mostly succeeded at instilling a rising level of irritation in the public, like an in-law who follows you from room to room at the family reunion, refusing to leave you alone until he's regaled you with the details of his latest feat. The business community is facing a deepening predicament. Business is working *harder* and paying *more* to pursue people who are trying to watch and listen *less* to its messages.

Back in the days when *The Beverly Hillbillies* could get a 50 or better share of the audience watching television on any given night, getting your message across to Americans was relatively easy. It wasn't hard for advertisers, like lucky Jed Clampett, to go "shooting for some food" and strike it rich with some "bubbling crude." Television literally made brands. Revlon's sales jumped 54% in 1955, the year it began sponsoring *The $64,000 Question* on CBS; in 1956, Revlon's sales soared another 66%. The quiz show put Revlon "on the map of corporate America," says Harvard Professor Richard Tedlow in his book *Giants of Enterprise.* In the 1950s, top-rated series like *The $64,000 Question, I Love Lucy,* and *The Texaco Star Theater* were regularly watched by half of households with TVs. Today, as Figure I-3 shows, a Nielsen rating of 21 wins the season. More shows and networks compete for viewer attention; the number of cable television networks has topped 200. There are more magazines (5,500 consumer titles alone, triple the number of 20 years ago). There are more radio stations (10,500, 1½ times the number 30 years ago). And, of course, there's the Web, which from a smattering of sites in the early 1990s has mushroomed to more than 30 million sites. In writing this book, we are competing for your attention with the mind-boggling 122,000 book titles that will be published this year in the U.S., up from 36,000 in 1970. The average American would have to read 334 books per day, go to 11,000 Web sites per day, peruse 15 magazines per day, and tune into 29 radio stations every day for a year to see everything available to him or her—and that's not counting the dozens of programs being beamed every day by the hundreds of television networks vying for viewers' attention.

With more to choose from, Americans are customizing their media consumption, creating further fragmentation. In 1980, there were 128 mil-

Figure I-3. Top Regular Series Network Programs 1950–2000

Traditional broadcast season: September through May for each year

Season	Program	Network	Rating	Share
1950–1951	Texaco Star Theater	NBC	61.6	81
1951–1952	Arthur Godfrey's Talent Scouts	CBS	53.8	78
1952–1953	I Love Lucy	CBS	67.3	68
1953–1954	I Love Lucy	CBS	58.8	67
1954–1955	I Love Lucy	CBS	49.3	66
1955–1956	$64,000 Question	CBS	47.5	65
1956–1957	I Love Lucy	CBS	43.7	58
1957–1958	Gunsmoke	CBS	43.1	51
1958–1959	Gunsmoke	CBS	39.6	60
1959–1960	Gunsmoke	CBS	40.3	65
1960–1961	Gunsmoke	CBS	37.3	62
1961–1962	Wagon Train	NBC	32.1	53
1962–1963	Beverly Hillbillies	CBS	36	54
1963–1964	Beverly Hillbillies	CBS	39.1	58
1964–1965	Bonanza	NBC	36.3	54
1965–1966	Bonanza	NBC	31.8	48
1966–1967	Bonanza	NBC	29.1	45
1967–1968	Andy Griffith	CBS	27.6	42
1968–1969	Rowan and Martin's Laugh-In	NBC	31.8	45
1969–1970	Rowan and Martin's Laugh-In	NBC	26.3	39
1970–1971	Marcus Welby, M.D.	ABC	29.6	52
1971–1972	All in the Family	CBS	34	54
1972–1973	All in the Family	CBS	33.3	53
1973–1974	All in the Family	CBS	31.2	51
1974–1975	All in the Family	CBS	30.2	51
1975–1976	All in the Family	CBS	30.1	44
1976–1977	Happy Days	ABC	31.5	47
1977–1978	Laverne & Shirley	ABC	31.6	49
1978–1979	All in the Family	CBS	30.5	48
1979–1980	60 Minutes	CBS	28.2	32
1980–1981	Dallas	CBS	31.2	52
1981–1982	Dallas	CBS	28.4	45
1982–1983	60 Minutes	CBS	25.5	40
1983–1984	Dallas	CBS	25.7	40

1984–1985	Dynasty	ABC	25	37
1985–1986	Bill Cosby Show	NBC	33.8	51
1986–1987	Bill Cosby Show	NBC	34.9	53
1987–1988	Bill Cosby Show	NBC	27.8	44
1988–1989	Roseanne	ABC	25.5	41
1989–1990	Roseanne	ABC	23.4	35
1990–1991	Cheers	NBC	21.6	34
1991–1992	60 Minutes	CBS	21.7	36
1992–1993	60 Minutes	CBS	21.6	35
1993–1994	Home Improvement	ABC	21.9	33
1994–1995	Seinfeld	NBC	20.5	31
1995–1996*	ER	NBC	22	36
1996–1997	ER	NBC	21.2	35
1997–1998	Seinfeld	NBC	22	33
1998–1999	ER	NBC	17.8	29
1999–2000	Who Wants to Be a Millionaire?	ABC	18.6	29
2000–2001	Survivor II	CBS	17.4	27

Copyright © 2001 Nielsen Media Research.

*Starting in 1995–1996, the traditional broadcast network season runs from September until mid-May.

lion TV sets in the U.S., or a little more than one per household. There are now more than 240 million televisions in the U.S., enough for every American over the age of nine to have his or her own personal set. According to our research, televisions have spread from the living room (about three in four households have one there) to the master bedroom (over half), to kids' bedrooms (more than one in three, in households with kids), the family room (about three in ten), and the kitchen, den, and guest bedroom (about one in ten each). About 2 million households have a TV in the bathroom. Computers are poised to follow a similar course. Large numbers of Americans are taking advantage of new laws that let people opt out of telemarketing calls, removing their phone numbers from the lists that telemarketers can call. Even Jed Clampett would be hard-pressed to hunt in this thicket. It's hard for a single medium to put a brand on the map, as television did for Revlon in the 1950s.

Political candidates and government officials face a similar dilemma.

Aside from times of national crisis, it's harder and harder for the federal government to get people's attention for major presidential addresses, political debates, and other forums that they watched as a matter of course in decades past.

At a time when the number of media is exploding and marketing is becoming more pervasive throughout life, the channel with the greatest influence in America is neither the traditional media of television, radio, or print advertising nor the new medium of the World Wide Web but the "human" channel of individual, person-to-person, word-of-mouth communication. The challenge, then, for society's institutions—businesses and government and the people who run them—is to adjust to this new reality in which word of mouth rules and to learn the word-of-mouth *rules.*

Which brings us to the Influential Americans. Our research suggests that the net effect of the changes of recent years—the emphasis Americans place on the word-of-mouth recommendations of others, the priority the public places on the social capital of conversation, the growing cacophony of media and marketing messages—is increasing the value of the Influential Americans. Influentials are much more likely than the average person to make a recommendation when they find something they like and to be sought out for their insights than other segments historically pursued as market movers, such as the affluent, the college educated, and people in executive or professional jobs. If word of mouth is like a radio signal broadcast over the country, Influentials are the strategically placed transmitters that amplify the signal, multiplying dramatically the number of people who hear it. The signal becomes stronger and stronger as it is beamed from Influential to Influential and then broadcast to the nation as a whole.

At a time when increased numbers of Americans are looking for leaders at the top (we know this from our research: almost half of Americans have been saying one of the major causes of the nation's problems is "a lack of good leadership"), the Influential Americans are the reliable, steadying leaders among us. They're engaged in the national conversation. They're more likely than the norm to be in on political discussions (even in 2001, an off year for elections, six in ten Influentials reported they'd had a discussion on politics during the previous week, more than double the response of the public as a whole). They're more likely to participate in online bulletin board discussions as well (Influentials are about twice as likely as the average American to have logged onto a bulletin board, 26 versus 13%). They're hooked into e-mail: two in three Influentials are regular users, about 1½ times the public as a whole, with four in ten Influentials using e-mail every day, double the rate of the total public.

Because they know many people and soak up a large amount of information, Influentials stand out as smart, informed sources of advice and insight. They know a lot about some things and something about a lot of things, and if they don't know the answer, they probably know someone who does. Influentials tend to be two to five years ahead of the public on many important trends, such as the adoption of major technologies (personal computers or cell phones) or new ideas, such as the movement of recent years to rebalance work and family. Influentials have a definite sense of themselves (character and values) and a clear sense about what's important and what's not important. Thus, when they talk, people tend to listen.

The result can spread positive word-of-mouth buzz for products. When personal computers experienced some of their strongest growth in the 1990s, Influentials were being sought out more for their advice and opinion about personal computers and were making more recommendations about computers. Influentials can help foster positive images of companies. Companies to which Influentials are strongly disposed, including Sony, Visa, and Frito-Lay (eight in ten Influentials have consistently had a favorable opinion of these companies in recent years), stand to benefit from Influentials' disposition to them. The rise of Japanese carmakers, such as Toyota and Honda, was recognized early by Influentials. By 1983, 55% of Influentials had a favorable opinion of Toyota, 12 points higher than the public as a whole; today about seven in ten do. The more recent rebound of the American carmakers was perceived by Influentials ahead of the rest of Americans as well.

The Influentials are evidence of something that many people know intuitively, that not all opinions are created equal. Some people are better connected, better read, and better informed. You probably know this from your own experience. You don't turn to just anyone when you're deciding what neighborhood to live in, how to invest for retirement, or what kind of car or computer to buy. You want to talk with people who speak with a sense of authority about what the schools are like, which mutual fund or brokerage will give you the best combination of returns on your investment and customer service, and which cars and computers are good deals and which are lemons—in words you understand.

Influence has been a topic of growing discussion in business and the society. In television political roundtables, business schools, best-seller lists, and countless conversations in settings in corporations, government, and homes, Americans have been engaged in exchanges on who has influence, who's gaining and losing it, and how influence works.

Malcolm Gladwell's *The Tipping Point* has arguably been "the tipping point" in this trend. The book popularized theories of *mimetics,* the spread of ideas, as explanations for sudden changes that seem to spread like epidemics in the popular culture and society, with examples that range from small, cool phenomena (the revival of Hush Puppies after their discovery by New York fashionistas) to the socially significant (the decline in crime in New York City by changing the cultural attitudes toward crime). Gladwell argues that these societal viruses share three key characteristics: (1) the support of a few key people, "mavens" who store up vast stocks of information and are willing to share it with other people, "connectors" who have vast social networks and can get out the word quickly, and "salesmen" who get everyone caught up with their passion for an idea; (2) a "stickiness factor" that makes them uniquely memorable and compelling; and (3) a "context" conducive to the idea.

With the Internet, argues Seth Godin in *Permission Marketing,* the old advertising technique of "interruption marketing" is wasteful. Businesses should instead use the new technologies (which enable you to learn more about people as you work more with them) to build relationships with the customer's "permission."

In *Anatomy of Buzz,* Emanuel Rosen posits that certain people are "hubs" who spread word-of-mouth influence across their social networks. The job for business is to identify and develop relationships with these hubs. Rosen cites the Roper Influential Americans as one "hub" who are "ahead of adoption," "vocal," and "avid travelers."

Academics are learning more about how influence works and why some people are persuasive. Dr. Robert Cialdini, in *Influence: Science and Practice* and *Influence: The Psychology of Persuasion,* after studying an array of instances of persuasion, including door-to-door salesmen, ad and PR execs, cult leaders, and other "compliance practitioners," decided there are six categories of persuasion: reciprocation, consistency, social proof, liking, authority, and scarcity.

Networking is receiving new respect. After interviewing hundreds of professionals about how they had gotten their jobs for his *Getting a Job: A Study of Contacts and Careers,* sociology professor Mark Granovetter found that personal contacts were by far the most common response.

The study of influence is not new. For many years, it was assumed that influence traveled down, with ideas formulated by the elites and then percolating through the social strata. The question was how to organize the process. Walter Lippmann, for example, in the landmark book *Public Opinion,* argued that it was a "false idea" to expect the public to direct public affairs. People believed what they were conditioned to believe, Lippmann thought. They had too many blind spots, were too subject to stereotypes, were too bound up in the social codes, and were too entangled in commitments and self-involvement to be knowledgeable about affairs of importance to the society. Lippmann believed that many were also none too smart. In fact, many were "mentally children or barbarians," he said. "The mass of illiterate, feeble-minded, grossly neurotic, undernourished, and frustrated individuals is very considerable, much more considerable than we generally suppose." Public opinion as a result was constantly backed up in "eddies of misunderstanding." Society was like Plato's metaphor of the cave: people see only the shadows. Lippmann's prescription was the creation of a "specialized class," "an expert organization" independent of political influence to make "the unseen facts intelligible to those who make the decisions" and "organize" opinion for the press.

Subsequent years produced a lively debate. A far-reaching 1940 study of the presidential election in an Ohio town by Columbia Professor Paul Lazarsfeld found that the mass media, in fact, had a "small" effect on how people voted "compared to the role of personal influence." Interviewing people about what influenced their decisions, the study found that, rather than starting from above and percolating down, influence appeared to be "horizontal." Each social stratum had its own opinion leaders—the neighborhood barber swapping insights throughout the day with his customers, for example. The media's effect was "two-step": the opinion leaders would digest the articles and broadcasts and then disseminate what they'd learned, mixed with their personal reflections, to their circle of friends and acquaintances. Subsequent research by Lazarsfeld and Elihu Katz, reported in their 1955 book *Personal Influence*, gave further support to the horizontal theory. Using the method of the earlier voting study, Lazarsfeld and Katz interviewed women in Decatur, Illinois about what influenced various decisions, such as groceries, fashions, movies, and civic affairs. They found that, in general, personal influence was most important. Young homemakers, for example, took their cues in grocery shopping most often from older women who were more experienced in such decisions.

Public relations executives have long appreciated the value of reaching opinion leaders. In op-ed page advertisements of the nation's major daily newspapers, of the type Mobil Oil pioneered during the 1970s, when oil companies were under a public opinion siege, and in public image commercials like the Archer Daniels Midland spots on Sunday morning news shows, they try to persuade opinion leaders to their point of view. Nonprofit organizations have used advertising toward a similar end to stir up public support for their issues. In consumer marketing, growing numbers of companies use high-profile events like the Academy Awards to distribute baskets of goodies to celebrities in the hope that, if *they* use the products, the rest of us will want to follow.

Roper became involved in influence research in the 1940s, when we were called in by the Standard Oil Company of New Jersey (now Exxon) to develop a research model for sifting out opinion leaders on public affairs. The goal was to help the company gauge its public image among the people who through their words and actions shaped public opinion in the larger community. The objective, as Elmo Roper later described it, was to find "the more articulate" citizens who were "better educated" and took "a higher degree of interest in the world around them." Such people would likely be the people "most articulate in their feelings about big corporations" and "most concerned to attack or defend them." These "politically active neighbors" would influence the thoughts and opinions of their more "politically inert" fellow citizens. They were the "alert citizens who strive to fulfill their obligations to society by performing the simple democratic function of voting and joining with others in groups in the expectation of making their voices heard."

Early research on the segmentation corroborated Roper's theory. Americans who were more politically and socially active did appear to be the thought leaders on public affairs. In a 1950 article in an academic journal, Roper concluded that the segmentation was "a promising tool" that could have "wider applicability and usefulness" in corporate public relations work.

After extensive testing by Roper researchers, what began as a battery of questions to discern political and social activists was distilled to one question that asked respondents which social or political activities they had performed in the past year. To qualify as an Influential, a person had to have done three or more of the items on the list. The natural human tendency of people is to want to answer in the affirmative to at least one thing because they feel that they "ought to." Hence, one item ("signed a petition") was added to the list with the express purpose of excluding it from the identification of politically and socially active Americans. Without this escape clause, it was thought, responses to the other eleven items would be exaggerated. (This was a prescient decision. To this day, upward of one in four Americans answers yes to signing a petition, the largest response of the total public on any item.) The target was to produce the 10% of the public that was most active, a figure that seems both philosophical (reflecting Roper's thinking that the politically active were about 10–12% of the society) and practical (yielding a sufficient base of respondents to produce meaningful data). The current Influential American question reads as follows:

Here is a list of things some people do about government or politics. Have you happened to have done any of these things in the past year? Which ones?

  a. Written or called any politician at the state, local, or national level
  b. Attended a political rally, speech, or organized protest of any kind

   c. Attended a public meeting on town or school affairs

   d. Held or run for political office

   e. Served on a committee for some local organization

   f. Served as an officer for some club or organization

   g. Written a letter to the editor of a newspaper or magazine or called a live radio or TV show to express an opinion

   h. Signed a petition

   i. Worked for a political party

   j. Made a speech

   k. Written an article for a magazine or newspaper

   l. Been an active member of any group that tries to influence public policy or government

Over the years, we have modified the question slightly to reflect changes in the society—adding "live radio or TV show" to item *g* to reflect the rise of call-in shows, adding "state" and "local" politicians to item *a* to reflect the emphasis on local affairs, and broadening item *l* from being member of a group for "good government" to influencing policy and government to reflect the increase in special-interest groups, such as environmental organizations.

The original idea was to use the Influentials to track the thinking of the society's opinion leaders on national issues, candidates, and the image of major companies. When the Roper Reports trend research study was launched in 1973, the Influentials segmentation was included because it was thought that it would help Roper Report attract public affairs and public policy clients. Along the way, however, we made an unexpected but very important discovery. Influentials stood out from the mainstream not only for being forward-thinking on social and political issues: they were forward-thinking, brought an activist approach, were engaged in ideas, were attuned to new developments, and exercised influence *virtually across the board.*

In 1978, in an effort to understand more about trendsetters, we asked Americans if they were "one of the first" people they knew to adopt various behaviors and perspectives or whether they were "somewhat later," "one of the last," or never or always did. The assumption was that the study might produce a group of "firsters" who led the way on everything. After testing a series of approaches, it was our conclusion that no such "magic" group existed. Some segments of the population were "more predictive than others," however, and among those groups, the Influentials stood out as "a thought leader, trendsetter group." The conclusion was reaffirmed by the results of another study in 1978 in which we asked a nationally representative sample of Americans if they were turned to by others for advice or insight on a variety of topics (we report the most recent results of this study in Chapter 1). Analysis of the results showed that "almost everyone is an expert on something" but that some groups were "sought more than others"—led by the Influentials. In a 1984 survey we tested whether people who were more likely to talk frequently with others about a subject also made a point of reading publications and articles about the topic or paying attention to ads on the subject. We found that the politically and socially active Influentials were overall the most engaged of any of the groups we regularly track, including segments defined solely by their affluence, education, or occupational status, on a range of topics including food, travel, health, sports, home, and investing.

In 1988, we released the first in a series of in-depth reports specifically devoted to the segment. The report, which for the first time used the "Influential Americans" label to describe the group, showed that the Influentials were not only leaders in their community but were also "pioneer consumers" who led the way in new ideas, such as the videocassette recorder (by 1982, 15% of Influentials had one versus 6% of the total public), the home computer (which 16% of Influentials had in 1984 versus 9% of the public as a whole), and catalog shopping (46% of Influentials had bought through a catalog in the past three months compared with 29% of the total public). In three subsequent reports, in 1989, 1992, and 1995, we delved further into the Influentials.

Now with 30 years of continuous research on Influentials, more than 250 studies that have produced a database of more than 10,000 questions and interviews with more than 50,000 Influentials and half-a-million Americans, we continue to see the same patterns. The Influentials may be America's foremost influence *generalists,* defining the mores for the mainstream on what's important (owning a computer, taking interesting vacations, or having strong local schools), spreading the word about new ideas in persuasive ways, and setting the context in which the society views the world—the dress codes in the office if not the fashions that come off the runway. Few important trends reach the mainstream without passing through the Influentials in the early stages, and the Influentials can stop a would-be trend in its tracks: they give the thumbs-up that propels a trend or the thumbs-down that relegates it to a short 15 minutes of fame.

To the discussion about word of mouth, influence, and how to market most effectively in today's fragmented media environment, then, we bring four new elements:

1. An *identified group* that influences change through their words and actions
2. A *database of research* on this group across a range of subjects from public policy and politics to product purchases, brand attitudes, social and personal values, and aspirations
3. The *ability to trend* their thoughts and behaviors through 30 years in most areas and 60 years on some topics
4. The *analytical experience* to project future changes in the broader society and marketplace based on Influentials' current attitudes and behaviors and to acquire an understanding of the two-step process through which Influentials take in information and disseminate it to others

In the chapters to come, we lay out much of what we know about Influentials: the characteristics that most define them (Chapter 1, Who Are the Influentials?); their mind-set (Chapter 2, The Influential Personality); how the influence process works (Chapter 3, The Influence Spiral: How Influentials Get and Spread Ideas); their leadership role in the trend we consider most important to understanding America today (Chapter 4, The Message of Influentials: The Age of Autonomy and the Rise of Self-Reliance); their insights on what tomorrow holds (Chapter 5, The Influential Vision: Seven Trends for the Future); and what they have to say about business, brands, and marketing (Chapter 6, Developing an Influential Strategy: Six Rules for Getting into the Conversation). Along the way, we draw on a trove of research on Influentials. We talk about what kinds of magazines they read and programs they watch—because these aren't the 1950s, when marketers could scoop up Influentials in that vast pool of Americans watching the same two or three programs every evening. We also introduce you to twelve real-life Americans who embody the Influential ideals, and we present charts, tables, and case studies from our research.

We think word-of-mouth influence will become more important in the years ahead. It's being increasingly recognized. Moreover, the word-of-mouth revolution is fueled by powerful forces. In addition to the rise of new technologies, like the Internet, and the fragmentation of the mass media, there are two trends that may be the major, driving forces of change today.

First, America is a vastly more educated nation than two or three decades ago. A high school diploma, a mark of status in Lippmann's time, is nearly universal. Today, more than eight in ten Americans 25 or older have graduated from high school. In 1960, when JFK was launching the new frontier with education as a central focal point, barely four in ten did. In 1940, only one in four Americans 25 or older had four years of high school. Today, college is a mainstream American experience. About half of Americans 25 or older today have attended at least some college, up from one in six in 1960 and one in ten in 1940. Growing numbers are college graduates. One in four Americans 25 years or older today have had four years or more of college, compared with only one in twelve in 1960 and one in twenty in 1940.

In our research, we have found that with education comes confidence. Americans may not be "smarter" than their parents or grandparents; it took smarts to run a railroad engine, take apart and repair a tractor, and the other tasks of past generations. Americans do seem to be more adept at critical-thinking skills, however, such as parsing arguments, challenging opinions, making calculations, and parrying with others—skills, not coincidentally, that serve people well in the kinds of conversation in which word-of-mouth influence is spread. We have consistently found in our research that education is a transformative experience; when people go to college, they are exposed to new people, ideas, experiences, and ways of thinking.

If Walter Lippmann were writing today, a good number of people reading him would be as educated as or more educated than he. Government efforts at propaganda increasingly are undermined not only by the mass media (which sometimes get to the front ahead of the troops) but by the "micromedia" of citizen counterpropagandists who feed live reports on their own through e-mail, cell phones, and Web sites that, in turn, often wind up on the evening news or in the morning paper. The window of "fooling some of the people some of the time" has closed. Media manipulation has become a parlor game; viewers analyze the spin in political debates along with political commentators; focus group participants spout their opinions in the argot of marketing. Books on influence and persuasion generate lively discussions on the Web and impassioned reader endorsements. "Wow, I am so glad I read this book," says one reader of Cialdini's *Influence* in an Amazon.com posting. "It will help me never be fooled again in the market."

Second, in addition to being more educated, the population is also older. More than one in three Americans are 45 years old or older. Between 1973 and 2000, the median age of Americans rose from 28 to 35. By the year 2010, four in ten Americans will be 45 years or older. Age may not make people wiser, but it does make people more experienced and, like education, tends to make people more certain of themselves.

We think it's logical that word of mouth has been growing as Americans have grown more educated and older. The U.S. may have a rich history of people marching to the beat of their own drums, blazing their own trails, doing it *their way,* following their bliss, doing their thing, and being pilgrims, pioneers, frontiersmen, lone rangers, gunslingers, jazz soloists, rockers, inventors, entrepreneurs, and free agents. But they still turn to others, and they like to be part of a community, feel a sense of comfort in belonging, and juggle many conversations in the course of a day.

More confident in themselves and more skeptical of the "official" wisdom, Americans are more willing to seek out answers from other people. Many families have designated experts, a brother, a sister, or a friend of the family who knows where to find information on the Web if a family member falls ill and knows how to navigate buying a home or how to find someone who knows. The conversation level is rising. The result is increasing the value of people who know more people, are interested in more subjects, and know more about more things—the Influentials.

In times of change, people naturally seek a guide, someone who's been out ahead of them, who's already identified the issues, addressed them in his or her own life, and can offer good, reliable, informed insights, advice, and information about what's going on now and what's to come, someone they trust. Americans instinctively know this. We believe this is one reason, in this time when messages are coming fast and furious at people from seemingly all directions, Americans are placing increasing stock in the simplest form of communication, word-of-mouth advice and information from people they know and trust.

Getting through to the Influentials is not easy. They're hard to reach. They are among the most critical citizens and consumers in the society. They hold business to higher standards, are harder to persuade, see through hype more easily, and drive a harder bargain than the average American. It's our belief, though, backed by decades of research, that those who take the time and effort to understand the Influentials will be rewarded, both in their success in the marketplace and society today and in the longer-range perspective they gain on where we are going.

For decades, we have used the Influentials to make sense of the present and gain insights on the future. The market is not what it used to be. Communications are not what they used to be. Tonight's meetings at schools across the country may be more important than a mass media ad campaign. For those trying to make sense of things today, we think the Influentials are an important missing link. You're about to find out who they are, what they're thinking, and how to reach them.

CHAPTER 1

Who Are the Influentials?

ABOUT 25 MINUTES north of New York City, Irvington, New York is the kind of town time forgot that is often idealized these days as the perfect place to raise a family. With its Hudson River setting, tree-lined streets, sense of history, and cozy size, it's easy to see why. The old-fashioned Main Street, devoid of national chains, is dotted with delis, restaurants, and other local businesses. Proprietors often know their customers by name. The cash register at Geordane's, the local grocery, usually has a petition on an issue facing the community (a stoplight for the elementary school or a town swimming pool) or a handbill for a local fund-raiser (a benefit concert to raise funds to buy a large piece of open space for a park).

Like many places, Irvington is scrambling to adapt to the forces of change. The qualities that make it attractive—the friendly, small-town atmosphere and proximity to Manhattan—have set off a frenzy of home construction. Since 1990, the population has jumped by 33% to 8,000 people. The streets, built for a small-town population, are increasingly clogged. The schools are building new additions to keep up with a booming student population. It's getting harder to find affordable housing. As testified by the petitions and handbills in the local grocery, though, these problems are spurring a response. People are getting involved. Like many communities across the nation, Irvington in recent years is experiencing a resurgence in grassroots activism.

Isabel Milano has been an active member of this movement. The 42-year-old mother of two was one of the organizers of the Irvington Education Foundation, begun in 1996. The group, formed to support educational enrichment programs that were threatened by budget cuts, has raised several hundred thousand dollars from the community through dinner dances, auctions, and other events. When school athletic programs were threatened by the budget ax, she helped start the Irvington Athletic Foundation to keep them fit. Earlier in her activism days, she helped stage a series of fund-raisers to build new playgrounds at the elementary school. She served on the long-range planning committee that helped secure the multimillion-dollar construction bond for the schools' new additions. She was one of the founders of a community-building group that brought moms together to share their experiences and talk about issues they faced. Recently, a group of local officials asked her to run for village trustee, saying it could strengthen ties between the school community and the village. She entered the race, and won.

In the process, Milano has become a leader in her community. People come to her when they have questions. Some involve civic affairs. "Who should I call in the Village to find out about this?" "What do you think of having a swap meet for athletic gear?"

Because she gets around and knows a lot of people, Milano is asked about other subjects as well. The questions range from recommendations of where to go out to eat to questions on parenting, like what she's heard about a center in a neighboring community that sponsors dances for teenagers. She once was asked if she knew how to secure a patent for an invention. She didn't, but it "was an interesting question," she says, so she researched and got the answer.

Isabel Milano is an Influential American. She is one of about 400 in Irvington, if the proportion of one Influential to every 10 persons in the adult population is true here—which seems to be the case, judging from the numbers of people working on fund-raisers, village and school committees, environmental and historical preservation groups, senior citizen programs, and the busy youth sports leagues. The results are reflected in the community. A four-story brick building that formerly housed the headquarters of a local industry has been renovated to create a spacious new library and affordable housing apartments. A long, green 11-acre park along the Hudson with views of Manhattan, a promenade for walkers, baseball fields, a senior citizens' center, and playgrounds has been created on a strip of land formerly occupied by warehouses. Several valuable parcels of woodland have been acquired for preservation.

Influentials are key conduits of information in Irvington, not only for community concerns like a parcel of land coming on the market or how many openings there will be this year on the school board or village trustees, but also on the best buys in the annual community thrift sale at St. Barnabas Episcopal Church, whether to go to the hip, big-city-like River City Grill that replaced the local restaurant institution Benny's Seafood, and the best place in Westchester County to get a stove or refrigerator when you're renovating your kitchen. They hear where people are traveling on vacation, get the lowdown on how good the destination was when people get back, and synthesize what they hear into cogent reviews that are disseminated to family, friends, colleagues, acquaintances, and other people, regularly updating their views as they take in more information, like a continuously replenished *Zagat's Guide to Restaurants*.

Because of their strategic placement at the center of the conversation in their communities—and, by extension, the nation—the Influentials are an important intersection for business, government, and the society. In computer terms, they are like the central processing units of the nation. Because they know many people and are in contact with many people in the course of a week, they have a powerful multiplier effect, spreading the word quickly across a broad network when they find something they want others to know about. The result can accelerate trends in the broader society or, with a negative experience, bring them to a crawl. To a large extent, they are the force behind the throne of government and business.

Who are these people? They are not your stereotype of who runs the country. They are not the familiar faces portrayed in the mass media as the change agents in society and the marketplace. Many have achieved material success, but they are generally not the richest Americans. They are well-educated but generally not the *most* educated Americans. They are accomplished in their careers but not at the top of industry. You won't often see them on the front page of *The New York Times* or *The Wall Street Journal* or on the evening network news. Their homes, recipes, wardrobes, and summer reading aren't likely to be parsed in celebrity magazines or on television programs. Some are elected officials or business leaders, and a few are celebrities. The vast majority, however—20 million-plus of the 21 million-strong group—*aren't* in Congress or the White House or the head of a federal agency, *aren't* CEOs of large companies or movie stars. They're more likely to be people who live in your neighborhood. At a time when people no longer believe that what happens at the national level usually matters very much to them personally, the Influentials across America are the people who increasingly set the agenda that influences the future of America's cities and towns and, ultimately, the nation.

How do you identify Influentials? Are they a certain age? Income? Education level? Occupation? Are there distinguishing markers to Influentials that make them recognizable as they walk down the street or take their place in a crowded meeting room? Do you know who they are when they speak? Are they "born" Influential or "made" by events and experience? Can anyone become an Influential?

Demographics Are Not Influence

Certain images usually come to mind when people talk about influence. The charisma of popular presidents, such as Ronald Reagan, Franklin Roosevelt, Theodore Roosevelt, and John F. Kennedy, who rally Americans to pursue great aims—renewing the national spirit, overcoming economic depression, winning wars, instituting major reforms, or putting a man on the moon. Some people associate influence with wealth and celebrity. Oprah Winfrey, through the simple act of endorsing a novel, can send droves of viewers of her talk show into bookstores and turn the book into a best-seller. The Rockefeller family, through their family fortune, support museums, international cooperation, and other good works. Performers from the Beatles to Madonna have popularized their passing interests. Businesspeople like Bill Gates or Steve Jobs inspire consumers to buy their products and investors to buy shares in their companies.

These can be described as influence. Decades of research on change and trends in the society have convinced us, however, that there is a major source of influence in America that lies with a larger group of Americans. After all, not everything attempted by the people at the top of the government, business, and celebrity worlds succeeds. New products fail at alarming rates. Presidential initiatives founder. Investors turn away from companies. The U.S. depends on the individual initiative of the people at the top, but it strikes us that it depends in a much larger sense on the collective consciousness of this larger group. The titular leaders of the society need the consent of this larger group for the initiatives to have mainstream success.

The Influential Americans are integral to understanding many of the significant changes in the marketplace and the society. Although there are sometimes mitigating factors in the failure of initiatives—well-organized lobbies, downturns in the economic cycle, and unexpected events—history suggests that this group is a critical link in whether initiatives succeed or fail. As a RoperASW colleague says, the Influentials are the "early majority" for the nation and the consumer marketplace. Through the millions of conversations they create and the examples they set, they shape attitudes and behaviors in the broader society.

Influential Americans share certain characteristics. They generally have an activist approach to life that extends from the community to the workplace to leisure time; a network of contacts broader not only than the norm for the society but also broader than the networks of people often labeled as demographically desirable, for example, the affluent; a tendency to be looked to by others for advice or opinion; restless minds that seem to be constantly engaged in and fascinated by problem solving; and a pattern of trendsetting in areas that have made a substantial difference to the mainstream society.

There is a certain demographic "center of gravity" to Influentials—college educated, midlife, in the child-rearing years, upper-middle income, in positions of responsibility in the workplace—but they are not a uniform group by conventional measures. They are about as likely to be women as men. In fact, with about a 50:50 split between men and women, the Influential Americans are much more gender balanced than the representative bodies of national or state government or the nation's corporate boardrooms and executive suites, which still skew far more toward men than women. In many ways, the Influentials are a reflection of the diversity of the United States at the beginning of this new century. They are young, old, and in between; come from the full range of income strata; represent the different races that make up America; can be found from the largest cities to small towns and rural areas; are from the Northeast to the West Coast, the Midwest, and South; are Democrats, Republicans, and independents; and are evident in occupations from executives and professionals to homemakers and students.

If you brought them together for a group portrait, they might look something like these people:

Larry Lee, Jr., a State Farm Insurance agent in Fort Pierce, Florida, is involved in so many groups in his community (including some he has started) he is referred to by his friends as "the Mayor."

Shelley Miller, a working mother and accountant returned to her hometown of Richmond, Indiana 10 years ago and became mayor of the city 2 years ago.

Rick White, a mutual fund manager in New York, has lent his time and expertise to help his brother's campaign to provide support and resources to land mine survivors around the world.

Sophie Glovier, a former Madison Avenue advertising executive and mother of two, is active in the land-trust movement and part of the new generation of power volunteers who have injected a sense of energy into communities since stepping off the career track.

Teresa Graham of Texarkana, Arkansas is a grandmother and Internet consultant who, having pulled herself up by the bootstraps, devotes herself to helping others turn their lives around.

Mike Williams, Chairman of the Intertribal Council of Alaska's Native American population and a member of the state Board of Education of Alaska and father of five, channels his energies (including riding in the 1,150 mile Iditarod dogsled race across Alaska) into championing tribal causes.

David Pendergrass, a schoolteacher and father from Kansas City, Missouri, is one of many Americans trying to create charter schools in their communities.

Leonard Pitt, a San Francisco Bay Area performance artist and teacher, merged two of the dynamic forces in his community—rap culture and environmentalism—to raise environmental awareness in inner-city youth.

Walter Arrowsmith, a rock-ribbed Republican in his seventies, after decades of involvement in the Kiwanis, Junior Achievement, United Way, and local and state politics, came back from a battle with prostate cancer to run for his old seat on the Lancaster, Ohio City Council—and won.

Tim Draper is a founder of one of Silicon Valley's leading venture-capital firms, an outspoken proponent for overhauling the nation's school system, and a founder of a nonprofit foundation for teaching entrepreneurism in schools.

Sarah Vokes, a recent college graduate living in Portland, Oregon, is part of a younger generation of activists for women's rights, environmental issues, and social justice.

And *Isabel Milano*, whom we've already introduced.

The Numbers: Shared Characteristics and Diversity

Influentials have in common some demographic characteristics. In particular, they tend to be educated. According to the aggregate data from the Roper surveys for 2001, shown in the accompanying figures, the vast majority of Influential Americans, almost eight in ten, have at least some college. Half of Influentials have graduated from college, and one in five has gone on to postgraduate work. All these measures are substantially higher than in the public as a whole. Influentials are more than 1½ times as likely to have attended college than the 18 and older public as a whole (80 versus 50%), are twice as likely to be college graduates (49 versus 23%), and are more than three times as likely to have done postgraduate work (21 versus 6%). The Influentials' high level of education is probably a significant factor in their influence, giving them the ability to analyze problems and express positions in ways that are persuasive to others. Given the increasing appreciation of education by the public as a whole—"more and better education" is the leading response when Americans are asked what would change society for the better (55% have been saying so for more than a decade, up 10 points from 1976)—their higher attainment in education probably also gives the Influentials status. In education, the Influentials already *are* where Americans want to *go*.

Majorities of Influentials share certain other demographic factors as well. Just over seven in ten Influentials are employed in the workforce in a full- or part-time job (slightly more than the total public). Almost three-quarters of Influentials are homeowners (again, ahead of the total public, for whom the figure is about six in ten). More than two in three Influentials are married (compared with about six in ten of the public as a whole). More than four in ten Influentials have children 17 years old or younger living at home (slightly more than the public as a whole). Four in ten are in two-income households, which, combined with their activism and parental status, suggests their families are on the go (see Figure 1-1).

Although perhaps not as significant as education, these factors also play a role in the Influentials' influence. Being in the workforce, being a homeowner, and having a family give people a stake in the community; they're more likely to care about tax rates or the quality of schools, for example. Being a parent creates an additional stake in the future: you want your children's world to be a place where they can feel safe and have a high quality of life.

Large numbers of Influentials have been through the kind of life stage events that leaven ego and broaden perspective. Upward of three in four, for example, have been through the experience of moving out on their own, getting married, and becoming a parent. Many have experienced personal loss. About half have been through the death of a father and one in three the death of a mother. Influentials are more likely than the public as a whole to have gone through a major career change, a major illness, or a serious medical condition. Some have experienced the last child moving out of the nest and, more than a few, the experience of an adult child moving back home. Some have been through divorce and remarriage. When someone says they are going through a rough patch, many Influentials can respond that they have been there and know what it's like (see Figure 1-2).

Figure 1-1. Demographics: Who Is the Typical Influential?

A man *or* a woman (50% each)

Middle-aged
.... 45.2 years old for median (+2.3 years from the total public)

Middle/upper-middle class
.... $55,300 median household income (+$17,900 from the total public)

College educated
.... 80% have attended college (+30 points from total public)
.... 49% are college graduates (+26 points from total public)

Married with children
.... 70% are married (+13 points from total public)
.... 53% with children at home

Homeowners
.... 74% own their own home

Employed
.... 72% are in workforce
.... 58% in full-time job

Executive or professional
.... 34% as the leading occupation (+19 points from total public)

Source: Roper Reports

What else describes the average Influential? Median age (meaning half of Influentials are older and half younger) is about 45 years old, about two years older than the adult population as a whole. Median annual household income is about $55,300 a year—not rich, particularly by the standards of big cities like New York or San Francisco, but middle to upper-middle class for the country as a whole.

Many Influentials have achieved the hallmarks of modern life. On the whole, they're technologically literate. More than eight in ten Influentials have used a personal computer in the past 30 days, eight in ten have been on the Internet in the past 30 days, and four in five have a personal com-

Figure 1-2. Experienced in Life

Most Influentials have experienced

. . . . Moving out on their own 95% (+4 percentage points from total public)

. . . . Getting married 83% (+9)

. . . . Becoming a parent 78% (+7)

In addition, many have been through loss

. . . . Death of father 46% (+5)

. . . . Death of mother 34% (+4)

. . . . Getting divorced 24% (+3)

Career changes

. . . . Major career change 34% (+17)

. . . . Losing job 23% (+3)

. . . . Retiring 19% (+3)

Personal changes

. . . . Surviving major illness 24% (+8)

. . . . Changing diet because of medical condition 23% (+8)

. . . . Remarrying 17% (+5)

. . . . Menopause 15% (–)

. . . . Midlife crisis 12% (+4)

Parental changes

. . . . Last child moving out 27% (+2)

. . . . Adult child moving back home 14% (+5)

Source: Roper Reports

– indicates no difference

puter in the household; all these figures are about 1½ times the rate in the total public.

They're also savers. About three in four have money in mutual funds, stocks, bonds, retirement accounts, or money market funds, compared with about half in the public as a whole. Again substantially more than the public as a whole (for whom the rate is 50%), 71% of Influentials regularly sock away money for retirement. Eight in ten Influentials have two or more cars, and three in ten have three or more vehicles (see Figure 1-3).

Although these last factors are probably not as important in explaining

Figure 1-3. The Typical Influential Is

A hard worker

.... 41% in dual-income households (+10 points from total public)

.... 22% own their own businesses (+10)

More opinionated than the norm

.... 45% are politically conservative (+9 from the total public)

.... 30% are "middle of the road" (-10)

.... 24% are liberal (+5)

But mostly moderate/centrist

.... Split between Republicans (36%, +12), Democrats (34%, -4), and independents (27%, -6)

.... Mostly in the center: 76% are moderately conservative (30%), moderately liberal (16%), or middle of the road (30%)

Computer savvy

.... 84% have used a PC in the past 30 days (+27 points from total public)

.... 77% have accessed the Internet in the past 30 days (+27)

.... 81% have a PC at home (+27)

In a multicar household

.... 78% own two or more cars (+17 from total public)

.... 30% own three or more (+9)

Saver

.... 71% regularly put money away for retirement (+21 points from total public)

.... 75% have money in mutual funds, stocks, bonds, retirement accounts, or money markets (+24 from total public)

Source: Roper Reports

the segment's influence as education or life stage factors, such as being a parent, they suggest that Influentials are adept at the tools of this era for creating influence. They know how to use e-mail to spread the word for an important planning board meeting, for example, or to warn everyone they know when they've had a bad experience with a product or service. Insofar as Influentials save for their financial security in retirement, they show the kind of foresight and smarts that can engender respect and encourage influence.

Many Influentials share these demographic characteristics, but large numbers in the segment do not. Many, for example, fall on either side of the median income of $55,300 a year. Indeed, Influentials are spread across the spectrum in income, with significant numbers in households making $30,000–$49,999 or less than $30,000 a year.

Similarly, although the median-aged Influential is in her mid-forties, large numbers are older or younger. About one Influential in six is in her fifties. About one in seven is 18–29 years old, and about one in ten is in her sixties or 70 years old or older. Like income, age is a not a particularly strong gauge of whether a person is an Influential.

Although a large number of Influentials are in high-profile executive or professional positions, occupation is a relatively weak indicator. Influentials are about twice as likely as the public as a whole to be in executive or professional jobs, at 34 versus 19% of the total public. This means, however, that about two in three Influentials are *not* executives or professionals. Some don't exactly fit into traditional occupational categories: Mike Williams made a conscious decision several years ago to step back from his job as a mental health counselor and devote himself full-time to his community involvements. Some Influentials are entrepreneurs. Isabel Milano, for example, owns several businesses in the area with her husband, Bernie, a corporate jet pilot (see Figure 1-4).

Political affiliation is not a strong barometer, either. Ideologically, Influentials are more opinionated than the norm, just under half describing themselves as conservative and about one in four as liberal; they are less likely than the norm to describe themselves as middle of the road. Despite their conservative leanings, Influentials are about equally as likely to be Democrat as Republican, and more than one in four say they are independent.

Even in areas strongly associated with Influentials, including education, home ownership, and marriage, the numbers also reveal that fairly large numbers have not been to college (one in five, or about 6 million Influentials), are single (one in three, or about 7 million Influentials), or are renters or have other living arrangements (again, about one in five).

Influence, then, is not purely a matter of wealth, occupational status, or geographic location. So how do you recognize an Influential?

Figure 1-4. Many Influentials **Don't** *Fit the Mold*

Broad age distribution

.... 13% are 18-29 years old (-10 from the total public)

.... 19% are 30-39 years old (-2)

.... 30% are 40-49 years old (+8)

.... 17% are 50-59 years old (+4)

.... 13% are 60-69 years old (+2)

.... 8% are 70 years old or older (-3)

Broad range of household income

.... 6% under $15,000 per year (-8)

.... 12% $15,000-$29,999 (-12)

.... 27% $30,000-$49,999 (-2)

.... 56% $50,000 or more (+23)

.... 30% $75,000 or more (+15)

Broad range of occupations

.... 34% are in executive/professional jobs (+19 from total public)

.... 20% are in white-collar jobs (-1)

.... 18% are in blue-collar jobs (-10)

.... 15% are retired (-1)

.... 8% are homemakers (-1)

.... 2% are students (-1)

.... 2% are unemployed (-2)

.... 2% fit other descriptions (–)

Source: Roper Reports

Who Are the Influentials?
THE ACTIVISTS

What most identifies Influential Americans is their activism. They are involved in life in the broadest sense, and the result shines through like the facets of a diamond in the areas of their lives, from the office to leisure time. The first way to identify the Influentials, then, is that they demonstrate an *activist orientation* to life.

This engagement in life is evident, first, in their involvement in the community. In the past year, three in four Influentials have attended a meeting on town or school affairs. Seven in ten wrote or called a politician to make their opinions known. Half served on a committee of a local organization. A comparable number served as officers of a club or organization. Between three in ten and five in ten wrote a letter to the editor or called a live talk show to express their opinions, attended a political speech or rally, were active members of a group trying to influence public policy or government, or delivered a speech. One in five wrote an article for publication or worked for a political party.

These numbers are significant for several reasons. First, they show that Influentials are actively working the levers that create change in their communities and the larger society, making their case in public forums from publications, meetings, speeches, and call-in shows to try to persuade others to their point of view; working in leadership positions in clubs and organizations; working on committees, groups trying to influence government, or political parties; and placing themselves in behind-the-scenes settings where they can learn more about issues and perspectives. These skills are mostly applied to local issues, but they are often applied to issues in larger forums, making their voices known on national issues. As we show in this book, these skills also come in handy when Influentials have a complaint or praise about a product or service and decide to alert others.

Second, the data in Figure 1-5 show that Influentials are markedly more likely to be engaged in these activities than the public as a whole (the differences generally range from 22 percentage points upward to a whopping 41–58 points). Influentials are substantially more likely to be engaged in this work than groups traditionally pursued by business and politicians, like college graduates (who lag Influentials' involvement by an eye-opening average of 31 points), people in households making $75,000 or more per year (who lag Influentials by an average of 28 points), and people in executive or professional jobs (for whom the gap is also 28 points).

Last, the numbers show that for every Influential who actually holds or runs for political office (a group that totals only 5% of the Influential segment), substantially larger numbers are involved in their communities in other ways. This last insight has relevance for business as well as government, affirming the idea that the opinion leaders in the society are a group who extend well beyond the relative handful of people who are the visible

Figure 1-5. Activists in the Community

Percentage of Influential Americans who have done activity in past year, with percentage point difference from total public

74%. . . . Attended public meeting on town or school affairs (+58 points from the total public)
68%. . . . Wrote or called a politician at local, state, or national level (+56)
50%. . . . Served on a committee of a local organization (+43)
48%. . . . Were officers of a club or organization (+41)
45%. . . . Attended a political rally, speech, or organized protest (+38)
40%. . . . Wrote a letter to the editor or called a live broadcast to express their opinions (+34)
35%. . . . Were active members of a group trying to influence public policy or government (+30)
31%. . . . Made a speech (+27)
25%. . . . Worked for a political party (+22)
21%. . . . Wrote an article for a magazine or newspaper (+18)
6%. . . . . Held or ran for political office (+5)

Much more involved than their demographic peers (average for all items)
Influentials 43%
Executives and professionals 15%
$75,000-plus households 15%
College graduates 12%

Source: Roper Reports

leaders of the society and suggesting that a large number of Americans have an activist mind-set and activist behaviors.

Other research underscores the conclusion that the Influentials are highly active in their communities. Influentials are among the core of people who volunteer. More than seven in ten Influentials devote at least some time to a cause or issue in the community during the course of a year. Six in ten Influentials do volunteer work of some type in a typical month. In both measures of volunteerism, Influentials are markedly higher than other segments. The proportion volunteering in a typical month, for example, is double the rate of the public as a whole and about triple the level of people in higher income households, executives and professionals, and college graduates.

The activist mind-set is reflected at work as well. Influentials are significantly more likely than Americans overall to view their work as a career rather than a job, fully 75% of Influentials in the workforce saying they consider their work a career compared with only 56% of workers overall. They're hard workers. Influentials are significantly more likely than the public overall to bring work home (22% regularly among employed Influentials, more than double the rate in the public as a whole). Influentials do not mind occasionally when work spills over into leisure time (about half say they at least sort of enjoy it). They like being where the action is at work. Half are "completely satisfied" with the opportunities the job gives them to influence decisions in the workplace (double the rate of workers overall) and to make a contribution to society (about 1½ times the response of all workers).

Influentials also lead busy personal lives. Majorities of Influentials have a long list of activities they do at least occasionally in their leisure time: they read newspapers, books, and magazines, listen to music, eat out, spend time on hobbies, call friends and family, and get behind the stove and cook (at least occasionally by about three in four or more Influentials). They exercise and play sports, take weekend trips, volunteer in the community, attend cultural events, browse in stores, and browse the Internet (half or more). They aren't doing all these things all the time, of course—rather, the findings suggest a breadth of interests. And they do make time for themselves: about three in four at least occasionally use leisure time to be alone.

Influentials are substantially more likely than the average American to pursue a range of activities during leisure time. Befitting their orientation to community service, they are about twice as likely as the average American to volunteer in their leisure time. As shown in Figure 1–6, they are more likely than the average to engage in a number of other activities at least occasionally, with differences of 10 points or more for going to cultural events, taking weekend trips, reading books and magazines, and spending time on hobbies, for example. About the only areas they are not more likely to pursue are *passive activities,* such as watching television (they watch TV, but at far lower rates than the public as a whole).

Such activities are possible points of contact, of course, both for Influentials, who can use them to meet new people or rendezvous with old

Figure 1-6. Influentials Lead Active Leisure Life

Influentials are more likely to use their leisure time for active pursuits
Percentage who "often" do activity, with point difference from total public (percentage who do it at least "occasionally")

	"Often"	Point difference	"Occasionally," point difference from total public
Read newspaper	58%	+21	(88%, +14)
Listen to music	51%	+7	(88%, +1)
Read books	49%	+22	(81%, +17)
Cook	49%	+7	(75%, –)
Read magazines	40%	+17	(81%, +17)
Get prepared for work	38%	+4	(58%, +4)
Spend time alone	36%	+7	(78%, +2)
Spend time on hobbies	35%	+11	(80%, +17)
Talk on phone with family, friends	35%	+4	(81%, –)
Make home improvements, repairs	31%	+11	(70%, +13)
Go online, browse Web	30%	+11	(52%, +14)
Eat out in restaurants	29%	+8	(83%, +3)
Volunteer work, community service	27%	+20	(67%, +35)
Exercise, play sports	26%	+10	(69%, +10)
Travel on weekends	21%	+12	(62%, +18)
Browse in stores	20%	+5	(62%, +1)
Go to cultural events	12%	+7	(63%, +24)

. . . and are less likely than the norm to use leisure time for passive pursuits

Watch TV	35%	-14	(77%, -11)
Watch sports	21%	-6	(56%, -3)
Watch videos	15%	-2	(61%, +1)
Nap	11%	-4	(45%, -5)
Go to movies	8%	+2	(51%, +6)
Play video games	7%	+1	(21%, -1)

Source: Roper Reports

friends, and for businesses looking to engage Influentials in conversation. As we see in more detail in the pages to come, sponsoring a cultural event and advertising in magazines are among the leading ways to engage Influentials.

People are often part of Influentials' leisure plans. They get together with people on a regular basis: about six in ten have friends over at least two or three evenings per month, 1½ times the rate in the total public. One in five have met friends or business colleagues for dinner at a nice restaurant in their town in the past month, again about double the public as a whole.

Influentials are active travelers—travel, like reading and culture, is a major theme in the segment. They're much more likely than the norm to have taken various kinds of trips in the past year, to the lake or seashore (roughly eight in ten in a typical year, versus about half of the total public), on a driving tour (four in ten, about double the average for the total public), to another country (one in four, again, about double the norm), or to a resort (one in four, again, double). One place to see them, then, is on a plane, in a nearby beach chair, or on some sort of adventure.

They are active in the religious life of the nation as well (another theme—their sense of values). Six in ten Influentials have been to a church, synagogue, or temple service in the past month, the majority going every week. One in three Influentials have been to some sort of social function at church or synagogue in the past month, about double the response of the public as a whole. Befitting their status as leaders in the community, more than one in ten currently has a leadership position in the church, synagogue, or another religious group, triple the rate of the public as a whole.

Influentials' activist approach to life is thus the logical starting point for understanding their role in the society. It places them where they can exert influence and gives them skills and experience that make them important to others.

PROFILES IN INFLUENCE

Isabel Milano

Isabel Milano fits the active profile of the Influential. Her civic involvement in Irvington, New York is only one side of a many-sided activist approach to life. Milano has launched three businesses, one on her own and two with her husband, Bernie. She opened the first, a restaurant named Isabel's, at age 19 when she was taking a break after deciding the college where she had started wasn't right for her.

She has gone on to run two businesses with her husband, a Mobil service station and a Harley-Davidson motorcycle dealership. The focus of the businesses—which reflect the passions of her husband, a car buff, more than her own—is not particularly important to her. "I love taking ideas and getting them up and running," Milano says. "I'm a firm believer that business is business. The same principles apply, regardless of what you're doing and what you're selling."

If she has a gift, she thinks, it's this kind of "orchestration" of ideas and people. She looks at life as "an adventure," presenting new opportunities to bring people together, strike out in new directions, and bring about change. Gather enough people with "positive energy," she believes, and you can solve problems that to many would seem insurmountable.

This mind-set has been the starting point for most of Milano's civic involvement. When the school district was coming off a divisive contract negotiation with teachers, she got together with a group of other parents and organized a celebration to mark the beginning of the school year, to help heal the divisions and move forward. Around the same time, she became involved in the Parent Teacher Student Association; because of her business background, she was asked to be treasurer.

Parents Connection, the mothers' group, grew out of informal conversations in that period with other mothers about issues in the community and their lives. They realized that the bonding within the group—"just being able to say, I know what you're going through, the simple things"— was something that could build relationships and a sense of community on

a larger scale within the town. The idea took off. It was a completely different kind of experience. It's nice to satisfy people by "taking care of their cars
or giving them a nice time on a Friday night in your restaurant," she says,
but the group showed what it was like to help people on a deeper level.
Being able to bring women who didn't know many other people into the
community was "very fulfilling." It was a valuable lesson. "When you volunteer, people think, 'Oh, you use so much of your time,' " she says. "But I
have gotten so much more back out of it."

This kind of sharing and connection is at the root of Milano's philosophy. She values bringing people together toward a common goal. "The
more people you can bring together, and the more who can benefit from it,
the better," she says. The people orientation is in her nature. She had much
the same approach in high school, when she was both junior and senior
class president. She thinks it probably started with being the oldest girl in a
family of seven. She doesn't see herself as an expert so much as someone
who knows "bits and pieces of this and that" and has a knack for connecting people with what they want.

So far so good. The businesses have been a success. Once set up, they
have afforded the Milanos the opportunity to focus on the big picture, on
family and community activities, and let managers run the day-to-day
operations. The Harley-Davidson dealership is set to move into a new location double the size of the current property. She gets a kick out the power
of the Harley brand: "we sell everything from coffee to baby clothes."

Although her inclination is toward family and people, the work the
Milanos have put into life has paid off in material ways as well. She and her
husband and children live in a handsome home they built 10 years ago.
Around the house are the modern-day signs of success: a Sony home theater system in the family room, a passel of computers, nice appliances, and
a batting cage in the backyard for her son to practice his swings. The family is able to get away on vacations, and she and two of her sisters have been
talking about taking a trip to Ireland, her family's ancestral home. They go
out to eat as often as they can.

She especially likes what she sees in the community, though—the new
park, the new library, the additions to the school, the renovation of the village hall, the volunteers who contribute their time, and the human interac-

tions large and small that contribute to change. "I love the human elements in all this," she says. "I'm in the thick of it, but there's a part of me that steps back sometimes and watches and just loves it."

Who Are the Influentials?
PEOPLE WHO ARE CONNECTED

Isabel Milano's emphasis on connections could describe Influentials generally. Combined with the Influentials' sense of activism, this focus on people is a major factor in the segment's influence in the society. Their contacts create new opportunities that bring them into contact with more people, in turn creating more opportunities and more contacts and an ever-widening network. Isabel Milano, for example, was asked to run for village trustee based on the contacts she had developed through her activism for schools. The friends who suggested she run saw her as someone who could bridge the older generation, which had always been active in village affairs, with the newer generation of parents whose main involvement in Irvington was through their children in the schools. Her school involvements seem to build one upon another in similar style. The back-to-school celebration led to more contact with parents, leading to PTSA and the Parents Connection, and a seat on the long-range planning committee, building contacts that led to the education and athletic foundations. The second way to identify the Influentials, then, is that in addition to being activists, they are connected.

Influentials have ties to a significantly larger number of groups than the average American. Like Isabel Milano, they feel a particularly strong sense of connection to the community where they live. When asked whether they feel they have a connection to various types of groups, almost all Influentials, 96%, feel at least "some" connection to the neighborhood or town where they live and more than six in ten feel a "strong" connection to the neighborhood or town. Among working Influentials, the workplace has a comparable sense of connection. Virtually all employed Influentials feel at least some connection to their workplace, and seven in ten feel a strong connection (recalculate to the total Influential population, and these numbers drop somewhat, because some Influentials are not in the workforce).

As further evidence of their beliefs and values, a wide majority of Influentials also feel a bond with a church, synagogue, or spiritual group. More than eight in ten feel at least some connection, and six in ten have a strong connection. Half or more of Influentials report at least some connection to five other communities as well: a political group, such as the major parties or a lobbying organization like the AARP; an alumni association; a group devoted to a hobby or interest—a reading club, a collectors group, or a fan of a particular sports team; and a youth-related group, such as youth soccer, Little League, scouts, or the PTA. Close to half report a link to a social activism or volunteer organization, including Sierra Club, Mothers Against Drunk Driving, and the kinds of community groups with which Isabel Milano is involved. Four in ten have a connection with a professional group or union: the American Medical Association, the American Association of Advertising Agencies, or the United Automobile Workers. Substantial numbers—between one in five and one in three—feel connected to an ethnic group, a demographic group (retired people, college students, or their own generational group), a support group like Al-Anon, AA, or Parents Without Partners, or a virtual or online community.

Influentials are far more likely than the average American to be connected to many groups. Indeed, there are differences of 20 percentage points or more—major differences—between the percentages of Influentials and the public as a whole who feel connected to political groups (29 points), alumni associations (28 points), social activist and volunteer groups (26 points), hobby and interest groups (22 points), youth-related groups (22 points), and professional groups or unions (21 points) (see Figure 1-7).

Influentials are more likely than the norm to feel *strongly* connected to many of these groups as well. In nine areas, there are differences of 10 points or more between Influentials and the public as a whole, starting with a neighborhood or town (21 points), social activist or volunteer group (17 points), and youth-related group (16 points). Supporting these groups' activities—a town's annual fair, the education foundation's fund-raiser, a town cleanup, or clearing land for sports fields—can be another way to begin a relationship with Influentials.

Being connected likely helps Influentials on various levels. It introduces

Figure 1-7. Plugged In: Connected to Many Communities

Percentage of Influentials saying they feel at least "some" connection to group, with point difference from total public (percentage who feel "strong" connection)

	At least "some" connection	Point difference	"Strong" connection, point difference
Neighborhood or town	96%	+7	(63%, +21)
Religious or spiritual group	85%	+6	(59%, +14)
Workplace	72%	+7	(51%, +12)
Political group	58%	+29	(22%, +13)
Alumni association for college or school	57%	+28	(20%, +10)
Group for hobby, interest	57%	+22	(22%, +10)
Youth-related group	53%	+22	(29%, +16)
Social activism/volunteer group	47%	+26	(25%, +17)
Professional group or union	43%	+21	(25%, +14)
Ethnic group	34%	-2	(14%, –)
Demographic group	33%	+2	(9%, -2)
Support group	22%	+5	(10%, +2)
Virtual/online community	22%	+6	(8%, +4)
Gay/lesbian	8%	+1	(2%, –)

. . . and they are much more connected than their demographic peers:
> Number of groups to which 50% or more in segment feel a connection
>> Influentials 7
>> College graduates 4
>> $75,000-plus households 3
>> Executives and professionals 3

Source: Roper Reports

them to different points of view and increases the opportunity to encounter information they might not otherwise get on subjects from social and political issues to everyday decisions—ideas about restaurants or vacation destinations. It can enable them to traverse economic or social boundaries and establish relationships with people whom they might otherwise not meet. It gives them contacts they can call upon if they have a question or are trying to rally support for an issue.

The research also sheds some light on how to engage Influentials. The groups to which Influentials feel a sense of connection are hubs for Influentials to encounter other people and perspectives. An obvious starting point for cultivating a positive image among Influentials is to support these kinds of groups through cause-related marketing programs and other kinds of involvement—sponsoring events for educational foundations or youth sports programs, for example. Companies can also encourage involvement by employees in these areas. Besides making a contribution, they get an opportunity to know Influentials personally. As we explain in Chapter 6, large numbers of Influentials expect companies to contribute and be part of the community.

The strength and breadth of the Influentials' connections in their communities also draws out the distinction between them and traditionally courted demographic segments, such as the affluent, the college educated, and people in executive or professional jobs. Most Influentials have a connection to seven different groups. In contrast, the typical executive or professional feels connected to only three groups; college graduates, only four groups; and people in $75,000-plus households, only three groups. Almost all executives and professionals, for example, feel connected to a workplace—it's where they spend most of their days, after all. About nine in ten feel connected to their town, and about eight in ten have some sort of religious connection. Work is the only area, however, in which a majority of executives and professionals feel a "strong" sense of connection.

The idea that affluence is not a gauge of influence, that money in and of itself doesn't buy power, is not an entirely new thought. Walter Lippmann noted 80 years ago in *Public Opinion* that many people "live in grooves, shut in among their own affairs" and "barred out of larger affairs." They have the resources to do more, but they "meet few people not of their own sort," read "little," and "always" talk to "the same people, with minute variations, on the same, old themes," Lippmann said. "Worlds of interest are waiting for them to explore, and they do not enter." Instead they move through life "as if on a leash, within a fixed radius according to the gospel of their social set." There's a relevant point here for contemporary business. Executives who talk only to people in their own social set miss out on a lot (including many Influentials).

We have focused on a specific way of measuring Influentials' connectedness, but there are many other examples in our research. Influentials are markedly more likely, for instance, to think that "the community I live in is an important part of who I am"; 74% agree at least "mostly" with the statement, 41% agreeing "completely," substantially higher than the responses of the average American (59 and 26%, respectively). Influentials are much more likely to agree completely with the statement than executives and professionals (27%), college graduates (29%), and people in $75,000-plus households (31%). Separately, almost all Influentials report at least a basic level of satisfaction with their relationships with their neighbors, 71% saying they're "very satisfied" with their neighbors, a level higher than in the public as a whole (55%) and among peers, such as executives (59%) and the affluent (58%). About nine in ten Influentials in the workforce express a basic sense of satisfaction with their relationships at work, saying they're "fairly well satisfied," with four in ten "completely satisfied" with their work relationships. The responses are comparable to those of executives and professionals, who are more apt to be single-mindedly focused on work.

Relationships seem to be key to Influentials' well-being. The Influentials' leading response to feeling down is not to withdraw but to call someone on the phone. Likewise, when asked what they do when they feel like indulging themselves, the Influentials' first response is to call someone on the phone.

As Isabel Milano's story shows, there's a value in having connections across different kinds of groups, with different interests, insights, and, probably, different demographic compositions. It brings people into contact with perspectives and information they otherwise might not obtain. It can enable them to traverse economic or social boundaries and to establish relationships with people whom they might not otherwise encounter. It builds networks that can be called on to organize support for a cause. It probably fosters credibility as well. If an Influential is attuned to what she sees or hears, when she speaks about an issue, she has a more informed, balanced perspective. Knowing how different groups feel, she can advance proposals that have better prospects for success. She's more likely to be listened to, as well. People know she has done her homework.

Who Are the Influentials?
PEOPLE WITH IMPACT

The third essential ingredient of Influentials is influence. They are people who are looked up to by others for their advice and opinion.

Influential Americans are about twice as likely as the average American to be asked for advice and opinions on a range of topics. Appropriately, Influentials report that they are most likely to get asked their advice or opinion about "what's going on in government or politics." Fully 55% of Influentials say they're asked for their perspectives on this subject, a remarkable 39 percentage points higher than that of the total public. Large numbers of Influentials report that they are asked their insights in many other areas as well (as shown in Figure 1-8). As much as Influentials are valued for their opinions on government and politics, they are almost as highly prized for tips on good restaurants. Almost half of Influentials are turned to for advice or opinions on cooking.

More than four in ten Influentials say people turn to them for advice or opinions on health problems. About four in ten Influentials say people seek them out for parenting insights on raising small children and teenagers. Comparable numbers of Influentials say people turn to them for their perspective on where to go on vacation and how to invest. About one in three Influentials say people ask them about computers, makes and models of automobiles, and career choices. Significant numbers, between one in four and one in three, say they're sought out on music, automotive problems and repairs, what's going on in professional sports, or tips on golf, tennis, or another sport. More than one in five say people ask them for advice or opinions on Web sites.

Influentials are not experts on everything. They are considerably more likely to be sought out on some subjects than on others. They're not particularly likely to be turned to about hairstyles or fashion. Young adults seem to rule the roost in clothing styles; people aged 18–29 are twice as

Figure 1-8. Opinion Leaders on a Wide Range of Topics

Percentage of Influentials who tend to get asked for advice or opinion on topic, with percentage point difference from total public

Point difference

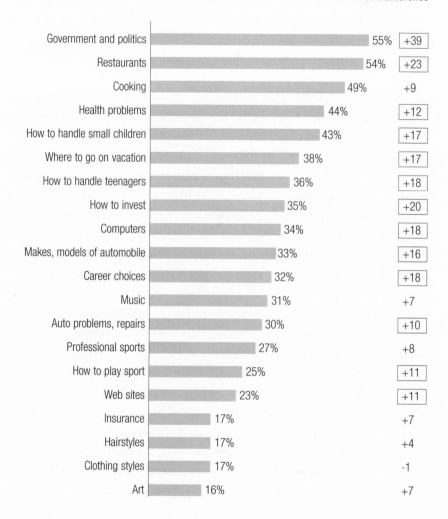

Topic	Percentage	Point difference
Government and politics	55%	+39
Restaurants	54%	+23
Cooking	49%	+9
Health problems	44%	+12
How to handle small children	43%	+17
Where to go on vacation	38%	+17
How to handle teenagers	36%	+18
How to invest	35%	+20
Computers	34%	+18
Makes, models of automobile	33%	+16
Career choices	32%	+18
Music	31%	+7
Auto problems, repairs	30%	+10
Professional sports	27%	+8
How to play sport	25%	+11
Web sites	23%	+11
Insurance	17%	+7
Hairstyles	17%	+4
Clothing styles	17%	-1
Art	16%	+7

Much more likely to be asked than their demographic peers (average for all topics)
Influentials 33%
$75,000-plus households 26%
Executives and professionals 24%
College graduates 23%

Source: Roper Reports

likely as Influentials to say they are sought out for advice and opinions on clothes (32 versus 17%). Women 18–49 years old are the society's leading source for perspectives on hairstyles (27 versus only 17% for Influentials). Although Influentials have some expertise in cooking, women are still the leading font of knowledge on cooking by a fairly wide margin (60 versus 49% for Influentials). Young adults are sought out more than any other group for music (41% among people 18–29 versus 31% for Influentials). Men 18–49 years old are a bit more likely to be turned to for advice on car repairs than Influentials (35 versus 30% for Influentials). Thus, influence is broadly distributed. As we said in 1978, "almost everyone is an expert on something."

At the same time, the research suggests (noted in our analysis when the question was first fielded in 1978) that the Influentials have the most influence across a *breadth* of topics compared with any of the other major segments. In 13 of the 20 areas we ask about, there are double-digit differences between the percentages of Influentials who are asked for their insights and the total public, led by government and politics (39 points), restaurants (23 points), investing (20 points), teenagers (18 points), computers (18 points), career decisions (18 points), vacations (17 points), and small children (17 points). In a number of areas, the Influentials are more likely to be asked for their advice and opinion than other groups such as executives and the affluent, traditionally pursued by business. In investing, for example, there is a 12 point margin between Influentials and executives. In travel, there is a 10 point difference between Influentials and executives. In 12 areas in all, Influentials are the most likely to be sought of any of the two dozen standard demographic groups we track. Influentials stand out as influence generalists, people who know a lot about some things and something about a lot of things and can usually track down the answer if they don't know it.

Isabel Milano is a case in point. As a village trustee with a background in civic involvement, she is one of the people who knows the most about what's going on in government and politics in Irvington. Because she travels in several circles, however (village government, the schools, the education groups, her business, her church, and her family and friends), she picks up insights in many other areas, "bits and pieces of this and that," as she puts it. As a result, she is asked by people for restaurant tips, about schools, for insights on parenting, how to apply for patents, and other topics. With her broad network of contacts, if she doesn't know the answer, she knows someone who does or who knows how to find it. Like many Influentials, she's an expert on expertise.

The data begin to give us a picture of where Influential Americans are most important, the subjects about which they are most likely to produce word-of-mouth insights. If you're involved in government and politics, restaurants, food, health, kids, travel, personal finance, technology, cars, careers, and culture, there's special reason to know what Influentials are thinking and doing. If you're only tangentially involved in these areas—for example, if you're an advertising copywriter wondering what Influentials are talking about so that you can depict them accurately—these are conversational hubs of Influentials: they're what Influentials talk about when they get together. Knowing what they're talking about and where they influence opinions in the society doesn't mean an advertising copywriter will be able to speak persuasively. In fact, without a broader understanding of Influentials, such as their expectations of business, the copywriter will likely have a very difficult time. We are, however, another step closer to understanding this important group.

PROFILES IN INFLUENCE

Larry Lee

To see what an Influential's life looks like in practice, consider Larry Lee, Jr. Though the 47-year-old Fort Pierce, Florida State Farm Insurance agent doesn't hold elected office, his reputation among his friends and neighbors as "the Mayor" is well-deserved.

Lee was the first African-American on the board of directors of the Port St. Lucie County Chamber of Commerce. He was a founding member of the Fort Pierce Jazz Society, dedicated to promoting the jazz tradition to the community. He founded the Treasure Coast Gospel Fest, an annual music festival that raises funds for local youth, drug rehabilitation programs for men and women, and a ministry to feed the hungry.

His number one priority these days is the local Boys and Girls Club. Last year, he joined the club's board of directors, which sets policy, approves the budget, allocates funds, and raises funds for the organization. The club serves about 1,800 youths through mentors, recreation programs, and field trips, even serving lunch in the summer.

Lee has two mottoes: "Do all I can while I can" and "I believe in reaching back and giving back."

A former schoolteacher and assistant high school football coach, Lee is a great believer in the Boys and Girls Club's mission: "giving young people the opportunity to get involved with other kids and be in programs that teach them how to be good citizens." He doesn't think it's possible to underestimate the importance of having connections. "Many kids fall into lives of crime because they don't have it," he says. "We try to create an atmosphere where they feel they belong."

Lee also is spearheading a $3.5 million drive to build the Human Resource Development Center, which will house youth activities and adult education, computer training, job training, and recreational programs for youth and other residents.

He is cofounder of the Avenue O Community Investment Club, an investment club of old friends from school days (most of them played on the Avenue O sandlot football league) who went on to do well—one's a cardiologist, another's a pharmacist—and left town for places like Miami, Chicago, and New York. The club operates like many of the investment clubs that have sprung up in recent years—members pool funds and invest in the market with a conference call once a quarter—with one exception. They're putting their profits back into redevelopment projects in a blighted area of their old neighborhood. The group, together for two years, is about to buy its first property.

Lee has been active in politics, campaigning for candidates on the local, state, and national levels and running several campaigns. He has been a member of the boards of the former Barnet Bank and Nationsbank. Cofounder of the Business Investment Group, another stock club, he was until recently a board member of the Workforce Development Board, a federal government agency. He is an elder at the Goodwill Presbyterian Church.

With his daughter, Latasha, now in college, Lee is making time for new pursuits. "I've started playing a lot of golf in the past two years," says Lee. With his wife, he is building what they call their "poet's and dreamer's garden" in their backyard. The garden, modeled on one they used to stroll in college, is sprinkled with inspirational quotations from favorite writers (Maya Angelou, Lorraine Hansberry, and George Bernard Shaw, among others). The Lees enjoy getting involved in design; like Isabel and Bernie Milano, they built the home they live in.

They enjoy travel and get away often, with annual trips to his childhood home in Statesboro, Georgia and to see her family near Atlanta. There are frequent weekend jaunts around Florida as well. Being in a stressful business, Lee says, it's rejuvenating to "just get away sometimes, remove myself from the environment in which I live and work."

Still solidly built, he was a star linebacker in high school and went on to play football at Livingston College in Salisbury, North Carolina. With dreams of the big time, he signed a contract with the Denver Broncos pro football team. After he was cut in the preseason, though, Lee came to the realization that "football was only a temporary part of his life—it had served a purpose in helping me to obtain an education." Now it was time to move on.

Things have worked out—and then some. As part of a campaign highlighting its agents' roots, State Farm featured Lee in a national advertisement, photographing him in front of the Jazz Society's House of Jazz music club. The campaign also put Lee on brochures distributed throughout State Farm's 16,000-office network. Like Influentials generally, Lee finds himself being sought out for advice and information. "A lot of the older people think that because I have done OK in insurance and a few other areas, I know more than I know. So they come to me for all sorts of things." He tries to help. "There were so many people who reached out to help me who did not have to," he says. "Without them, I would not be where I am today." Giving back, he says, "is the least I can do."

Who Are the Influentials?
PEOPLE WITH ACTIVE MINDS

When Larry Lee, Jr. takes off on one of his weekend trips, he doesn't turn off his mind. Rather, he turns it loose. He got the idea for the Fort Pierce Jazz Society, for example, on a trip to the birthplace of jazz, New Orleans. "I like meeting people, seeing how other communities work." If he sees "something positive in another community," his first thought is to think of a way to "start a movement to get it here."

Lee's restless intellect is fairly typical of Influential Americans. An active mind is the fourth major characteristic of Influentials. Influential Americans are continuously taking input from what they see, hear, and read and turning it over in their minds for new insights and ideas.

The Influential Americans' high level of education is one tip-off of their involvement with learning. It is not the only one. Life continually presents opportunities to learn something new. Many Influentials would agree with Isabel Milano, who likes to "learn through people and experiences."

Influentials are not the kind of people who slog through their days, performing the same rote behaviors over and over again.

Learning temperament comes through in various ways. Influentials are much more likely than the public as a whole to maintain interests in a number of areas. Befitting their positions in the community, they express the highest level of interest in news and current events. Almost all Influentials are at least moderately interested in what's going on in the world. More than nine in ten Influentials express interest in the environment. Most Influentials (80% or more) are interested in fitness and health, nature and animals, music, politics, history, and technology. More than three in four express interest in science, different countries and people, and cooking (see Figure 1-9).

Not everything piques their curiosity. Only about one in three Influentials, for example, admit to being interested in famous people and celebrities. Influentials are not as likely to be carrying the banner for the celebrity culture as other groups, including young adults (55%) and women 18–49 (54%). Similarly, only 41% of Influentials are interested in fashion, further evidence that they're not as important to the designer set as working

Figure 1-9. Active Minds: Many Interests

Percentage of Influentials who are "moderately" or "very interested" in topic, with percentage point difference from total public

Point difference

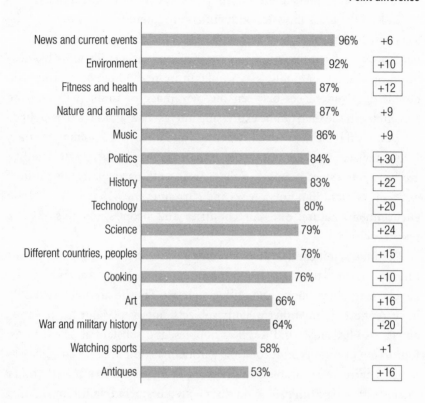

Topic	Percentage	Point difference
News and current events	96%	+6
Environment	92%	+10
Fitness and health	87%	+12
Nature and animals	87%	+9
Music	86%	+9
Politics	84%	+30
History	83%	+22
Technology	80%	+20
Science	79%	+24
Different countries, peoples	78%	+15
Cooking	76%	+10
Art	66%	+16
War and military history	64%	+20
Watching sports	58%	+1
Antiques	53%	+16

Percentage who are "very interested" (ranked by difference from total public)

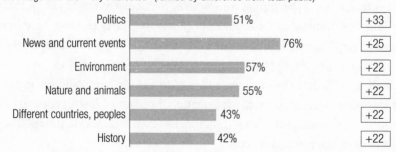

Topic	Percentage	Point difference
Politics	51%	+33
News and current events	76%	+25
Environment	57%	+22
Nature and animals	55%	+22
Different countries, peoples	43%	+22
History	42%	+22

Source: Roper Reports

women (69%), women generally (61%), or young adults (58%). Influentials are interested in sports, but they're not as passionate as men 18–49 (76% of whom express interest in sports versus 58% for Influentials).

Still, in the areas in which Influentials are interested (as with the subjects on which they're most likely to be asked their advice or opinion, these tend toward substantive, meaty areas), they are substantially more likely to be engaged than the public as a whole. In more than ten areas, there are double-digit differences between the percentage of Influentials and the percentage in the total public expressing interest in a subject, led by politics (30 point difference), science (24 points), and history (22 points). Further, Influentials are markedly more likely than the average person to say they are "very interested" in many of these areas, with particularly large differences in politics (33 points), news and current events (25 points), and the environment, nature, different countries and peoples, and history (22 points each).

Reading, significantly, is their leading hobby (cited by 68%); as we see time and again in the pages to come, Influentials are heavy readers of newspapers, magazines, books, and online material. They're not interested only in current events and other weighty subjects, however. Majorities of Influentials also list music and travel as hobbies, and substantial proportions, four in ten or more, count cooking, gardening, computers, and exercise as hobbies or interests. Sizable numbers (one in five or more) pursue 12 other interests ranging from pets to outdoor activities, including fishing, hiking, camping, and bicycling, and photography, investing, and golf. In a number of these areas, again, Influentials are more likely to claim these as hobbies and interests than the public as a whole, particularly travel (27 points), reading (26 points), and computers (21 points). They're not into everything: fewer than one in five Influentials claims bowling or extreme sports as a hobby, for example (see Figure 1-10).

Still, as with the subjects they're turned to for advice or opinion and the topics they're interested in, the Influentials' breadth of interest bespeaks a breadth of knowledge and insight that makes them valuable to others. They tend to keep their minds sharp.

Lee is a case in point. He reads the local newspaper and *The Wall Street Journal* every day and *Money* and *Black Enterprise* magazines every month.

Figure 1-10. Active Minds: Many Hobbies

Percentage of Influentials saying item is hobby or interest of theirs, with percentage point difference from total public

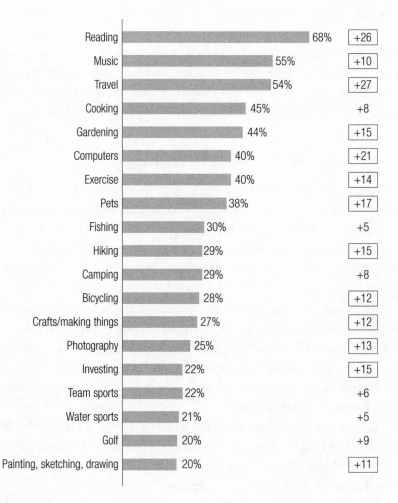

Point difference

Hobby	Percentage	Point difference
Reading	68%	+26
Music	55%	+10
Travel	54%	+27
Cooking	45%	+8
Gardening	44%	+15
Computers	40%	+21
Exercise	40%	+14
Pets	38%	+17
Fishing	30%	+5
Hiking	29%	+15
Camping	29%	+8
Bicycling	28%	+12
Crafts/making things	27%	+12
Photography	25%	+13
Investing	22%	+15
Team sports	22%	+6
Water sports	21%	+5
Golf	20%	+9
Painting, sketching, drawing	20%	+11

Source: Roper Reports

He tries to read a few books a month, usually self-help and business titles. His television tastes run to informational programming; he watches the news and financial shows, CNN, CNBC, and *Moneyline.* A big fan of the Home and Garden Cable Network, he uses it for ideas and inspiration for his garden and other home projects. He loves game shows: *Weakest Link, Jeopardy,* and *Who Wants to Be a Millionaire?* are recent mainstays. He watches them, he says, because they're educational and entertaining and a good way to "test my mind." He tends to think such mental activity will keep him younger as he ages. "I have a lot of friends who are 80-plus years old, and one of the things I've learned from them in terms of how to live and age is to keep your mind active, read a lot, do crossword puzzles."

A Product That Works: The Cell Phone

Longtime cell phone users sometimes joke about the old days when cell phones weighed a ton, cost a fortune, and used up batteries faster than you could dial 911. Larry Lee, Jr. remembers those days well. He bought his first cell phone in 1989. "It was one of those real big ones," he recalls. "I bought it in Port St. Lucie at a U.S. Cellular store that one of my policy holders ran."

His pioneering purchase reveals another side of the Influentials' value to their friends and family, as well as the marketplace and society. Because they are interested in a variety of subjects and have a breadth of resources providing a steady stream of information, from their reading and viewing to their network of contacts, they tend to hear about new products like cell phones ahead of the masses.

To Lee, the unwieldiness of his first cell phone ("imagine walking around with a brick and an antenna all day") was worth the convenience it offered. Lee had a beeper, but "it was not a good way to stay in contact." When he saw a client haul out a cell phone, he was sold.

The benefits were clear to the busy Influential. The phone increased his efficiency, making it possible to keep up with work while doing something else. It also erased geography, making it possible to stay linked with the office while somewhere else, a huge boon for anyone in a service position.

"A lot of times, when I'm out of the office, a client will call with a question, and rather than telling the person I'm out, my staff can say, 'Let me check with him and we'll get back to you,' " says Lee, who today carries a sleek black Ericsson R289LX he bought at a local AT&T store. "They call me, ask me the question, and I tell them what to do. In many cases I call the customer back myself."

Influentials were integral in building the market for cell phones. By 1992, when fewer than half of the public as a whole had heard of them, mobile phones had virtually universal awareness among Influentials. Within two years the product was gaining a foothold in the segment. Prospects for the category's growth looked promising: many Influentials voiced interest in getting a cell phone in the next year or two. By 1995, 14% of Influentials had a cell phone, double the penetration in the total public.

By 1997, the penetration of mobile phones among Influentials had reached 40%, 16 points higher than the total public. As of 2001, 62% of Influentials had a cell phone, versus 44% of the total public. As shown in Figure 1-11, Influentials have been about three years ahead of the total public on cell phones.

Today, Influentials are ready for cell phones to do more. The jury seems to be out on what Influentials want their cells to do, however. The growth of text messaging seems assured from their perspective, with 56% expressing interest. Services that enhance convenience, such as being able to access e-mail from remote by cell phone (46%) and being able to get news updates and traffic information (about 40% each), stand the best chances of other services. But Influentials are wary of loading too much into their mobiles. There is comparatively little interest, for example, in using mobiles for electronic payments (see Figure 1-12).

Who Are the Influentials?
TRENDSETTERS

Although we originally studied the Influentials for their role as opinion leaders in public policy, the Influentials tend to be pioneer consumers as well, as Larry Lee was with his mobile phone. This is the fifth major characteristic of Influentials. In addition to being people who are actively engaged in the community and many areas of life, have a broad network of

Figure 1-11. The Adoption Trend: Cell Phones

Percentage who have cell phone

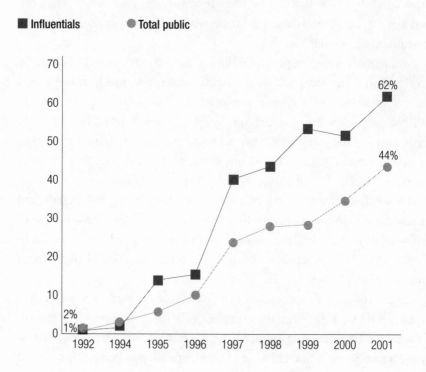

Source: Roper Reports

connections, are looked to by others for their advice and insight, and have active minds, Influential Americans tend to be trendsetters for the larger society.

The Influentials are not "the most voracious consumers," as the first in-depth Roper report on Influentials said in 1988. Compared with the affluent, Influentials "are not the group with the most of everything or the one that routinely purchases the most expensive products." Influentials, however, have a way of finding important things well in advance of other segments of the society. Being "assiduous experimenters," they also often serve as a test laboratory for the mainstream market.

Figure 1-12. Varying Interest in Doing More with Cell Phones

Interest among Influentials in performing function with cell phone, with percentage point difference from total public

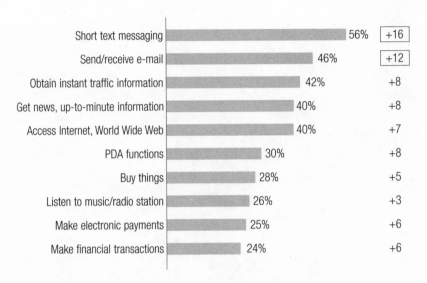

Point difference

		Point difference
Short text messaging	56%	+16
Send/receive e-mail	46%	+12
Obtain instant traffic information	42%	+8
Get news, up-to-minute information	40%	+8
Access Internet, World Wide Web	40%	+7
PDA functions	30%	+8
Buy things	28%	+5
Listen to music/radio station	26%	+3
Make electronic payments	25%	+6
Make financial transactions	24%	+6

Source: Roper Reports

Influentials were among the first to have a personal computer. Since then, the Influentials have been about three to five years ahead of the total public. In 1983, only a few years after the first PCs hit the consumer market, 9% of Influentials had their own computer, double the rate in the total public. By 1986, almost one in three Influentials had a PC (more than double the total public). By 1995, more than half of Influentials had a PC (again, double the total public). As of the year 2000, three in four Influentials had a PC compared with half of the total public (see Figure 1-13).

Influentials were among the first to recognize the potential of the Internet as well. In 1996, 40% of Influentials were accessing the Internet, compared with 19% of the public as a whole. Within four years, the Net had

Figure 1-13. The Adoption Trend: Personal Computers

Percentage who have personal computer in household

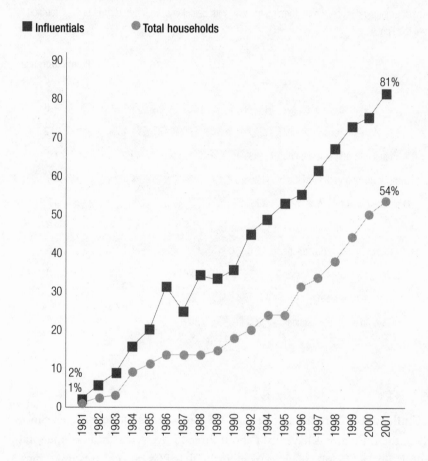

■ Influentials   ● Total households

Source: Roper Reports

been integrated into the everyday life of the majority of Influentials. By 2000, 80% were accessing the Internet (versus half of the total public); of that 80%, virtually all were online regularly (see Figure 1-14).

Influentials were among the first to bypass bank tellers and to bank using automated teller machines. By 1998, 32% of Influentials were using ATM cards to make consumer purchases (10 points higher than the total public). Influentials were in early on VCRs as well. In 1982, only a few years

Figure 1-14. The Adoption Trend: The Internet

Percentage accessing Internet or online service

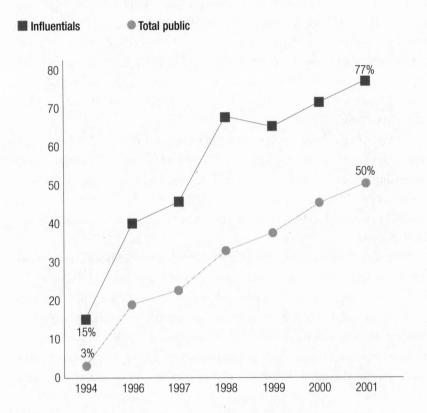

Source: Roper Reports

after VCRs were introduced, 15% of Influentials had one (9 points higher than the total public). The Influentials were among the first Americans to switch their home moviemaking to video camcorders; by 1988, 13% of Influentials had a camcorder (8 points higher than the total public).

They got in early on the retirement accounts, mutual funds, and stock market booms. In 1982, when the ink on the legislation creating IRAs had hardly dried, about one in five Influentials had an IRA (double the rate of the total public). By 1995, as changes in the tax laws made 401(k) accounts more attractive, more than one in three Influentials had an IRA or 401(k) account (about double the rate in the total public). By 2000, more than half had one (versus about one in three of the total public). As the stock market slipped in 2000–2002, they took a step back (see Figure 1-15).

Over the years, we've been able to forecast trends in the larger society based on patterns in Influentials. Observing the early data on personal computers, we predicted in 1988 that "the home computer market will experience sustained growth in the future." Looking at Influentials' increased thirst for bottled water, in the same report we wrote that "bottled water has a bright future."

The record has held up. A subsequent report in 1992 predicted that "cellular telephones look strong." A 1995 report found Influentials were increasingly focused on creating an "integrated life," in which work and leisure are in "balance," foreshadowing a larger cultural shift, as well as products and services that enabled people to take back time, from takeout foods to new technologies.

Influentials have led the way in the ups and downs of health and fitness trends. Influentials started pounding the pavement in the mid-1970s in the early days of jogging. By the early 1980s, though, as the jogging craze was catching on with the rest of the country, Influentials were getting bored and moving on. The numbers of joggers in the general public didn't start to decline until several years later. Influentials were among the first to try out alternative medicines in the 1990s and to sort out those that worked and didn't work.

They've been predictive of changing political winds: 10 months before the 1974 crisis that forced Richard Nixon to resign from office, two-thirds of Influentials described themselves as "critics" of the president. At the same time, Influentials believed the nation could withstand the constitutional test of Watergate. When many others thought the nation was in some way fundamentally broken, the Influentials maintained that the government would survive, the Constitution was sound, and "no fundamental changes were needed."

They helped sow the seeds of the modern consumer movement. About the same time in the 1970s that they were calling for a change in the White House, more than three in four Influentials thought "big business" had "too much power." In contrast, they were also more likely than the general pub-

Figure 1-15. The Adoption Trend: New Investment Tools

Percentage who have money in 401(k), IRA, or other retirement account

■ **Influentials**   ● **Total public**

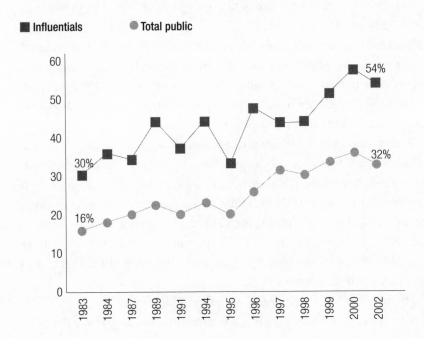

Percentage of Influentials who have money in mutual funds

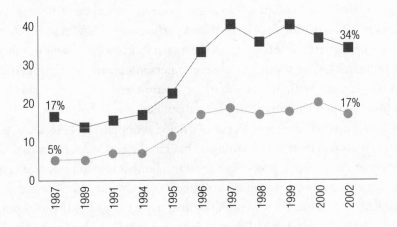

Source: Roper Reports

lic to think that "consumer protection groups" had "too little power" (49 versus 35% for the total public).

They were early to express skepticism when national brands didn't deliver on value. More than four in ten Influentials in the early 1970s judged store brands "a better value" than national brands (43 versus 26% for the total public). About half said they were buying store brands at least "quite often," versus about four in ten of the total public.

Before the nation as a whole flocked to small cars, more than one in four Influentials in late 1973 had a compact car, a response 1½ times higher than in the public as a whole. It was even more forward-thinking than it looks: it was only at that time that OPEC's oil price increase sent a shudder through the world (October 17, 1973); the Gulf states announced their boycott (October 21), with the rest of the petroleum-producing companies increasing prices by 60–80% by year's end. Driving a compact car was clearly ahead of the curve in 1973.

On the other hand, Influentials have foreshadowed declining markets as well. By the early 1980s, with gas prices dropping, Influentials led the market back out of small cars.

Getting in early on the first wave of a trend often leads the Influentials to be early on subsequent waves as well. Computers are a good example. Influentials have gone from among the first to buy computers to among the first to try new computer applications. In 1996, large numbers of Influentials regularly used computers to e-mail (one in five), access databases for news and information (one in five), and participate in bulletin boards (one in seven); all were triple the rates of the total public. By 2001, large numbers of Influentials were starting to use computers in new ways—viewing digital images (half had), listening to music (four in ten), and filing taxes (one in four), at rates twice those of the total public.

Realizing early the convenience of catalog shopping (by 1988, six in ten Influentials had bought something by mail in the past three months, double Americans overall) probably helped Influentials also to recognize early the benefits of shopping online from their PCs. By early 1999, one in five Influentials had bought something online, triple the rate in the total public. By 2001, the number had risen to over four in ten, double the rate in the total public.

Influentials are often asked about products whose profiles are rising. Compared with the 1970s, Influentials are far more likely now, for example, to be buttonholed by someone for their thoughts on investing (35%, up 15 points from 1978), reflecting the public's growing participation in the stock market, mutual funds, 401(k)s, and other financial topics.

The trends also reveal how consumer interest can move on and leave businesses scrambling in its wake. As Americans have gotten their fill of health scare headlines, questions about health issues have decreased. Although more than four in ten Influentials are still asked their advice about health, this is down a lot from 1987, when more than half were. As Americans have adopted more casual dress codes, the Influential word-of-mouth buzz on fashion has diminished; 31% of Influentials said in 1987 they were turned to by others for advice and opinion on clothing styles, but only 17% say so currently.

As the personal computer market exploded, the percentage of Influentials asked about computers rose proportionally, jumping from 25% in 1987 to 36% in 1995. Since then the figure, although still high, has plateaued, a signal to the computer industry that it's time for the next generation of new technologies.

Influentials have the ability to surprise. Thomas Miller, who wrote the first in-depth study of Influentials in 1988 and who is now a managing director of RoperASW and head of our U.S. and global consumer trends research, says his prototype for an Influential was U.S. Senator Paul Sarbanes of Maryland. To Miller, who grew up near Sarbanes and interned for Sarbanes when he was in college, the senator fit the criteria for Influentials—smart, well-educated, affluent but not rich, independent-minded, in the prime of his life, a family man. The son of Greek immigrants, Sarbanes grew up busing tables and washing dishes. He worked hard in school as well, winning a scholarship to Princeton, becoming a Rhodes Scholar, then going to Harvard Law School. A 2002 *New York Times* profile described Sarbanes as a "low-key" but "formidable" legislator who has played a key role in important legislation, including the sweeping post-Enron 2002 "Sarbanes Bill" reform of the accounting and securities industry, which he shepherded through the Senate as chairman of the Senate Banking Committee. The commonsense, independent streak was evident in his personal life as well: Miller recalls Sarbanes being one of the first people he knew to have a Volkswagen Beetle.

To Miller, it's logical for people to turn to Influentials. To be an Influential, "you have to be smart and articulate, and be in a position to communicate, persuade, and convince. If you're all alone in the forest, who's going to hear you? These are respected members of their community, and being respected means people look up to them in a number of ways." The influence extends beyond what they say. "What they do speaks as loud as their words," including the decisions of daily life. "People will be aware they drive a Beetle, and it sets an example."

A Product That Can Wait: E-Books

When Stephen King bypassed the traditional publishing houses and self-published his new novel *The Plant* over the World Wide Web in the summer of 2000, it created a sensation. It made front-page news in the national media. Soon, major publishing houses were setting up e-publishing divisions as a flurry of new products and services broke out. Book contracts were rewritten to include e-book rights. Many believed they were on the cusp of a technological breakthrough.

The predictions of revolution proved short-lived. King, who promised to keep writing chapters as long as most readers who'd downloaded the book paid for installments, soon discontinued the novel. The broad revolution heralded by *The Plant* never really took root.

The Influentials predicted as much. In January 2000 we surveyed them on their interest in e-books. Their response? As an idea, it was not yet a best-seller.

Most Influentials expected e-book devices to be part of technology's future. Six in ten said they thought electronic handheld reading devices could be part of everyday life in America within 20 years, a response substantially higher than the overall public's (four in ten).

Only three in ten Influentials, however, said they *personally* would like to have such a device. The response, although higher than the total public's two in ten, placed e-books among the technologies Influentials were *not* particularly excited over.

Considering the Influentials' usual enthusiasm for technology and their love of reading, which one would have expected to have heightened their interest further, this was a surprising response. The Influentials seemed to be saying that e-books may well be part of technology's future but they're not likely to be a big part of "my future," at least not as things currently stand.

Without the Influentials' endorsement, this is not likely to change in the near term. This isn't to say the concept is headed for the virtual remainder pile. For some purposes, such as academic research, electronic features like full-text search or the ability to download a semester's worth of reading (rather than schlep to the library for the reserved reading articles) make good sense.

Still, the lukewarm interest suggests that to become a major success, e-books will probably have to become more "bookish"—cheap, light-weight, as pleasing to the touch as paper, and easy on the eyes (no small concern for a middle-aged population moving headlong into the bifocal years). All this is not out of the question—science will no doubt in time produce inexpensive reading matter that looks and feels like paper while being able to carry digital text—but the PCs, PDAs, and PC-like reading devices that are the current transmission devices aren't there yet.

Case Study: The Entrepreneurial Wave

Companies can associate themselves with trends by aligning with Influentials. Ernst & Young did so by engaging Roper to conduct a 1998 study gauging Influentials' feelings about entrepreneurism. At the time, entrepreneurism was beginning to become a force in the society.

Our preliminary research suggested that Influentials were strong advocates of entrepreneurism. Despite their association with the civic realm through their political and social activism, when asked what they would most like, Influentials by a more than 2:1 margin said they'd rather own their own business than be the top executive of a large corporation. By a comparable margin they claimed they'd rather own their own business than hold down an important position in government or politics.

A sizable number were entrepreneurs themselves, about one in five of the Influentials who are in the workforce, double the rate in the total public.

The Ernst & Young study revealed that Influentials saw a brighter future for entrepreneurism. Eight in ten of the Influentials said they believed entrepreneurism would be the "defining trend of the business world" in the new century. The same number said they believed entrepreneurism would increase throughout the world, even in nonindustrial countries in Africa and the Middle East. By an almost 2:1 margin, Influentials ranked entrepreneurs ahead of government as a driver of the economy's success; most put entrepreneurs ahead of corporate America. Nine in ten said they thought entrepreneurism would be important to the next generation.

The results prompted Gregory K. Erickson, Ernst & Young's national director of entrepreneurial services, to project that "the Twenty-First Century may very well be known as the 'Entrepreneurial Age,' in much the same way as the Industrial Age is associated with the Nineteenth Century and the Corporate Age with the Twentieth Century."

Most Influentials expected entrepreneurism to continue to grow in the decades to come. Partly this reflected their thoughts on the nature of entrepreneurism; seven in ten Influentials believed entrepreneurs were more responsive to change than large corporations. Many factors pushing the trend—technology, economic conditions, social conditions, such as two-income families, a global economy, deregulation, and large companies' relatively poor performance in innovation relative to entrepreneurs—were all cited by majorities of Influentials as major, driving forces in the rise of entrepreneurism.

Now, five years later, it still looks like the Influentials were on the money. The 2000–2001 Internet shake-up, stock market shakeout, and economic slowdown may have slowed the trend. The other drivers are still in place, however—such forces as technology, globalization, two-income households, and deregulation are hard to roll back.

Most Influentials saw broad social changes resulting from the trend. Their responses bode well for continued business opportunities for serving not only entrepreneurs but also workers and Americans generally who adopt entrepreneurial behaviors and attitudes. The three changes Influentials most expect are a greater emphasis on personal fulfillment, increased innovation, and more creative schedules and work arrangements.

Are Influentials Born or Made?

About this time you may be asking a chicken-or-egg question. Are Influentials born or made? Is influence genetically programmed, like eye or hair color? Or is it something that people learn? The issue usually comes up with us in one of two ways. One, we're asked by people who are curious about the Influentials, are considering becoming involved in some way in the community and want to know: could *I* become an Influential? We also get this question from clients who want to know how best to reach Influentials. Can you identify someone as an Influential (say, Larry Lee, Jr. or Isabel Milano) and track them for the rest of their lives?

U.S. history offers anecdotal evidence of leadership running through families (for example, George Herbert Walker Bush being followed into the presidency by his son, George W., with another son, Jeb, governor of Florida). History also makes a case that some people work their way into leadership. Harry Truman, for example, worked his way up from the son of a farmer to contribute significantly to shaping the post–World War II world as president.

Our research shows that there is a great deal of fluidity in our Influential Americans segment. Some people become involved in a group or issue and stick with it for life, but many seem to come into groups for a few years—becoming involved with school issues when their children are in schools but not being led into local government, for instance, as Isabel Milano has been.

One study, which was undertaken specifically to find out how long Influentials had been performing the 11 activities that comprise the question we use to define Influentials, shows that most Influentials have been involved for five years or less. On average, about one in three (34%) have been active less than one year, and a comparable number (31%) one to five years. A little more than one in ten (13%) have been involved in the activities an average of six to ten years, and one in five (20%) more than ten years.

Some activities seem to lend themselves to newcomers. For example, among those who have attended a public meeting on town or school affairs in the past year (the activity most done by Influentials, as we saw earlier in this chapter), two in three have been doing it either for less than one year (37%) or for one to five years (29%). Similarly, among those who have written or called a politician in the past year (the activity that draws the second largest number of Influentials), about three in four have been doing it either less than one year (35%) or for one to five years (39%). Going to meetings and writing letters, as those who are involved in their communities know, are "entry-way" activities, giving large numbers of people the opportunity to try out the idea of getting involved, to learn about the process and see if they like it. To our friends who ask if they can become Influentials, our answer is "go to a meeting—it's how a lot of Influentials got their start."

Once someone's involved, opportunities for advancement can come pretty quickly. Among those who have served on a committee for some local organization in the past year, a somewhat smaller, more select group than those who turn out for meetings or write letters, more than six in ten have been on the committee for less than one year (30%) or for one to five years (34%). Similarly, among those who have been an officer of a club or organization in the past year, also a somewhat smaller, more select group, about two in three have been doing it less than one year (32%) or for one to five years (33%).

Demographics appear to underscore the idea that many people enter into community involvement at a particular stage of life, some continuing as they get older and others moving on to other things. Those who have done an activity less than a year are largely in their thirties to mid-forties (38%), with the next largest group in their mid-forties to fifties (28%). The remaining 34% are fairly equally split between people 18–29 years old or 60 and older. People who have been involved for one to five years follow a similar age profile. Those who have been involved six years or more tend to be older, with fairly equal numbers in the 30–44 (30%), 45–59 (32%), and 60 and older (30%) age groups. These "wise old heads," of course, are a smaller group.

For companies that want to track Influentials, the group's fluidity poses some challenges. At least some of those who are Influential today won't be in a couple of years.

From a civic standpoint, the fluidity in the Influentials strikes us, on the whole, as a good thing. It poses some challenges, such as higher levels of stress as successive waves of "newbies" learn the ropes, but it also probably helps explain some of the energy of community activism in the U.S. (something that newcomers to the U.S. have been remarking on since the first colonies were settled). Just as the U.S. Army has its "citizen soldier," the nation, it seems, has its "citizen leader," who becomes involved for a period of time and then retires to the pleasures of garden and grandchildren—a Cincinnatus of the suburbs.

Importantly, this fluidity is probably also good for the vital word-of-mouth network, replenishing it continuously with new people who bring a new sense of energy and excitement to conversations, investigation, and opinions about all manner of topics, from what's going on in the local schools to what's a good place to go to on your next vacation. Thus, the word-of-mouth conversation never ends—it moves to a new phase.

CHAPTER 2

The Influential Personality

A T FIRST, SHELLEY MILLER was not sure she should run for mayor. For four years she had been city controller, essentially the chief financial officer for the city government. During that time, she had established new financial controls that had placed the city on firm financial footing. She had centralized the information network, installed a new accounting system, and, with the help of the bull market on Wall Street, increased the city's investment income by 500%. If she ran, she would be the front-runner.

She would also be the first woman mayor of Richmond, Indiana, the city where she had been born and grew up, graduated from high school (class of 1975), where her parents still lived, and where, five years before, she had returned.

Miller, however, already had one "m" title in her life—"mother" to two children. When she and her husband, Joe, moved back to Richmond after a dozen-plus years of climbing the career ladder through various moves around the country, the goal was to slow the pace of their life and be more family focused. Several years earlier, she had made a conscious decision to step back from her career as an accountant. Miller took three years off from work to be a full-time mom—making sandwiches, shuttling her kids to practices, joining the PTA—and had only reentered the workforce in 1996.

Maintaining balance between work and family had been foremost in her mind when she went back into the job market. Being city controller for this city of 39,000 on Indiana's eastern border was not exactly what she'd had in mind. It was too good to pass up, though, not just in the specifics of the job but in the opportunity to develop programs and policies to address issues facing Richmond. If not exactly 9 to 5, there was a rhythm to the job: council meetings every other Monday evening, longer hours during budget time, but stretches of reasonable, predictable periods as well. The mayor's position would be a bump up in hours, with more weekend and evening activities, with speeches and ceremonial commitments like ribbon cuttings. As head of the city government, she would be more "on call."

There was yet another issue holding her back. For as long as Miller could remember, she had a fear of public speaking. She had grown accustomed to addressing council meetings, but beyond that she got butterflies. It was "a big issue" for her. She was comfortable with most of the other aspects of being mayor. "I knew how things worked. I knew the projects and programs. I knew the parties involved." She felt good about the direction the city was going and was confident she could handle the challenges of being mayor. Her concern for her family and the anxiety about public speaking gave her pause. She knew running for mayor was the next step up from being controller but didn't know if she was ready.

So when Mayor Dennis Andrews announced in the fall of 2000, early into his second term, that he was resigning as mayor to enter a Presbyterian seminary, Shelley Miller was in some fundamental ways uncertain whether she should run.

It came down to a couple of conversations. Miller talked with her husband, who was "very supportive," she said. She talked with her children. "My daughter said, 'Mom, this is something you need to do.' " Her younger child thought it would be "cool" to have a mother who was mayor. She talked with Mayor Andrews and members of the administrative team. There was a clear sense that city officials wanted to continue the work they had begun (something that would not be assured if there were a new mayor from outside the group).

"I kept looking at what it meant to the community. I couldn't help but feel that I still wanted to contribute to the growth of the community." As for the fear of public speaking, after wrestling with the anxiety, she woke up one morning with a sense of determination to fight it. "It was more important for me to overcome that weakness and move forward with what I wanted to do," she recalls, "than to let it hold me back."

She threw her hat into the competition for mayor, which by this time included several candidates. That meant persuading the precinct chairs of the Republican Party: according to Richmond bylaws, if a mayor leaves office in the middle of a term, his or her party chooses the successor. Over a two-week period, she met with 26 of the 31 chairs, spending from five minutes to three hours with them about what she wanted to do for the community as mayor. When the vote came, she emerged as the hands-down winner.

The Influential Personality:
A CLEAR SENSE THAT "THIS MATTERS"

Shelley Miller did not have to run for mayor of Richmond. Nothing required her to do so, just as nothing required Isabel Milano to become active in her children's school or Larry Lee, Jr. to become involved in his city. A sense that some things are simply important and warrant attention, participation, and commitment—that "this *matters*"—is characteristic of Influentials. It sets the Influentials apart from the crowd. Their ability to sort out what is important and commit to seeing it through often draws Influentials into involvement in the larger society. It helps them persevere through the inevitable frustrations and disappointments that arise from being mayor or starting a new association. It often spurs them to overcome personal hurdles, like a fear of public speaking.

In many ways, Influentials' attitudes and values are similar to those of the mainstream. They're more optimistic than the norm, but not uniformly optimistic. Between July 1999 and July 2001, a time of transition in the U.S., with a new century, a change in presidents, and the economy tipping toward recession, Influentials were substantially more likely than the typical American to say they were "generally optimistic" about their personal situation—remarkably optimistic, with an average of 83% saying they were optimistic about their personal prospects in eight surveys during the period, 12 points higher than the public as a whole.

The Influentials were only *somewhat* more optimistic, however, than the average American about the prospects for the country (64% on average versus 56%) and the economy (55 versus 50%). Influentials were fairly evenly divided on whether the country was "going in the right direction" or "on the wrong track," an average of 49% saying it was moving in the right direction, virtually indistinguishable from the 47% response of the public as a whole during the two-year period.

Influentials' consumer confidence, as measured through a question asking them whether they think it's "a good time to buy" the things they want and need, "a good time to wait," or "someplace in between," was somewhat higher than that of the public as a whole: 38% on average thought it was a good time to buy, modestly higher than the 33% for the public as a whole.

Influentials do not come off as Pollyannas. They don't look at the world through rose-colored glasses. Rather, they are selective and discriminating, able to see cause for confidence when it's appropriate but skeptical when the facts warrant skepticism and able to appreciate nuances to make a smart, informed decision.

When Influentials talk about what's most important to them, they tend to emphasize the same things as most Americans: a family, a house with a yard in a safe neighborhood, a measure of financial security, and a sufficient amount of leisure time to be able to enjoy yourself. Similarly, our studies show that the Influentials have changed in some of the same ways that Americans as a whole have changed. They're more centered on family and community, more focused on finding balance between work and personal life, and more accepting of the idea that it's all right to enjoy life and material pleasures like a nice vacation or meal out. In many, but not all, ways, the priorities they emphasize are the same as those to which their neighbors are drawn. They are descriptive of William James's quotation of an acquaintance of his, that "There is very little difference between one man and another, but what there is is *very important*."

Sometimes the Influentials seem to be the keepers of the flame for the ideas that are central to the larger society. In learning about Influentials' values, we also learn about the values of the nation, the ideas that resonate in the public generally, but that most people don't think about that much (relying on the Influentials to do it for them). In spring 1998, for example, a relatively quiet, prosperous time when many Americans were focused inward, our research showed that Influentials had a clear sense of what set America apart and made it "great." Their level of engagement with the issue contrasted with that of the public as a whole.

What the Influentials were drawn to—the American Idea—seems a good reflection of the changes in America since the 1970s. Compared with their responses in the 1970s, more Influentials pointed to America's status as a nation of people who work hard as a source of its greatness. More also cited the nation's status as "a melting pot," also its "pioneer heritage," with its emphasis on exploration and self-reliance, the "free-enterprise system," with its offer of opportunity, and the nation's "moral principles" and "religious beliefs," which gave it a foundation on which to grow and change. All of these reasons were up notably from 1974. In addition, the Influentials cited a number of ideas that resonated in the earlier period, in particular the U.S. "Constitution and form of government," with its focus on ensuring individual rights and balance of power, and the nation's "natural resources," which have provided the nation with room to grow and plenty of land for agriculture and natural parks.

Influentials laid out, in retrospect, a thoughtful vision of the modern U.S.—energized by new waves of immigrants and the new "pioneers" of technology, self-reliant, more concerned with reconnecting to its moral foundation, and appreciative of the nation's natural beauty and system of government. Influentials were substantially more likely than the public as a whole to cite most of the items, with disparities of up to 27 percentage points—major differences. Of the items cited by the majority of Influentials in 1974, only one was down notably: "our system of public education for all people," which, other Roper studies showed, was a rising concern of the opinion leaders and an increasingly important agenda item in communities, state legislatures, and the nation as a whole (see Figure 2-1).

That sense of discernment, of being able to sort through information and select the most important ideas ("this *matters*"), is reflected in their thinking on the nation's problems as well. Recent years' studies show that Influentials think the U.S. has been doing well in some areas. Most are optimistic about "the basics"—the prospects for "quality of life" in the U.S., what technology will offer for the society and individual Americans, the economy's capacity to create growth for the nation, and the U.S. system of government and ability to get along with other countries. In these areas Influentials generally express more optimism than the average person.

Influentials are highly critical in other areas, however. Influentials are

Figure 2-1. The American Idea: What Sets the U.S. Apart

Percentage of Influential Americans and total public saying factor is among "the major causes" of the United States' greatness, with percentage point change between 1974 and 1998

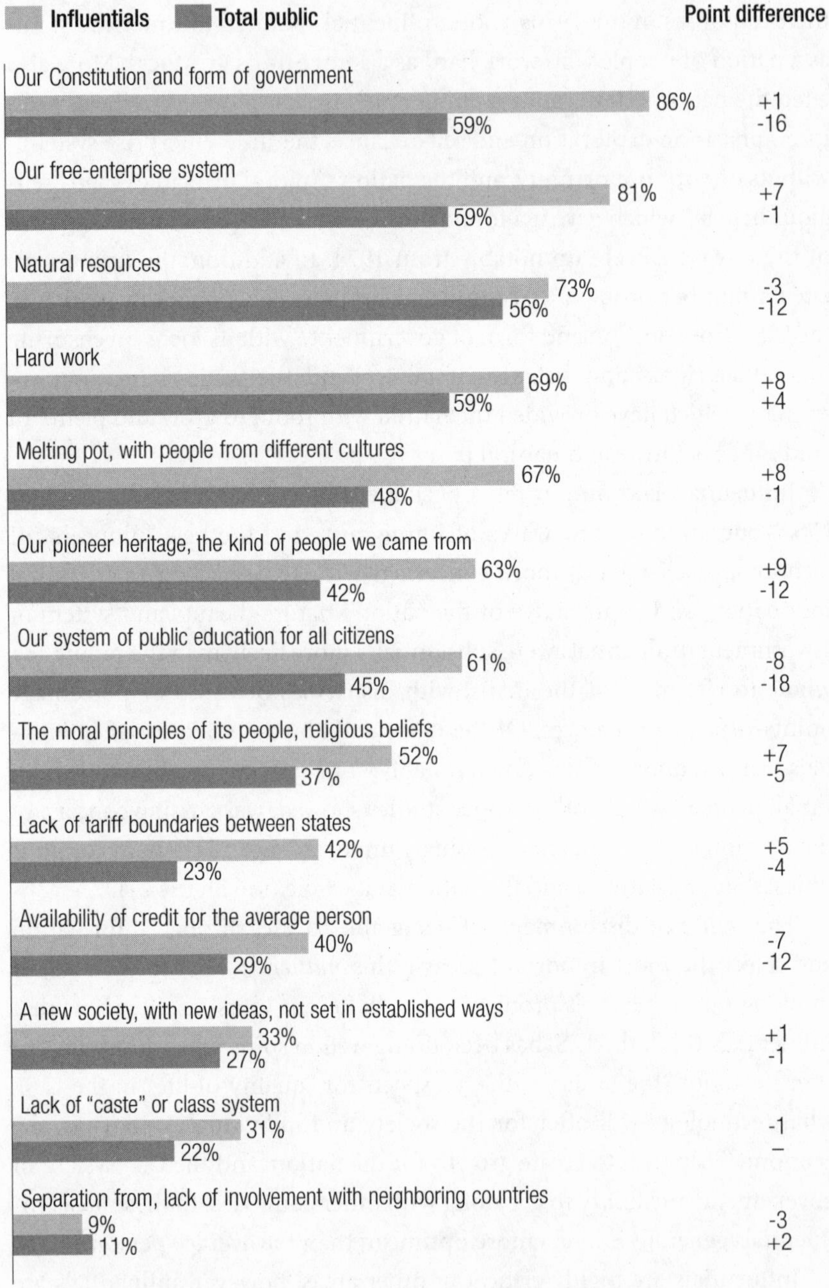

■ **Influentials** ■ **Total public**   **Point difference**

Our Constitution and form of government

86% +1
59% -16

Our free-enterprise system

81% +7
59% -1

Natural resources

73% -3
56% -12

Hard work

69% +8
59% +4

Melting pot, with people from different cultures

67% +8
48% -1

Our pioneer heritage, the kind of people we came from

63% +9
42% -12

Our system of public education for all citizens

61% -8
45% -18

The moral principles of its people, religious beliefs

52% +7
37% -5

Lack of tariff boundaries between states

42% +5
23% -4

Availability of credit for the average person

40% -7
29% -12

A new society, with new ideas, not set in established ways

33% +1
27% -1

Lack of "caste" or class system

31% -1
22% –

Separation from, lack of involvement with neighboring countries

9% -3
11% +2

Source: Roper Reports

far from the boosters that many people think of when the image of civic-mindedness comes to mind (images that have been part of the popular consciousness since the Lynds' study of *Middletown* and Sinclair Lewis's novels of Middle America in the 1920s). In some areas, more Influentials than not are *pessimistic,* with levels of pessimism higher than in the public as a whole. Such is the case in education, the environment, the health care system, the state of morals and ethics, and crime and violence in the society. In the Influentials' view, these major issues deserve significant efforts on multiple fronts, from government through individual Americans.

Influentials' ability to sort through things is reflected on life's big questions as well. Influentials are more likely than the norm to question religious or spiritual conformity. Although Influentials are more likely than the average American to go to church every week and to be active in the church, they're not significantly more likely than the norm to say religion is *very important* in their lives (about half do). They are not strict in their religious observance. Although a fairly large number of Influentials describe themselves as "strong" followers of a particular religion (39%, about the same as the total public), many Influentials characterize themselves as "religious but not very active" (29%, 10 points lower). A substantial number of Influentials, disproportionate to the public as a whole, say they fall into neither of those two categories and instead portray themselves as "spiritual but uncomfortable with organized religion" (22%, 10 points higher).

The Influentials' ability to sift out what matters is engagingly evident in their personal interests—a reason they are so important to business. Ask an Influential for an opinion on a car or for their assessment of whether this or that new consumer electronic, technology, or kitchen gadget is worth getting and you will get a lively, informed reply. Influentials delve deeply into their passions. Take food, which we've seen is both an interest of Influentials and something they're frequently queried about. Influentials are significantly more likely than the average person to like a broad palette of foods, from mainstream cuisine like Italian (enjoyed by 78% of Influentials, 16 points higher than the public), Chinese (74%, 11 higher), and Mexican/Tex-Mex (68%, 13 higher), to a global pastiche of Greek and Middle Eastern (35%, 20 higher), Japanese (29%, 12 higher), French (29%, 12 higher), and Thai (27%, 13 higher), in addition to plain "American" (enjoyed by seven in ten) and regional cuisines like Cajun/Creole (enjoyed by more than four in ten). Similarly, in music, Influentials share the popular American taste for rock but also like classical (which ties country as the second most popular music of Influentials, at 46% of Influentials, 24 points higher than the total public), jazz (36%, 12 higher), and blues (36%, 15 higher).

You may not get a long discourse when you ask an Influential for an opinion, however. Although the Influentials tend to know a lot, they do not come across as know-it-alls. Judith Langer, senior vice president and director of the Roper/Langer Qualitative Division of RoperASW, who has conducted focus groups of Influentials, has found that one of their main characteristics is that they're "good listeners." Focus groups of Influentials, she says, are often exchanges of ideas. During the course of sessions, it's not unusual for participants to change their point of view as they get more information. It's rare for one person in a group of Influentials to dominate or for the group to try to say things to please the moderator (the bane of moderators).

Listening appears to play a large part in many Influentials' leadership styles. Shelley Miller considers her "most effective" forums to be after her speeches, when she turns the floor over so that citizens can talk about what's on their minds. Our studies show that Influentials put a high *priority* on listening skills. Two-thirds of Influentials rate being a good listener to be "essential" in a boss, a response more than 10 points higher than in the public as a whole. Influentials are word-of-mouth leaders and are significantly more likely to be asked their advice and opinion than the average, but they probably end at least some responses with *a question of their own.* They're interested in what others have to say.

Aspirations: The American Dream, the Good Life, and Life's Necessities

The Influentials' sense of priorities comes through on three key questions that we have used for years as gauges of Americans' aspirations—their ideas on what the American Dream and "the Good Life" are and what they consider to be life's "necessities." Influentials place a much higher value on certain aspirations than the public as a whole: interesting, enjoyable work that contributes to the greater society; the opportunity for people to pursue their dreams; freedom to choose the life you want to lead; college education, particularly for one's children; and technologies that help them accomplish more, like personal computers, the Internet, and a home office.

Influentials are substantially more likely than the public as a whole to say their vision of the Good Life includes a job that "is interesting" (70% say so, 17 points higher than in the total public) and "contributes to the welfare of society" (42%, 17 points higher). They are much more likely than the norm to say having "a job you enjoy" is part of what the American Dream means to them (72%, 12 higher). They place a higher priority than the average on living in an open society in which "everyone has an equal chance" (78%, 11 points higher than in the public as a whole) and on people having "freedom of choice in how to live one's life" (78%, 8 higher); only owning a home rates as high in their vision of what the American Dream means. As important as college education has become to Americans as a whole, it is even more important to Influentials, substantial numbers rating college for one's children and oneself not only to be part of the American Dream but part of the Good Life as well (62%, in particular, saying college education for their children is part of their vision of the Good Life, 11 points higher than in the total public). Influentials are also a little more likely than the public as a whole to associate the American Dream with climbing the career ladder and rising through the ranks to become the head of a company (see Figures 2-2 and 2-3).

The Influentials' ideas about the Dream and the Good Life do share some common characteristics with the average American's. More than 70% of Influentials and the public as a whole rate owning a home of your own as part of their idea of both the American Dream and the Good Life. Majorities would have a yard (probably with a picket fence) around that home. Wide majorities aspire to happy marriages and having children. Two-thirds in both groups associate the American Dream with being "financially secure enough to have ample time for leisure pursuits" and having "a financially secure retirement." About six in ten of both Influentials and Americans as a whole regard having "both a rewarding career and family life" to be part of the American Dream. Both value the modern conve-

Figure 2-2. What the American Dream Means to Influentials

Percentage of Influential Americans saying item is "very much" what the American Dream means to them, with percentage point difference from the total public

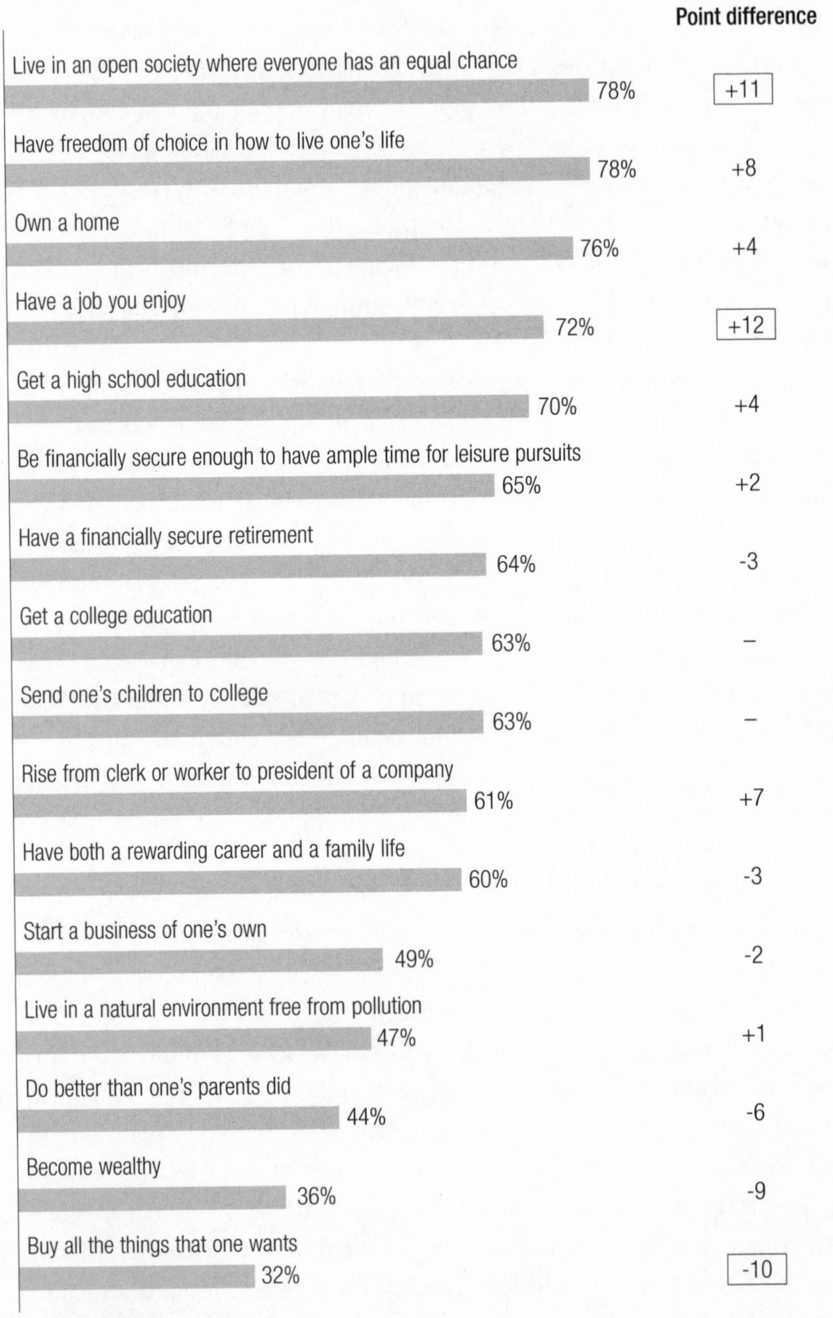

Point difference

Live in an open society where everyone has an equal chance
78%   +11

Have freedom of choice in how to live one's life
78%   +8

Own a home
76%   +4

Have a job you enjoy
72%   +12

Get a high school education
70%   +4

Be financially secure enough to have ample time for leisure pursuits
65%   +2

Have a financially secure retirement
64%   -3

Get a college education
63%   –

Send one's children to college
63%   –

Rise from clerk or worker to president of a company
61%   +7

Have both a rewarding career and a family life
60%   -3

Start a business of one's own
49%   -2

Live in a natural environment free from pollution
47%   +1

Do better than one's parents did
44%   -6

Become wealthy
36%   -9

Buy all the things that one wants
32%   -10

Source: Roper Reports

Figure 2-3. What "the Good Life" Means to Influentials

Percentage of Influential Americans saying item is for them "part of the good life, the life you'd like to have," with percentage point difference from total public

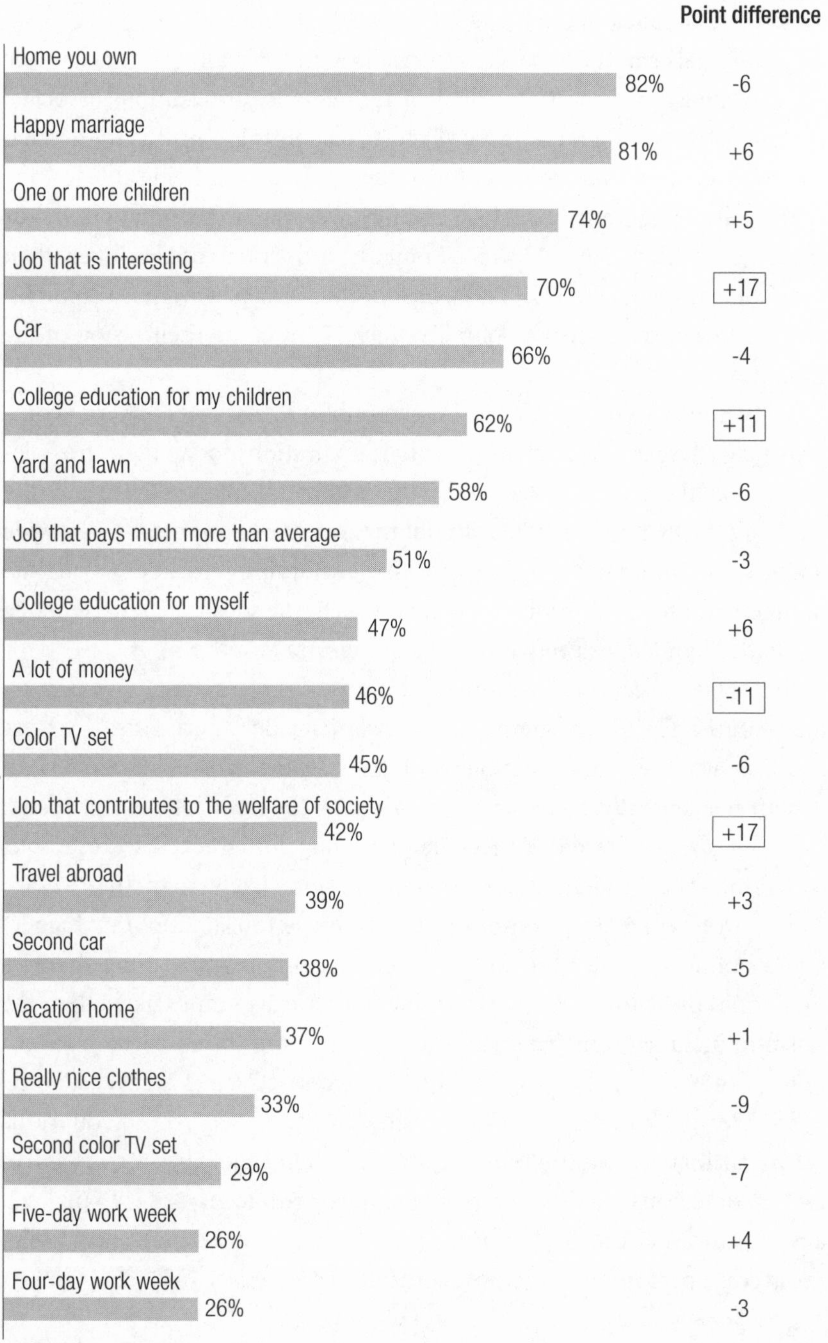

		Point difference
Home you own	82%	-6
Happy marriage	81%	+6
One or more children	74%	+5
Job that is interesting	70%	+17
Car	66%	-4
College education for my children	62%	+11
Yard and lawn	58%	-6
Job that pays much more than average	51%	-3
College education for myself	47%	+6
A lot of money	46%	-11
Color TV set	45%	-6
Job that contributes to the welfare of society	42%	+17
Travel abroad	39%	+3
Second car	38%	-5
Vacation home	37%	+1
Really nice clothes	33%	-9
Second color TV set	29%	-7
Five-day work week	26%	+4
Four-day work week	26%	-3

Source: Roper Reports

nience of a car and, for many, a second car. They place about equal value on foreign travel (which, as it has become more affordable, has risen in the overall public's idea of the Good Life).

Influentials stand out as less materialistic in their aspirations than the average American. Fewer than half of Influentials, for example, associate the Good Life with "a lot of money" (46%, 11 points lower than in the total public). Well under half think of the American Dream as being able to "buy all the things one wants" (32%, 10 points lower than in the total public) or "become wealthy" (36%, 9 lower). Similarly, Influentials are less likely than the public as a whole to cite "really nice clothes" (33%, 9 lower), a color TV (45%, 6 lower), or a second color TV (29%, 7 lower) in their vision of the Good Life.

Influentials aren't ascetics. As in the public as a whole, material comforts play a larger part in the Influentials' aspirations today than three decades ago. Like Americans generally, the Influentials place a lower priority on their jobs than in the 1970s. It's not that work is unimportant. The wide majority of Influentials want interesting, enjoyable jobs and substantial numbers want to have a job that contributes to the society. There is merely more focus on *balance* between work, home, and family.

Influentials seem to have utilitarian attitudes to material possessions, life's "stuff." The list of items Influentials consider "necessities" has expanded over the years, as it has with most Americans. Compared with Americans generally, however, Influentials have a practical, commonsense mind-set about life's necessities. There are huge differences, for example, on computers. Influentials are markedly more likely than the average American to consider a computer for office use (50%, 22 points higher) and a home computer (46%, 21 higher) necessities rather than luxuries they could do without. Likewise, Influentials are also more likely than the norm to include on their necessities list such commonsense gear as a second car (48%, 15 higher), online/Internet access (32%, 14 higher), a home office (23%, 11 higher), clothes washer (89%, 10 higher), credit cards (46%, 10 higher), multiple bathrooms (like multiple cars, a godsend in two-income households and growing families with teens; 45%, 10 higher), and a dishwasher (40%, 8 higher). In contrast, they are a bit less sold than the average person on TV remote controls as a necessity (38%, 6 lower).

Influentials' necessities will likely grow in the years to come. To make the grade, however, an item must prove itself. In time, personal digital assistants (or whatever the technology evolves into) may do that. At this point, though, the jury's out; only 2% of Influentials view PDAs as necessities. Influentials, again, are more selective; they focus on things that make the most difference to them.

Affluent Americans, in contrast, tend to view *everything* as a necessity, including, for example, the remote control (49%, 11 higher than among Influentials). The Influentials' selectivity probably contributes to their being trusted advice givers; they seem to have a clear sense of how much difference a product will make in someone's life (see Figure 2-4 on page 92).

The Influential Personality:
BELIEF IN GROWTH AND CHANGE

In deciding she was not going to let fear hold her back, Shelley Miller says, she drew on wisdom that had been instilled in her from childhood. She learned early from her parents to "work hard and do your best. Don't focus on the barriers. If you want to do something, do it." That old-fashioned advice still rings true to her. "I think we have to overcome hurdles every day in life," she says. As mayor, she continues to try to "grow and adapt" to the challenges of the job. Growth and change are part of life, she believes. The attitude you bring to problems means "everything" in how far you go.

These are not empty words to her. Reframing her attitude was the starting point for addressing her qualms about public speaking, Miller says. It created a reserve of confidence that she could tap into before giving a speech—the OK-I-can-do-this moment with which many speakers reconnect before taking the stage. It also gave her motivation to find resources to break down the problem into smaller, more addressable problems. She searched the Internet for a prayer that she'd seen in her doctor's office that had always inspired her: "Slow me down, Lord. Slow down the beating of my heart. . . ." She now keeps a copy of the prayer with her to bring out when she wants to center herself (at this point, she needs to remember only the first line).

Influentials think that people have more control over their fate than is

Figure 2-4. Utilitarian: What's a "Necessity" to Influentials

Percentage of Influential Americans saying they personally think of item as "a necessity" rather than "a luxury you could do without," with percentage point difference from total public

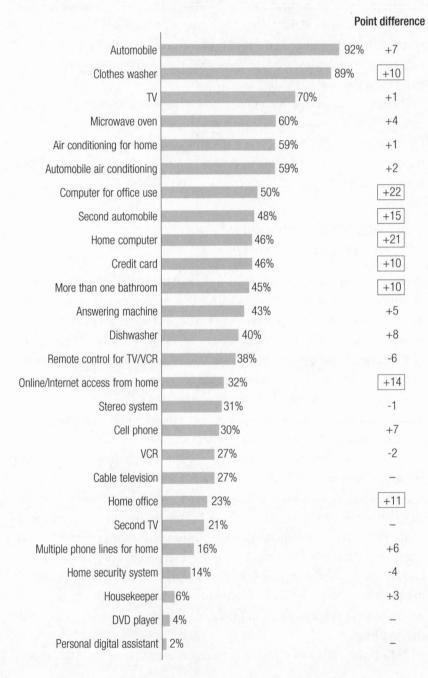

		Point difference
Automobile	92%	+7
Clothes washer	89%	+10
TV	70%	+1
Microwave oven	60%	+4
Air conditioning for home	59%	+1
Automobile air conditioning	59%	+2
Computer for office use	50%	+22
Second automobile	48%	+15
Home computer	46%	+21
Credit card	46%	+10
More than one bathroom	45%	+10
Answering machine	43%	+5
Dishwasher	40%	+8
Remote control for TV/VCR	38%	-6
Online/Internet access from home	32%	+14
Stereo system	31%	-1
Cell phone	30%	+7
VCR	27%	-2
Cable television	27%	–
Home office	23%	+11
Second TV	21%	–
Multiple phone lines for home	16%	+6
Home security system	14%	-4
Housekeeper	6%	+3
DVD player	4%	–
Personal digital assistant	2%	–

Source: Roper Reports

often believed. They believe so of themselves. The wide majority of Influentials believe that "how my life turns out is pretty much within my personal control and depends mostly on what I do or don't do" (82%) rather than that the outcome of their lives is "pretty much beyond my control" and "depends mostly on outside forces which I have no control over" (4%). Influentials are significantly more likely to feel that they control their destiny than the average person (by 19 points) and, in fact, are more likely to believe so than other segments traditionally associated with success, such as the affluent, executives and professionals, and college grads (who lag the Influentials by 13 points).

Fully 93% of Influentials agree that "if you have an unhappy life, you can change it if you really try." Although this belief in the ability of people to make their lives better is something ascribed to by most Americans, it is more strongly held among Influentials (by 13 points over the public as a whole).

These two ideas are worth pausing over. In the course of this book, we see that Influentials' politics range widely, from people like Shelley Miller, who probably is a "compassionate conservative," to Walter Arrowsmith, a Goldwater Republican; Tim Draper, a free-market Republican; Sarah Vokes, a left-leaning student activist; Democratic centrists like David Pendergrass; a few lifelong Democrats; and numerous "social liberal/fiscal conservatives." The Influentials come from all walks of life. They live in different settings, from cities to suburbs to rural outposts like Akiak, Alaska.

Virtually to a one, however, Influentials share this sense of confidence in people's ability to effect change, particularly in their own lives. Aside from their activism (which, since it defines them, is universal), their commitment to family and community (which is often the source of their activism), their sense of curiosity and passion for learning, and a few other things (the aspiration to a happy marriage and owning a home, for example), little is shared so completely among Influentials as this 90%-plus belief in individuals' ability to change their lives to be happier and 80%-plus confidence that they control their own destinies.

Influentials tend to think change is a good thing and that people, communities, and the society are capable of change, more than is commonly believed. Just over 60% of Influentials, 18 points higher than in the total

Figure 2-5. Belief in Growth and Change

Percentage of Influential Americans who agree with statement, with percentage point difference from total public

93%. . . . . If you have an unhappy life, you can change it if you really try — +13

82%. . . . . How my life turns out is pretty much within my personal control and
depends mostly on what I do or don't do — +19

66%. . . . . A person can change his or her personality if they try hard enough — +4

62%. . . . . Most people don't change things in their lives often enough to experience
all that life has to offer — +18

60%. . . . . Prospects of achieving personal concept of "Good Life" are "very good" or
have "already achieved it" — +21

54%. . . . . I am well on the road to achieving my vision of the American Dream
(at least 7 on a scale of 1-10) — +18

43%. . . . . The American Dream is "very much alive" (88% at least "somewhat alive") — +9

41%. . . . . I like to make changes in my life–variety is the spice of life — +4

Source: Roper Reports

public, think "most people don't change things in their lives often enough to experience all that life has to offer" (see Figure 2-5). They tend to place a higher priority on finding work that enables them to effect change. They are much more likely than the average worker to express satisfaction at the opportunities their job gives them to influence decisions in their workplace (49% are very satisfied, 23 points higher than in workers overall) and to effect change in the broader society (49% of employed Influentials report, in fact, being "very satisfied" with this aspect of their job, 15 points higher than in workers overall).

Influentials look forward to the future in large part because of the changes it will bring. Their optimism about the new century is predicated on their belief that the next 100 years will bring dramatic changes in the way people live their lives. The year 2000 itself was, to most Influentials, "no big deal." It was what was to come *after* that counts. This belief in the future, combined with their utilitarian mind-set, is probably a major force in Influentials' enthusiasm for technology and for meaningful (note *meaningful*) advances generally.

Influentials don't extol change for change's sake, though, or prescribe change as the solution for all scenarios. Only four in ten Influentials agree that change is always good because "variety is the spice of life." They're not more likely than the average person, for example, to think people can change their basic personality: about two-thirds in both groups agree. "Changing personality for what?" would probably be an Influentials' response. "Variety" to what end? Influentials seem to stand out most where there is a goal in sight—that utilitarian, pragmatic mind-set at work again—changing an unhappy life into a happy one; taking responsibility for one's decisions; experiencing more of life; looking forward to the tangible changes that the future will bring; addressing problems in the community; and influencing decisions and making a contribution through their work.

The consensus view of Influentials (90%) is that an individual has at least "some small effect" on the course of the nation. At the same time, though, half of Influentials think an individual can have at least a "*real* effect, even if not a substantial one" on the country, and a large number (19%) believe that an individual can have a "very substantial" effect on the course of the nation. Influentials don't see individuals' powers as limitless, then. In getting involved, though, they believe you can have at least a small effect, often a real effect, and sometimes a substantial effect. Many Americans also believe in people power, but the idea is more strongly held among Influentials.

Probably because of this confidence and belief in change, Influentials tend more than Americans generally to think that they'll achieve their goals: 60% of Influentials, for example, believe their prospects of achieving the Good Life are "very good" or feel they've *already* achieved it, 21 points higher than in the public as a whole. Just over half of Influentials (54%) think they're well on the road to achieving the American Dream, placing themselves at 7 or higher on a scale of 1–10, with 10 meaning they've achieved it. Those scores are on a par with people in households making $75,000 or more per year ($20,000 above the median Influential), who presumably because of their affluence have more financial wherewithal than Influentials to reach their goals. What they lack in financial resources Influentials make up in their grit, drive, and brainpower.

The Influentials' confidence probably reflects their clear-headedness about their priorities to some extent. They don't "want it all." They don't aspire to over-the-top riches. They're focused instead on opportunity, freedom, a home, marriage, children, meaningful work, enough leisure time to enjoy life, a secure retirement, college for oneself and one's children, balance, achievement, and so on. Still, being clear about goals doesn't ensure they'll be achieved. A happy marriage can be pretty elusive, as can meaningful work—much less a financially secure retirement or "ample" leisure time. The Influentials' confidence thus suggests that they have a clear sense of their objectives *and* ideas about how to reach their goals. The relatively high numbers of Influentials saying they feel they have already achieved the American Dream (22%, 8 higher than in the total public) and the Good Life (17%, 6 higher) suggest a good number *did* figure out how to reach their goals.

The successes of the Influentials we have profiled so far offer proof: Shelley Miller's becoming mayor (as well as figuring out how to overcome a deep-seated fear); Larry Lee, Jr.'s success in insurance, appointment to important boards in his community, and leadership in new ventures like the jazz society; Isabel Milano's success with her husband, Bernie, as an entrepreneur, her involvement as a parent in the schools, and her election to the village trustees. These Influentials may not yet have fulfilled all their dreams, but they've got solid achievements under their belts. The Influentials' confidence is backed up by experience.

The weight of opinion among Influentials is that you *can* reach goals. This belief is probably in large part what leads the Influentials to insert themselves into problems in their community. "I'm a firm believer that attitudes can be changed," says Isabel Milano. "It's part of my nature." "You're going to be confronted by negatives all the time in life," says Shelley Miller. "It's just a matter of, are you willing to step up and address them?"

Shelley Miller

Since becoming mayor, Shelley Miller has done many of the things you would expect the mayor of a small city in contemporary America to do. She is leading efforts to attract businesses to Richmond, promoting the city to the outside world, encouraging public works projects like parks improvements, and trying to bring more state and federal aid for programs like downtown redevelopment.

She is also trying some new and interesting ways to create change from within in Richmond. She has launched a multipronged effort to encourage people to become more active in their neighborhoods and communities. The more that the city can become stronger than the sum of its parts, she believes, the more it will be able to reach its goals.

The first major effort was a campaign to enlist residents in putting a fresh face on the city. Dubbed the "spring cleanup blitz," the effort sent out teams of street and parks department workers on six consecutive weekends with trucks, equipment, and lots of bags to trim trees and help residents remove debris and spruce up their neighborhoods. Landfill fees were waived to encourage residents to discard refrigerators, tires, and other debris that had gathered in their yards and garages. Advertisements were placed in utility bills and the media to get out the word. An educational program was launched to talk up property owners' responsibilities to maintain their properties. Grant money was secured to help property owners with a fresh coat of paint and make overdue repairs. "We didn't want to collect fines," Miller says. "We wanted to see properties improved." Although the city was prepared to issue citations for properties in serious disrepair and to take further actions against public hazards, the goal was to spur action.

Miller pushed through the idea after hearing the issue coming up in several contexts. In a series of neighborhood meetings, residents expressed concern that trees, sidewalks, and curbs weren't being adequately maintained. Separately, Richmond's police chief told her that doing more maintenance work in neighborhoods would go a long way to preventing crime.

Well-trimmed trees create more exposure for streetlights and give criminals less shadow to operate in. It might also encourage more citizen involvement in fighting crime. They talked about "the broken windows theory," formulated by criminologists James Wilson and George Kelling, that a single broken window left unrepaired engenders a sense of lawlessness that can quickly multiply into a building full of broken windows and a relaxed attitude toward crime generally in a community.

It was worth a try. Miller brought together an interdepartmental task force to make the cleanup blitz a reality. The plan was put into place and became a success. More than 3,500 residents participated in the cleanup. In all, 867 tons of refuse were carted to the landfill, including 13,000 tires, 450 Freon units, and 4,800 containers of household hazardous waste. More than $123,000 in fees was waived. Moreover, the effort generated considerable goodwill: letters to the editor, phone calls to the administration, and, perhaps most important, a jump in membership in the city's 19 neighborhood associations—the first step toward involvement.

There's still a long way to go. Like many small towns outside the belts of major cities, Richmond has had more than its share of struggles in recent decades. Many of the big factories that once generated solid middle-class incomes and benefits for blue-collar workers and white-collar managers, producing farm equipment, school buses, machine tools, auto parts, and other heavy-duty industrial items, have left town. A number of residents joined the exodus, particularly young families. Although the city's median age, 36, is only a year older than the median for the nation, K-12 enrollment in the city's schools has slipped to 5,100 from 12,000 in 1971–1972, when the city's population topped 43,000.

But there are encouraging signs as well. Richmond's favorable location astride Interstate 70, one of the nation's major east-west routes, has turned it into a regional shopping hub. The north and east sides of town, where there is easy access to the interstate, have been sprouting stores and restaurants attracting travelers and day-trippers who come in for the day to stock up at the big discount and hardware stores, stroll the shopping mall, or eat at one of the restaurants along East Main Street. Reid Memorial, the city's hospital, has become a regional health center with a clutch of new services like sports medicine. Growing interest in environment and local history has given rise to new ventures, including a 100-plus acre environmental center. The local Indiana University extension has had rapid growth. A national drive was recently begun to reclaim Richmond's history as "the birthplace of recorded jazz" with a new museum and performance area—luminaries like Louis Armstrong, Bix Biederbecke, and Hoagy Carmichael cut discs at Gennett Records here. A series of CD reissues of Gennett recordings has begun. Murals of 1920s recording artists have sprung up around town.

Miller sees her role more as facilitating change than making it. The recent history, from the cleanup to the local historical preservation and environmental movements, has proven there's energy to create change within the community. Part of her mission as mayor is to "support those who can create change," as she sees it. "There are a lot of problems that government on its own can't fix," she says. She wants to "get better at breaking down barriers" and use her connections as mayor to bring together groups with complementary resources and common interests—a group with financing, for example, with another group without funding.

She tends to take a methodical approach to issues. She sees it as part of her "conservative, practical" CPA nature. "I don't make snap, emotional decisions," she says. Instead, she prefers to "gather information" and "be clear what's going on." She believes those traits help her get her points across. Before announcing a controversial decision to throw out a vote by city street workers to organize (it's her belief that in a small town it shouldn't be necessary to call in outside representation), she drafted a release to put her reasons down in words, and set up a meeting with the editorial board of the local newspaper so she could present her case. "If you take the time to show people the process you go through when you make a decision, they may not agree with you, but they'll be more able to say, 'I accept it.' "

Miller shows the same sense of focus in her personal life. She allots her time where it matters most—in particular, family—and prioritizes accordingly from there. As a consumer, she will pore over details if a decision is big enough—a home renovation, for instance. She has created a few areas in which she lets go of that practical, conservative side, in particular a lifelong love of sports cars (currently in abeyance with a city-owned car and family-practical minivan). In the main, though, she tries to be as efficient as possible. For that reason, she's brand loyal in most purchases, especially in the supermarket. "I tend to find something I'm satisfied with and stick with it." Knowing what brands to buy gets her out of the store and onto more important things, such as her family and her work.

The Influential Personality:
BALANCING COMMUNITY AND SELF

A seminal idea that Alexis de Tocqueville contributed to the understanding of America was the ability of Americans to see the connection between their self-interest and the interests of the community. Tocqueville believed this concept, which he called "self-interest properly understood," to be the country's main defense against individualism run amok. Whereas Europeans preached "the beauties of virtue" for its own sake, he thought the more practical Americans saw that a better reason to act in the interest of the community was that "virtue is useful." "By serving his fellow man," Tocqueville said, the American "serves himself." Among Americans, there was "hardly any talk" of virtue for its own sake; rather it "gives them pleasure to point out" that decisions to "give part of their time and wealth" for the common good benefited them through better, more stable communities and a generally "orderly, temperate, moderate, careful, and self-controlled" citizenry.

That connection of self-interest and community good continues to be a thread today. Criticisms of the state of the society in recent years, such as Harvard Professor Robert Putnam's book *Bowling Alone,* have in one form or another called for a return to the interconnectedness of self-interest and community. The idea resonates with Influentials. There is a strong sense of relationship between the individual and the community among Influentials. The two seem to go hand in hand. For example, Shelley Miller says that being mayor enables her to support her community and create the kind of community she wants for her children.

More than other Americans, Influentials tend to consider both their individual interests and the interests of the community to be important and to consciously seek out a balance between the two. Like Americans generally, Influentials place a strong value on the rights of the individual. They feel a little more strongly than the average American that government should "stay out" of people's personal lives and let the individual have sovereignty over his or her personal choices about relationships, sex, and family life (66% agree mostly or completely with the statement). About half of Influentials feel that they "should be able to do whatever I want" so long as no one else is harmed. There is also an undercurrent of belief (although not a majority view) that parents and property owners should be free to make decisions as they see fit and that "what other people do is none of my business."

However, there is a *strong* sense of the importance of community among Influentials. Fully 84% of Influentials feel they "have responsibilities to my neighbors and community beyond what is required by law," the highest level of agreement among the group on any of ten statements on the relationship. Three-fourths of Influentials say "the community I live in is an important part of who I am." Two in three Influentials think people generally have "a definite responsibility" to "help the people in their community who are less fortunate than they are." Most Influentials feel that business has an obligation to the society as well: 78% believe business "should consider what is good for society, not just what is good for profit." A significant number of Influentials (but short of a majority) think parents should sacrifice personal interest and "stay together for the sake of their children," even if they have fallen out of love (see Figure 2-6).

Many Americans share the idea that community is important, but it's much more of an article of faith among Influentials. Influentials are substantially more likely than the public as a whole to feel a sense of responsibility to their neighbors and community (by 21 points), to see their community as an "important" part of their identity (by 15 points), and to believe people have an obligation to help those who are less fortunate (by 14 points). On the other side of the equation, Influentials are significantly *less* likely than the norm to feel that they should be able to do whatever they want (by 12 points) and that what others do is none of their business (by 15 points).

The importance of community has been growing. Since 1995, there's been a 14-point increase in the numbers of Influentials saying people have a responsibility to help those who are less fortunate, a 10-point increase

Figure 2-6. Balancing Community and Individual Interests

Percentage of Influential Americans saying they agree "mostly" or "completely" with statement, and percentage point difference from total public

84%. . . . I have responsibilities to my neighbors and community beyond what is required by law   `+21`

78%. . . . Business should consider what is good for society, not just what is good for profit   +6

74%. . . . The community I live in is an important part of who I am   `+15`

69%. . . . People have a definite responsibility to help the people in their community who are less fortunate than they are   `+14`

66%. . . . Government should stay out of people's personal lives, that is, their choices about relationships, sex, family life   -3

48%. . . . I should be able to do whatever I want as long as it doesn't harm anyone else   `-12`

41%. . . . Parents should be able to raise their children however they want   -5

39%. . . . There shouldn't be any restrictions on what one can do with his or her own private property   -3

37%. . . . What other people do is none of my business   `-15`

33%. . . . Parents should try to stay together for the sake of their children, even if the parents have fallen out of love   +1

Source: Roper Reports

in Influentials saying business should consider society's interests, and an 8-point gain in Influentials feeling a responsibility to their neighbors and community. Many Influentials appear to be taking the message to heart. Growing numbers say the causes they're involved with are one of the things that says the most about them. More also feel enriched by involvement, particularly in church (up 21 points since 1979).

Larry Lee, Jr. likens the synthesis of self and larger causes to his high school experience on the football team. During his junior year, his town's all-white and all-black high schools were integrated. The football team became a flashpoint of the racial tensions in the schools. Over the course of the season, though, the players rose above the stresses. "It was like *Remember the Titans*," a movie about a similar experience in Arlington, Virginia, Lee says. The team went on to a perfect 13-0 record and the state championship. Nine players (including Lee) went on to college with football scholarships, and a handful went on to at least short careers in the pros, with one playing 14 years. "It taught me about teamwork—no matter what color you are or what your background is, if you have a common goal, you can accomplish great things."

The Influential Personality:
VALUES: FAMILY AND ENGAGEMENT FIRST

Community is important to Influentials, but it's not all-important. We've already seen this in the Influentials' vision of the Good Life. Altruism doesn't define the Good Life to Influentials. Instead, the Good Life begins with home ownership, a happy marriage, children, and an interesting job. Even a car, a yard, and a job that "pays much more than average" are more important to Influentials than the altruistic aspiration to have a job that "contributes to the welfare of society." Similarly, the Influentials' vision of the American Dream is a *blend* of ideals like opportunity and freedom of choice plus material aspirations, such as owning a home, having ample time to enjoy leisure pursuits, and having a financially secure retirement.

When asked what most defines "success" to them, Influentials rate family first, far ahead of anything else. Fully 55% of Influentials say that being a good spouse and parent "comes closest" to their idea of success. The proportion of Influentials citing family as the measure of accomplishment has risen substantially in recent decades, climbing 20 points since 1985 (placing them at the fore of an 11-point rise, to 48%, in the public as a whole). Influentials place a much higher priority on such intangibles as being a good parent and spouse, being true to God (44%), being true to themselves (42%), and having friends who respect them (22%) than outward success, such as being powerful (4%) or wealthy (7%) or even doing or making things that are useful to the society (12%) and being knowledgeable and

Figure 2-7. Family and Values Define Success

Percentage of Influential Americans saying item comes closest to their personal idea of success, with percentage point difference from the total public

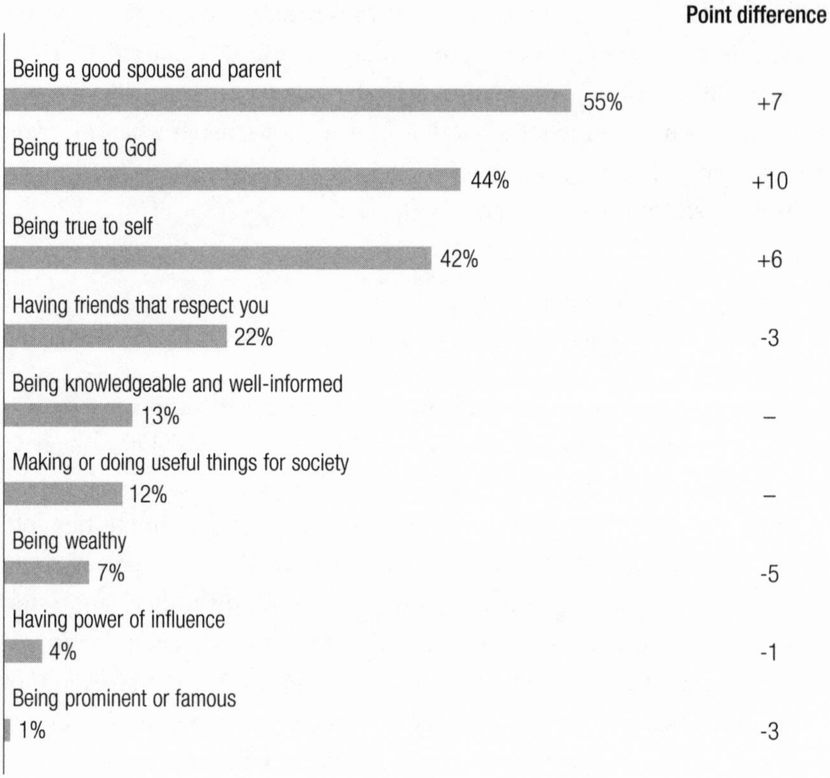

	Point difference
Being a good spouse and parent	
55%	+7
Being true to God	
44%	+10
Being true to self	
42%	+6
Having friends that respect you	
22%	-3
Being knowledgeable and well-informed	
13%	–
Making or doing useful things for society	
12%	–
Being wealthy	
7%	-5
Having power of influence	
4%	-1
Being prominent or famous	
1%	-3

Source: Roper Reports

well-informed (13%). Community is important, material success is great, but to Influentials, family comes first. Their other relationships—with their friends, with their God, with themselves—are more important than outward symbols of achievement (see Figure 2-7).

Influentials share many of the core values of Americans as a whole—family, honesty, freedom, authenticity, love, relationships—but they ascribe to them more intensely than the average person. They also place a particular emphasis on certain values that the average American does not include in his core set of values, in particular "knowledge" and "learning." This blend of values no doubt contributes to Influentials' status in the community. Because they share many values with others, they can make connections with people. At the same time, the importance they place on knowledge and learning makes them more likely to cull out ideas and insights ahead of others, making it worthwhile for others to seek out their opinions. The Influentials' blend of sharing the values of their fellow citizens, *but more so,* with a particular bent toward learning and knowledge, makes them valuable. You can be relatively confident when you talk with Influentials that they speak your language, share common values, and have something new to contribute.

Influentials have a clear sense of their values. We know because we ask on a regular basis which of 57 different values are most important to them. Family—specifically, "protecting the family"—is their leading value; 65% of Influentials say it is extremely important to them, according to our 2001 surveys. "Honesty" (58%) and "freedom" (51%) rate second and third. "Authenticity" (48%), "enduring love" (48%), "stable personal relationships" (44%), "knowledge" (41%), "justice" (40%), and "learning" (39%), "faith," "self-esteem," and "friendship" (tied at 38%) round out the Influentials' top ten.

Influentials place more importance on many of these values than the average person, particularly enduring love (for which there is a 16-point difference between Influentials and the public as a whole), knowledge (15 points), authenticity, stable personal relationships, and learning (13 points), and freedom (11 points). "These *matter,*" to use the phrase we introduced earlier in this chapter.

A number of other values are also held more closely by Influentials than the public as a whole, such as "duty" (33%, 10 higher), "social tolerance" (29%, 9 points higher than the total public), "open-mindedness" (28%, 9 higher), "fulfilling work" (28%, 9 higher), and "creativity" (21%, 7 higher). These responses round out the picture of Influentials' philosophy toward life: they care deeply about family and personal relationships, aspire to being ethical ("honest" and "authentic"), place high importance on ideas like freedom and justice, believe in growth and change ("learning" and "knowledge,"), and have a sense of responsibility to others ("duty") but are not rigid, valuing open-mindedness, tolerance, and creativity. (Indeed, based on their responses, Influentials are less likely than the average person to take things "on faith." The public as a whole places faith among their top four values; among Influentials, it only ties for tenth.)

Meanwhile, certain things *don't matter* particularly to Influentials. "Live for today" is not a core idea to them (only 17% rate it an extremely important value). Influentials don't place a priority on power (only 2% say it is extremely important to them), status (3%), looking good (4%), or wealth (5%), placing them at the bottom of their values.

The message to business: America may be a materially affluent country, but its opinion leaders are motivated by more than material possessions. At the end of the day, family, relationships, ideas, and learning drive the Influentials.

Influentials place a high value on experiencing life. They are strong proponents of travel. When asked what makes their lives "richer or fuller" (another way to approach values), Influentials rate the experience of "traveling to see new places" first. Some 56% of Influentials say traveling to new places makes their lives richer or fuller, 17 points higher than in the total public. Travel rates slightly ahead of being involved in church or religious activities (53%, 21 higher) and doing volunteer work in the community (50%, 27 higher). Being involved in the community is important, but it's not all there is to life.

Influentials are markedly more likely than the average American to say a whole *range* of pursuits enriches their lives, including getting to know new people, being in love, reading, physical activity, pets, hobbies, taking a class, being involved in a group with similar interests, creative or artistic pursuits, and gardening, all with differences of 10 points or more. To Influentials, life seems to be a kaleidoscope, with many facets that are ever-shifting and ever-engaging (see Figure 2-8).

Other studies have underscored the importance of family, learning, the outdoors, home, and other interests. Asked, for example, what is most important to them in their leisure priorities, Influentials rate "spending time with family" first; three in four say it's "very important" to them. "Helping others" is important but is down on the list, after relaxation and learning

Figure 2-8. A Multifaceted Approach to Life

Percentage of Influential Americans saying activity makes their life "richer or fuller," with percentage point difference from total public

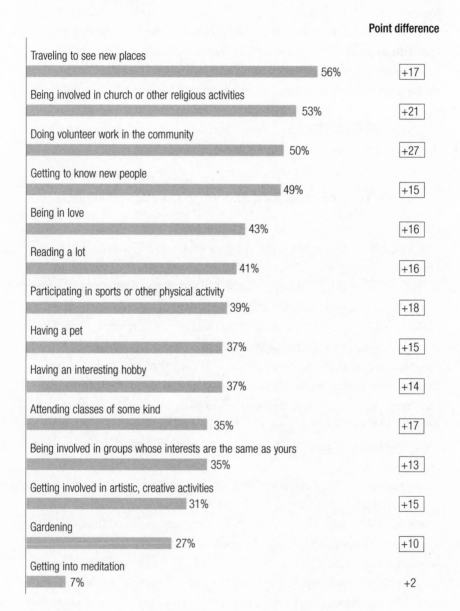

Point difference

Traveling to see new places — 56% — +17

Being involved in church or other religious activities — 53% — +21

Doing volunteer work in the community — 50% — +27

Getting to know new people — 49% — +15

Being in love — 43% — +16

Reading a lot — 41% — +16

Participating in sports or other physical activity — 39% — +18

Having a pet — 37% — +15

Having an interesting hobby — 37% — +14

Attending classes of some kind — 35% — +17

Being involved in groups whose interests are the same as yours — 35% — +13

Getting involved in artistic, creative activities — 31% — +15

Gardening — 27% — +10

Getting into meditation — 7% — +2

Source: Roper Reports

new things and on a par with being outdoors and having time to oneself, for example.

Asked which one or two things say "the most" about them as a person, Influentials put the causes they contribute to or work for first (family and relationships were not offered as an option), at 38%, 14 points higher than in the public as a whole. Significant numbers, however, also say the home says the most about them (33%, about the same as the average person). Hobbies (28%, 8 higher) and jobs (25%, 5 higher) are also cited by large numbers of Influentials as saying the most about them.

Where They Are Satisfied and What They're Working On

Perhaps because they are clear about what they're after—"what matters"—Influentials tend to be somewhat more satisfied with their lives than the average American. Across 15 areas of their personal lives they are on average most likely to express "complete" satisfaction than the public as a whole by 11 points. Influentials are particularly likely to feel fulfilled in two areas that are very important to them, their values and personal relationships. Six of the seven areas in which Influentials are most likely to express satisfaction involve values and relationships: the moral code they've decided to live by, their marital status, the way their parents treated them, their friendships, their marriage or romantic relationship, and the way they treated their parents. In addition, they're substantially more likely than the average to be happy with their career or field of work, another area of importance to them.

Again, just as they are not 100% optimistic, there are some areas in which most Influentials are *not* satisfied. Just under half of Influentials, for example, feel completely satisfied about how they've raised their children. As parents, they apparently feel they can and should do better. Factoring out Influentials who don't have kids under 18 at home—that is, those who aren't actively parenting young children—only raises the figure to a little over half, still significantly below the two-thirds of Influentials completely satisfied with how their parents treated *them*. Parenting is thus a significant concern.

Similarly, only about four in ten are really happy with their house, a

Figure 2-9. Fulfilled—but Not Completely

Percentage of Influential Americans saying they are "completely satisfied" in area of life, with percentage point difference from the total public (average 1997–2001)

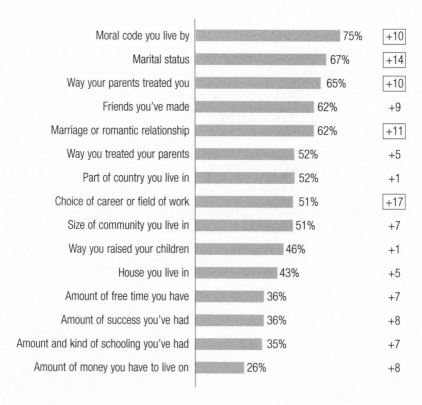

		Point difference
Moral code you live by	75%	+10
Marital status	67%	+14
Way your parents treated you	65%	+10
Friends you've made	62%	+9
Marriage or romantic relationship	62%	+11
Way you treated your parents	52%	+5
Part of country you live in	52%	+1
Choice of career or field of work	51%	+17
Size of community you live in	51%	+7
Way you raised your children	46%	+1
House you live in	43%	+5
Amount of free time you have	36%	+7
Amount of success you've had	36%	+8
Amount and kind of schooling you've had	35%	+7
Amount of money you have to live on	26%	+8

Source: Roper Reports

subject that we return to later in this chapter. Only about one in three In-fluentials are entirely satisfied with the amount of free time they have, the amount of success they've had, and the level and type of schooling they had, and only one in four is fully satisfied with the amount of money they have to live on (see Figure 2-9).

These areas of dissatisfaction keep coming up as places that the Influentials are working on. They are the issues they're striving on in their lives: the amount of time and level of care and skill they bring to parenting, their homes, the amount of time they have for leisure, their success relative to their ambition, how much learning they have relative to how much they'd like, and how much money they have. They're the areas in which Influentials are putting energy and open to new ideas: products and services that help them be more efficient during the workday so they can free more time for their kids and have meaningful, fun experiences with their kids; get more leisure time; help them reach their ambitions in their careers and activities in the community; increase their learning; and help them earn more and build wealth. Computers, cell phones, vacations, museums, performances, books, magazines, learning-oriented television programs, investment guides, 401(k)s, home ideas, family-friendly restaurants and getaways, the World Wide Web—the products and services in which Influentials lead the mainstream—relate back to the problems in their lives. Influentials appear to see their lives as works in progress. This sense of unfulfilled goals, like their confidence, is probably one of the keys to their success, giving them motivation to persevere. This mind-set, as we also see in the chapters to come, is poised to create a demand for new ideas in the future from business, government, and other sources and to keep those entities focused and on track, too.

PROFILES IN INFLUENCE

Rick White

Values such as family, honesty, authenticity, and learning seem to fit Rick White well. The 41-year-old mutual fund manager likes to be intellectually engaged. He is usually reading a clutch of books: *The Long Walk,* a World War II memoir of a Polish prisoner of war's trek home; *The Last River,* a memoir of a kayaking adventure; and Thomas Pynchon's epic *Gravity's Rainbow* are recent examples.

He values the problem-solving aspects of his job, such as evaluating market conditions, assessing companies' prospects, and figuring out how to reach his objectives. Some of his favorite experiences have been in building new businesses for the companies he's worked for, both for the business challenge ("Here's a blank sheet of paper. Build an asset management business.") and the team aspects of the assignments. "The notion of a common goal and vision, the social dynamic when you have a joint cause and are working with high-quality people," appeals greatly to him, he says.

His preference is to engage in activities from which he can learn. A lot of the attraction of starting a business is the education he gets from the experience. He has always tried to find positions where he can work with "people I can learn from." Like a number of the Influentials we've interviewed, he periodically considers going back to school for further education. "The ultimate liberal arts guy," he says with a self-deprecating smile. The books he reads are usually books he can benefit from—history, religion and spirituality, business, science (though, of the three books he's reading at any given time, he reserves one for pure fun).

He is inquisitive. When his mother enrolled later in life in divinity school, it struck a chord. Conversations with him can slip easily into discussions of how people live out their values and what it means to be true to your values. When he and his wife, Rebecca, started looking for a church, it seemed that Quakerism, with its openness to individual spiritual experience, skepticism of accepted wisdom, and value on involvement in society, was a good fit. Although he has been successful in his career and has many of the trappings of success—a nice home, good cars, and regular vacations—he has tried to make it a point not to get caught up in materialism.

Family is very much the center of his life. He and Rebecca have three children, ages five to nine. White typically is out of the house and off to work before sunrise so that he can put in a full day's work and get home to spend time with the kids before they go to bed. Weekends are usually wall-to-wall family: soccer games, going to the beach, trips to the museum or zoo, and First-Day School and church on Sunday morning. The family spends a lot of time outdoors; summer means camping, boating, and raft rides; winter brings family ski trips. Colorado (where Rebecca's family lives) and Utah are favorite vacation haunts.

The value placed on family, children, engagement, and learning have led both Rick and Rebecca White to be busy in the broader world. They're both active in their Friends Meeting, for example, Rick on trustees, Rebecca in children's programs; the family usually turns out for cleanup days.

White's major commitment is the Land Mine Survivors Network. He became involved in the international organization, created to support victims of land mines and to lobby for a global ban on land mines, through his brother, Jerry, who is one of the cofounders of the group and a land mine survivor. Jerry White lost a leg in 1983 when he stepped on a land mine while on a student trip to Israel. When Jerry, after recuperating from the horrible accident, informed Rick that he was forming an organization to try to turn his tragedy into something that could benefit others, Rick enlisted in the effort. His work has mostly been behind the scenes, helping with fund-raising, serving on the board of directors, organizational assistance, and "thoughts and counsel." He has accompanied representatives of the group on international trips, including missions showing donors the group's work in other countries, such as Jordan and Cambodia, and has met with dignitaries, including Jordan's Queen Noor. The Land Mine Survivors Network, which is premised on the self-help idea that a victim can help another victim in a way that no other person can (a concept underlying some of the most successful outreach organizations in the past century), has grown to the point that it is now operating in six countries. It has made its mark in other ways as well. It was part of the land mine coalition that won the Nobel Peace Prize in 1997.

White has found the experience of being involved with the Land Mine Survivors Network to be both inspiring and harrowing: "It's hard to understand that something you can put in your pocket and costs three bucks—which is typical for a land mine—can forever alter someone's life. Land mines are indiscriminate in whom they choose for their victims. Jerry was the classic example of a land mine victim. The mine he stepped on was left over from a conflict 20 years before." It's "sobering" to see the impact firsthand, but also motivating—to do something about it.

Case Study: Green Marketing—the Influential Balance

One of the ways Influentials synthesize their values and their lifestyles is to prod business and government to focus on what will benefit society. This comes through clearly in their values. The finding that 78% of Influentials think business should "consider what is good for society, not just what is good for profit" is one example. One area in which Influentials have been pushing government and business hardest in recent decades is the environment. Influentials have been among the staunchest advocates for expanding national parks and clamping down on pollution.

At the same time, they've seen clearly that there are limits to how far green marketing can take consumers and companies and have become proponents for finding new solutions to balance environmental protection and human needs for economic growth and steady supplies of energy. This likely is a portent for a shift in the national discussion on the environment in the years to come. The Influentials' position suggests that environmental impact statements should be part of all companies' thinking: how much waste will be generated by a product, what the opportunities are for recycling and using renewable materials, and in which areas of environmental cause-related marketing a company can get involved. The Influentials' openness to new ways of thinking also suggests that business, government, and the other organizations involved in environmental issues need to be open to questioning conventional wisdom.

Take green marketing. On balance, Influentials are strong environmentalists. They believe environmental protection laws and regulations "have not gone far enough" (52% agree with the position) rather than gone "too far" or "struck the right balance," according to Roper Green Gauge, an ongoing tracking study of Americans' views on the environment. On a scale of 1–10, with 10 the best possible environmental situation, Influentials give the U.S. only a middling grade of 5.5 on environmental quality (their communities score slightly higher, 6.2; the world slightly worse, 4.7).

But many Influentials are critical of products marketed as green by business. A substantial number of Influentials (44%), when asked the major reasons not to buy environmentally marketed products, say such products often "don't work as well" as the products they are meant to replace. Almost half of Influentials (49%) say green products are "too expensive." The message: business needs to make green products competitive with other products in price and quality.

It is not too much to ask that green products reflect the price-quality value formula they expect elsewhere in the marketplace, Influentials argue. Higher mileage requirements and emissions standards have not deterred the car industry from producing higher quality sedans, they say. Some might argue that there shouldn't be separate environmental product lines at all. Rather than being a side product or line extensions commanding premium prices, environmentally minded features should be integrated into companies' core product lines.

Achieving that goal of integrated environmentalism will probably not be easy. The impression the research gives us is that Influentials understand that long-term progress on the environment will not come through easy fixes.

They also seem to be open to compromise. This could lead to some surprising developments. For example, Influentials appear to be willing to relax on energy exploration under the right conditions. Just over half of Influentials accept the idea that there are now ways to extract oil, coal, and natural gas from the ground "with only minimal damage to the environment." This doesn't mean they are yet open to going ahead on drilling in areas they deem valuable, such as the coastline or inland treasures. The discussion is beginning, however.

Not surprisingly, there is resistance among Influentials (like most Americans) to stricter regulations on SUVs, one of the ideas often discussed in the environmental community. Applying car emissions standards to SUVs draws well under majority support from Influentials, for example. The desire for safety that has led many Americans, the Influentials included, into larger vehicles still holds sway. Although midsize sedans are the most commonly owned vehicle among Influentials (49% own one), large numbers of Influentials count a gas-guzzling SUV (23%), pickup truck (32%), full-size car (30%), van (8%), or minivan (19%) among their households' vehicles.

One way out of the big car conundrum may be hybrid fuel or alternative fuel vehicles. There's a surprisingly high degree of interest in gas-electric hybrid cars among Influentials. Just under half of Influentials have said in surveys in recent years that they're at least "somewhat interested" in getting a hybrid car, with a substantial number in that group "very" interested. There are similar levels of interest in alternative fuel vehicles. The current hybrids, mostly small sedans like the Toyota Prius and Honda Insight, should probably be considered only the starting point. Although their 70 mpg mileage generates a lot of "gee whiz" sentiment, the big question is how far the technology can carry the larger, family-friendly sedans and people haulers in Influentials' lifestyles.

Influentials don't hold out a lot of hope that science and technology will bail out the U.S. In fact, only 30% of Influentials think new technologies will "come along to solve environmental problems before they get out of hand." Influentials are significantly *less* likely to place their hopes in technology saving the day than Americans overall (with a 16-point difference). Influentials are great fans of science and technology, but they are not especially likely to think scientists and engineers will even play "the most important part" in preserving the world's environment (52% agree, 10 points less than in the public as a whole). To Influentials, environmental progress depends on a concerted effort on multiple fronts, decisive leadership and effective enforcement from government, better environmental products from business, and more effort from Americans generally.

Many Influentials seem to be ready to do more than recycle their newspapers, bottles, and cans (which most already do regularly). Many say they would pay premiums for products that are better for the environment. On average, Influentials, for example, say they'd pay 10% more for an automobile that would be one-third less polluting to the air. They would pay a comparable premium for gas that is one-third less polluting. They would pay even more of a premium, 15%, for major appliances that require one-third less energy or water to run and would pay 13% more for electricity generated from renewable resources, such as wind or solar, that are one-third less polluting and as a result contribute less to global warming.

Of course, these are hypothetical options. Our other research suggests that these cars, gas, appliances, and energy would have to continue to meet Influentials' needs without trade-offs in quality or reliability. Otherwise, they will be merely novelty products. Still, if the big breakthroughs aren't yet readily evident to Influentials, it's clear that the environment is front and center to them. Only a relatively small number of Influentials (28%, compared with 42% in the total public) think that economic security and well-being come first, "*then* we can worry about environmental problems."

Politicians should take note. Almost half of Influentials say they will vote against a candidate who is not for stronger protection of the environment. The environment is an area that matters to Influentials.

An Idea That Works: The Integrated Home

One of the ways Influentials lead trends is through adapting what they see elsewhere—ideas, products, and services, for example—into something new that works for them. One example is the integrated life, a trend that we saw emerging in Influentials in 1995. Through piecing together such new technologies as computers and cell phones and new ideas like flex-time schedules, Influentials very consciously seemed to be reshaping their work schedules to be able to devote more time to family, activities in the community, and hobbies and interests. Rather than separate from each other— the "workday" and "the rest of life"—work and personal time were brought together in new ways to make life work better.

The trend toward integration has led to far-reaching changes in Influentials' lives, in particular in the home. The American home—as defined by Influentials—is increasingly the "integrated home." The typical home of Influentials has become a hub for a growing number of pursuits, from the traditional haven from the world, to family center, entertainment space, work space, gallery, and natural preserve. The result has created a growth path for business.

As Figure 2-10 shows, the majority of Influentials see the home as serving at least eight functions. The traditional role of "private retreat," where one can "relax and get away from it all," continues to be the leading function of the home to Influentials; 88% say the idea describes their homes "mostly" or "completely." Comparable numbers see the home as "a family haven" where their family members can "come together to relate and connect" (84%), another traditional role. *How* they connect is changing, however. Just over eight in ten Influentials say the home is "an entertainment center" where they can "have fun and enjoy" themselves. Six in ten view the home as "a social hub" where people come to socialize; a "learning center" where they can learn or teach others; an important financial asset; and "a hobby center." Half say it's "an office/workshop" where "I do work." Influ-

Figure 2-10. The Integrated Home

Percentage of Influential Americans agreeing mostly or completely that statement describes their home, with percentage point difference from total public

88%. . . . My home is a private retreat; at home I can relax and get away from it all   -3

84%. . . . My home is a family haven; it's a place where family come together
to relate and connect   +5

82%. . . . My home is an entertainment center; it's a place where I have fun and
enjoy myself   +4

61%. . . . My home is a learning center; at home I learn or teach others   +13

60%. . . . My home is a social hub; I often socialize with others there   +5

60%. . . . My home is the most important financial asset I have   -3

57%. . . . My home is a hobby center; it's where I keep up with my hobbies   +4

52%. . . . My home is an office/workshop; it's a place where I do work   +22

42%. . . . My home is like a gallery; I enjoy purchasing and collecting nice things
to display or use at home   +4

33%. . . . My home is a high-tech zone; it's wired with the latest technology   +9

16%. . . . My home is a way station; I use it mostly just for eating, sleeping,
and bathing   -7

Source: Roper Reports

entials are significantly more likely than the average person to view their homes as serving certain roles, particularly as an office (22 points higher). Moreover, some roles are becoming increasingly important. Since 1998, the percentage saying the home is "a high-tech zone" with "the latest technology," although not a majority, has leaped 10 points, to 33%. More also view the home as an entertainment center (up 14 points).

People at one time had only one choice—go out—but they increasingly have an option to stay home. For example, with the home office, the idea isn't to do *all* one's work from home but to have it as an option. The typical Influential doesn't want to work from home every day but to do about one-fifth of their work from home—a day a week. The functions of the modern city have migrated into the home, from multiplex theaters (home theaters) to workplace (home office), library (the Web), gym (home gym), spa (home spa), parks (garden), and on and on. The point does not seem so much to be to pull up the castle gate and escape as to have more options, so that homeowners can do what suits their mood—without leaving the nest. Thus, if in ancient times all roads led to Rome, in the modern American community, all roads lead home.

The Influential Personality:
IDIOSYNCRASY

Ability to sift out what matters. Belief in growth and change. Balance of community and self. Focus on family and being engaged in life. Putting together the pieces, we begin to get a sense of what the Influential personality is like. There's one piece that is missing in this equation: the element of idiosyncrasy that is part of the Influential personality. This element is more evident in some Influentials than others and, fittingly, comes out in different ways in different Influentials. It is, however, a key element in the Influential personality.

Breaking the word down into its Greek origins, *idiosunkrasia, idio* being one's own and *sunkrasia* a mixture, the word in essence means "mixing one's own." The Influentials mix their own. They're comfortable creating a position for themselves outside the mainstream. These rough edges add an element of unpredictability, quirkiness, richness, and style to Influentials' personality.

We've seen this element of idiosyncrasy in the Influentials' perspective on the environment, in their skepticism that science will save the day, their openness to new ideas, and their steadfastness that the environment matters and should not take a backseat to the economy. We've seen earlier in this chapter as well how much more clear they are on certain issues, like the U.S. pioneer heritage being a source of its greatness, the high priority they place on certain values, and their blending of intangibles, like religious belief, with very tangible things like owning a home, taking trips abroad, and being interested in Thai food and rhythm and blues.

This idiosyncrasy is reflected in their political ideas. Our studies have shown Influentials generally support the position that women should have the right to legal abortions. Majorities also support the position that prayer should be permitted in public school. More than half of Influentials support equal rights for homosexuals (at levels significantly above those in the public as a whole).

At the same time, most Influentials take the position that communities should be able to limit sex and violence in the media. Six in ten Influentials favor requiring young people to participate in national service programs, a subject that is not currently a major element in the political discussion. Influentials don't favor everything—far from it. Fewer than half favor big rollbacks in government regulation of business. In some areas, they want more regulation of business. The picture that comes through is that, in terms of the orthodoxies of the established political parties, Influentials are mavericks. Many are loyal to their political party, but there's a streak of independent mindedness. Large numbers seem to question their parties' stance on issues.

This "mixing your own" is reflected in the marketplace as well. Despite being relatively skeptical of materialism, fairly large numbers of Influentials told us in one 2000 survey that they'd like to have a vacation home (two in three), have a beautifully decorated home (half), stay in luxury hotels (half), travel abroad frequently for fun (half), eat in expensive restaurants (just over four in ten), and fly first class (just under four in ten). One in four said they'd like to own an expensive car. The responses here and elsewhere suggest that, after satisfying their obligations at the office, meeting their commitments in the community, and enjoying their time with family and friends, Influentials use such desires—cars, hotels, eating out, art, medieval history, "the integrated home," or whatever their passions are—as rewards, indulgences, and R&R.

Shelley Miller's enjoyment of convertibles is, for her, a way to take a break from her "conservative, practical" side and have some fun. It's also a great way to decompress after a long day of meetings—"put the top down, and drive out, and the stress just dissipates and you feel good," she smiles. She owned a Mitsubishi Eclipse until recently. "Barcelona red with tan interior, turbo, the whole thing—not a practical car for a mother of two, not to mention an accountant. I really loved that car," she laughs. Miller downsized the car when she was given a city-owned vehicle (common sense prevailed), but she keeps up with the new models and eventually will own another Mitsubishi.

This idiosyncratic thinking has already made a beachhead in the consumer marketplace. Consider the success of the new retro car designs like the 1940s-like Plymouth PT Cruiser, the revived VW Bug, the revived British Mini, the revived Ford Thunderbird, and the new generations of roadsters.

Influentials appear to be doing their part to raise a new generation of self-confident, idiosyncratic thinkers. Influentials are significantly more likely than Americans as a whole to value the qualities of being "self-confident" and an "independent thinker" in their own children (particularly, interestingly, their daughters).

They're doing their part to encourage self-confident, independent-minded thinking in the political process, too. The Influentials are significantly more likely than Americans as a whole to value presidents who display "personal courage in fighting for their beliefs." During the 2000 presidential race, 46% of Influentials said it was one of the two or three most important qualities to them in a president, 14 points higher than the response of the total public. Only "honesty" (67%) and "intelligence and brains" (55%) ranked higher. Factors like political philosophy (24%) and the candidate's party (7%), meanwhile, were rated far down the list.

This mix-it-yourself approach by Influentials means they are willing to experiment when they think it can make a difference in their life. Influentials are significantly more likely than the average person to "like to experiment with cooking" (44%, 12 higher than in the total public), be "always looking for new and unusual flavors" in cuisine (36%, 11 higher), and be "very interested in foods from different countries" (30%, 9 higher). The openness to experimentation is also reflected in the eclectic idea of the integrated home, where they've mixed and matched technologies and ideas to produce homes that better meet their wants and needs.

Influentials seem to like looking at things differently from others, even money. When asked what "money" means to them—a not unimportant subject in a society focused on having more money and building financial security—Influentials are less likely than Americans as a whole to say "pleasure" (only 43%), "achievement" (34%), or "status" (10%) and more likely to say "security" (83%), "independence" (78%), and "helping one's children" (75%)—money in the service of values, like family and being engaged in life. As elsewhere, Influentials take in the same information as other people. They parse it differently, though, and ultimately pick out what matters. In so doing, they set an example for others.

CHAPTER 3

The Influence Spiral

HOW INFLUENTIALS GET AND SPREAD IDEAS

IT'S NOT UNUSUAL for Sophie Glovier to come home to find a dozen or more messages on her answering machine. In the five years since leaving a high-profile job with the Madison Avenue ad agency Young & Rubicam, the Princeton, New Jersey mother of three has become a power volunteer. She organizes the annual major fund-raiser for the Delaware Raritan Greenway, a land preservation group that has acquired 3,300 acres for park and open space in New Jersey in the past 11 years.

Together with other mothers from her play group in Princeton, she formed Hudibras (named after a beloved pub from their college days), to bring area residents together four times a year to meet people outside their usual circle and to have fun, from an old-fashioned barn dance in a real barn to a scavenger hunt through the boroughs of the Princeton area. The group quickly grew to 100 couples.

She has served on the board for Teach for America, the national organization dedicated to placing the best and brightest of the nation's college graduates into teaching positions in poor school districts. For two years she pulled together the major annual fund-raiser for Trinity Counseling Service, a local agency providing help regardless of need. Active in her church, she is a regular participant in an all-women book club, and she recently joined the town garden club.

Because she knows so many people—her red address book-cum-calendar is crammed with a few hundred names—and in turn seems to be in the know, Sophie Glovier is an information nexus for a wide cross section of the Princeton community. Several years ago, she read in the local newspaper about an organic farm coop and convinced her husband, Curtis, to join. Next, she asked a friend if she wanted to sign up; now a dozen of her friends trundle off to the Stonybrook Millstone Watershed Organic Farm every week for fresh organic fruit and vegetables. Through a similar process, a large circle of acquaintances now have organic milk delivered regularly to their homes from Moo Milk Express, a delivery service.

Sophie Glovier is a quintessential Influential. The most engaged Americans, Influentials are conduits of information for their community and the nation. Their activist bent, many connections, and active minds, as well as the sheer force of their personalities—their clear sense of priorities, belief in growth and change, passionate approach to life, and infectious sense of confidence—make the Influentials natural intersections for intelligence. They tend to know more than others, to hear about things first, and to broadcast what they know to many people. People share interesting ideas and useful insights with Influentials and trust their opinions enough to come to them when they have problems to solve.

The Spiral of Influence

The result of Influentials' involvement often creates what we call a spiral of influence. As the Influentials' efforts at learning something new bear results, it inspires them to learn more about the subject, to share what they've learned with others, and to seek out others with expertise in the area. This inspires them to further exploration and experimentation, which yields further results—which they share with others, and inspires them to learn, explore, and experiment more—and share what they've learned with others: an ever-widening circle of influence and change. Adoption of a product leads to integration of the product, which leads to exploration and change, which leads to adoption of something new, and the cycle begins again. In turn, the Influentials' word-of-mouth impact tends to be not merely larger than the norm but to rise exponentially when they become interested in a subject (see Figure 3-1).

The Influence spiral is evident in the pattern of trendsetting and word of mouth we have detailed so far in this book. The Influentials' interest in

Figure 3-1. The Influence Spiral

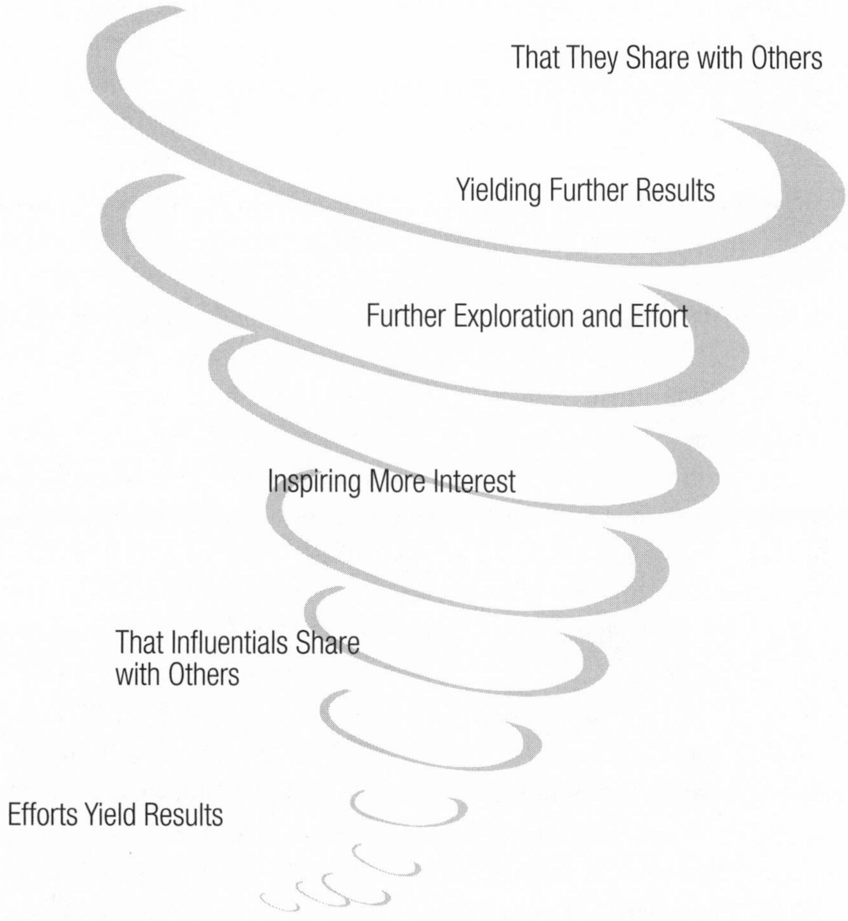

That They Share with Others

Yielding Further Results

Further Exploration and Effort

Inspiring More Interest

That Influentials Share with Others

Efforts Yield Results

computers, which as we described in Chapter 1, was evident by 1981, led them to acquire computers ahead of other Americans and to learn first-generation applications like word-processing. This in turn led them to see the potential benefits of PCs ahead of others and to take advantage of these opportunities ahead of others, from using computers to work from home to tapping into the Internet to keep up with news, communicate with others, shop, bank, invest, file taxes, and store and disseminate their photos. We see this pattern in our research. Between 1996 and 1998, access to the Internet and online services among Influentials jumped 27 points to 67%. As Internet access grew, Influentials started experimenting with and integrating other uses. As Figure 3-2 shows, by 1998, half of Influentials were using or had used a computer to send and receive e-mail; by 2002 the figure had grown to 72% (32 points higher than in the public as a whole). More started using their computers to connect to news and information databases (by 2002, 56% of Influentials, 30 points higher than in the total public) and read magazines and newspapers (by 2001, 41% of Influentials, 23 points higher than in the total public). More started using their computers to consult books like medical guides and encyclopedias (by 2002, 51% of Influentials, 27 points higher than in the total public). Growing numbers started using their computers to buy things (by 2002, 47% of Influentials, 24 points higher than in the total public), giving rise to the e-commerce industry, a subject we discuss in further detail later in this chapter.

New computer uses cropped up, like viewing photos and videos (by 2002, 40% of Influentials, 19 points higher than in the total public) and listening to music (by 2002, 40% of Influentials, 17 higher). Using the computer for household bookkeeping began to get a boost (rising to 54% by 2002, 32 points higher), as did using the computer to keep track of personal records (47%, 25 points higher). Majorities were using computers for the traditional uses as well: word processing (63% in 1998; 67% in 2002) and playing games (58% in 1998; 61% in 2002). At the same time, some uses did not take off. For example, the proportions of Influentials connecting to online bulletin boards, although sizable, has bounced between 26 and 35% since 1998. Playing games with others via computer network has only recently shown signs of taking off, rising to 21%. Filing taxes via the PC, although showing promise, does not yet appear to have hit its full potential with Influentials. Using the computer to do office work from home, for a variety of reasons we focus on more in Chapter 5 ("High Pace/High Peace"), became less compelling; after hitting 50% by 1998, the percentage of Influentials doing so slipped to the low to mid-40s in subsequent years (see Figure 3-2).

As the Influentials' expertise grew, they were sought out more by others for advice and information. As computers became more of a mainstream product, the proportion of Influentials being sought out for their insights

Figure 3-2. Experimentation and Integration: Computers

Percentage of Influential Americans saying they now do or have done activity with a personal computer, 1998–2002, with point differences from the total public in parentheses

Activity	1998	2000	2002
Send/receive e-mail	51% (+30)	60% (+30)	72% (+32)
Word processing	63% (+34)	63% (+28)	67% (+31)
Play games	58% (+28)	61% (+25)	61% (+25)
Access news, information databases	41% (+24)	51% (+30)	56% (+30)
Household bookkeeping	44% (+23)	44% (+20)	54% (+32)
Consult books, reference material	39% (+23)	44% (+24)	51% (+27)
Keep track of personal records	50% (+29)	42% (+23)	47% (+24)
Buy things	20% (+12)	36% (+21)	47% (+25)
Do office work from home	50% (+29)	43% (+25)	44% (+26)
Read magazines, newspapers online	20% (+9)	38% (+23)	41% (+23)
Make bank transactions	21% (+13)	23% (+12)	26% (+11)
Accessing discussion bulletin boards	31% (+18)	35% (+20)	26% (+13)
File income taxes	16% (+10)	16% (+9)	15% (+5)
Playing games with others via a network	14% (+9)	18% (+11)	21% (+14)

Source: Roper Reports

rose substantially. Today 34% of Influentials (just over 7 million Influentials) are regularly asked for their advice and opinion about computers, up from 25% in 1987, a significant change. The same pattern will likely be repeated in the next growth phase of computers.

Influence spirals are evident in other areas. From being among the first to take advantage of Individual Retirement Accounts in the 1980s, Influentials moved on to learn more, do more, and help forge the way in 401(k) retirement accounts (as shown in Figure 1-15) investing directly in the stock market and making the most of new tools from Web-based stock and mutual fund investing services, to financial media from daily newspapers, to magazines, TV programs, cable networks, and Internet sites. In tandem, the numbers of Influentials asked their advice and opinion rose as others followed them into the markets, so that 35% of Influentials (about 7½ million Influentials) are now queried by others for their insights on investing. Over the course of this book, we describe more such spirals.

There is a high correlation between subjects in which Influentials are interested, pursue in their leisure time, are asked their advice and opinion about, and start word-of-mouth buzz on. This pattern can be seen in particular in politics and government, the area that defines the segment. Large numbers of Influentials play active roles in their community (76% going to a meeting on town or school concerns, 50% serving on a committee, and 49% being an officer of a club or organization, for example, all 40-plus points higher than the public as a whole); place a high priority on involvement in the community (67% doing volunteer or community-service work at least occasionally in their leisure time, 35 points higher than the public as a whole); and take a special interest in topics that will help them in their involvement in the community, such as news and current events (which they are almost universally interested in), politics (which 84% are interested in, 30 points higher than in the public as a whole), and history (an interest of 83%, 22 points higher than in the total public). Influentials are also sought out by others for their perspectives on politics and government (55% on a regular basis, 39 points higher than in the public as a whole).

This intersection of interest, activity, and opinion leading is also evident in other areas. Travel is one example, with Influentials substantially more likely than the average American to see this as a special hobby or interest (54%, 27 points higher), pursue the interest in their leisure time (for example, 62% taking weekend trips at least occasionally, 18 points higher), enjoy learning about new places (78% saying "different countries and people" is an interest of theirs, 15 points higher), and to be sought out by others for advice and opinion on places to go on vacation (38%, 17 points higher).

Restaurants and food are another subject, with many Influentials expressing interest in food (76%, for instance, in cooking, 10 higher than in the total public), eating out regularly (83% at least occasionally in their leisure time, slightly higher than in the total public), and being asked regularly for their insights on where to eat (54%, 23 higher than in the public as a whole). Culture, too: large numbers of Influentials use their leisure time to attend cultural events (63% at least occasionally, 24 higher than in the total public), express interest in culture (66% in art, 16 higher), and are asked their for advice and opinion (31% on music, 7 higher; 16% on art, 7 higher). We use these figures not to overwhelm you with numbers but to make a point: the statistics show high levels of involvement and, generally, substantial differences between Influentials and the public as a whole.

One reason environmentalism has become a "third rail" in politics, like Social Security, virtually untouchable (as President George W. Bush found in his unsuccessful attempt to drill in the Alaskan wilderness), is that environmentalism shows up across our studies as an important priority to Influentials. Nine in ten Influentials express interest in the environment and related areas, such as nature and animals, and large numbers enjoy spending leisure time outdoors in nature and speak out on environmental issues.

Academic research suggests that there are "strong-tie" and "weak-tie" influences on word-of-mouth decisions. "Strong ties" mean that people are part of a tight social circle with the decision maker and "weak ties" are more casual acquaintances. How much the consumer relies on strong-tie versus weak-tie sources depends on various factors, including the kind of information important for the decision and the difficulty of the decision ("Influences on Consumer Use of Word-of-Mouth Recommendations," Duhan et al., *Journal of the Academy of Marketing Sciences*, 1997). Because of their strong connections to many groups, Influentials seem to have more strong-tie connections than the average person and have a sufficient breadth and depth of expertise often to be influential in others' decisions when their links to the decision maker are not strong-tie links.

Influentials are not at the center of national conversation on every topic. They have a utilitarian approach to shopping, for example: browsing stores is not a particular leisure-time activity or interest. They're not especially engaged in the latest styles in fashion or in video games, as we saw previously. They don't appear to be "know-it-alls" who have to tell everyone their opinions whether they have something worthwhile to say or not. The research suggests there is good reason for the people in this segment to be sought out for their insights. The subjects on which Influentials are seen as experts, from concerns in their community, to national issues, to such topics as travel, eating out, technology, culture, health, and the environment, are areas in which they are interested and involved, usually on many levels. As a result, they probably have something worthwhile to say.

Like Sophie Glovier, they dispense what they know on a regular basis. We have seen this in multiple studies through the years that have tested the thesis of the Influentials' leadership. One such study, for example, showed that in the past month four in ten Influential Americans had been "asked for an opinion about a product or service" (43%, to be exact), double the response of the public as a whole (21%) and also higher than in other groups traditionally pursued as opinion leaders, such as $75,000-plus income households (32%), executives and professionals (33%), and college graduates (30%).

PROFILES IN INFLUENCE

Sophie Glovier

Sophie Glovier is a case in point. "I've always been a good networker," says the 36-year-old. In turn, she is often sought out by others and tends to "give a lot of recommendations." It is a fluid process, part of the give and take of conversations that naturally unfold in her daily rounds. "Someone will mention they need a window washer. I say, 'I've got a great window washer.' Someone else overhears the conversation. Then I'm giving three people the window washer's number."

At the same time, she is continuously gathering bits of information throughout the day, from the three papers she reads each morning to the car radio (including "a great deal" of National Public Radio) she listens to as she drops the kids off at school, does errands, and goes to meetings and especially from the people with whom she interacts throughout the day. "I regularly get tips from chatting with friends," she says. "I'm usually crunched for time, so it's rarely over coffee." The leisurely conversations that for decades have been a staple of movies, television, and commercials are not part of her everyday life.

More often it's in "chit-chat before meetings, at the kids' school, or while we are working on something," she says. "I was with a friend taking the kids to a movie and I mentioned that I was looking for a light fixture for our kitchen," she recalls. "That night she dropped by a packet of information on light fixtures that she put together when she was renovating her home."

One day the subject might be how to set up a fund-raising event—which corporations to contact for corporate sponsorships, which people to call to arrange for location, menus, and other details for the event, which artists to seek out to create art for the event, which firms to ask for direct-marketing help, and who to contact in the media for advance promotion—the basics of "getting the right people in the right place," as Glovier says, that are key to creating a successful event.

Another day it might be Moo Milk Express, or the Stonybrook Millstone Watershed Organic Farm, a window washer, a book that she read in her book club (*Divine Secrets of the Ya-Ya Sisterhood*, for example) or currently on her nightstand (David McCullough's biography *John Adams*, which she was "really excited to read").

"I find most ideas come out of conversations with people building on what's just been said," says Glovier. "It's a very natural serendipitous process for me. I really want to help people find the things they need—even friends. It's satisfying when it works out. We don't normally set out with an agenda. We just respond to what comes up in conversation. There's no structured tip-sharing."

Glovier found her new home through networking. While collecting boxwood for a church fund-raiser, she told an older woman whose door she knocked on how much she loved the neighborhood. "Why don't you look at my house?" the woman piped up. "It's for sale." Glovier and her husband did, and bought it; they have just completed a major renovation on a 150-year-old Colonial farmhouse, set on eight acres amid nature—one of Glovier's passions—next to a wildlife preserve.

Like many Influentials, Glovier defies conventional stereotypes. A product of affluence—the Chestnut Hill section of Philadelphia, Ivy League schools (undergraduate degree in political science from Princeton; Masters of Business Administration from Columbia)—she is also idiosyncratic. Though her professional background was marketing and advertising, she says, "I try to keep my life as unimpacted by business as possible," making a conscious effort to avoid marketing messages. She tends to keep cars forever. Her primary vehicle is a seven-year-old Ford Taurus station wagon. "I pride myself on not having a status car," she says. She reads *The New York Times* and *The New Yorker* regularly but also indulges herself with *People* and *Martha Stewart Living*.

Like most Influentials, Glovier leads a highly focused life. There is little wasted energy. "I always have my to-do list," she says. "I read really fast, and I'm not easily distracted." She lets go of some of the details of life, for example, maintaining a short, practical hairdo, which means less time for hair care. Her description of herself as "pretty organized" may be an understatement. Her orientation is to lead a productive life. She is highly aware of her orientation and, generally, thinks she is "able to get a lot more done in the same amount of hours" than other people.

Her mind-set carries over into the marketplace. Glovier's shopping style is get in, get out, and get on with life as quickly as possible. In day-to-day purchases, she doesn't do a lot of comparison shopping. "I will have five minutes in a store," she says. "I usually know what I want, and if it's right there, I just get it." She has more important things to do.

She is drawn to products and services that make her life demonstrably easier. The Internet is one example. Like many Americans, she first discovered the Internet at the office, while working on a new product development assignment for AT&T. She started buying books through Amazon.com, then branched out from there. "I've bought everything from Palm Pilots to nursing bras to strollers online," she says. Last summer, she and her daughter bought the required summer reading books for her school online. She likes the efficiency of buying online. "I love it when a site knows me so I don't have to fill out all the address and credit card information again."

On the other hand, Glovier doesn't fit the traditional image of the avid consumer. She "hates" to go to the bank and doesn't much like to shop. "Really the only business" she does, she says, is by phone, by computer, or going to the grocery. "I do a lot of shopping on the computer," she says. Marketing messages run a daunting gauntlet. Glovier pays attention to advertising for things she's in the market for, particularly ads that are rich in information that helps her make smart decisions. She's not easy to reach, though. There's little room for stray messages. "I almost never watch television," and she has "such limited time" for magazines that she "generally" doesn't read the ads. Direct mail "gets thrown out unopened" and telemarketing calls "never work." E-mail marketing messages "generally get deleted."

She concentrates on what she cares about—*family, learning, and the environment.* Her experience with the open-space preservation group has spurred her to consider pursuing the subject further, perhaps through an advanced degree. A lot of the land around Princeton that she first knew as "beautiful farms" has sprouted housing developments. She gets "a visceral feeling" when she drives past "bulldozers bulldozing up" land. The idea that "we need to be taking care of this land" has become "a spiritual belief," she says. *Tradition.* Before moving into their current home, the Gloviers lived in another old home with a broad front porch near the Princeton campus. Her decorating style reflects her tastes—antiques, floral prints, silver-framed family photos, an old-fashioned milk box on the front porch, lots of flowers. *Growth and change.* She's toyed with the idea of going to divinity school. She is finishing up a four-year class at her church that began with reading the New and Old testaments, continued with church history and incorporated a lot of discussion toward a goal of helping people decide and refine their mission in life, a fitting endeavor for an ever-exploring Influential.

The Water Station

The conversation-steeped decision-making process that Sophie Glovier uses is not the way the major institutions of business and society traditionally have liked to think the marketplace works. People in leadership positions in business and society have generally been taught to think top-down. A business or candidate creates a message, then delivers the message to the consumer/citizen through advertisements; the consumer, persuaded by the power of the message, goes to the store and buys the product.

To the extent that a conversation is perceived to exist between business and consumers, it's thought of as top-down as well. Word of mouth, the idea of getting consumers to spread recommendations for products or services, is in turn often practiced as a top-down dialogue. Many businesspeople seem to imagine it as a relay race. Businesses give a message to the consumer. The consumer then passes it on, like a baton, to someone else. A really powerful word-of-mouth carrier—a person like Sophie Glovier or Influentials generally—then takes the message to a whole lot of people.

The problem is, at least with Influentials, it doesn't work that way. Decisions are often a group conversation, as in Sophie Glovier's book club. The message enters the group. It's dissected, analyzed, and discussed by the group and meshed with other sources of information. More voices make it easier to cut through the marketing to the key issues. Is this really something new? Is the quality good? Does it solve a problem? Can it be used some other way to solve a problem? What comes out the other side can be something altogether richer, more nuanced, and different from what began—and a better idea. Sign up for Moo Milk. Buy this lighting fixture. Use this bank.

Influentials generally are not waiting for a product or service, like a relay runner waiting for a baton and running for dear life when they get it. They want what they want when they want it. A more apt image is a water station along a marathon course. The passing runner wants water, gets the water, and goes on with the race. It's not top-down, it's a one-to-one engagement. Sometimes they don't want water at all. Got Gatorade? What about something out of the ordinary? Every year, a local group sets up a stand along the Brooklyn leg of the New York Marathon offering soup, bagels, and oranges. It's not an official New York Road Runners Club site. It's not promoted. But every runner who has done the Marathon remembers it—and talks about how the soup warmed them up on a really cold day or the bagel gave them a much-needed carbohydrate boost.

The race metaphor is not inappropriate for Influentials; this group is usually racing to get things done (and sometimes literally running; Sophie

Glovier is probably not alone in keeping a baby jogger on her porch). Influentials' predilection for *seeking out* the water stations rather than waiting for batons is part of what makes Influentials a driving force in creating markets for initiatives, ideas, messages, products, and services. Since they aren't waiting for you to deliver the water (or anyone; they're too busy), the key is placing your water station along *their* route, which as we've seen is sometimes different from other people's.

There are rules for their road:

- Influentials use multiple sources of information.
- They put people first, rating their interactions in their word-of-mouth network substantially more important than traditional media.
- They believe in sharing what they know with others and are far more likely than the average not only to be turned to for advice and information but also to go out of their way to recommend things to others, a characteristic that, combined with their tendency to have connections with many groups, creates a powerful multiplier effect.
- They most value word-of-mouth insights from people, but they are voracious readers and draw on other sources from the Internet to television to build up their knowledge on subjects.
- Companies must practice "continuous provement," creating meaningful improvements in their services and communicating them in compelling ways, or risk being overtaken by a competitor who is continuously improving and becoming part of the Influential conversation.
- Word-of-mouth buzz is not guaranteed, and once achieved, there's no assurance it will last on its own. Influentials are always interested in something that will make a substantial contribution to their lives, but they don't go out of their way to keep up with what's new in many areas, another reflection of the clearly delineated sense of priorities that is part of their temperament.
- Influentials trust their instincts. They count on word-of-mouth insights from others, but in the end they base their decisions on their personal experiences, assessments, and sense of priorities.

These factors, besides helping Influentials make decisions, also make for interesting conversations. This, in turn, can build and strengthen relationships and help get things done, priorities that are dear to this achievement-oriented, people-connected, growth- and change-directed group.

So how do businesses become part of the conversation?

Principles of Influence:
MULTIPLE SOURCES OF INFORMATION

In swapping news, insights, and information with her friends and gleaning more from multiple sources throughout the day, Sophie Glovier is doing what comes naturally to her. To Influentials, many of their daily contacts— human interactions, the newspapers and magazines they read, the programs they see and hear (even the occasional marketing message on a subject in which they are interested)—have the potential to create or strengthen connections and solve problems.

Call it the "law of the many." Influentials use many more sources than the norm, whether to get news and information or to communicate. In some ways, they are rather like human parallel processors, taking in information, rating it, sorting it, sifting out the element that's useful or interesting, and storing it away for future purpose.

Many Influentials consume an eclectic mix of media. Sophie Glovier is a good example. She keeps up with local news with the local papers and with what's going on in the region, nation, and world through *The New York Times,* NPR, and *The New Yorker,* picks up the occasional tidbit through *People* or *Martha Stewart Living,* and is usually reading a book for her book club or to learn more about "things that interest me." Like many of those interviewed, she is often reading a spiritual book. In addition, she says, "every once in awhile if I find a good review, I'll read a book about urban policy or nature." She doesn't watch TV and limits her kids to videos.

Influentials use more channels than the average for trying to keep abreast of current events or looking for information on a variety of different subjects (see Figure 3-3). Nine in ten Influentials turn to television and newspapers to keep up with events and get information on a breadth of topics. Three in four use radio as a source of news and information, and

Figure 3-3. Multiple Sources of Information

Percentage of Influentials who turn to source when they are "trying to keep abreast of current events or looking for information on a variety of different subjects," with percentage point difference from total public

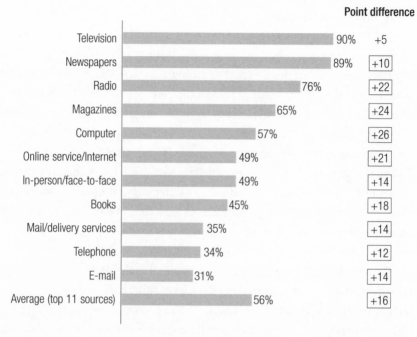

Point difference

Source	Percentage	Point difference
Television	90%	+5
Newspapers	89%	+10
Radio	76%	+22
Magazines	65%	+24
Computer	57%	+26
Online service/Internet	49%	+21
In-person/face-to-face	49%	+14
Books	45%	+18
Mail/delivery services	35%	+14
Telephone	34%	+12
E-mail	31%	+14
Average (top 11 sources)	56%	+16

Source: Roper Reports

two in three turn to magazines. Six in ten use computers and half the Internet and online sources, further testimony to the growing importance of the new media. About half turn to in-person, face-to-face interchanges for news and information, a comparable number to books. Smaller but substantial numbers consider other sources to be good sources as well, including the phone and e-mail, cited by about one in three each.

True to their nature as "information sponges," Influentials are much more likely to draw on a variety of sources for news and information than the average person. In most of the responses just cited, there are differences of 10 points or more between Influentials and the public as a whole. In several areas, there are differences of 20 points or more (computers, magazines, radio, and the Internet). As with Sophie Glovier, piecing together insight and information throughout the day, most Influentials don't rely on one source for their perspectives, balancing what they see, read, and hear from multiple sources. What they hear from any one source—a presidential address, an insight from a neighbor, or an ad on the radio—thus will likely not become gospel.

The same is true when they deliberately seek out education and training to learn new things or sharpen their skills. Influentials typically draw from a number of sources. Books are the leading source when Influentials want to learn, sought out by seven in ten. Computers are the second most common source when Influentials want to learn something new; the majority of Influentials now use computers as a learning channel. Face-to-face learning is the third most important source for learning, turned to by about half in the group. Influentials are substantially more likely than the public as a whole to draw on these sources, particularly computers, for which there is a 24 point difference. Influentials are more likely than the norm to turn elsewhere as well, notably to magazines (used by about one in three, roughly double the rate of the public as a whole).

Their habit of going to multiple sources makes the Influentials good researchers when it comes to making decisions. More than eight in ten Influentials (82%) say that before stereo, TV, and video equipment, "I gather information from specialized sources," a response 13 points higher than the average. Influentials are twice as likely as the norm to call *Consumer Reports* recommendations one of the most important factors to them in brand decisions.

The law of the many holds true in communications as well. Sophie Glovier prefers in-person interactions for keeping in touch, but she also keeps up through numerous phone calls and e-mail. There are 250 names on her Christmas card list. Although she is "not addicted to it," she has a cell phone and used it "a lot" to keep in touch with the contractors on the renovation of her new home. She also has a fax machine. Influentials use far more channels than the norm to communicate with others. The average Influential uses six channels to communicate, from the phone and in-person interactions (used universally) to the mail and delivery services (used by three in four), computers and e-mail (two in three), and online services

Figure 3-4. Multiple Channels of Communication

Percentage of Influentials who use channel to communicate when they "want to express ideas to another person either verbally or in written form," with percentage point difference from total public

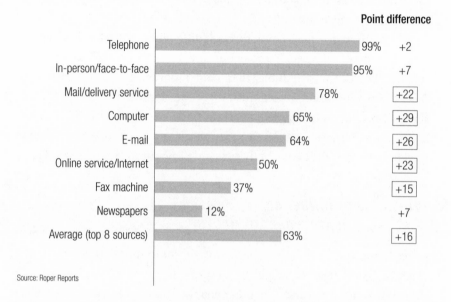

		Point difference
Telephone	99%	+2
In-person/face-to-face	95%	+7
Mail/delivery service	78%	+22
Computer	65%	+29
E-mail	64%	+26
Online service/Internet	50%	+23
Fax machine	37%	+15
Newspapers	12%	+7
Average (top 8 sources)	63%	+16

Source: Roper Reports

and the Internet (half). In contrast, the average person uses only three (the phone, in-person interactions, and the mail). Influentials are more likely to use not only mail but e-mail *and* computers to communicate than the public as a whole is to send a letter (see Figure 3-4).

Glovier ascribes her passion for creating connections—to put on a fund-raiser to create a stronger sense of community in Princeton or just to help her friends learn to square dance or get better quality milk and produce—to two traits. The first is a good, old-fashioned Protestant work ethic. "I feel dopey if I'm not doing something," she says. The second is pleasure. "It's fun to be able to put people together and know they'll have a great time. Different people have different gifts, and one of my gifts is being able to get groups of people together." She's not alone. Recall Isabel Milano, who sees herself as someone who knows "bits and pieces of this and that" and has a knack for connecting people with what they want, "orchestrating people to come together to create an idea or program where people benefit." Or Larry Lee, Jr., who consumes media—*The Wall Street Journal, Money, Black Enterprise,* CNN, CNBC, quiz shows—to use it. He enjoys reading, watching, and listening, but it's not passive entertainment. It's a tool that makes him smarter in his job and interests and a way to strengthen connections.

It's common for those going through difficulties to reach reflexively for a book. When Larry Lee's father's business hit hard times, Lee turned to spiritual books, first the Bible, then contemporary books like *Prayer for Jabez* to turn the situation around. "It got me closer to God," says Lee. He started working on his garden, which in turn drove him to *HGTV (Home and Garden Television)* to learn more about gardening. He then recommended to others the books, activities, and programs he found helped him.

Principles of Influence:
NOTHING BEATS WORD OF MOUTH

Considering their profile—leaders in their community, well-read, motivated, self-sufficient—it would be tempting to conclude that Influentials don't think they can learn from other people. This is far from the case. They draw on a variety of sources, but Influentials consider the recommendations of people the best well of new ideas. Personal recommendations of others are one of the most important criteria for them in choosing a brand, much more so than whether a brand is well-known and advertised. Although there are some exceptions, as a general rule nothing beats word of mouth.

The centrality of word of mouth in Influentials' decision making shines through when they talk about specific decisions. More than eight in ten Influentials rate friends, family, and other people among the best sources for ideas and information on restaurants to try. Seven in ten or more Influentials rate people among the best sources for ideas and information on new meals to try, prescription drugs to use, hotels to stay in, and places to visit. Half or more rate people among the best sources on videos to rent or buy, the merits of one car versus another, movies to see, retirement planning, ways to save and invest, ways to improve their health, improving the appearance of their home, which brands are "best," where to find the best buys, computer equipment, and clothes (see Figure 3-5).

Figure 3-5. Word of Mouth's Value to Influentials

Net percentage of Influentials who believe people—family, friends, or others—offer "the best ideas or information" in most areas (with the specific groups in parentheses)

84%. . . . Restaurants to try (68% friends, 43% family, 16% other people)

75%. . . . New meals or dishes they'd like to try (57% friends, 44% family, 10% other people)

75%. . . . Prescription drugs to use (59% friends, 21% family, 11% other people)

73%. . . . Hotels where they'd like to stay (52% friends, 38% family, 24% other people)

71%. . . . Places they'd like to visit (49% friends, 42% family, 16% other people)

68%. . . . Videos they'd like to purchase or rent (51% friends, 36% family, 12% other people)

63%. . . . Relative merits of one make of new car versus another (33% friends,
32% family, 21% other people)

63%. . . . Movies they'd like to see (43% friends, 37% family, 9% other people)

60%. . . . Retirement planning information (34% friends, 34% family, 21% other people)

58%. . . . Ways of saving or investing (31% friends, 23% family, 23% other people)

58%. . . . Ways of improving their health (32% friends, 25% family, 18% other people)

56%. . . . Improving the appearance of their home (34% friends, 21% family, 21% other people)

55%. . . . Best brands of different products (36% friends, 31% family, 16% other people)

53%. . . . Where to find the best buys on products they want or need (34% friends, 29% family,
15% other people)

53%. . . . Computer equipment to buy (30% friends, 23% family, 18% other people)

53%. . . . Clothes they'd like to own or buy (32% friends, 22% family, 14% other people)

46%. . . . Web sites to visit (30% friends, 20% family, 12% other people)

42%. . . . Where to find new jobs (24% friends, 18% family, 17% other people)

Source:Roper Reports

Isabel Milano speaks for many Influentials when she says she learns "through people." Larry Lee turns to friends in real estate for tips on neighborhoods that are turning around and could be good investments. How did he learn about the importance to kids of a sense of belonging? "Research." Some of it came from Norman Penner, the director of the Boys and Girls Club, some through workshops the club sponsors, some from casual conversations with other board members who work in schools, the courts, and job training: "everybody brings a different aspect." Given the value Influentials place on connections—the fact, for example, that six in ten Influentials feel not only a connection but a *strong* connection to their community— it's logical they would value the insights of the people in their social networks in their personal decisions.

People are probably the most useful medium to Influentials. No other source comes close to a telephone conversation or an in-person, face-to-face interaction when it comes to communicating. Only a handful of sources are as good as or better than an in-person setting for buying things, getting news and information, or learning something. A surprising number of Influentials (four in ten) say in-person interactions are one of their main sources for entertainment. As New York City Mayor Michael Bloomberg said during his successful 2001 mayoral campaign, "I think this is not a job for anybody that doesn't like people." The people orientation is a connecting thread in the lives of Influentials.

Sophie Glovier's feeling that "most ideas come out of conversations with people building on what's just been said" is typical. Influentials rate people as the top source of information and ideas in almost every one of eighteen different types of purchase decisions we ask about. Even in the categories for which they are not the leading source, people rank high in the mix, behind newspaper advertising when it comes to where to find new jobs and behind advertising generally for movies to see and clothes to own.

The Influentials' reliance on the word of others comes through in other ways as well. When asked to rank what is most important to them generally when deciding among brands, Influentials are much more likely than other groups to say "personal recommendations of others." Six in ten say so, compared with only about one in three of the total public and fewer than half of their demographic peers (the affluent, college graduates, and executives and professionals).

Word of mouth seems to be particularly important in decisions that count the most, categories in which the stakes are high, new developments are happening all the time, or Influentials have strong personal interest (see Figure 3-6). Influentials are about twice as likely to seek advice and information on money matters than the average person. Virtually all Influentials turn to someone for financial advice. They're most likely to seek out friends and relatives. Large numbers, however—one in four or more—consult accountants or CPAs, bank officers, financial planners, and lawyers. Quite a few go to other people as well, such as insurance agents, stockbrokers, financial advisers, financial publications, and television or radio commentators. Only a few Influentials rely only on themselves in financial decisions—something not true of the public as a whole. Self-reliance, for Influentials, does not mean going it alone. One in three Influentials has sought out advice about investments in the past month, three times the response of the public as a whole.

In technology and electronics, two categories in which there has been considerable product news, word of mouth also counts for a lot. Two in three Influentials say personal recommendations are one of their leading sources for finding new Web sites. Eight in ten Influentials say the recommendations of friends and acquaintances influence their choices in stereos, TVs, and video equipment. Four in ten Influentials say they "rarely" try a new restaurant unless someone has recommended it to them. The purchase doesn't have to be expensive. Three in ten Influentials say personal recommendations are among the most important factors to them in deciding what brand of iced tea to drink.

In a society increasingly oriented to talking through decisions, then, the Influentials are among the leading proponents of conversation. The cue for institutions from business to government should be obvious: the door should always be open for Influentials when they have a question or concern. Those who represent the company—particularly salespeople, customer service representatives, investor relations personnel, and others in public positions—should be well-informed about the business and its

Figure 3-6. Moneyline: Many Turn to Others on Finances

Percentage of Influentials who turn to source for "advice and expertise" on financial matters, with percentage point difference from total public

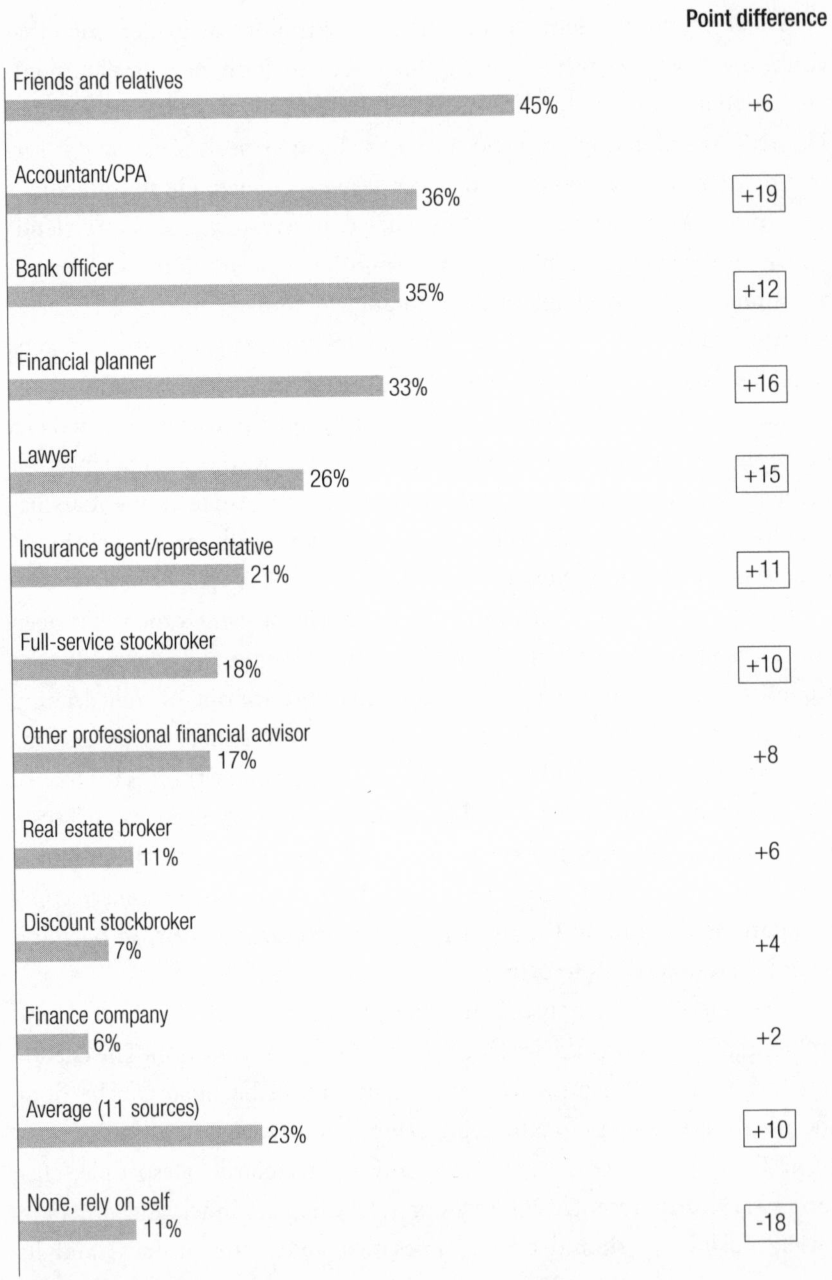

	Percentage	Point difference
Friends and relatives	45%	+6
Accountant/CPA	36%	+19
Bank officer	35%	+12
Financial planner	33%	+16
Lawyer	26%	+15
Insurance agent/representative	21%	+11
Full-service stockbroker	18%	+10
Other professional financial advisor	17%	+8
Real estate broker	11%	+6
Discount stockbroker	7%	+4
Finance company	6%	+2
Average (11 sources)	23%	+10
None, rely on self	11%	-18

Source: Roper Reports

products and be empowered to address concerns or put them on a fast track to be resolved.

Principles of Influence:
IF YOU GET IT, SHARE IT

Sophie Glovier's telling her friends about the Stonybrook Organic Farm, Moo Milk Express, or the efficiencies of buying online instead of schlepping to the store has a lot in common with Larry Lee, Jr. telling his friends when he became a convert to cell phones.

Influentials don't hold back their opinions when they find something they like or don't like. We've seen this already in the high rates to which people turn to them for advice and opinion when they have a question. It's also reflected in other research as well—most importantly, perhaps, in their propensity to make recommendations when they find something they like. The research underscores the conclusion that the segment's influence extends beyond political and civic concerns. Influentials are much more likely than the norm to recommend products and services to others when they find something they like.

Over the course of a year, the Influentials have an aggregate impact of millions of word-of-mouth recommendations. The segment is particularly likely to wield a powerful word-of-mouth force through recommendations in areas that by now should be familiar areas of expertise, including restaurants and food, travel, technology, media, cars, and personal finance. Almost nine in ten Influentials say that in the past they've found a restaurant that they've liked so much that they've recommended it to others. Two in three have seen a movie that they liked enough to recommend to others. More than half have recommended a vacation destination. A comparable number have recommended a television show. About four in ten have recommended a type of car or a store. Substantial numbers, roughly one in five or more, have made recommendations in 12 other areas in the past year: cars, retail stores, hotels, magazines, clothing, computer software, Web sites, insurance, investments, computer hardware, consumer electronics, and long-distance phone services (see Figure 3-7).

On average, Influentials are twice as likely to have made a recommen-

Figure 3-7. Influentials' Word-of-Mouth Influence: Recommendations

Percentage of Influentials who have recommended item to others in the past year, with point difference from total public, and how many recommendations were made by the average Influential making recommendations

Item recommended	% doing	+/- Total public (percentage points)	No. people told last time made recommendation
Restaurant	85%	+26	4.7
Movie	67%	+19	5.4
Vacation destination	54%	+30	4.7
TV show	54%	+16	4.7
Car	38%	+17	3.9
Retail store	37%	+16	4.2
Hotel	32%	+18	4.2
Magazine	32%	+16	3.7
Clothing	31%	+10	3.6
Computer software	28%	+16	4.4
Web site	27%	+13	5.6
Insurance	24%	+11	3.2
Investment (stock, mutual fund, CD, etc.)	23%	+13	3.8
Computer hardware	20%	+11	4.4
Consumer electronics	20%	+10	3.5
Long-distance phone service	19%	+9	4.0
Cosmetics	18%	+6	2.6
Airlines	16%	+11	3.4
Office equipment	13%	+8	4.3
Beer, wine, or liquor	13%	+3	5.0
Credit card	9%	+4	2.3
Pay-cable TV network	5%	+2	3.8

Source: Roper Reports

dation in the past year in the 22 categories than the average person (30 versus 17%). The differences are largest, once again, in many categories in which word of mouth is key: vacation destinations (for which there is a 30-point difference), restaurants (26 points), movies (19 points), cars (17 points), computer software (16 points), magazines (16 points), TV shows (16 points), retail stores (16 points), Web sites (13 points), and investments (13 points). The research is further evidence that companies in these categories need to pay particular attention to this group. In other categories in which the percentage point difference is not as large, the Influentials still wield disproportionately large influence. In airlines, for example, Influentials are three times as likely to make a recommendation as the average person (16 versus 5%). In consumer electronics and office equipment, Influentials are twice as likely to make a recommendation. In some categories they are on a par with segments usually considered the experts, such as computer-owning households for computer equipment, Internet accessors for Web sites, or young people for movies.

In many areas, Influentials are more likely to make a recommendation than demographic peers (the affluent, executives and professionals, and college grads), with particularly large differences in vacation destinations (with an 11–16 point gap in the percentages of Influentials and people in these groups making recommendations in the past year), magazines (12–13 points), restaurants (8–12 points), and insurance (8–11 points). Influentials may not watch as much TV as other people, but when they find a program they like, they tell others (with 14–18 point differences between them and the total public, execs, college grads, and the affluent). Although this is probably learning-oriented television, like Ken Burns's historical documentaries (*Civil War* and *Jazz*), areas in which the Influentials have particular interest, it likely also means entertainment programming as well.

Moreover, when they make a recommendation, Influentials usually broadcast it to a large network of friends, relatives, and acquaintances. Thus, they have a large "multiplier effect," multiplying the scope of their word-of-mouth influence beyond the size of their group. In three categories, the typical Influential told five or more people the last time they made a recommendation: movies, Web sites, and alcoholic beverages. In 11 other categories, the typical Influential told four or more people the last time they made a recommendation: restaurants, vacation destinations, TV shows, retail stores, hotels, computer software, computer hardware, long-distance phone services, and office equipment. In seven other categories, the typical Influential told three or more people the last time they made a recommendation: cars, clothing, insurance, investments, consumer electronics, airlines, and pay-cable networks. In only two categories did the typical Influential tell fewer than three people the last time they found something they liked: cosmetics and credit cards.

On a national scale, multiplying the percentage of Influentials who have made a recommendation by the average number of persons they told the last time they made a recommendation (probably a conservative estimate of their power, since they likely make recommendations on multiple occasions in the course of a year), and projecting this to the national scale based on the Influentials proportion in the population (one in ten), shows they generate tens of millions of recommendations a year. In the past year they made 84 million restaurant recommendations, the category in which they had the largest impact. They made 76 million movie recommendations. In two other categories, vacation destinations and television shows, they generated 53 million recommendations each. They made more than 30 million recommendations for retail stores, cars, and Web sites and more than 25 million recommendations for hotels and computer software. It goes on: more than 20 million recommendations for magazines and clothes; more than 10 million recommendations for investments, insurance, computer hardware, consumer electronics, long-distance phone services, airlines, office equipment, and alcoholic beverages; and more than 5 million recommendations for cosmetics.

Influentials seem to have an aversion to keeping things to themselves. This is probably a reflection of their values. They believe it's important to give others information that could help them. Probably it stems from the nature of their work. It's not a coincidence that many Influentials work in fields or volunteer in positions in which either through the responsibilities of the job or through having a leadership role, people come to them with their problems, concerns, and questions. Mayor. Village trustee. Stockbroker. Insurance agent. Board member. Educator.

Also, Influentials know so many people, have strong connections in many groups, and have many interactions throughout the day. Glovier's description of herself ("I've always been a good networker") applies to Influentials generally and makes them part of the flow of ideas in their community.

Principles of Influence:
CONTINUOUS PROVEMENT

Making it onto the Influential radar screen does not guarantee staying there. Influentials are busy people and have a clear sense of priorities—and business, as Sophie Glovier says, has only a passing connection to what is important to them. Companies thus need to practice what we call "continuous provement." They need continuously to re-prove their value to consumers. It's the water station metaphor again: Influentials need what they need when they need it.

In certain categories, the study on word-of-mouth recommendations shows, at least some companies have done well enough to garner the Influential seal of recommendation. Restaurants, movies, vacation destinations, TV shows (at least some), and cars, for example, are generating large numbers of word-of-mouth buzz from Influentials. Other categories, like credit cards, do not appear to be generating a lot of interest.

The research also suggests that things change. It's possible to turn things around and get more buzz—or lose it. Influential word of mouth is not static. Since 1995, there have been many changes. The percentage of Influentials who had recommended a restaurant jumped by 11 percentage points, a substantial shift. The proportion recommending vacation destinations and movies rose 9 points apiece. The percentage recommending a magazine increased 7 points. The percentage recommending TV shows and insurance rose 6 points, not as significant a change, but interesting. Web sites came on the scene and generated a considerable amount of buzz, about as much as investments, for example, a bit more than computer hardware or software (a telling sign of shifting fortunes in the tech industry), and more than many traditional categories, such as alcoholic beverages or airlines.

Projecting on a national basis, there have been huge increases in the aggregate number of recommendations from Influentials in some categories. There are 10 million-plus more recommendations than in 1995 for restaurants and movies. There are 5 million-plus more recommendations for vacation destinations and TV shows. There are also notably more recommendations for retail stores, hotels, magazines, investments, insurance, and airlines (see Figure 3-8).

On the other hand, some categories haven't gone up. In certain categories, the likelihood an Influential would recommend a product or service has actually declined. The aggregate number of recommendations has slipped in computer software (down 3 million to 26 million) and hardware (down 3 million to 18 million), alcoholic beverages (down 6 million to 14 million), and credit cards (down 5 million to 4 million). These products, it appears, have fallen out of the Influentials' conversation.

Doing business in a category in which Influentials have a high level of interest doesn't appear to be much protection. Because Influentials are interested in technology and computers doesn't translate to a continuous stream of conversation from Influentials on computer hardware and software. New advances in related areas—the Internet and Web sites—can keep the spiral of influence growing just fine. PC hardware and software makers need to reconnect with the segment, probably by getting out ahead and setting up a "water station" of new products and services that leverage the Internet and other new technologies (for more on the Influentials' vision of the future of computing, see Chapter 5).

The up-and-down pattern in the changes in Influential word-of-mouth buzz suggests that the economy, which was booming during that period, was not as important a factor in the shifts as dynamics within the various industries. Other research corroborates this point of view. Since 1996, there's been a marked drop, for example, in the percentage of Influentials saying they're always looking for something new in computer-related products (down 14 points to 20%); the percentage saying they pretty much stick with the same brands has jumped 12 points to 46%.

The implication is that news counts a lot more than "newness." Compared with the excitement of the early days of computing, computer hardware and software were mature categories by 2000. Deals in long-distance phone service were big news in the 1980s after deregulation; by the 2000s,

Figure 3-8. The Multiplier Effect: Recommendations

Estimated number of recommendations made per year by Influentials per category, with change from 1995

Item recommended	National projection	Change from 1995
Restaurants	84 million	+14 million
Movies	76 million	+14 million
Vacation destinations	53 million	+9 million
TV shows	53 million	+8 million
Retail stores	33 million	+4 million
Web sites	32 million	*
Cars	31 million	+2 million
Hotels	28 million	+3 million
Computer software	26 million	-3 million
Magazines	25 million	+5 million
Clothing	23 million	-1 million
Investments	18 million	+6 million
Computer hardware	18 million	-3 million
Insurance	16 million	+4 million
Long-distance phone service	16 million	+2 million
Consumer electronics	15 million	-1 million
Beer, wine or liquor	14 million	-6 million
Office equipment	12 million	no change
Airlines	11 million	+3 million
Cosmetics	10 million	*
Credit cards	4 million	-5 million
Pay-cable TV networks	4 million	-1 million

Source: Roper Reports

* Not asked

the word-of-mouth conversation had moved on. Many of the major inno-vations in credit cards (mileage and rewards programs, zero annual fees) occurred years ago. The conversation has moved on to other areas of finan-cial services. The effort of American Express to extend its brand umbrella to financial services, in this context, was strategically smart. One of the strengths of the AmEx brand is that it has been more than charge cards and credit cards. Its status as the world's number one travel agency, in addition to being the number one issuer of charge cards, links the brand to one of the passions of Americans generally and Influentials in particular, and one of the subjects for which Influentials are most likely to create word-of-mouth buzz. That kind of expansive thinking has made AmEx one of the marketplace's leading brands (number 17 in the world, in *Business Week*'s 2001 ranking), which in turn helps it weather tough economic times and gives it a platform for introducing new products and services.

In truth, although companies often like to think opinion leaders are constantly scouting out new products and services, the majority of Influentials usually have more important things on their minds—their family and friends, work, and community activities. Most aren't on the lookout for the latest things to buy. The largest number say they are "always" looking for something new in places to go for vacation (42%), a subject, as we've seen, in which they're highly engaged. Influentials are often not substantially more likely always to be looking for something new than other segments of the population.

In no way do we wish to suggest that Influentials have closed minds. On the contrary, just as there is a clear sense of priority in Influentials' lives, there is a clear imperative to businesses trying to court them. To get their attention, you must contribute something meaningful, a product or service that makes life demonstrably better, connects with a passion of theirs, or contributes to the causes and concerns in their community and elsewhere that they care about. You must position yourself at the water station so you're there when their thirst makes you relevant.

The periodic silencing of buzz from Influentials appears to affirm the value of continuously proving the worth of products and services through significant, meaningful improvements *and* finding compelling messages and ways to communicate the news to people. For many years, businesses have preached the gospel of continuous improvement, learning from experience always to make the product better. Apple Computer continued to be an innovator in software (desktop icons) and design (candy-colored, swivel-top Macs), and more recently video and the iPod. The result naturally predisposes people to look to Apple for innovation. In a society in which choice is always an option, thanks to globalization and technology, companies must continuously prove that they are worthy of consumer choice. When there's nothing going on in a company or with a product, there's little to talk about. In the word-of-mouth society, "death by conversational inattention" is one of the major threats.

Case Study: Influential "Inflection Points" and "Plateaus"

In mid-2000, a large, midwestern packaged foods company came to us with an interesting question. Using our best judgment from our consumer insights, what do we see as the future of convergence? It's a question that today remains on a lot of minds, not only in computer, Internet, and consumer electronics companies, which have a direct stake in the questions of how and to what extent the computers, televisions, and other technologies in Americans' homes converge into one system. Many companies in other areas have a vested interest in how Americans' lives will change as new technologies come onto the scene.

Paul Leinberger, senior vice president in our Southern California office, used the prism of the Influentials to answer the question. In part, it was because Influentials have a history of trendsetting in technology. The more important reason was Influentials' record of being what Leinberger calls an "early majority" market. As such, Influentials can be a better proxy of what's to come in the broader market than early adopters, the small group of technology buffs who are always the first to buy new technologies. Not everything the technology buffs buy goes on to mainstream success. Influentials, on the other hand, tend to "mirror the behavior of the total public—just out ahead of it." Perhaps because Influentials have other, more important concerns, including community involvement, family, and work, they bring a utilitarian mind-set to technology. Influentials like technology, a large number saying it's "exciting" and "I use it as much as I can." When it comes to integrating technology into their lives, however, Influentials focus on the here-and-now questions—"how can this make my life more efficient?"—rather than becoming carried away with new technologies.

The analysis suggested that the tech industry had come to a crossroads of a sort. The Internet was still on the rise among the public as a whole, but among Influentials it was beginning to flatten in some telling ways. The proportions of Influentials citing connecting to the Internet as a major reason to buy a PC, for example, which had soared 36 points to 65% among Influentials between 1996 and 1998, had flattened since then. The same applied to communicating electronically (which rose 27 points to 55% between 1996 and 1998 but has not changed appreciably since). That this flattening was occurring while interest in the Net and e-mail was still soaring in the total public seemed especially significant. From an "alpha" point (the inflection point in the mid-1990s at which PC penetration sailed past 50% in Influentials and began a rapid ascent into the mainstream in the total public) it appeared to have reached a "beta."

Such plateau points are critical for growth industries. At such a point, something has to change to kick-start a new growth period: "a new technology has to take hold, or something in the environment shifts to change how you use a product dramatically," said Leinberger. Otherwise, the industry begins to stagnate. People like the Influentials turn their attention elsewhere. "Basically, the Influentials were telling us, 'you've gone through the adoption phase with the Internet; you're entering a new stage.' "

"It looks like the Influentials are ready for something else," Leinberger concluded. Exactly what that would be was, unfortunately, not readily apparent. The Influentials themselves, at that point, "probably couldn't tell us what that would be." Even here, there was an important lesson for marketers: Convergence would probably go more slowly than at least some in the tech industry wanted. For all the imperatives in the industry for growth to move quickly, "consumers *walk* into the future, one step at a time," Leinberger said. The "early majority" Influentials, for their part, had to "still figure out for themselves what convergence will mean for them." Meanwhile, the Net was integrated in people's lives; "the thrill is gone."

Some of the same patterns are still evident in the research two years later. Influentials' interest in the Internet, although high, remains at a plateau. There are interesting things Influentials are pursuing with their computers (and, as we see in more detail in Chapter 5, some further-out computer applications that intrigue them), but they still haven't gravitated to a "killer app" that will lift the tech industry to the next level like the Internet did in the 1990s. The crosscurrent in public opinion that Leinberger described, with Influentials' interest plateauing while the public interest was still rising, appears to have had an impact on word of mouth on computers. Americans are still turning to Influentials for advice or opinion on computer equipment at higher rates than in the 1980s, but the rates have flattened in recent years. The word-of-mouth buzz Influentials were going out of their way to create through making recommendations on computers also started to decline (as we saw in Figure 3–8). Moreover, the plateau we saw in Influentials began to spread. In early 2002, the percentage of Americans saying they or someone in their household was interested in connecting to the Internet flattened; the percentage of Americans saying they or someone in their household was interested in 22 different computer functions declined by an average of 6 points from 2001, a significant decrease. The shift to beta that we saw in the Influentials in 2000 proved to be prescient.

So what happens if a spiral of influence stops? The research we just discussed, from the convergence study to the declines on recommendations and interest in new products, suggests that word-of-mouth buzz moves on to something else, with consequences for the business that loses its word-of-mouth edge.

Principles of Influence:
MEDIA: IN THE BEGINNING WAS THE WORD

So how do you become part of the conversation? Where do you set up your water station? For many Influentials, the starting point is the printed word. We may live in the age of television and the Internet may for the foreseeable future be the technology that is on the rise, but the printed word is more influential with Influentials than any other medium, traditional or new. Most Influentials would probably agree: In the beginning was the word. Among the traditional media, Influentials turn to the printed word first, use it more often, and value it most. Sophie Glovier's reliance on the printed word to stay informed applies to many Influentials—how she "gets lots of information" from the newspapers to which she subscribes and reads them "pretty carefully." As does her affection for the printed word, even the self-indulgent ones. "I *love People,*" she enthuses. Not only because it's an intellectual box of chocolates: it's also a conversation starter, no small thing to people-oriented Influentials. "Since lots of people read it, it's fun to compare notes on the news," she says.

Influentials are, as a rule, big readers. That should be apparent to those who have taken special note of their interests, hobbies, and leisure time pursuits. Reading is in the top tier of Influentials' leisure time activities (reading newspapers, books, and magazines accounting for three of the five activities they're most likely to do often), is their leading hobby (claimed by two in three people in the segment), is one of their primary means to keep up with events and learn new things, and is an area they enjoy talking about, as we've seen in the word-of-mouth buzz they generate (like their 24 million recommendations a year for magazines).

Reading is ingrained in their daily lives. Nine in ten Influentials read a newspaper at least two or three times a week (compared with only three in four of the total public). Three in four read a magazine at least several times a week, and seven in ten read a book this regularly (among the total public, the responses are a little over half and about half, respectively). Influentials are much more likely than the average to read various different kinds of magazines regularly (reading at least three of every four issues), from general editorial titles and newsweeklies to home service and home magazines, women's and men's magazines, health and fitness titles, business and financial titles, and more specialized interest titles in areas from parenthood to gardening to sports. More than eight in ten Influentials are regular readers of at least one magazine, compared with about two in three of the total public. They browse across an even broader range of titles. Eight in ten read a general editorial magazine at least occasionally, more than half a newsweekly, home service or home magazine, and women's magazine and one in four or more a national newspaper, business or finance magazine, health and fitness, parenthood, or science and technology title (see Figure 3-9).

In a number of areas, Influentials rate print as one of the best places to get good ideas. On average, 27% of Influentials rate newspapers among the "best" sources for ideas in 18 categories, and 24% say so of magazines, not as strong as word-of-mouth sources of friends, family, and other people, but higher than TV (which averages 20%) and radio (6%). While the Inter-

Figure 3-9. Power of Print: Influentials and Magazines

Percentage of Influentials who "ever read" magazine in category, with percentage point difference from total public

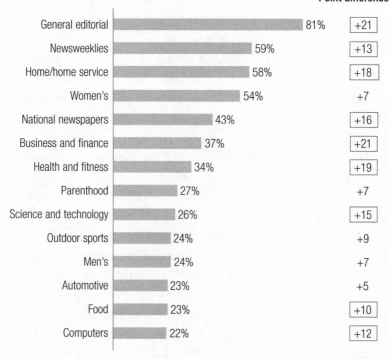

Percentage of Influentials who regularly read magazine in category (three of every four issues), with percentage point difference from total public

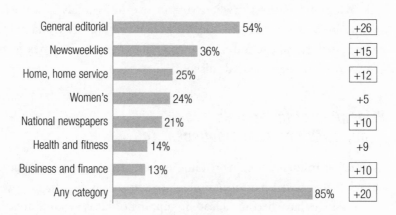

Source: Roper Reports

net has been growing in importance, it still lags newspapers and magazines, with an average of 17%. Newspapers, for their part, seem to have carved out a niche with Influentials as a source of ideas for new jobs (57%), best buys on products (47%), movies to see (35%), and restaurants, clothes, and which brands are best in different categories (33% each), testimony, probably, to the traditional newspaper staples of help-wanted ads, movie listings, restaurant reviews, and consumer news. More than one in four Influentials rate newspapers a leading source of ideas for ways of improving health, places to visit, ways of saving and investing, and the merits of different cars.

Magazines, meanwhile, have carved out a niche as a source of ideas about improving the appearance of the home, places to visit, and new meals or dishes to try, clothes to buy, ways of improving health, and the merits of one car versus another—cited by about 30–40% of Influentials. In addition, one in four or more Influentials rates magazines among the top sources for ideas on ways of saving and investing, information on retirement planning, and where to find the best buys (see Figure 3-10).

Books don't have the immediacy of newspapers or magazines, but they serve a practical niche as well, as we've seen with the large numbers of Influentials who turn to books for general education and career skills. Books are more of an entertainment medium to Influentials than the other print media; half of Influentials say they turn to books for entertainment, compared with four in ten who say so of magazines and one in four who say so of newspapers. In terms of ideas, books rate highest on retirement planning and saving and investing (where one in five Influentials says books are among the best sources of ideas, only slightly lower than magazines or newspapers). Significant numbers turn to books for ideas for health, home appearance, and new meals or dishes.

Principles of Influence:
BUT THEY USE OTHER SOURCES, TOO

As much as Influentials enjoy reading and use it to keep up, learn more, or just relax, they soak up information in other areas as well. The Internet and online sources have become a leading supplier of ideas in some areas. Log-

Figure 3-10. Invaluable in Some Categories

Magazines: Decisions for which Influentials are most likely to turn to them for ideas or information

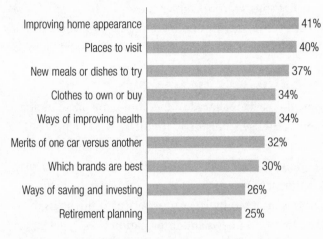

Improving home appearance	41%
Places to visit	40%
New meals or dishes to try	37%
Clothes to own or buy	34%
Ways of improving health	34%
Merits of one car versus another	32%
Which brands are best	30%
Ways of saving and investing	26%
Retirement planning	25%

But not where to find jobs (7%), movies to see (7%)

Newspapers: Decisions for which Influentials are most likely to turn to them for ideas or information

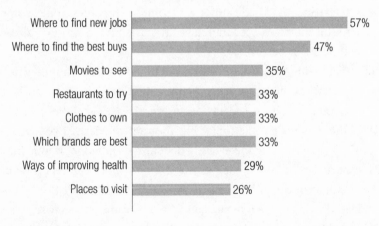

Where to find new jobs	57%
Where to find the best buys	47%
Movies to see	35%
Restaurants to try	33%
Clothes to own	33%
Which brands are best	33%
Ways of improving health	29%
Places to visit	26%

But not prescription drugs (13%), Web sites (13%)

Source: Roper Reports

ically, it's turned to most for ideas on Web sites to visit (34%). A comparable number say the Web is one of the best sources for ideas on where to find new jobs (34%), a tribute to online job search boards. Large numbers say the Web is one of the best sources in consumer categories from cars (27%) to computer equipment (25%), saving and investing (24%), where to find best buys (24%), places to visit (20%), and hotels to stay at (20%), to retirement planning (19%), which brands are best (16%), and improving health (13%) (see Figure 3-11).

Computers may be the "jack of all trades" medium—not a bad designation in an era that appreciates generalists and multitasking. PCs may not be the "masters" of any one use; they're not as strong an entertainment option as television, or as good in quality or dependability as newspapers or magazines for news and information (which never get jammed from having too many users). Computers are used by large numbers of Influentials, however, to communicate (65%), get news and information (57%), get education and training (55%), get entertainment (37%), and buy things (31%). No other medium has that level of versatility, which by extension gives the computer industry a broad expanse in which to develop new products and services. This kind of flexibility could give the industry an edge in comparison with television-based consumer electronics companies in developing next-generation interactive technologies; in marketing terms, PCs already have a positioning of flexibility.

Influentials value the printed word more than television, but they don't look at television as the vast wasteland one might suspect. In truth, Influentials have mixed opinions about television. As activists, they're not as partial as the general population to positioning themselves passively in front of the TV and letting the evening drift away. Only one in four Influentials "especially like" using their leisure time to watch television (about half the response of the public as a whole). Large numbers of Influentials, indeed, feel "the bad outweighs the good" in television (45% say so, versus 38% who feel the good in TV outweighs the bad), a feeling not shared in the total public, the majority of whom feel the medium's influence has been positive. One is a lot more likely to find people who aren't plugged into television culture among Influentials. The Glovier family, for example, mainly uses it for videos.

Figure 3-11. Where the Internet or TV Is Valuable as a Source of Ideas

Internet: Decisions for which Influentials are most likely to turn to it for ideas or information

Web sites to visit	34%
Where to find new jobs	34%
Merits of cars	27%
Computer equipment	25%
Ways of saving and investing	24%
Where to find best buys	24%
Places to visit	20%
Hotels to stay at	20%
Information on retirement planning	19%

But not videos (4%), new meals or dishes (6%)

TV: Decisions for which Influentials are most likely to turn to it for ideas or information

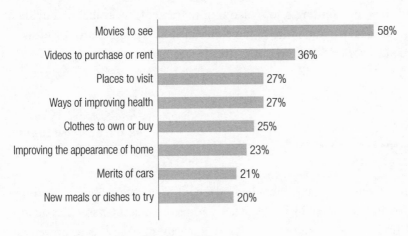

Movies to see	58%
Videos to purchase or rent	36%
Places to visit	27%
Ways of improving health	27%
Clothes to own or buy	25%
Improving the appearance of home	23%
Merits of cars	21%
New meals or dishes to try	20%

But not new jobs (4%), retirement planning (6%)

Source: Roper Reports

Still, most Influentials agree that television has utility for some things: 70% consider the television "a necessity" rather than a luxury they could do without, about the same as the national average. Nine in ten turn to the TV for news and information, about as many as turn to the newspaper. A comparable number use TV for entertainment, a response considerably higher than for any other medium. A certain number, about three in ten, see TV as one of their prime sources of education and training. Nine in ten Influentials watch TV at least two or three times a week, a percentage comparable to that in the total public.

Influentials generally aren't thinking "idea" when they turn on the television, but there *are* areas in which the TV is one of their leading sources for new ideas. Six in ten Influentials say TV is one of the best sources of ideas for movies, a reason to run movie previews during programming watched by Influentials. About one in three Influentials say TV is one of the best sources for ideas for videos to buy or rent, and one in four regard TV as one of the best places to get ideas about places to visit, improving health, clothes, and improving home appearance.

The connecting thread is "visual." Home, clothes, vacation destinations, videos, and movies are all categories in which image counts as much or more than information. TV doesn't do as well in information-dependent decisions, like finding a job, planning retirement, investing, or buying a computer; fewer than one in ten think of it as a good source of ideas in these categories. Sometimes, a picture is worth a thousand words.

PROFILES IN INFLUENCE

Teresa Graham

Teresa Graham is, quite literally, a merchant of information. From a three-bedroom apartment in Texarkana, Arkansas, she conducts searches on topics from Roberts Rules of Order to how to start a suicide prevention hotline, to the laws on incorporation, for clients ranging from churches to nonprofit organizations, private businesses, and, in one case, a motorcycle club. The work is done under the aegis of her company, ECE, Inc., Eleazar's

Consulate of Erudition—from a favorite Bible passage, "Eleazar" being the son of Aaron and the ancestor of all the later high priests; "consulate" reflecting her goal to offer "assistance on neutral ground" to anyone in need; and "erudition" for learning, the most important service to Graham.

Graham's work has brought her into contact with all kinds of people in Texarkana and has sent her across Sunbelt states from California to Atlanta on assignments. "One pastor said, 'Teresa, you know everybody,' " she jokes. "I said, 'No, I don't.' But then I thought about it and said, 'Well, yeah, I guess I do.' "

Graham describes herself as an "information person." Like many Influentials, she is a clearinghouse for information seekers. "People come to me and ask about everything: political, criminal, social, health, mental health, and drug abuse and alcoholism questions," she says. "They think that if I don't know the information, I can get it. And nine times out of ten, I think I can."

The 42-year-old mother of three grown children and grandmother of five (and informal maternal figure to numerous kids in the area who call her "grandma") finds a lot of what she needs in one of the many file cabinets in her apartment where she has neatly organized and filed away documents she has collected through the years. Or in her extensive personal library of books. If it's not there, it's usually on the Internet. Graham has a ferocious appetite for information sites on the Web. Or she gets information from someone she knows. She did not go through formal training. "I just do what I know how to do," she says.

Graham's larger goal is to offer transitional services to help low-income residents of Texarkana jump-start their lives. She has filed for 501(c)3 status as a not-for-profit corporation and applied for funding to buy two houses to set up shelters for single mothers and their children. Her plan is to have a facility where residents can stay for six months to a year, during which time they would receive help in finding jobs, housing, education, and "wraparound services," such as counseling in parenting, alcoholism and addiction recovery and prevention, mentoring, health assessments, credit assessments, "everything they need to help them become successful." Upon employment, half of their income would be placed into an escrow account intended to pay first and last month's rent, lights, gas, furniture, and other living needs when they leave and get their own places. The goal is to enable clients to "be independent, and take care of themselves and their family without welfare"—consistent with ECE's motto "building lives through empowerment, education, and equipping."

Graham started on this path in part from work she has done over the past decade for the Bibleway Ministries and World Outreach Church, where she has been secretary and personal assistant to Bishop David E. Wilson and coordinated various church programs. It's also the result of her values.

She has bootstrapped her way up. "I've lived the rough life," says Graham. "I know that's not where it's at." Growing up poor, she learned what works—and what doesn't. She is a "stickler" for respect and standards. "You set the bar high," she says, "and you make people come up to your level." She also knows her limits. "As a woman, you have the power to change *anything*. But you have to believe in yourself. Resources are not going to change your life. You have to *want* to be helped. I tell people, ten percent of this job is me; the other ninety percent is *you* and what *you* make of it."

Texarkana has a large subpoverty population, so there is no shortage of need, or of problems that often accompany poverty, including addiction, alcoholism, and despair. "You have to take people by the hand and teach them they are worthwhile, they are somebody," Graham says. It's a message she continues to apply to her own life.

She started the information search business out of her own frustration when trying to find basic facts. By providing the service, she figures, she enables people to avoid the tedious task of going through "the 50 yards of digging around, when the answer's right there." She thinks of it as a calling. "I feel that if someone comes to me and they want to do something positive, and I have the information, I'm obligated to give it to them. As a Christian, I should not keep information from people who need it."

It's also fun for Graham. Reading is one of her joys. She collects books from bookstores, thrift shops, yard sales, "anything that's interesting." She likes to buy books by the box ($10 buys quite a few) and dig in from there. Among her recent reading is a book on the German positivist philosopher Ludwig Wittgenstein. She reads the local Texarkana paper, the *Dallas Morning News, Inc.* magazine for entrepreneurial advice, and novels for fun. "I believe knowledge is power. I know it sounds like a cliché, but I believe that when you stop learning you cease to live. You always have to be ready to learn."

She learns a lot from people as well, constantly drawing on the network of contacts she has built up over the years, from members of her congregation to people in government, business, and universities. When she reads something she doesn't understand, like an unfamiliar marketing or business term in *Inc.*, she calls someone up. "I always feel if you don't know, ask," she says.

Last, Graham learns by doing. She learned how to put on workshops by doing programs for her church, and learned the Internet to help out the church. She volunteers "a lot" for nonprofits because it's always a good learning experience, and once took a telemarketing job to get some first-hand experience in marketing. The latter taught her the "100, 80, 10" principle, which she has gone on to apply in her work: "Talk to 100 people; 80 are going to say they don't want to hear it; 20 are going to say they don't know; but 10 will say yes." The experience taught her a valuable lesson: to accept rejection as part of life. "When you're calling people on the phone, you learn to accept no and it doesn't bother you. You have to weed through the no's to get to the yeses."

An Idea That Works but Should Work Better: E-Commerce

Where have you gone, Sockpuppet? In the mad-mad-mad-mad world of the late 1990s gold rush, the dopey-looking homemade puppet got its 15 seconds of fame as the icon for Pets.com, a short-lived Internet pet supplies retailer. It was part of an advertising tidal wave for fledgling e-commerce sites that tried everything from celebrities (William Shatner and Whoopi Goldberg) to the absolutely bizarre (shooting gerbils at a target) for businesses flogging everything from groceries to medical services over the Web. Most of the ad campaigns wound up on the scrap heap, along with a good number of the brands and companies behind them (and a number of investors' dreams of striking it rich).

Behind the smoke and mirrors and hype and Mr. Toad's ride up and down, an interesting thing happened. E-commerce grew, with dollar volume rising to $51.3 billion in 2001, according to Forrester Research. Because it has captured the imagination of Influentials—and moreover, *works* for them—we expect e-commerce will continue to grow. Shopping online has momentum. Since 1997, the percentage of Influentials saying they had bought something online has almost quadrupled, rising from 12 to 47% (among the total public, it grew from 4 to 23%; see Figure 3-12). Three in ten Influentials in early 2002 said they had bought something online in the past three months. Most Influentials use the Internet to research products even if they aren't necessarily buying online (in all, about two in three, compared with about one in three of the total public).

Based on the Influential trendline, the online audience will likely continue to grow. There's a caution flag as well. Among Influentials, the large growth in interest in shopping online was in 1996–1997. During that period, the percentage of Influentials saying they or someone in their household was interested in shopping online leaped 16 percentage points to 48%. Since then, it's plateaued. In the five subsequent years, 1998–2002, it rose a total of 13 points, to 61%, an average annual gain of less than 3 points. There is still a fairly sizable spread between the percentage of Influentials expressing interest in shopping online and the percentage who have done it (61% interest – 47% use = 14 points, or about 3 million Influentials), but the data suggest that the period of easy growth for the industry has ended. Success is now dependent on the nuts-and-bolts issue of making the existing audience feel better about shopping online, so they'll buy more.

This will mean some changes. In the first phase of the industry, much of the focus of e-commerce was on differentiating itself. Proponents talked about how different e-commerce was. Traditional retailers "just don't get it." The distancing helped get attention on Wall Street, but it has limited utility now. E-commerce and traditional retailing will be increasingly compressed and interdependent.

Research shows that, if anything resonates with online shoppers, it's "convenience." Convenience is the "USP," the unique selling proposition of online shopping. The benefits that Influentials who are online cite highest as major advantages for nonstore shopping generally (as well as shopping online) relate to convenience: the ability to save time, shop anytime or from anywhere, take your time, and not have to deal with crowded stores. Large

Figure 3-12. The Adoption Trend: Shopping Online

Percentage who have bought something online

■ **Influentials**　　● **Total public**

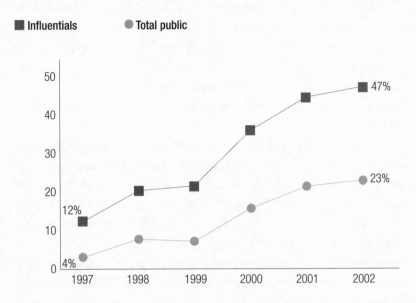

Percentage saying they or someone in their household would be interested in buying things online

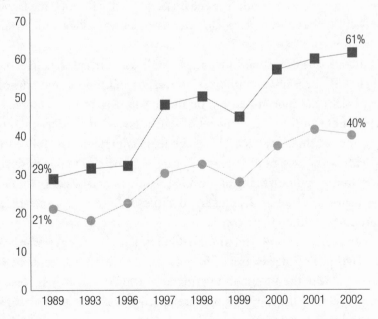

Source: Roper Reports

numbers also appreciate the ability to comparison shop and access a wide variety of hard-to-find items, all benefits that reinforce its convenience.

The convenience positioning, however, places high demands on e-commerce. Sophie Glovier praises online shopping as "quick, easy, and satisfying" and loves it when a site recognizes her so she doesn't have to re-keystroke personal information. She also sees it as a good medium for networking, always a benefit for the people-oriented Influentials. "I know others who shop online, and we swap tips, mostly about sites to get things we want," she says. "A friend will tell me, 'you should get X,' and I'll just go get it." On the other hand, Glovier is "easily frustrated" with the online shopping experience. The complexity of searches and irritation of spam add to the frustration. "Many times it's not time-efficient to find things online, especially compared to *real* word of mouth," she says.

Sometimes it's quicker just to go to a store. After the September 11 attacks, like many Americans, Glovier wanted to buy a U.S. flag. She began calling her friends for ideas when the area stores sold out and lines started snaking around the block to place orders for the next shipment. Glovier and her friends went online and started searching for sites with flags for sale—to no avail. In the end, "I ended up getting a flag from Home Depot," she says. "My friend who placed an Internet order was still waiting for hers two months later."

If there is one thing that Influentials would ask "virtual" retailers to do, it would be to be seamless with "real" stores. For online book and music retailers, bricks and mortar may not be an impediment. You can still read an excerpt online or listen to a snippet of music. For most products, though, seeing and touching matters. This is the main complaint that Influentials have with nonstore shopping generally (as well as being a major complaint with online shopping). Many of the other major complaints also center on convenience—out-of-stock items and the "hassle" of returning or exchanging products—although privacy is also a significant concern.

E-commerce has powerful forces behind it. The movement toward convenience is one of the key trends in retailing of the past half-century. The trend began with the advent of supermarkets (which made it possible to do in one weekly trip the shopping that previously was done in several stops at mom-and-pop grocery stores, butchers, bakers, florists, and so on). It accelerated with the rise of shopping malls and one-stop shopping (no more driving from location to location to location to shop) and marched forward in the 1980s with the boom in direct-mail catalogs (no more driving at all: consumers could shop from the comfort of the living room sofa). With e-commerce, people don't even have to wait for catalogs to arrive, or have a catalog handy when they decide to make a purchase. They can compare products and prices handily without even getting up from their keyboards. To Influentials, though, it's still not "there." The promise hasn't been achieved yet.

Principles of Influence:
THEY TRUST THEIR INSTINCTS

One of the complaints of modern life is that there is simply too much information for human beings reasonably to process. Given this, it would be easy to make the leap that Influentials, since they are the nexus of so much information, are even more bogged down and confused. This is sometimes the case. Perhaps because they have a clear sense of priorities, however, they can step back, evaluate the options, and make decisions. They trust their instincts.

When asked about the most important factors to them in making consumer decisions, the far-and-away leading responses are based on their own judgment. Almost nine in ten (88%) cite their own "past experience with the brand." The same percentage (88%) cite their assessment of the quality of a product or service in comparison with other brands. On both, Influentials are substantially more likely to give the response than the public as a whole (with a difference of 17 points on past experience and 27 on quality, marked differences). Other things factor into their decisions. Well over half, for example, cite whether the brand is reasonably priced (three in four) and others' recommendations (cited by six in ten, as noted earlier in this chapter). They are twice as likely to cite the endorsement of *Consumer Reports* as influential with them (see Figure 3-13). But in the end, the opinion that Influentials trust most is their own.

This ability to trust their instincts, of course, runs deeper than marketplace behaviors. It's consistent with the self-confidence and optimism that

Figure 3-13. Trust Yourself: Brand Decisions Begin with Personal Experience

Percentage of Influentials saying factor is among most important factors in brand purchase decisions, with percentage point difference from total public

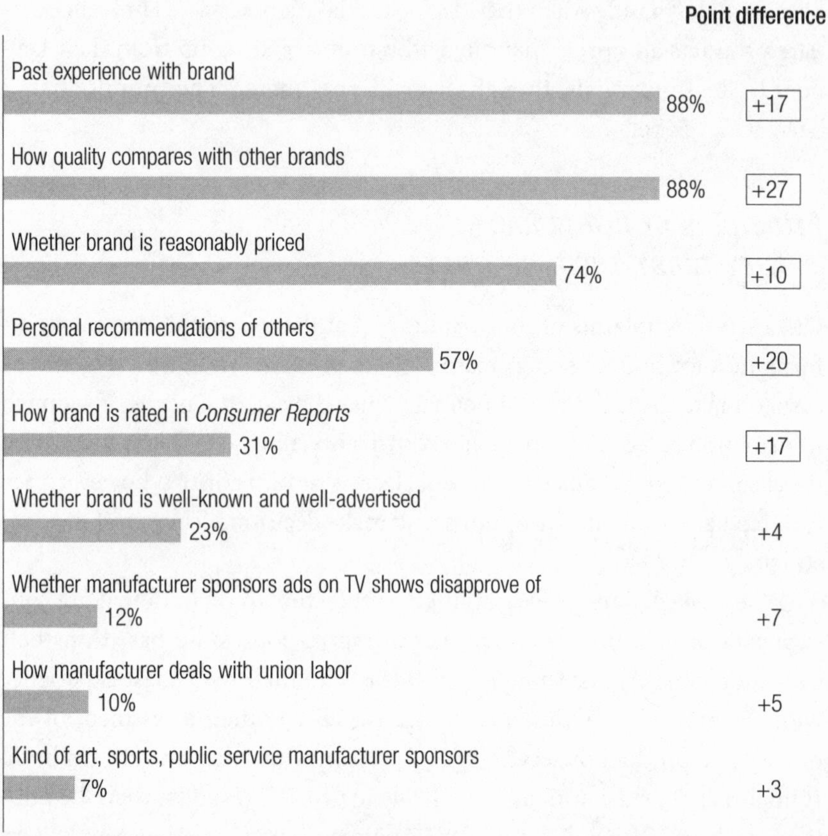

Point difference

Past experience with brand

88%   +17

How quality compares with other brands

88%   +27

Whether brand is reasonably priced

74%   +10

Personal recommendations of others

57%   +20

How brand is rated in *Consumer Reports*

31%   +17

Whether brand is well-known and well-advertised

23%   +4

Whether manufacturer sponsors ads on TV shows disapprove of

12%   +7

How manufacturer deals with union labor

10%   +5

Kind of art, sports, public service manufacturer sponsors

7%   +3

Source: Roper Reports

pervades the group. As Shelley Miller says, "you either let the inevitable negatives in life stop you or put them into perspective and work to overcome them."

Many seem to have the imperative to action traditionally associated with pragmatism. To borrow from William James, the American philosopher and father of pragmatism, everything operates under "rules for *ac-*

tion." What they read, hear, and see is "in the production of habits for *action.*" This sense of self-reliance is probably a major factor in why Influentials are leaders in the society and the marketplace. It enables them to decide what's important, what's new, what's interesting, what's useful, and what stands in the way—and to build word-of-mouth buzz.

CHAPTER 4

The Message of Influentials

THE AGE OF AUTONOMY AND THE RISE OF SELF-RELIANCE

E VERY MARCH, Mike Williams, a Native American of Alaska's Yupiaq tribe, bundles himself up for the Alaska cold and sets off behind a dozen huskies on the Iditarod dogsled race. Over the next two weeks, he and 70 fellow Iditarod "mushers" will travel 1,150 miles through some of the wildest, most beautiful landscape in North America, along icy rivers, dense forests, open tundra, and rugged mountains, from Anchorage to the finish line in Nome. On the way, they will brave bone-chilling temperatures, blinding winds, the occasional ice- or snowstorm, and long hours of solitude.

Mike Williams doesn't have to do it. A leader in his community and the larger world, the outgoing, 49-year-old father of five has plenty of responsibilities without plunging off into the wilderness on the Iditarod. He is chairman of the Alaska Intertribal Council, an advocacy group formed by Alaska's 220 tribes to represent the interests of the state's 100,000 Native American population—"the chief of chiefs," he jokes. The group has been active in fighting to preserve and protect the tribes' rich traditions and culture.

Williams is also a member of Alaska's State Board of Education and Juneau area vice president of the National Congress of American Indians, a national advocacy group for Native American rights, and he sits on the boards of the Alaska Humanities Forum and the Native American Rights Fund. At any given time, he has a fistful of other projects going as well. For example, he helped bring a new public library with Internet access to Akiak, the small village where he lives. He has a full family life as well, with his wife, Maggie, and five children ranging from four years old to their early twenties, some of whom are starting their own families now. He is a proud grandfather of two grandsons.

Williams does the Iditarod in part because it connects him to his roots. He grew up with the old ways, going to fishing camp in the summer and riding dogsleds from an early age. He has raced dog teams since he was in his teens. Being on the trails is like being a kid again, he says. "I enjoy being out there. I want to do it as long as I can. I love the challenge, and I love wild Alaska."

The major reason he does the Iditarod is to raise awareness for the Alaska Federation Native Sobriety Movement. Every year since 1991, he has collected signatures from people who have pledged to stay sober for one year. He brings the names with him on his dog team races. By 2002, he had collected 60,000 signatures.

The problem of alcoholism hits close to home. Williams lost six brothers to early deaths from drinking. "They got into snow machine accidents and boating accidents. Three of them drowned," he says. All "were tied to alcohol abuse." Rather than giving in to bitterness, he made a conscious decision to turn around his grief to try to help others. "I don't want anyone to go through what my family went through. I've seen so many people suffer from abuse of alcohol." At a certain point, he "just had to do something. I needed to take this public."

The Self-Reliance Movement

Mike Williams is part of a larger movement of Americans who have decided to do something about the problems facing their community and the challenges in their personal lives. This movement toward self-reliance and local, grassroots activism has become an animating force in the culture. It is a theme that connects many of the changes in the society today, from the growing priority Americans place on saving for retirement to their willingness to learn new technologies and the comeback of traditional values, such as family and accountability, to the growth of new organizations like the groups with which Mike Williams is involved, the education foundation that Isabel Milano helped start, and the jazz society Larry Lee, Jr. created.

Rather than looking to forces beyond themselves—their congressman or senator, the White House, the nation's major corporations—Americans have increasingly looked to themselves for answers. They are saying, in effect, "I'm a resourceful person. I can figure out a lot on my own. And I can connect to others to help me solve the problems I cannot resolve with my own resources, to create the life I want."

The result is reflected in our research in a higher priority on individual initiative, responsibility, family, and community. It is evident as well in the increasing adoption of self-reliant tools and behaviors. There are growing signs that Americans are becoming more involved in their communities as well, from going to meetings, to participating in churches and other spiritual activities, to starting and joining new groups dedicated to creating connections and change.

We at Roper have been tracking the growth of the self-reliance movement over the past decade. We first reported the mood shift in early 1993 in a special report to clients in our newsletter *The Public Pulse* on the "25 major trends shaping the future." "Americans seem to be taking greater responsibility for their actions," we wrote in the newsletter. People were becoming more involved in such issues as protecting the environment. Financially, they seemed to be "sobering up." Overall, there was a "more realistic attitude." There was "growing evidence" of "an emerging ethos of personal responsibility among Americans." "On many fronts," ranging from attitudes toward health and safety to concern about social problems, there was a feeling that "individuals need to protect and restrict themselves."

On the national level, we saw that Americans were "prepared to address critical issues." Efforts to reduce the federal budget deficit spoke to a "determination to correct some of the more evident excesses" of prior years. Still, a lot of the focus was to "look inward for solutions." "The public was not letting government and business leaders off the hook," but had "come to realize that when the wheels of progress are slow or mired in bureaucracy, it makes sense to do what you can yourself." The signs pointed to "a new period" in the nation's history.

In another report in 1993, we keyed in on what we believed was an important marketplace manifestation of the emerging trend of self-reliance, a phenomenon we called "the tactical consumer." Our research showed that Americans were more focused on "shopping around" and "getting the best deal." They were consciously looking for product promotions and sales. The trend was born in the recession of 1990–1991, but it outlasted the recession and, indeed, showed every sign of becoming a long-term, ingrained behavior. There were clear implications for the big brands that for decades had dominated the consumer marketplace. Consumers were "rejecting brands that carry a premium price," we wrote. There was still room for brands, and some measures showed that brand loyalty was rebounding. The days of charging a premium were over, however. Marlboro Friday—the day when Philip Morris dropped the price of its venerable cigarette brand—rather than being a concession, as many at the time interpreted it ("Are Brands Dead?" was a common headline in newspapers and magazines), was in fact pointing the way to the future. The brands that succeeded would be brands that understood the priority today's shopper placed on getting quality *and* a good price—the "value" equation. Consumers had "learned that they can safely shop for price without having to sacrifice much in terms of quality." Having learned to be "smart shoppers," consumers weren't likely to turn back.

The conclusion, once again, came out of the research. There had been dramatic shifts in consumer priorities. One of our studies, for example, showed double-digit gains in the numbers of women saying price was their top criterion now, even in larger purchases like small appliances (up 12 points since 1984), televisions (up 18 points), even cars (up 17 points). Growing numbers were trying private label brands and new, value-oriented retail formats like discount stores and warehouse clubs—and liking what they found.

By 1995, as evidence of the trend toward self-reliance continued to accumulate, we gave the movement a name, the "Age of Autonomy." At the center of the movement was an increasingly autonomous consumer. In another *Public Pulse*, we wrote to our clients that it was clear that the 1990s represented a major transition in the attitudes and behaviors of Americans. It was an era of "choices and change," the "breakdown of old orders and construction of new orders." Rather than coming from the top down, from big corporations and big government, the change was bubbling up from the public, from "individual Americans pushing the nation forward through collective self-interest."

Change was rapidly unfolding on multiple fronts. The job insecurity from the recession plus waves of corporate restructurings were spurring workers to be more "self-directed in their careers." New technologies like the Internet, meanwhile, were "making it easier to be self-reliant." Americans saw the change. When asked who they thought was doing the most to "solve the nation's problems," fully 53% of the public cited "individual Americans." Larger numbers said individual Americans were solving the nation's problems than cited political leaders and government officials, including Congress and the president. Tellingly, we added in the article, the Influentials, the opinion leaders for the society, were "twice as likely to say individual Americans are solving the nation's problems as Congress," 55 versus 27%.

Corroborative evidence was all around. It seemed to us to be "no accident" that news of a fault in Intel's then-new Pentium computer chip surfaced in an online user group—*individuals* detecting a problem and getting the word out to demand better products—at the same time that a grassroots movement of parents was swinging into action to arrest the decline in education—*individuals* demanding higher standards; *individuals* creating new groups to raise funds to bail out school programs. A volatile electorate was playing Democrats and Republicans off against each other, much the same way they were playing brands against each other to get better value in the consumer marketplace—*individuals* leveraging the one thing they have, the vote, to exercise their demand for more accountability on the national level. "Everyday low pricing" took hold in the marketplace— the institutionalization of the demand for value from tactical consumers. Americans were starting businesses and "sending e-mail around the world"—*individuals* using new channels to create change.

"Call it the self-serve society," we wrote at the time. "Or call it the YOYO effect (you're on your own)." People were looking at things in new ways. The power was shifting and likely would continue to shift. Institutions and listeners who didn't pay heed would "be in for a rude awakening." The result was making it both a "challenging" and "exciting" time. "Little wonder that the icons for this era are sport-utility vehicles, thick-soled boots, casual

Fridays, and a high-powered computer with an online connection," we wrote in that 1995 article. "You need a hard shell and a quick mind to get ahead today."

Succeeding years have seen further integration of the idea, and more change. A 1998 study showed that growing numbers of Americans thought that an individual person could have an impact on the course of the nation. Fully 78% believed that an individual could have at least a "small effect" on "the directions America takes." Just under four in ten thought an individual person could, indeed, have at least a "real effect, even if not a substantial effect" or could wield "a very substantial effect," and the proportion who thought so was 7 percentage points higher than in 1974, a significant shift (see Figure 4-1).

Entrepreneurism has become a model for getting ahead in the workforce. Even after NASDAQ stocks sank in 2000, puncturing the bubble of the dot-com economy, Americans by more than a 3:1 margin said they would rather own their own business than be a top executive of a large corporation (38 versus 12%), and by a more than 5:1 margin said they would rather own their own business than hold an important position in politics or government. If the dream of the 1960s was to follow JFK's "think not what your country can do for you but what you can do for your country" call to public service, the dream of the 1970s was to follow the Woodstock siren song to go back to nature, and the dream of the 1980s was an MBA and a position in a conglomerate. The dream of the past decade has been to follow your own path and be master of your own destiny.

The spirit has had an obvious impact in the broader society. This era will likely go down as one of the more invention-minded periods in America's history. According to government statistics, more than 105,000 patents have been issued per year since 1989, more than double the rate of the 1900s up to that point (46,900 from 1901–1988), and almost 20 times the rate of the 1800s (when it averaged 6,700 per year).

Americans have been busily trying to take in as many of these changes as they can. Products and services that empower people to do more for themselves have made enormous inroads into the American lifestyle. The percentage of households in the total public with personal computers, as we noted earlier, leaped from 18% in 1990 to 54% in 2001. In only 10 years,

Figure 4-1. Individuals' Effect on the Society

Percentage in a group agreeing with statement

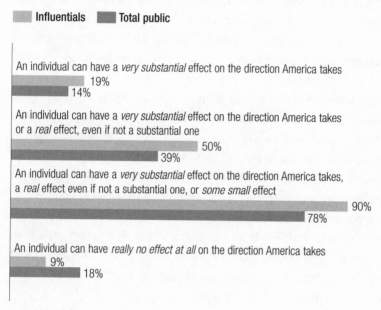

Influentials   Total public

An individual can have a *very substantial* effect on the direction America takes
19%
14%

An individual can have a *very substantial* effect on the direction America takes
or a *real* effect, even if not a substantial one
50%
39%

An individual can have a *very substantial* effect on the direction America takes,
a *real* effect even if not a substantial one, or *some small* effect
90%
78%

An individual can have *really no effect at all* on the direction America takes
9%
18%

Source: Roper Reports

the percentage of Americans using the Internet went from basically nil to majority status; by the end of 2001, fully half of adult Americans—more than 100 million people—were using the Net. Legions of Americans have signed up for new financial products to build up their assets, what's been called "the democratization of Wall Street," itself a major trend of this era, with the advent of mutual funds, 401(k) and IRA accounts, discount brokerages, online transactions, and media for the individual investor like the cable channel CNBC, beefed-up coverage of financial services in the nation's newspapers and magazines, and a slew of Web sites. Between 1991 and 2000, the percentage of Americans with money in a 401(k), 403(b) Individual Retirement account, or other self-directed retirement plan almost doubled, jumping from 20 to 36%.

New devices such as cell phones and PDAs that give Americans more autonomy over life—calling long-distance to Mom in California while walking the dog, for instance—have had rapid rises. Having climbed from 1 to 44% penetration between 1992 and 2001, cell phones now have an active user base of 88 million adult Americans, one of the steeper new product adoption curves in history. Other new devices have given consumers more control over other areas of their lifestyles. DVD players and home theater entertainment systems, for example, make the home an increasingly attractive alternative to going out for a movie.

Perhaps most germaine to the premise of this book, Americans are looking to *each other* more for solutions. Word of mouth has surged as a source for all manner of decisions: the percentage of Americans citing their friends as one of their best sources of ideas and information about where to get the best deals (a subject at the heart of being a tactical consumer) is, at 37%, 8 points higher than in 1977. Community mindedness has gone up as well. More Americans, for example, agree that "people have a definite responsibility to help people in their community who are less fortunate than they are" (55%, up 6 points from 1995). More Americans say the causes they contribute to or work for are among the one or two things that "say the most" about who they are (24%, up 5 points from 1996).

Family and personal relationships are being valued more. When asked about their personal idea of success, almost half of Americans (48%) today say "being a good spouse and parent," up 11 points from 1985, making this far and away the leading definition of success today. ("Being true to yourself," the leading response in 1985, has slipped to a distant second, at 36%.) Although having money is more important today than in the past—more, for example, say having "a lot of money" is part of their idea of the good life—being "wealthy" ranks far down the list of Americans' criteria of success, at only 12%. Despite the allure of celebrity, only 4% say that, for them, success means "being prominent or famous." Family, today, is first.

As Americans have gained more confidence in their ability to set their own course, they've reset their goals to be more ambitious. This goal mindedness is apparent in many areas of life (their hopes for what they'll do in retirement, for instance), but it is probably most evident in their personal finances (appropriately, since their finances will be the foundation for their future life). Interestingly, their ambitions rose early in the new millennium despite the recession and two consecutive years of stock market declines. When asked about their two or three main goals, fully 52% of Americans in early 2002 included "be financially independent of others," up 8 points from 1999, when the stock market and economy were both roaring, and 18 points higher than in 1995. Dreams of untold wealth may have faded, but the desire to be in control of one's financial destiny was still strong. They were substantially more likely to cite financial independence as their goal than the more existential concern of "having enough to live as well as we can now," which did rise from 1999, probably because the turbulent events of 2001 were putting more focus on the moment, but was, clearly, the second priority (39%, up 7). Americans' commitment to save for their retirement years has also risen (at 36%, it's now up 5 points from 1995), another indication of self-reliance. In addition, more are aiming at the goal of early retirement (12%, now up 4 from 1995; see Figure 4-2).

Influential Americans have played a key role in many of these shifts in attitudes and behaviors. The increasing emphasis on financial independence, for example, was presaged by the opinion leader group. Between 1995 and 1997, the percentage of Influentials setting their sights on being financially independent of others jumped 31 points; currently 56% of Influentials cite financial independence as their leading goal. Their presence was visible in other areas as well. The Influentials' belief that people have a definite responsibility to help people in their community who are less fortunate than they are, strongly held already, rose higher than it did in the public as a whole, climbing to 69%, up 14 points from 1995 (more than double the increase in the total public). The value they place on being a good spouse and parent as a definition of success, similarly, has risen 20 points to 55% since 1985, compared with an 11 point gain to 48% in the total public. Elsewhere, they have been generally in tune as well. Despite their involvement in the community, the growth-and-change, community-oriented Influentials seem to believe that the best channels for creating change today are outside the traditional channels. This thinking is reflected in their ideas at work as well. Like the public as a whole, Influentials are substantially more likely to want to own their own business (39%) than be a top exec of a large corporation (11%) or hold an important position in politics or government (12%).

Figure 4-2. Americans' Leading Financial Goals

Percentage of Influentials and all Americans saying item is one of their two or three main financial aims at this stage of life, with percentage point change from 1995

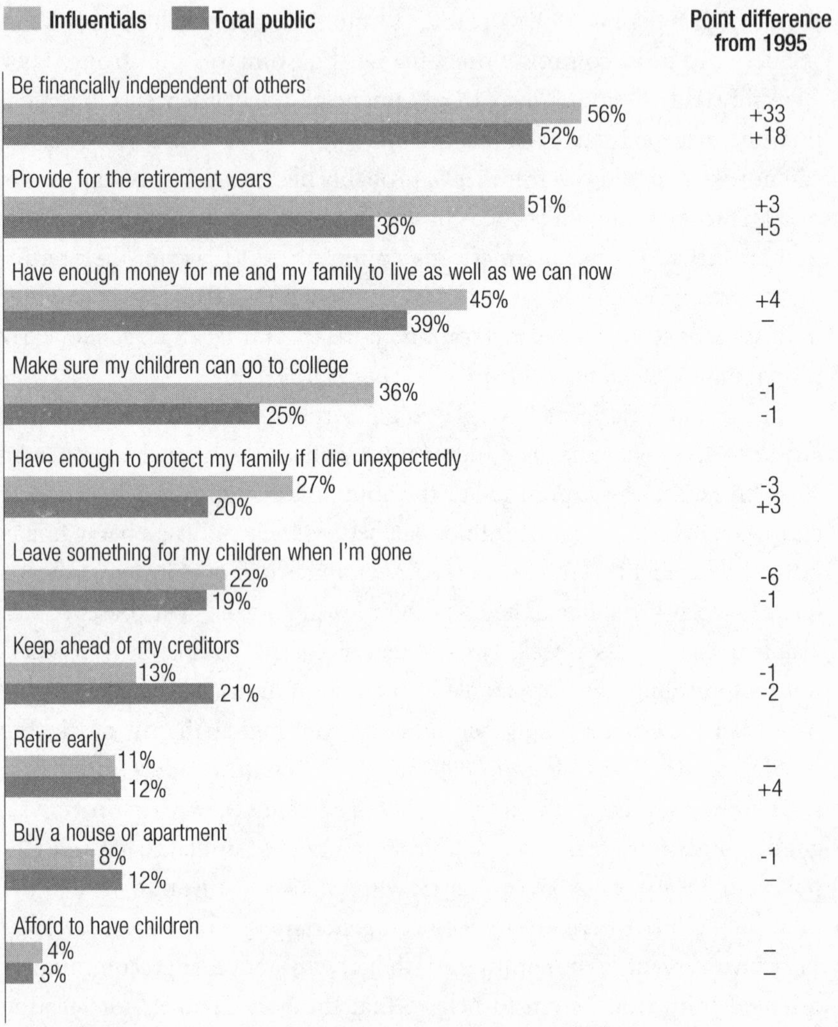

	Influentials	Total public		Point difference from 1995

Be financially independent of others

Influentials 56% · +33
Total public 52% · +18

Provide for the retirement years

Influentials 51% · +3
Total public 36% · +5

Have enough money for me and my family to live as well as we can now

Influentials 45% · +4
Total public 39% · −

Make sure my children can go to college

Influentials 36% · -1
Total public 25% · -1

Have enough to protect my family if I die unexpectedly

Influentials 27% · -3
Total public 20% · +3

Leave something for my children when I'm gone

Influentials 22% · -6
Total public 19% · -1

Keep ahead of my creditors

Influentials 13% · -1
Total public 21% · -2

Retire early

Influentials 11% · −
Total public 12% · +4

Buy a house or apartment

Influentials 8% · -1
Total public 12% · −

Afford to have children

Influentials 4% · −
Total public 3% · −

Source: Roper Reports

The New Century: The Changes Come to the Surface

By the turn of the century, the groundwork had been laid. America, in the opinion of Americans, was changing. There was also a growing sense in the public that the changes *worked*. We at Roper started to see confidence about the prospects for the future in both Americans as a whole and the opinion leader Influentials. The change was crystallized in their views on the new century. Rather than taking the dire outlook that the new century would bring calamity (the "millennnial panic" that some pundits predicted), wide majorities of Americans said they were "looking forward" to the new century. In all, 83% in the total public voiced that confident opinion, including 91% of Influentials, 60% of whom voiced "strong" agreement. Solid majorities in both the total public and Influentials thought that lifestyles would "change dramatically" in the new century (66% in the total public and 75% of Influentials). The feeling was that, on the whole, those changes would be for the better.

Even in spring 2001, after the economy had slipped into recession and the stock market was in the dumps, there was a strong current of confidence in the public mood. Compared with the mid-1990s, when optimism about the nation's institutions sank to an all-time low (even as Americans, individually, were beginning to take control of their destiny), substantially higher proportions of the public said they were "generally optimistic" about the future of quality of life in this country (58% of the total public, for example, 10 points higher than in 1995). The majority of Americans were optimistic about the effect technology would have on the society into the future (57% of the total public).

On a number of fronts, there was a sense that the country, even with its problems, had turned a corner in the past decade. For example, the institution of marriage and family, the subject of considerable worry by both the public and its leaders in the mid-1990s, when out-of-wedlock births and divorce rates seemed to be spiraling out of control, was seen by more Americans (although far from all) as something to be optimistic about (52% saying so, up 11 points from 1995). The efforts Americans had made to draw attention to the family—evinced, among other places, in the increased call for responsibility that we saw in 1993—appeared to be having an impact.

Official statistics showing declines in out-of-wedlock births and other markers of social problems appeared to bear them out. More Americans expressed optimism on other fronts as well, from the ability of the U.S. to get along with other countries in the world (52%, up 5 from 1995) to the U.S. system of government and "how well it works" (50%, up 14), "the soundness of our economic system over the long haul" (49%, up 14), and even, probably in part because of the call for higher standards and more support, the public education system (39%, up 7).

The public wasn't optimistic on all fronts. Substantial numbers continued to describe themselves as *"pessimistic"* on a number of issues, particularly crime (58%), moral and ethical standards (49%), the health care system (42%), the education system (36%), and, reflecting the debacle of the 2000 presidential election, with its disputed ballots, the way the nation chooses its leaders (an all-time high of 35%). Still, there was a clear sense, reaffirmed in a number of studies, that things had changed. After years of spiraling out of control, we told clients in our annual perspective on trends in the consumer marketplace, there was a sense of things "spiraling *into* control."

When the 9/11 terrorist attacks on the World Trade Center and Pentagon occurred, this resilience, resolve, and renewed sense of faith in the nation came to the surface. Based on what we had seen unfold since 1993, we believed that the public would "surprise people"—perhaps even themselves—"with their resilience, strength, and courage." Consumer confidence as measured by the percentage of the public saying it was "a good time to buy" fell, predictably, to recession levels as the public sorted through the events, but faith in the nation surged. In our first study after the events, fielded the weekend after the attacks, a solid 59% of Americans expressed optimism about the future of the country. An even larger 70% were optimistic about their own, personal future. Despite the jolt the economy had absorbed, a surprisingly large number (49%) were optimistic about the economy as well. The numbers were, if anything, a little stronger than what we had seen in the months leading up to the attacks. Rather than sinking, the spirit of Americans rose.

The resilience and resolve might have come forward without the events of the preceding decade, the turning inward for solutions, "more realistic attitude," "determination to address critical issues," and "taking greater responsibility" that we saw in 1993. It probably would not have happened as readily, quickly, or strongly, though. Meaningful trends (as opposed to fads) tend to unfold over a long period of time. The spirit that many saw in the nation in 2001–2002 had been building for more than a decade.

Older, More Educated, and More Adept

There is good reason to believe the movement toward self-reliance will continue to be a defining theme for years to come. It seems to be "the" message both in Influentials and in the public as a whole. Businesses and institutions that interact with Americans need to take account of these attitudes and behaviors of autonomy in their products, services, communications, and operations.

The trend has strong forces behind it. A wealth of new technologies and businesses are now predicated on it, from the mutual-fund industry, to the technology industry, to retailers like the Lowe's and Home Depot home improvement chains, which are based on the greater involvement of consumers. Further, the trend taps into values traditionally associated with America and closely held by the opinion leader Influentials, including belief in growth and change, initiative, family, learning, the ability to sift out what matters, and the utilitarian synthesis of self-interest and the interest of the community that Tocqueville called "self-interest properly understood."

Self-reliance is, of course, deeply rooted in the American psyche. Many of the themes being sounded today have been articulated for centuries—most famously, in Ralph Waldo Emerson's essay "Self-Reliance," which, although more than 160 years old, captures much of the mood of modern America with its famous counsel of self-trust (*"Trust thyself.* Every heart vibrates to that iron string"), meaningful work ("Do your work, and you shall reinforce yourself"), following your own path (genius is "to believe your own thought." "Whosoever would be a man must be a nonconformist." "What I must do is all that concerns me, not what others think"), integrity ("Nothing is at last sacred but the integrity of your own mind"), not being afraid of striking out on a different course ("A foolish consistency is the hobgoblin of little minds")—even not being a slave to labels ("I am ashamed to think how easily we capitulate to badges and names").

In a more practical realm, there are powerful demographic forces propelling the trend to acting and thinking in more self-reliant, self-confident ways. This is where "the older, more educated, more adept" theme really comes to the fore. Americans are more experienced than 20 or 30 years ago, are carrying around a *lot* more information that they can tap—and share with others—and they have more tools to address problems and reach out to others when they don't have the solution. Consider: the median-aged American today (35 years old), having been born in 1967, has lived through four recessions (1974–1976, 1980–1982, and 1990–1991, and 2001), including the two worst recessions since the Great Depression (1974–1976 and 1980–1982) and, arguably, the next most disconcerting one as well (1990–1991). She has lived through a lot of awful disruptions in her 35 years, from the dismaying days of the late 1960s and early 1970s—Vietnam, Watergate, the oil price shock and energy crisis, and runaway inflation of the Carter administration (of which she may have early memories), through the Rust Bowl scouring of the industrial heartland of the 1970s and 1980s, the depressing shared national experience of the *Challenger* space shuttle explosion, the end of the social contract between workers and management in the 1990s restructurings, and periodic fears of downward mobility and the end of the American century (to cite only a few). At the same time, she would have lived through long periods of economic expansion, the bull market of the 1980s and 1990s, and all the changes of the past decade. That combination of up and down, dispiriting and invigorating, would give her experiences to draw on as she faced new challenges, and, quite possibly, a more balanced perspective.

In contrast, the median-aged American in 1975 (age 29), having been born in 1946, would have lived most of her life to that point in a great building up: the advent of the social contract between management and labor that paved the way for the middle-class prosperity of the 1950s and 1960s, the U.S. rise to economic superpower status (while most of the rest of the developed world was struggling back from WWII), the "guns and butter" expansion of government in the 1960s, the idealism of the youth culture of the 1960s, and possibility-opening movements in civil rights and women's rights, authority-tweaking cultural shifts like the sexual revolution and street protests, and booming consumer markets (including growing numbers of products and services catering to teens and young adults like her). When that all came to an abrupt, bitter end in Vietnam, Watergate, the 1974–1976 recession, the long bear market of the 1970s, the oil crisis, and so on, she would have had nothing to compare it to. The prior recessions she had been through had been relatively mild (nothing like what was to come in 1974–1976, 1980–1982, and, probably, 1990–1991). A world where everything pointed *up* became a world that had been suddenly *turned upside down.*

The median-aged American in 1981 (age 30), having been born in 1951, had even more reason to be pessimistic, given the worsening of inflation, the scouring out of the industrial heartland, and so on, between the mid-1970s and the early 1980s and few positives to hang onto other than the Reagan rhetoric of better days ahead and (if they were really tuned in) the new technology of the personal computer. It was a breeding ground for pessimism, which, we see in our research, was basically the mood of America in the early 1980s.

A case can be made that the commonsense response of Americans since the early 1990s is the kind of response one would expect from people with more *maturity* under their belts.

The further shift of being more educated—having more information at your disposal, the means to access information that you don't have on hand (through the Net or a friend or calling a specialist), and the confidence to voice opinions and go your own way—would seem to be further fuel. People not only have more experience, they have more *wherewithal* to rely on themselves. Having more tools to achieve these ends (the Internet, cell phones, mutual funds) gives them not only more wherewithal but more *means* to achieve their ends.

Means, wherewithal, maturity, older, more educated, more adept: this is a good set of ingredients for brewing more responsible, self-reliant workers, consumers, and citizens.

This blend of individual and community mindedness could well become a theme beyond the U.S. as well in the years to come. The ethic of initiative doesn't seem to be unique to one country. At the 2002 World Economic Forum, shifted from Switzerland to New York in a show of global unity after the terrorist attacks, Gloria Macapagal Arroyo, the president of the Philippines, called on the world's nations to combat terrorism not just militarily but by fighting poverty through "promoting self-reliance."

One of the major challenges for institutions from business to government to other organizations is determining how best to adapt to this new era of independent-minded, tactical, self-reliant, autonomous consumer-citizens. Institutions have a very different role to play. Rather than being counted on to *provide* a solution, they are seen more as resources to *facilitate* solutions in tandem with consumer-citizens, who, especially because they are older and more informed than ever, are more equipped to be full partners (if not leading in the decisions affecting their lives).

This individual and local orientation does not mean that government is fading away. Indeed, to the extent that government has learned to recognize the changes going on in the broader society, there's been growing recognition by the public of government's value. This was not always the case. In the early 1990s the public thought that *nothing* was working. We registered record low levels of confidence in institutions. Between 1992 and 1995, the percentage of Americans calling for a "major effort" by government on various problems dropped an average of 8 percentage points, a marked decline.

Sometime after the 1994 midterm elections—when the public seemed to deliver a sharp rebuke to the Clinton administration for the errors it had made, in the form of major Republican congressional wins, and the public outcry when the GOP subsequently overreached and was rebuked—something began to change. The government seemed to become more focused, concentrating on several key issues, including inflation, the federal deficit, crime, and welfare reform, and began to win back the public's confidence.

Business also started to be viewed more favorably, through both the new products and technologies it was bringing to market (which, though only in some categories, seemed to create a halo effect for business generally) and by integrating consumers' low price-plus-quality value equation.

In turn, government and business seemed to be viewed more as part of the solution than part of the problem to be slogged through. This is not to say the problems the public perceived have gone away: far from it. The mood today seems to be a willingness to allow government and business to be in on the equation. For example, when asked who is doing the most to solve the nation's problems, the public as a whole and Influential Americans continued to rank "community groups" highest and to rate "individual Americans" as high or higher as entities high up in the chain of government, including the president and Congress. In what seems to be a recognition that government had taken steps to address the "critical issues" facing the nation, however, the marks that Americans gave government improved. Although state government has recorded the largest gains, more in the public give higher scores to federal officials as well, including the perennially low-rated Congress (50%, up 8; see Figure 4-3).

There is still considerable skepticism of government. Only 16% of Americans in 2002 were "very confident" (they could depend on what they were told by government leaders); the largest numbers were only "fairly confident" (53%) or "not at all confident" (28%), only a modest improvement over the levels of the 1990s, which themselves were at Watergate-era levels. Despite being more involved in government and politics than the average person, only 18% of Influentials were very confident and 50% fairly confident they could depend on what they were told by government leaders, and 32% were not at all confident.

At the same time, though, there was a growing sense among the public that government is the best route to address some issues. From the nadir of the mid-1990s, the percentage of the public calling for major effort by government began to climb for a number of issues, particularly crime and drugs, health care, education, nuclear proliferation, and terrorism (all of which, even before 9/11, were considered deserving of major effort by government by 65% or more of the public).

We talk more in detail about the public's perceptions of business in Chapter 6, but the data showed a similar upturn. Businesses that responded to consumers' growing appetite for everyday low prices, innovative, easy-to-use technology, quality at a reasonable price, information, and a consumer-first mind-set, meanwhile, saw their sales and brand value grow,

Figure 4-3. Pulling Together—At Least Sometimes

Percentage of Influentials and all Americans saying group is doing "a fair amount" or "a good deal" to solve the nation's problems, with percentage point changes from 1995

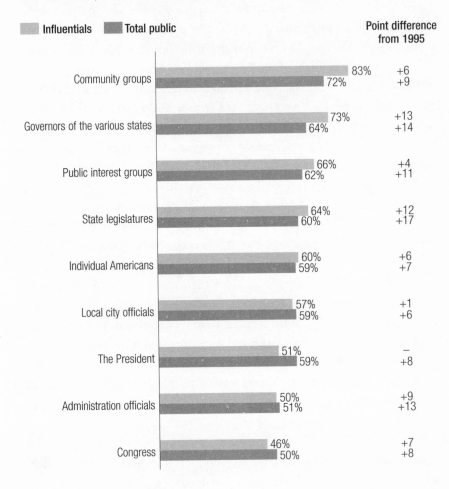

	Point difference from 1995
Community groups	Influentials 83% +6 / Total public 72% +9
Governors of the various states	Influentials 73% +13 / Total public 64% +14
Public interest groups	Influentials 66% +4 / Total public 62% +11
State legislatures	Influentials 64% +12 / Total public 60% +17
Individual Americans	Influentials 60% +6 / Total public 59% +7
Local city officials	Influentials 57% +1 / Total public 59% +6
The President	Influentials 51% – / Total public 59% +8
Administration officials	Influentials 50% +9 / Total public 51% +13
Congress	Influentials 46% +7 / Total public 50% +8

Source: Roper Reports

including Wal-Mart, Southwest, Microsoft, Home Depot, Nokia, Charles Schwab, Dell Computer, Starbucks, and FedEx, to cite some of the names that by 2002 were consistently showing up on *Fortune*'s most admired companies lists.

The job for business and government is to understand better the themes of the Age of Autonomy so that they can be there with goods, services, and the right words when people need them—"water station" marketing for the consumer "runners" in this era of change.

The Role of Influentials

Influentials have played a dual role in the self-reliance movement. As we've seen, they've led the way in adopting many of the new products and services that enhance self-reliance: computers, the Internet, cell phones, self-reliant retirement plans, and the iterations that have followed those products. They were among the first Americans, for better or worse, to be enrolled in health maintenance organizations. As such, they've had to learn how to think more for themselves in personal health. They've been early and important proponents of some of the key ideas of this era, such as trying to create change outside the traditional channels of government and business.

In other ways, however, the Influentials haven't changed. The values they have today are basically the same values we found in Influentials when we wrote our first in-depth report on them in 1988. Some have grown stronger, such as the importance of family, but the foundation was there. This is important. To a large extent it's been the public that has changed more than Influentials. If we go back to the charts and tables we have used so far in this chapter, we see that the public as a whole has changed more than Influentials on the issue of how much effect an individual can have on the society. In 1974, 52% of Influentials believed that an individual could have a "real effect" and in 1998, 50% agreed; a 2-point change in the Influentials is not statistically significant. The major change on the question of the individual's impact on society was in the public as a whole (where a 7-point change is significant).

Many of the points of view to which Americans have come around are positions that Influentials have long advocated: community involvement, people power, saving for tomorrow, thinking ahead, and solving problems. This is not a new thought. In our 1992 report on the Influentials, we foresaw that the Influentials had the potential to be "role models" for "the national agenda for the 1990s," one that would be "considerably different" from the "corporate raiders, highly leveraged developers, and financial market makers" of the 1980s. This was a group of "homegrown" and "more proximate" leaders whose messages, although "prescient," were "too often ignored" during "the frenetic 1980s."

With an older, more educated, more adept public, it's logical that Americans are coming around to the Influentials' point of view. The Baby Boomers and Generation X have moved into the family years. As they have done so, their concerns have taken more of a family bent—schools, neighborhoods, community, and the safety of their children when they send them out into the world in the morning. There's good reason for the Influentials, who have always been educated and have always had a midlife demographic profile, to be listened to more and to be role models both for those who are navigating midlife and for those in business and government who want to understand what is to come in the larger society.

Moreover, Influentials are among the leading proponents of the idea that the changes of the past decade are working. They are motivated to extend the trend of self-reliance into the future.

Opportunities and Challenges

As with all unfolding trends, much is still to be worked out in the self-reliance trend. In what seems to be evidence of Tocqueville's "self-interest properly understood," for the total public and Influential Americans there is growing appreciation of community *and* self. This likely will be an ongoing source of tension. NIMBY (not in my backyard) protests aren't likely to go away. There are new rules to work out (when and where it's appropriate to talk on a cell phone) and what generally are the boundaries between community and self.

Some of the seeds of future tension are evident in our studies. On the one hand, as we noted previously, there's growing belief that "people have a definite responsibility to help the people in their community who are less fortunate than they are." In addition, more Influentials say they "have responsibilities to my neighbors and community beyond what is required by law" (84%, up 8), and they think business "should consider what is good for society, not just what is good for profits" (78%, up 10). Although there might be argument over the means for accomplishing these ends, those trends would be those most Americans would find compatible; majorities in the total public agree with both positions.

The growing emphasis on community and family also contains some currents that are likely to set off sparks, however. For example, although it's not a majority position, more Influentials and Americans generally believe that "parents should try to stay together for the sake of their children, even if the parents have fallen out of love" (up 17 points to 33% among Influentials between 1995 and 2000 and up 9 points to 32% in the total public, substantial changes). Buck up, a number of Influentials appear to be saying. Stop placing your own selfish interests first. The recent debate among psychologists about the effect of divorce appears to be matched by a rupture in the broader public, with the Influentials leading the change.

There's also a fissure opening up on property rights. Again, it is only an undercurrent to the majority opinion, but there's been a sharp increase among Influentials (and a smaller gain in the public as a whole) in the view that "there shouldn't be any restrictions on what one can do with his or her own private property" (up 13 points to 39% among Influentials since 1995 and up 4 points to 42% in the total public). This shift may be a micro-level manifestation of the openness among Influentials to looking at new ways to meet the needs of environmental protection and economic vitality (see Chapter 2). Such a sentiment is understandable to homeowners who have crossed swords with the local zoning board, but it poses obvious problems on other issues, including the control of development and the preservation of green space, which many Influentials (including Sophie Glovier) strongly support.

There's likely to be further debate generally on the place of individualism versus community. In addition to being more community spirited, the public is also more inclined to believe "what other people do is none of my business" (up 8 points to 52% since 1995). Most Influentials *don't* share that laissez-faire stance (only 37% of the opinion leaders, the same as in 1995, think what others do is none of their business; see Figure 4-4).

There are many loose ends. Self-reliance hasn't tied everything up into a neat package. Such is evident in the news on any given day. How much are people willing to sacrifice in their rights to have more protection from ter-

Figure 4-4. More Community Minded and More Individualist

Percentage of Influential Americans agreeing with statement, with change from 1995, with agreement of total public and point change from 1995 in brackets

84%. . . . I have responsibilities to my neighbors and community beyond what is
required by law (+8)   [63%, –]

78%. . . . Business should consider what is good for society, not just what is good
for profit (+10)   [72%, +3]

69%. . . . People have a definite responsibility to help the people in their community
who are less fortunate than they are (+14)   [55%, +6]

39%. . . . There shouldn't be any restrictions on what one can do with his or her
own private property (+13)   [42%, +4]

37%. . . . What other people do is none of my business (–)   [52%, +8]

33%. . . . Parents should try to stay together for the sake of their children, even if
the parents have fallen out of love (+17)   [32%, +9]

Source: Roper Reports

rorists? Where should new public works like power plants be built? There are often elements of the ethic of self-interest properly understood on both sides of the argument. Vouchers for public school education, for example, which allow parents to have more choice in what's best for their kids—echoing themes of self-reliance in "choice" and "family"—have generated support among African-American parents. "We are desperate for decent education for our children," one parent wrote in a *New York Times* op-ed piece. Vouchers are staunchly opposed by others, who see them as anti-community.

Companies probably will find themselves in the middle of the conflict. Self-reliance has become in many ways the basis for interaction between company and consumer. The result has democratized industries, turning old power structures upside down and creating growing markets for products and services that break down the walls between doctor and patient, company and customer, Wall Street and Main Street, and so on.

It also opens up new questions. The current debates on privacy regulation (how much is enough?), regulation of 401(k) accounts (should there be limits on how much employees can invest in their own company?), and health care (should there be price controls on prescription drugs?) share some common threads. What should the relationship be between individuals and institutions in this new era? What are the boundaries of individual responsibilities? When should government, employers, and other institutions step in? On what services should institutions focus?

With their positions of responsibility in the community and the workplace and their position at the center of the word-of-mouth conversation about the important issues of the day, the Influentials will play a key role in the outcome of these and other debates. From analysis of our studies on Influentials and the public as a whole, there are certain key themes that we think can guide businesses, government officials, and others interested in this important dynamic in the society and the marketplace:

1. A different kind of activism
2. Thinking out of the orthodox box
3. Return to values
4. Levels of confidence
5. Self-improvement and learning

The Age of Autonomy:
A DIFFERENT KIND OF ACTIVISM

For those who have worried about the state of civic democracy in America, the movement to self-reliance offers some encouraging news. Looking inward for solutions has led many Americans into the community. The result has given rise to a number of new groups dedicated to addressing issues. It has also generated new approaches. This "different kind of activism" should not exactly be a surprise. It's consistent with the antiorthodox, out-of-the-box mentality that spurred many of the innovations of the past decade. It has brought a new sense of energy to many communities, but the new activism also presents challenges to traditional organizations and processes and to institutions accustomed to using traditional mind-sets for solving problems.

We see the change in our studies on activism. Americans are doing some things more than they were a decade ago, but they are involved in other areas less than in the past. The U.S. has become much more of a meeting-going nation. Between 1987 and 1994, the percentage of Americans saying they had attended a meeting on town or school affairs fell from 17 to 12%—the bottoming out of a long decline in civic activism. After 1994, though, the percentage started to climb again. By 2000, it was back up to 17%, a gain of 5 percentage points. Estimated on a national basis using U.S. Census data for the respective years, this means about 36 million Americans went to a meeting in 2000, up from 23 million in 1994. The signs you see in Isabel Milano's community of Irvington, New York, for meetings on school fund-raisers, important board meetings, and local environmental issues, which give the impression *there are a lot of meetings going on around here,* are not an anomaly.

The 5-point changes reported in the preceding paragraph are in this case significant. Because the percentages on going to meetings are drawn from all of the in-person studies conducted during the course of a year, there is significantly less margin than in a single study. For the total public, there were 13,945 or more respondents in each of the years; among Influentials, there were 1,361 or more respondents per year.

Influentials shared in the increase—in fact, appear to have been in on it early. The percentage of Influential Americans attending a meeting on town or school affairs rose from 71% in 1987 to 75% in 1991. By 1999–2000 it had reached 76%.

Other measures have also shown increases. For Influentials, most of the changes occurred between the late 1980s and the early 1990s. If "the bottoming out" of apathy for the public as a whole was the early to mid-1990s, for Influentials it seems to have started in the 1980s. From 1987, our studies suggest, more Influentials became involved in trying to improve government in various ways. Between 1987 and 1991, the percentage of Influentials belonging to groups "interested in better government" rose 6 points to 23%. Between 1987 and 1994, the percentage of Influentials writing letters to the editor to make their opinion known rose by 6 points to 35%. Over time, the percentage of Influentials getting their views out by writing articles for newspapers or magazines inched up as well, rising from a low of 17% in 1987 to 21% in 2000–2001.

Volunteering has also gained new stature. More Americans say that volunteering in the community "makes life richer or fuller" (23%, up 7 points from 1989)—more than gardening (17%) or meditation or yoga (5%), pursuits that have received considerable media attention in recent years. Almost as many identify volunteering as life enriching as cite being in love (27%). The percentage of Americans who consider volunteering and charity work to be "in" rose from 54 to 64% between 1994 and 1999.

According to *BusinessWeek,* 2000 was a record year for volunteering. On a consistent basis, about one in three adult Americans since 1997 have told us that they perform volunteer work and community service at least occasionally in their leisure time, as many as go to cultural events. About one in five Americans—over 40 million people, on a national basis—report that they volunteered in the past month. In addition, 13% of Americans participated in a community-oriented activity, such as a neighborhood cleanup, food drive, or coaching a youth sports team, in the past month. (Among Influentials, participation rates and attitudes toward volunteering and community service are substantially higher than in the total public.) According to our studies, youth organizations draw the largest numbers of volunteers, appropriate to a nation with a large number of its citizens in the child-rearing years. Religious charities and community groups come next.

Large numbers are pitching in, from separating recyclables (done on a fairly regular basis by more than half of Influentials and more than one in three of the total public), to cleaning up the neighborhood (done by half of Influentials and about one in four of the total public), to joining a neighborhood watch group (which has been done by 39% of Influentials and 17% of the total public in the 1990s as crime rates were rising). In addition, more Americans say being involved in a group with similar interests makes life enriching (22%, up 5 from 1989).

Much of Americans' energies has gone to new ventures. Recent decades have seen a boom in new groups. According to the U.S. Census Bureau's

Statistical Abstract, more than 7,500 new nonprofit associations were formed between 1980 and 2000, an increase of more than 50%. The U.S. in 2000 had 1,068 more associations for health and medical concerns than it did in 1980, for example: 821 more educational and cultural associations; 809 more associations for public affairs concerns; 687 more associations for business, trade, and commercial concerns; 553 more associations for hobbies and interests; 354 more associations related to religious concerns; 278 more associations for sports and athletics; and 117 more associations for ethnic, nationality, or fraternal interests.

Many of the new groups that have come into being in recent decades have become part of the fabric of their towns, cities, states, and the nation. Mothers Against Drunk Driving has been instrumental in passing scores of new laws while promoting its mission to end drunken driving, aid the victims of drunk drivers, and discourage teenage drinking. The Gay Men's Health Crisis offers support services and resources for those with AIDS or HIV. Teach for America strives to place the cream of the crop of recent college graduates in poor urban and rural public schools to give kids there a better chance. The New York New Media Association has become a hub for networking for Silicon Alley Internet workers.

The Internet has added a new twist. With the fluidity of the new medium, it's possible quickly to build up informal networks around particular issues (the Millennial student activists are masters of this form of organizing), then disassemble them just as rapidly when the need is no longer there. Technology has become the focus of some groups as well. Geekcorps, created by Ethan Zuckerman, age 29, sends teams of volunteers into the Third World to teach computer programming, Web site management, and other IT (Information Technology) skills. "We've taken a lot of our inspiration from the Peace Corps," Zuckerman told Gannett News Service. "Only we're looking to send people to live in cities and work with businesses rather than into the fields like the Peace Corps."

Many of the Influentials we profile in this book have devoted at least part of their activism to new groups. Some of the Influentials have helped create new groups—Isabel Milano, for example, with Parents Connection, the Irvington Education Foundation, and the Irvington Athletic Foundation. The Intertribal Council and Native Sobriety Movement in which

Mike Williams is involved are relatively recent groups. The idea to race the Iditarod to collect sobriety pledges and raise awareness about alcoholism, something that Mike Williams does on his own, is emblematic of another type of involvement in the new activism. A number of Americans are undertaking independent ventures by raising money for a charity of their own choosing while riding a bike race or running a marathon or walking across a part of or the whole nation to raise awareness of an issue.

The Age of Autonomy:
THINKING OUT OF THE ORTHODOX BOX

Along with this different kind of activism has been a different mind-set toward involvement. There seems to be more of an emphasis on being effective and relevant. Sophie Glovier says she made a conscious choice to become involved with the Delaware-Raritan Greenway's land preservation group, which is relatively young, rather than volunteer for an older, more established environmental group. "I assume I would have gotten the, 'Well, honey, you can come in and stuff envelopes' response from some traditional groups," she says. "That's not the kind of involvement I look for. I'm happy to stuff envelopes, but I want to do other work, too. I like having an impact." For volunteers like Glovier who come to nonprofit groups with skill sets honed through their careers, it's logical to want to make use of their talents. This combination of desire and skills to make a significant contribution is probably one of the unexpected by-products of a more educated workforce and as such will likely be a growing theme in the years to come as more educated workers retire and look for outlets to make a difference through volunteering.

Befitting the out-of-the-box mind-set and ingrained skepticism that have been two of the hallmarks of the self-reliance movement, the new activism also tends to "think" outside traditional channels as well. We see this in Influentials. Large numbers of Influentials—larger than in the public as a whole—think that traditional interest groups on *both* sides of issues have too much power in the society today. Influentials think both "left-wing political groups" (51%, 18 points higher than in the total public) and "right-wing political groups" (53%, 20 points higher) have too much power; that "fundamentalist church groups" (43%, 15 higher) and "civil liberties groups" (43%, 16 higher) have too much power; that "antiabortion groups" (36%, 6 higher) and "pro-abortion groups" (46%, 9 higher) have too much power. Some groups in particular are thought to wield too much influence, including "business and industry organizations" (51%, 11 higher), "lawyers' organizations" (67%, 11 higher), and the "medical and health insurance industry" (66%, 17 higher). In the Influentials' thinking, traditional groups, with their traditional thinking and vested interests, often stand in the way of progress. It's smarter and better to become involved with a group outside the mainstream, they seem to be saying; you can make more of a difference there.

Therein lies the rub for government, political parties, and other traditional organizations. Americans are going more to meetings, volunteering more, and placing a higher priority on community involvement, but they are still avoiding some other types of civic engagements. This is even true among Influentials. Although they're doing some things more (going to meetings, joining groups to influence government, and expressing their opinions in public) and are involved in multiple areas with their community, they are doing some things less than in the past. Although half serve on committees or hold leadership positions with clubs or organizations, the percentages doing so are down (down 7 points to 50% since 1991 for committees; down 10 points to 48% since 1987 for serving as an officer of an organization or club). "Committee" and "chairperson" seem to be anathema to the effectiveness-oriented mind-set of the new activists (especially to those who have sat through interminably long committee meetings).

Going to rallies, protests, and political speeches also declined (down 6 points to 43% between 1991 and 2000). Protests may make good television, but it's in meetings that decisions are made. Because meetings are also where ideas are exchanged by people with different points of view, you can learn more from a meeting as well. Until recently, working for political parties was down markedly, too. The percentage of Influentials who had worked for a political party in the past year fell by 8 points to 19% between 1987 and 2000 before rebounding 6 points to 25% in 2001. Perhaps the close presidential race of 2000 brought more Influentials back to the party;

perhaps events are pointing them back to the political process (as Isabel Milano evolved from volunteering on school issues to running for village trustee; see Figures 4-5 and 4-6).

Still, it's too early to say political parties have Influentials back in the fold. There's still considerable skepticism of the political process and parties and of government the further you move from the local level. This is probably one reason Americans and Influentials have for years favored a split (some might say deadlocked) government, with one party in control of Congress and the other in command of the White House. Skepticism of traditional politics is probably also a factor in why half of Influentials, despite their nominal alliances to the Democrats and Republicans, for much of the 1990s expected a new political party to emerge to challenge the traditional parties.

There are lessons for business in the unorthodox position. Winning loyalty is increasingly dependent on opening up processes—being open to new ideas and creating avenues for people to express their opinions. Businesses should also be sure they are using their energy in the areas in which their consumers are using their time and effort. With the new channels being created for expressing community activism, it's important not to assume that what was true 10 or 20 years ago still works. At the same time, companies should be aware that they court controversy if they give their dollars to groups that Influentials think already wield too much interest. This is not to say that controversy is necessarily bad—it can bring attention, which sometimes is what you want. Companies should be aware in advance what they're getting into, though.

Underscored, as well, is the importance of bringing opinion leaders into decision making. As Sophie Glovier says, Influentials "like having an impact." Nonprofit foundations are being advised to develop policies now in anticipation of the $6.7 trillion expected to flow to charities by 2018 from the transfer of inheritance to a new generation. There is no guarantee that existing charities will get those funds, Professor Paul Schervish of Boston College's Social Welfare Research Institute tells *The New York Times*. "New philanthropists are setting higher standards and seeking to be more involved in the application of their money."

Democratizing the decision-making process is easier for some entities

Figure 4-5. Americans' Activism: More Meetings

Percentage of Americans who have done activity in the past year, total public

	1987	1991	1994	1997	1999	2000	2001
Attended public meeting on town or school affairs	17%	15%	12%	15%	14%	17%	16%
Wrote or called a politician at local, state, or national level	15%	13%	11%	12%*	12%	13%	12%
Served on a committee of a local organization	8%	7%	6%	8%	7%	7%	7%
Was officer of club or organization	10%	7%	6%	6%	6%	7%	7%
Attended rally, speech, or organized protest	9%	7%	6%	7%	5%	6%	7%
Wrote letter to editor or called live broadcast to express opinion	5%	5%	4%	6%*	5%	7%	6%
Was active member of group trying to influence public policy or government	2%	3%	3%	5%*	4%	5%	5%
Made a speech	5%	4%	3%	4%	4%	5%	4%
Worked for political party	4%	3%	3%	3%	2%	3%	3%
Wrote article for magazine or newspaper	2%	2%	2%	2%	2%	3%	3%
Held or ran for office	1%	1%	1%	1%	1%	1%	1%

Source: Roper Reports

Base: 13,945-plus respondents per year

* Wording changed on item beginning with year noted

Figure 4-6. Influentials' Activism: Some Things Up, Others . . .

Percentage of Influential Americans who have done activity in past year

	1987	1991	1994	1997	1999	2000	2001
Attended public meeting on town or school affairs	71%	75%	73%	73%	76%	76%	74%
Wrote or called a politician at local, state, or national level	62%	64%	62%	67%*	71%	69%	68%
Served on a committee of a local organization	54%	57%	54%	53%	55%	50%	50%
Was officer of club or organization	58%	54%	51%	45%	51%	49%	48%
Attended rally, speech, or organized protest	48%	49%	48%	47%	44%	43%	45%
Wrote letter to editor or called live broadcast to express opinion	29%	32%	35%	38%*	43%	45%	40%
Was active member of group trying to influence public policy or government	17%	23%	21%	37%*	38%	37%	35%
Made a speech	32%	33%	33%	30%	33%	32%	31%
Worked for political party	27%	25%	24%	25%	22%	19%	25%
Wrote article for magazine or newspaper	17%	19%	18%	18%	19%	21%	21%
Held or ran for office	5%	7%	7%	6%	6%	5%	6%

Source: Roper Reports

Base: 13,945-plus respondents per year

* Wording changed on item beginning with year noted

than others. A growing number of government agencies, since the reinventing-government movement of the past decade, have made efforts to be more responsive to citizens. Efforts to shift tax filing and application processes online, which no doubt upset established practices, are one example. Political parties, on the other hand, appear to face a more daunting challenge. The special interests that bug Influentials generate a lot of campaign money. The risk, though, is loosening loyalties, increasing tune-out, and heightened volatility at election time, trends that at present seem likely to continue into the years to come.

As the younger, Internet-integrated generation ages, the trend is likely to accelerate. The story is unfolding on college campuses, where "there has been a decrease in participation in formal extracurricular activities like student government—and an increase in self-organized groups," according to George Kuh, professor at Indiana University and director of the National Survey of Student Engagement. One of the upshots is a surge in the number of a cappella singing groups on campus. There are now 873, four times the number of 20 years ago.

PROFILES IN INFLUENCE

Mike Williams

Mike Williams is in many ways a model for making a difference today. Since he decided to use his passion for dog team racing to raise awareness of the problem of alcoholism, stories on Williams and the sobriety movement have become fixtures of the Iditarod. He is one of the featured mushers on Iditarod web sites. Twice he has been named the race's most inspirational musher. He gives speeches for the sobriety movement and makes personal appearances, going to schools and talking with kids. He meets with government officials on the local, state, and national levels to lobby for programs promoting sobriety. Through his efforts and those of others working on the issue, in 2001 Congress appropriated funds to support sobriety projects in Alaska. Villages regularly mount alcohol-free activities, dances, parades, and potlucks.

"So far, it's working," Williams says with the characteristic understatement that, like his droll sense of humor, is part of his persona. Williams views the Iditarod as "a lifetime commitment," part of a larger mission to create "healthy communities" and help unhealthy people "change their lives and become productive once again."

He has also established himself as a top dogsled racer, showing that personal passions and civic involvement can intersect. He has finished as high as eighteenth in the Iditarod, finishing the course in 10 days, 15 hours, and 45 minutes in 1997. He usually finishes among the top 30 racers. Six times he has earned prize money.

Self-reliance is a thread that runs through much of his work. The sobriety movement's goal is to encourage people to make positive changes in their lives. The Tribal Council and other Native American organizations are dedicated to giving Native Americans the right to pursue their traditions by securing and protecting fishing and hunting rights and preserving the language, customs, rituals, stories, and values the tribes have practiced through time.

After being a delegate to a national conference in Washington, D.C. in 1991 and advocating for libraries and information resources in rural areas, Williams was able to bring a community library to his own town. Now, he goes there regularly to browse the out-of-town magazines and newspapers that he doesn't read already at home and to surf the Internet. Like most Influentials, Williams is a big proponent of the Net.

Shortly after marrying, he decided he wanted to build his own home. The family still lives in the 1,200-square-foot wood-frame house. "I like my independence," he says. The home was an example. "I wanted to build my own house with my own two hands."

Williams traces his attitudes to tradition and pride. "Everything that was taught to me by my Yupiaq elders, I have stored in my heart and mind," he says. "I have my identity intact. My language is intact. I know exactly who I am." He grew up with the traditional ways of the Yupiaq. His family traveled with the seasons, to "hunting camp," "spring camp," and "fishing camp." By the standards of 1950s and 1960s America, it was a modest lifestyle. "No phone, no television, no electricity for the most part," he recalls, but "they were some of the best times I ever had. I spent most of my time listening to my grandmother telling me stories, or learning how to hunt and fish." He also learned how to travel by dog team.

From his parents, Williams also learned the value of knowing the ways of the wider society. When he was young, every winter his parents sent him and his siblings to a small school in the village run by the U.S. Bureau of Indian Affairs. "They thought that it was important for me to learn the white man's way of education to protect our interests." The decision put him on a road that both took him away from home and brought home the challenge of living in two worlds. After going as far as he could in the BIA school, he was sent off to Chemawa Indian High School in Salem, Oregon. Upon graduating, he was drafted into the U.S. Army and sent farther from home, to South Korea. Travel opened him up to new ways of looking at the world. He developed an interest in other cultures and peoples, an area that continues to engage him and give him insights to apply in his work. He is usually reading a book on such subjects as "how people have used the democratic process to overcome poverty" or people "from different walks of life, particularly Latino people and American Indians."

His parents' belief that "if we are ever going to deal with the land issues our people face, we need to have a formal education in order to be at the table and negotiate" has become part of Mike Williams's own outlook. His life is a blend of tradition and modernity. Family is central—starting with his wife, Maggie ("my biggest support"), whose teaching salary is the primary source of income since Mike quit his job as a mental health counselor to focus full-time on his work for the tribe and community and his interests in education and the sobriety movement. Between their four-year-old daughter and their grandchildren's visits, the house often echoes with children's voices. The family has a TV but limits its use. The general policy is "no TV," he says. In many ways, the family follows the Yupiaq traditions. Summers in the camp, with fish drying, still are "the best times."

There are modern twists, though. Williams drives a Toyota pickup truck. He values the Toyota brand; in addition, Toyota has sponsored him on the Iditarod, which defrays the costs of training for the race (such as maintaining a passel of dogs). Even at fish camp, Williams makes it a point to check his e-mail every day (hooking up his PC to a portable generator and phone line). He carries a cell phone and fax machine as well. As chairman of the consortium of 220 tribes, often with legislative items, regulatory proposals, court cases, and other business affecting them on the state and federal levels, he needs to stay in touch. Issues like fishing rights have been the subject of ongoing battles that have brought tribes both in Alaska and elsewhere in the U.S. into conflict with environmentalists and the fishing industry, among other groups. "I need to be in contact with people at a moment's notice." He maintains a regular media diet, reading a stream of magazines through the local library and the *Anchorage Daily News* and keeping up with *The Los Angeles Times* and *The New York Times* via the Internet.

With the nearest supermarket 450 miles away in Anchorage, the family is savvy in the modern hunting and gathering of shopping by catalog and the Internet. A few times a year, the family makes a shopping expedition to town that usually includes a long stopover at Wal-Mart. When he's traveling on business, he makes a point to pick up staples like rice and sugar. The system isn't easy by the standards of most Americans, but "it works."

Despite some modern improvements—running water, electricity, a sewer system, the library, a new school, and a community public television station—life in the small rural community of Akiak continues to mean a disproportionate amount of hardship for many of its residents. Services and living standards have improved, but Akiak is still "Third World" in comparison with the rest of the nation, with "not enough jobs" and "a harsh environment" in the view of many of its residents, Williams says. Skepticism of government and other institutions tends to run high.

To Williams, the traditions and customs of the Yupiaq are the way up from poverty, despair, and the social problems they engender. "A sense of identity is one of the best tools in the battle against alcohol," he says. You can hold onto language, stories, rituals, dances, the seasonal camps, fishing, hunting, and dogsleds. You can hold onto and find strength in them during times of hardship. "For generations, organizations came up here and told us not to speak our language," he says. Some tribes literally lost their language. To Williams the mission to "restore the native language and culture, dance and stories," more than establishing a connection to the past, is building a connection to the future.

The Age of Autonomy:
RETURN TO VALUES

The efforts of Mike Williams and others to preserve Native Alaskan customs and traditions and create healthy communities would likely strike a chord with many Americans. An emphasis on values and tradition is one of the characteristics of the self-reliance movement. It manifests itself in various ways.

There is increased appreciation of the traditions and customs that make up the society. Growing numbers of Americans believe that people from different cultures, traditions, and countries should feel free to "maintain a good many of the traditions and customs of their individual heritage," both Influentials (37%, up 10 points from 1974) and Americans as a whole (31% agree, up 12 points). In contrast, there's been a sharp decline in the view that people should "concentrate on adopting the customs of *this* country" and forgo their traditions, with a 10-point decline (to 21%) among Influentials and a 7-point decline (to 27%) in the public as a whole (see Figure 4-7).

There is also comprehension that the *lack* of values and morals has been a major problem. Indeed, among Influentials and the public generally, the decline in values is the leading cause of the nation's problems: the problem comes from inside, not from such outside factors as the nation's leaders. Fully 75% of Influential Americans, up 15 points from 1973, cite "a letdown in moral values" as among the "major causes of our problems in this country." The other factors that Influentials are most likely to cite among the sources of the nation's problems sound similar themes: "permissiveness of parents" (71%, up 20 from 1973), "selfishness" (68%, up 19 from 1973), and "too much emphasis on money and materialism" (58%). Influentials are significantly more likely to cite these issues than "wrongdoing in government" (cited by 48% of Influentials), "a lack of good leadership" (47%), "too much commitment to other nations in the world" (33%), "radical attempts to force change" (19%) or "growing conservatism" (18%), "too much technology" (10%), or "too little interest in other nations" (10%; see Figure 4-8).

Influentials aren't saying that values are the *only* problem in the U.S.

Figure 4-7. Ethnic Heritage a Growing Part of Nation's Identity

Support among Influential Americans and total public for different statements regarding how much of their traditions and customs people from different cultures, religions, and countries should maintain, with percentage point difference from 1974

	Influentials	Total public		Point difference from 1974

Maintain a good many of the traditions and customs of their heritage

37%		+10
31%		+12

Maintain a few of the traditions and customs

39%		-1
37%		-1

Concentrate on adopting the customs of this country

21%		-10
27%		-7

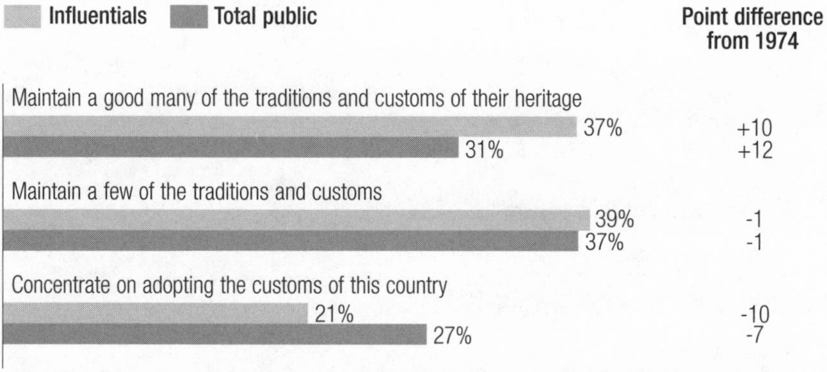

Source: Roper Reports

What Influentials seem to be saying is that, without an "inner" change, "outer" reforms can only go so far to make the U.S. better. The message is consistent with what they say elsewhere—that people have a definite responsibility to help the people in their community who are less fortunate, parents should place a higher priority on their children's interests, and being a good parent and spouse is the number-one measure of personal success.

Much of the responsibility for these changes is seen as beginning with the individual, but other entities are seen as having roles as well. Large numbers of Influentials in surveys in recent years have said that groups beyond parents have a responsibility to teach values to children, particularly churches (half or more Influentials say these groups have a definite responsibility here). Substantial numbers of Influentials, one-third or more, have said in surveys that they think it's at least highly desirable for the music industry, TV networks, the motion picture industry, and newspapers, for example, to teach children values. Although none of these groups are seen by

Figure 4-8. Morals and Values Integral to Nation's Well-Being

Percentage of Influential Americans and total public saying item is among "the major causes" of "our problems in this country today," with percentage point difference from 1973

Influentials   **Total public**

Point difference from 1973

Letdown in moral values

75%   +15

63%   +13

Permissiveness of parents

71%   +20

52%   +9

Selfishness

68%   +19

49%   -2

Too much emphasis on money and materialism

58%   +1

44%   -2

Permissiveness in courts

49%   -1

42%   +3

Wrongdoing in government

48%   +1

47%   -4

Lack of good leadership

47%   -7

47%   -2

Too much commitment to other nations in the world

33%   -6

30%   -18

Radical attempts to force change

19%   +5

17%   -2

Growing conservatism

18%   +11

10%   +4

Too much technology

10%   -4

12%   +6

Too little interest in other nations of world

10%   —

7%   +1

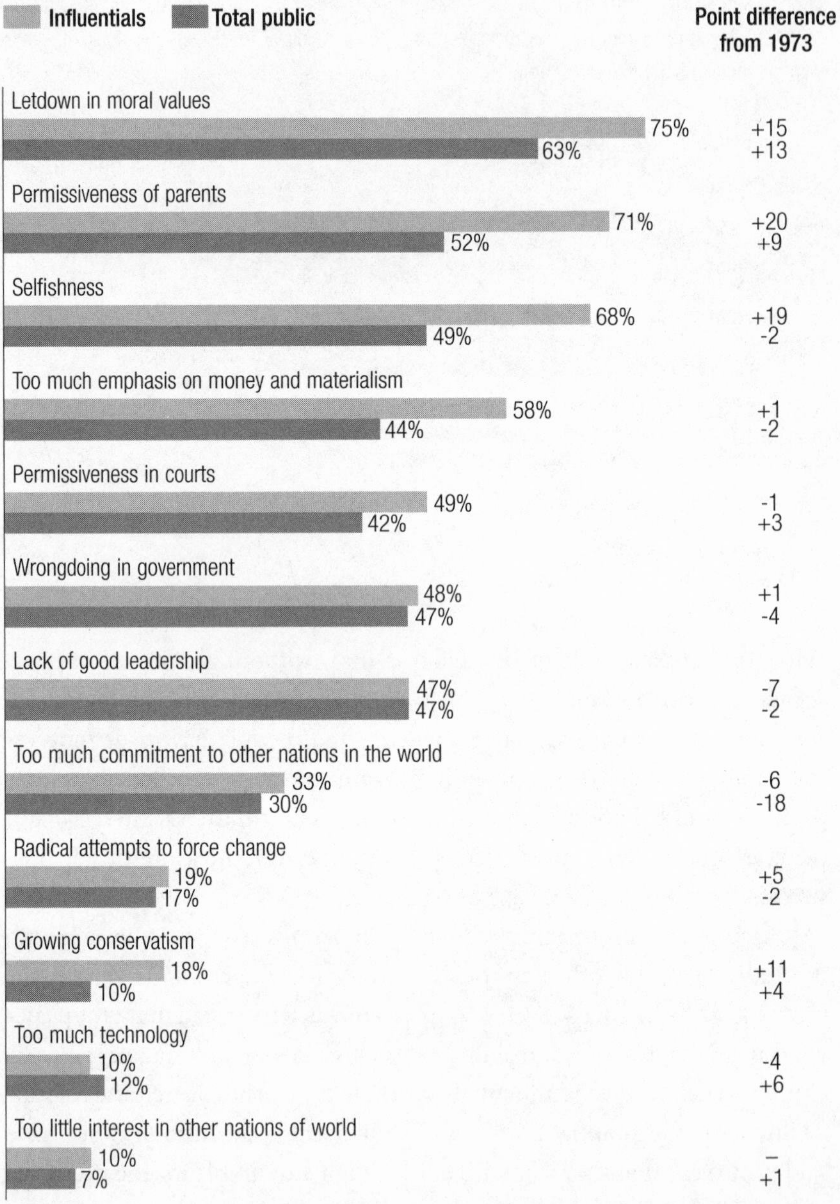

Source: Roper Reports

a majority of Influentials as fulfilling the responsibility, during the course of the 1990s Influentials gave modestly higher grades to some, particularly state and federal government.

The values message has other implications for business as well. Companies are being asked more to communicate their values. It's probably no accident that the companies consistently rated highly in *Fortune*'s most admired rankings are companies that place a high priority on communicating their corporate values through their marketing (customer-first advertising like Microsoft's "Where do you want to go today?"), the low-price high-quality formula (Dell and Wal-Mart), and design (the living room-like ambience of Starbucks coffee bars). Cause-related marketing is increasingly factored by consumers into their purchase decisions. It's also being recognized. More than half of both Influentials (55%) and the public as a whole (58%) credit business with using advertising to "promote good causes and social responsibility," evidence that business can be part of the solution.

The Age of Autonomy:
DIFFERENT LEVELS OF CONFIDENCE

The motivation to become financially independent of others, which has become more important to both Americans as a whole and the Influentials, doesn't mean they know what kind of investments will enable them to become financially independent. Wanting a lot of money (which, although not paramount, has become a more important part of the Good Life) also doesn't mean the average American or Influential has all the answers about how to make a lot of money. Being self-reliant doesn't mean being expert in all areas.

People bring different levels of confidence to different subjects. One of the keys to operating in a society that gives a high priority to self-reliance, then, is to achieve as firm a grasp as possible of the degree of confidence people have in an area and to keep up with it as it changes. One of the hallmarks of this era is that, sometimes little by little, sometimes in great leaps, people are always learning more. People know more about cell phones, the Internet, 401(k)s, and health maintenance organizations, for example, than they did 10 years ago. One of the easiest ways to offend Americans today is to assume too little—or too much—of a level of knowledge about a subject. Think of all the advertisements mired in financial or technological jargon, or, at the other extreme, filled with patronizing language, that in one way or another leave you saying, "Who do they think they're *talking* to?" On the other hand, in a society and marketplace placing a growing premium on "the conversation," where people are increasingly given to talking through decisions, relying more on the word-of-mouth expertise of family, friends, and other people, and like to create word-of-mouth buzz when they find something or hear something they like (a restaurant, vacation spot, or simply an idea), finding a meeting of the minds creates a sense of confidence in the person with whom you're speaking.

Finding this meeting of the minds is particularly important in engaging Influentials. Because they tend to be well-read and to be connected with many groups and people in a variety of settings, Influentials come to most conversations with higher levels of confidence than Americans as a whole. They don't profess expertise across all areas, however, and within most subjects, they feel confident about some aspects and they admit they aren't particularly confident about others. Appropriate to their position in the community as supergeneralists—people who "know a lot about some things and something about a lot of things"—they aren't know-it-alls.

Let's look at financial services, appropriately the dominant example in this chapter: investment has become one of the main areas of life that has changed as the population has aged, education levels have gone up, changes in technology and the marketplace have opened up more options, and the self-reliance movement (which feeds off these three trends) has taken hold. Influentials are much more likely than the public generally to feel comfortable making financial decisions, with double-digit differences in many areas. The majority of Influentials feel "quite competent" in deciding how to save money (59%, 15 points higher than in the total public). Large numbers feel quite competent planning their family's financial future (43%, 14 points higher), planning for retirement (42%, 11 higher), and deciding how to invest money (40%, 10 higher). They're not more likely to feel quite competent buying life insurance than the public as a whole (33%), and they don't exude confidence when it comes to the stock market. They're more comfortable than the average person with the nitty-gritty of how to buy and sell stocks, that is, whom to call, how to place an order, and other details of the transaction, but only 22% feel quite competent at it. Although the Internet is drawing growing numbers of Influentials (like other investors) to check information and make transactions online, only 15% of Influentials feel quite competent with making transactions and investments online. Only 15% of Influentials feel quite competent at "how to make money in the stock market," "what to buy and when to buy it." Stated another way, Influentials have only a third as much confidence in figuring out how to make money in stocks and how to make transactions online as they do in planning for their family's financial future and their retirement and only a quarter as much confidence as they have with the basic, family budget decision of how to save money.

Larger numbers feel at least "somewhat competent" with these decisions, as shown in Figure 4-9. Nine in ten Influentials, for example, feel at least somewhat competent in deciding how to save money, and more than 75% feel at least somewhat competent in planning for the future and retirement, making basic investment decisions, and buying insurance. The consensus on savings is that it's no big deal—about as many Americans as a whole feel the same—but in the other areas Influentials are substantially more likely to feel at least a little comfortable sitting down to make a decision than the public as a whole. When it comes to stocks, however, although they're more comfortable than the public generally, only half feel even somewhat confident. On the contrary, as many Influentials as not admit that they are "not very competent" or "totally at a loss" when it comes to knowing how to make money in the stock market (48%), the mechanics of buying and selling stocks (46%), and making investments and transactions online (55%; see Figure 4-9).

"The Best Places to Have Money"

Knowing where Influentials do and don't feel competent gives financial services companies a parameter for starting the conversation. "You probably know a lot about saving and know some things about planning for your family's future and your own retirement and the basics of investing. But how do you put that into practice in today's stock market?" Or, cutting to the chase, "are you as comfortable as you'd like to be making transactions online and with the nuts-and-bolts of how to make an investment?" Even though some financial services firms have made great strides in the art of starting the conversation with opinion leaders, many of the communications from this industry still assume too much or too little knowledge or begin with a pitch (like the telemarketer's "have we got a stock for you") rather than a question in which investors are interested. A scan of the business section of the Sunday newspaper finds some ads that get it. "You've

Figure 4-9. Confidence with Financial Decisions

Percentage of Influential Americans saying they feel "quite competent" making financial decision, with percentage point difference from total public.

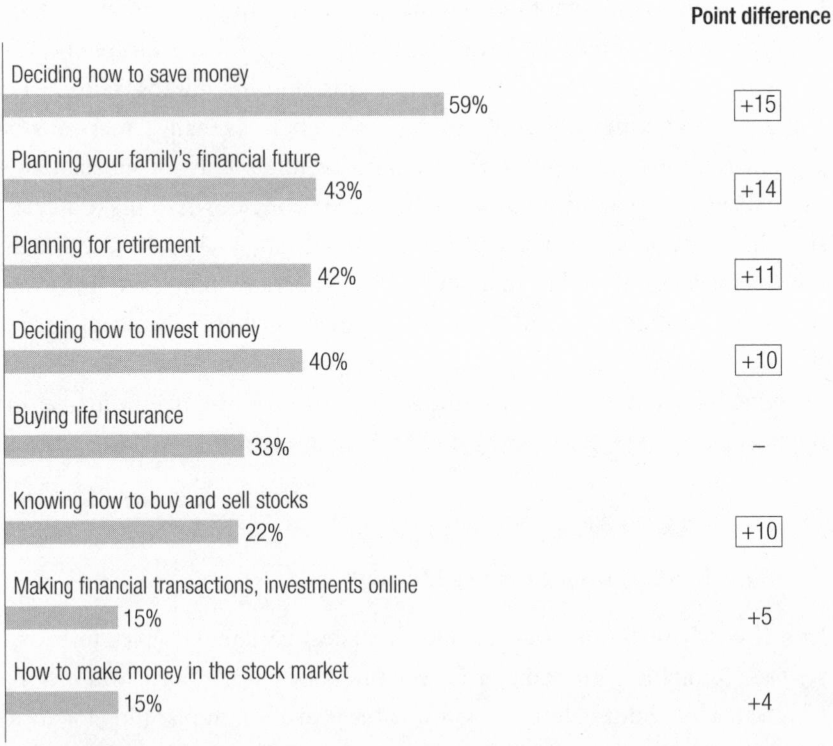

Point difference

Deciding how to save money
59% +15

Planning your family's financial future
43% +14

Planning for retirement
42% +11

Deciding how to invest money
40% +10

Buying life insurance
33% –

Knowing how to buy and sell stocks
22% +10

Making financial transactions, investments online
15% +5

How to make money in the stock market
15% +4

continued next page

Percentage of Influentials who feel at least "somewhat competent" making financial decision

Deciding how to save money

93% +6

Planning your family's financial future

86% +14

Deciding how to invest money

81% +13

Planning for retirement

79% +11

Buying life insurance

78% +8

Knowing how to buy and sell stocks

53% +21

How to make money in the stock market

50% +17

Making financial transactions, investments online

42% +15

Percentage who feel "not very competent" or "totally at a loss" making financial decision

Making financial transactions, investments online

55% -13

How to make money in the stock market

48% -15

Knowing how to buy and sell stocks

46% -17

Planning for retirement

20% -10

Deciding how to invest money

19% -12

Buying life insurance

18% -10

Planning your family's financial future

12% -12

Deciding how to save money

5% -7

Source: Roper Reports

been cautious, waiting for signs of strength in the stock market . . . it's a different market, which may call for a new strategy . . . guard against inflation . . . make sure you're adequately diversified . . . we can guide you," Prudential Financial says, in one example that invites a conversation. Schwab's plan to grade all listed stocks through a "fact-based" quantification, which was incorporated quickly into its investor ads, practically invites investors to call in or log on to find out their stocks' grades. On the other hand, other ads seem to be more about the company's strategy than the question on the investor's mind, urging investors to consolidate their retirement accounts with the company in tones that border on nagging.

There are other ways to start a conversation with Influentials on money and investing. On a regular basis, we ask where people think the "best places" to have their money are "during the coming year" and where they have their money. Not surprisingly, after the turbulence of 2000–2001, there was more uncertainty in Influentials' reading of the markets. A number of investments went down in their estimation. As of February 2002, there was no clear consensus that any one or two places were best to invest money (something that was the case in the late 1990s, when 401(k)s and IRAs, mutual funds, and stocks all leaped up the list). Just over half of Influentials continued to rate retirement and pension plans as among the best places to have money. Despite the widely covered meltdown of many employees' 401(k)s in the crash of the former high-flier Enron Corporation, Influentials continued to prefer self-directed 401(k) and IRA plans over company-directed traditional pension plans by a wide margin, 48 to 23%. ("Company pensions can fail, too; I prefer to trust myself," an Influential would likely say.) Mutual funds were the next most favored investment, at 36%. Retirement plans, pensions, and mutual funds were down double-digits from 2001, however, and stocks, though still favored by 21%, were down double-digits as well. Uncertainty over corporate prospects and the economy and frustration with low rates appeared to unsettle other investments as well. Only one area showed anything approaching a notable uptick: real estate investments (up 7 to 32%). With interest rates low and home prices holding, to Influentials the climate looked right for buying investment properties (see Figure 4-10).

Figure 4-10. The Best Places to Have Money in 2002?

Percentage of Influential Americans saying in February 2002 that they thought investment was one of "the best" places to have money in the coming year, with percentage-point difference from 2001; the percentage of Influentials who currently have money invested, with percentage point difference from 2001; and "gap" between the percentage of Influentials who consider an investment among the best places to have money and percentage who have money in it

Investment	"Best place"	Point difference from 2001	"Have money in"	Point difference from 2001	"Best" vs. "Have" gap (points)
Retirement/pension plan (net)	54%	-19	63%	-4	-9
401(k), 403(b), IRA, etc.	48%	-14	54%	-3	-6
Traditional pension	23%	-15	29%	-4	-6
Savings account	37%	+2	71%	+1	-34
Mutual funds	36%	-13	34%	-3	+2
Real estate investments	32%	+7	19%	+3	+13
Bank CDs	26%	-6	24%	-5	+2
Bonds (net corporate, muni, U.S.)	25%	-5	14%	-3	+11
Stocks (net U.S., overseas)	21%	-10	29%	–	-8
Cash	17%	-2	22%	+3	-5
U.S. savings bonds	15%	-5	14%	-3	+1
Money market funds	15%	-13	25%	-2	-10
Gold	12%	+1	4%	-1	+8
Annuities	11%	-6	10%	-1	+1
Art, jewelry, collectibles	9%	-2	15%	+2	-6
Cash-value life insurance	9%	-9	17%	-7	-8

Source: Roper Reports

However, as Figure 4-10 shows, the Influentials were not panicking. They weren't making major changes in where they had their money. The results suggest they were still confident in their long-term strategy and would only be making small adjustments to make sure they had money where they thought there would be growth in the coming year.

The gaps between where Influentials had money and what they regarded as the best places to have money suggested that there were opportunities for starting conversations with Influentials about their investments. The study suggested the best opportunities were in real estate (32% said it's one of best places to have money but only 19% had money invested in real estate, a gap of 13 points), bonds (25% considered it one of the best places to have money but only 14% had money in bonds, a gap of 11 points), and gold (12% put it among the "best" but only 4% had money in it, a gap of 8 points). "You've been thinking about making an investment in real estate (or 'bonds' or 'gold')," the conversation might begin. "What advice and information do you need to help you make a decision?"

Starting a dialogue with Influentials is fruitful—and not just because they're more likely to be sought out for an opinion. Influentials are more likely than the average person both to have opinions on what's a good place to invest and to have money in most investments. For example, Influentials were still significantly more likely to have a 401(k), IRA, or other self-directed retirement account than the average American in early 2002 (54 to 32%) and, even in an uncertain investment climate, to consider such plans one of the best places to have money (48 versus 30%). As a result, when someone comes to them with a question about investing (which 35% of Influentials say happens, 20 points higher than in the public as a whole) or they decide to make a recommendation (which 23% have done in the past year, 13 points higher), the Influential is more likely to be able to speak from experience—the kind of quality that builds spirals of influence.

This isn't to say that the average Influential is a Wall Street expert. Some are (like Rick White, who works in the field). The typical Influential stands out not for being *the* expert—their main investment, after all, is a pretty basic one, a 401(k) plan—but that they're *more* expert than the average person. Influentials have different levels of confidence; if you deal with Influentials, be familiar with their subtle distinctions.

Implications for Government and Institutions

The rules about degrees of confidence also apply in government and institutions. Influentials have more confidence in some areas than in others. They don't have *complete* confidence in any one institution in the society. The results suggest that the most effective solutions to Influentials are those that are multilevel, drawing on different levels of government *plus* individual Americans, for example, or the marketplace and technology in combination with groups outside government.

The Influentials' confidence in the nation's political leaders has grown over the past decade, but opinion leaders are nonetheless substantially more likely to express a "fair amount" or "great deal of confidence" in the nation's *business* leaders than in its *political* leaders (75 versus 59% in 2000). Military leaders generate more confidence than either group (81% in 2001), suggesting that in times of conflict, the opinion leaders believe the nation is in good hands.

Scientists, inventors, and technology are held in the highest esteem. When asked which groups have done the most to change society for the better in recent decades, Influentials choose scientists and inventors first hands-down (72%). About half cite business and industry leaders. Large numbers say groups outside government have done the most to change society for the better, particularly environmental groups (54%), women's groups (47%), and religious groups (45%). The responses are recognition, no doubt, of the stimulus these groups have provided to preserve and protect the nation's environment, create equal opportunities for women, and return values to the mainstream discussion, three issues of substantial importance to Influentials. In contrast, only one in three Influentials says government leaders have contributed the most to change society for the better; government leaders may be able to shepherd change, but they're not the society's leading change agents.

Similarly, when asked what they are optimistic about, recent surveys consistently show half of Influentials cite the nation's system of government. A comparable number cite the way the nation chooses its political leaders—not bad considering the debacle of the 2000 presidential election, with its flawed balloting. However, over half cite the nation's economic system, and about two in three are optimistic about technology, specifically "the effect of technology on this society." Other studies have shown basically the same results, for example, that Influentials are generally confident that the political system and government will continue to work but *more* confident that "advances in technology will benefit the average citizen" (see Figure 4-11).

The results suggest that although the opinion leaders have more confidence in government and political leaders than in the dark days of the early 1990s, they have *more* confidence in technology and have considerable confidence in the free-enterprise system. Thus, marketplace solutions likely will continue to be seen as a viable option for a number of problems. Not all problems, though: even when the stock market was booming, Influentials were not enthusiastic about 100% privatization of Social Security, with most favoring giving people only an "option" to invest "some" of their funds in the market, and large numbers opposing the government investing directly in the stock market. Although their confidence in political leaders went up in some other measures as the war on terrorism began, continued skepticism about the credibility of the nation's political leaders suggests that support for political leaders is not unlimited and, as with all kinds of leadership today, needs to continually be re-earned. The *best* solutions to Influentials are probably those that bring it back home—programs that include people on the local level. Given the 10 years of momentum of the self-reliance movement, this is likely to continue to evolve with more partnerships between government, technology, the marketplace, and individuals and community groups in the years to come.

The Age of Autonomy:
SELF-IMPROVEMENT AND LEARNING

A major component of the self-reliant mind-set is learning. By learning more about, say, how to make investments and transactions online, you learn how to make investments for yourself. By learning more about planning for retirement, you learn how to think through the issues that come up as you approach and begin your retirement. And you can share what

Figure 4-11. Where Influentials Have the Most Confidence

Groups that have caused the most change for the better in society in Influentials' view; confidence in leaders (percentage saying they have "great deal of confidence" or "fair amount of confidence"); areas in which Influentials are most likely to be optimistic about future, of 12 areas (average 1997–2001)

Change agents
. . . . 1. Scientists, inventors (72%)
. . . . 2. Environmental groups (54%)
. . . . 3. Business, industry leaders (51%)
. . . . 4. Women's groups (47%)
. . . . 5. Religious groups (45%)

Confidence in leaders
. . . . 1. Military leaders (81%)
. . . . 2. Business leaders (75%)
. . . . 3. Labor leaders (66%)
. . . . 4. Political leaders (59%)

Areas of optimism
. . . . 1. Quality of life in this country (64%)
. . . . 2. Effect of technology on the society (64%)
. . . . 3. Our ability to get along with other countries (55%)
. . . . 4. The institution of marriage and family (54%)
. . . . 5. Soundness of economic system over long run (54%)

Source: Roper Reports

you know with others, which raises your influence with others, information being the currency of the word-of-mouth marketplace.

A key question that marketers should bring to communications with consumers should be "what can the consumer *learn* from this?"

Influentials don't feel a need to know everything about certain subjects. They prefer to entrust major electrical repairs, for example, to someone skilled in that work. Such areas are relatively few and far between, however.

The priority Influentials place on education should be clear by now. There are, however, two points we'd like to make before moving on. The first is that the emphasis that Influentials place on learning is increasingly shared by the public as a whole. The percentage of Americans who believe that "the more college-trained people" the society has "the better the society" has roughly *doubled* since the 1970s, rising from 33% in 1974 to 64% by the late 1990s, a seismic shift (among Influentials, it also doubled, to 60%). The pursuit of pleasure is still Americans' number one leisure time priority, but about half of Americans today say that if they had more leisure time they would spend it "learning more about things" or doing things that would combine learning and fun. Many colleges are reporting increasing adult enrollment; the median age on college campuses has steadily crept upward.

Learning is going on beyond the classroom as well, in reading clubs, church discussion groups, and educational programs like those Sophie Glovier attends, and even television. Almost half of Americans say they watch informational programming fairly often, up from one in three in 1995. More report they watch how-to programs as well (32%, up 12 points from 1995). (Among Influentials, information-oriented television rates even higher; 62% of Influentials, for instance, say they watch informational programming at least occasionally, 16 points higher than in the total public.) Larry Lee, Jr.'s passion for personal finance programs, game shows, and other TV fare from which he can learn something is not an anomaly. This learning orientation could receive more focus as the retirement age population increases and generate further opportunities for entities from colleges to the media to publishers. It also will create opportunities for information resources generally, including consumer product information. Two-thirds of Influentials say they have gone online to do research before making a purchase.

The second point is that, with all this learning, the value of word-of-mouth, person-to-person exchanges of information—"the conversation"—will only *increase* in the years to come. The leading-indicator Influentials are pointing the way. There have been substantial increases from the 1970s in the percentages of Influentials saying that the word of mouth of family is among the best sources of ideas, on decisions from movies to see (up 25 points to 37% since 1977) and new meals to try (up 19 to 44%) to improving the appearance of the home (up 18 to 34%), restaurants to try (up 17 to 43%), and places to visit (up 16 to 42%). Friends, always important, have become more important in a few areas, especially new meals to try (up 17 to 57% since 1997). People outside the normal circle of family and friends are turned to more for ideas and information, particularly on health issues (up 16 to 32% since 1992), on which experts can parse conflicting information. These increases suggest that it's going to be more important than ever to be part of the word-of-mouth conversation. Giving the consumer a new insight or piece of knowledge may be the best way to get there.

PROFILES IN INFLUENCE

David Pendergrass

Being self-reliant doesn't mean everything always turns out the way you want. Sometimes your result isn't what you originally sought. Sometimes you have to persevere. David Pendergrass has learned these lessons. For the past two years, Pendergrass has been part of an effort to launch a charter school in Kansas City, Missouri. Although the school hasn't yet opened its doors, he feels he has had an impact.

As with many Influentials, Pendergrass's path began with going to a meeting. "My wife said, 'Hey, there's a meeting about new kinds of schools. Why don't you go check it out?' " So he went to the library and heard about charter schools. A university instructor and parent of two school-age children living in the heart of Kansas City, a city whose schools have been troubled for years, he found the idea of starting a school intriguing. The charter school movement, which has given rise to 2,300 new schools in the U.S. serving 575,000 students (essentially nontuition-charging private schools within the public school system), was intriguing as well. Pendergrass signed up for a charter school task force to evaluate the idea of starting a school. He plunged into the literature and began drawing up a design for a charter school.

He had always been interested in learning and memory, which were dinner table conversation topics while he was growing up. His parents were educated in the field; his father has an education doctorate and his mother a master's degree. The interest led Pendergrass to graduate study—he has a Ph.D. in biochemistry—and his academic specialty of neuroscience.

The charter school's focus was to be problem-based, interactive learning. Instead of learning, teachers present students with a problem. Students are encouraged to work out the solutions. In resolving problems, students would learn to think for themselves (in effect, be more self-reliant). The focus was in part a response to problems Pendergrass saw in the classroom as a teacher. "Even my medical students, who are some of the brightest students in the state, from some of the best schools, have not had really good critical thinking skills. They weren't challenged to think well. They're good at memorizing, but not critical thinking."

The problem-based focus, he believes, is more consistent with how people really learn. "Like a lot of education designs, the lecture style, where you stand up and lecture while students take notes, doesn't take advantage of how the brain works," he says. In truth, he believes, people "are really scientists" at heart. They learn through the scientific method, testing and refining ideas.

At this point, the project is waiting for funding. In 1999, the first year charter schools were funded by the state, 17 charter schools were approved in Kansas City, the equivalent of 10% of the district's children. Pendergrass had hoped his school would be in the second round, but funding crunches have intervened. No new charter schools have been approved since the first round.

He had hoped to send his own kids to the school. It didn't happen and both are now in college. He feels he has had an effect, however. The district invested $2 million in facilities at the college prep high school his kids attended, in part, he thinks, because of the proposal for the new school. Such is often the case. "A charter school challenges the schools in its district; sometimes they start using their resources better." He'd still like to see the charter school become a reality and has been to the state legislature to lobby. With the tighter economy of the 2000s, this may or may not come to pass.

Meanwhile, as a believer in volunteerism he stays involved in other ways. "It's important to care about yourself and to use that caring for other people." He's on the social ministry committee of his church; the church sponsors a Habitat for Humanity mission in Russia and a shelter for mothers and children. He is active in youth soccer as an administrator and coach.

Pendergrass is optimistic about the prospects for change. "I think we're in a period where a lot of ideas about life and community are in flux, and, consequently, communities are more amenable to change." Partly he thinks the culture is generally more accepting of change, that "change is part of the fabric of life." The success that change has brought to parts of life has also made a difference—from the social movements of recent decades, to the Internet, which "brings people solutions and information quicker than in the past," to the free-enterprise system, which by its nature "supports the concept of change and new solutions."

A Time for Building Up

America's history has arguably been a history of tearing down and building up. Periods when everything is being torn down are followed by periods in which the nation "builds up" and rapidly adopts new ideas, technologies, and processes. The Revolution (tearing down the ties that bound the U.S. to Britain) followed by nation building, the Civil War (destruction) followed by the industrial leap forward of the last half of the nineteenth century, and so on to the present day. Economic turmoil has often cleared the way for subsequent economic leaps forward. Some of the greatest technological innovations of the past 20 years (the first Apple Computer in the mid-1970s and the World Wide Web in the early 1990s among them) were incubated during recessions. No nation in history has been a better laboratory for what the economist E. F. Schumpeter meant when he wrote about the "creative destruction" of capitalism.

The 1970s was probably the beginning of a 20-year cycle of tearing down, not only in the traumatic events they witnessed but, our studies suggest, also the deeper sense of rejection the events instilled in the American people. In those events, though, were also the seeds of change, the turning away from "the establishment" leading to the road for creating a new establishment that would better meet people's needs. It's hard to pinpoint exactly when the building up began: perhaps with the first PC or perhaps President Reagan's pronouncement that "people who talk about an age of limits are really talking about their own limitations, not America's."

What's clear to us is that by the early 1990s, the seed had taken root in the nation's opinion leaders and was spreading into the broader society. Having spent two decades spiraling out of control, America at the beginning of the 2000s was spiraling *into* control. If this period lasts as long as the 20-year period of destruction that preceded it—and our study of Influentials suggests that this is the case—the building up from this decade-old Age of Autonomy may not have run its course yet, despite the recession and turmoil in the stock market of this decade's early years. The question for the immediate future, then, is how self-reliance will grow from here.

CHAPTER 5

The Influential Vision

SEVEN TRENDS FOR THE FUTURE

T HE DINOSAURS in *Jurassic Park* didn't learn how to move on their own. They had to be programmed by the computer animators for Steven Spielberg's science fiction thriller of dinosaur cloning gone massively awry. To figure out how the creatures should move—what it's actually *like* when a seven-ton T. Rex thunders toward you—the animators turned to Leonard Pitt. The Berkeley-based actor used his talents to help the film's animators make the creatures snarl and rumble like their real-life predecessors 65 million years ago.

For those who know Leonard—or "Lenny," as he is often called by friends, befitting the energy and enthusiasm the 60-year-old Pitt brings to his various projects—the assignment was all in a day's work. For most of his life he has been at the edge, where the past, present, and inspiration blur together to create visions of the future, a place Influentials often seem to occupy for the broader culture.

Passionate, creative, and independent minded, Pitt has long gone his own way. In the early 1960s, before Vietnam, campus protests, the rock 'n' roll rebellion, and other events that would shape a generation of Americans (and inspire its artists), he moved to Paris to study with master mime artist Etienne Decroux. He stayed for seven years. Since his return, he has built a reputation as one of the Bay Area's most inventive performers, with a series of one-man shows (*Meantime, Not for Real,* and *2019 Blake*) that have won critical acclaim and toured the U.S. and abroad. He has taken on interesting projects, such as consulting on the films *Jurassic Park* and *Dragonheart.*

He has followed some intriguing detours as well—traveling to Bali for an extended stay to immerse himself in that country's traditional mask theater in the 1970s (elements of which became part of his shows); periodically leaving for months to study and teach abroad (he recently returned from Sweden); cofounding a theater school and theater company; and following his intuition into nontheater projects. He is currently writing a walking guide on the urban transformation of Paris, which he has sold to a French publishing house. He is also working on another book, on Valentine Greatrakes, a seventeenth-century Irish mystic healer.

Leonard Pitt probably reached his broadest audience, though, with a project called *Eco-Rap,* which he neither performed nor wrote. *Eco-Rap* brought together an improbable combination of two prominent themes of contemporary life in the San Francisco Bay Area, environmentalism and rap music, with an ambitious goal: to bridge the gap between two very different communities, raise awareness for environmental problems in the inner city, and encourage inner-city youths to look beyond themselves. In five years, it grew from a moment of inspiration ("Boing! A light went off in my head," as Pitt puts it) to a force for social change that drew thousands of Bay Area residents to rap concerts to hear environmental messages written and performed by urban, mostly African-American youths. *Eco-Rap* became a media hit, attracting coverage from the cable TV news network CNN, the music video channels VH1 and MTV, National Public Radio, and local media and drawing sponsorships from foundations. It made an impact in the community, educating hundreds of kids on environmental threats in their midst and giving them the opportunity to do something about it and gain something for themselves in the process.

With no experience in rap or environmental politics, Pitt admits, "I didn't know what I was getting into." This didn't stop him. "I just followed my nose," he says with a shrug, "and started meeting people in those fields who could help me put it together. It was just sheer intuition, but I knew I had a good idea."

A Window onto the Future

How Leonard Pitt started *Eco-Rap* and, in a larger sense, his entire multi-faceted career is emblematic of how Influentials create change and in doing so help create the future. Moving back and forth between different communities while keeping their eyes open to the world around them, Influentials catch ideas well before they move into the mainstream. Through their sense of priorities—"what matters"—and their ability to engage others in what they care about through their activism and broad social networks, they drive the ideas into the broader culture.

Their orientation toward growth and change inevitably leads Influentials to think more about the future than the average person. This future-mindedness is even present in their daydreams. Four in ten Influentials say they daydream about the future. They are less likely to be preoccupied with "getting rich" than the average person and more likely to be thinking about what's coming next. The process makes Influentials perhaps America's clearest window on the future—"the early majority," what the majority of Americans will be doing in two to five years or more. The subjects that interest them, the projects they're involved with, the activities they're pursuing, and the products they're intrigued by are leading indicators of what is to come for the broader culture.

Influentials have a different vision of the future from that commonly portrayed in contemporary popular culture. Like most people, they think the future will bring severe problems. They are more likely than the average American to see certain issues becoming severe problems in the future, particularly problems related to technology, like privacy and technoterrorism.

The Influentials are not crippled by these problems, however. As elsewhere, problems seem to be spurs for action. Influentials do not seem to share the pessimism of much of contemporary culture, which sees doom, failure, and entropy everywhere—society in decline, life getting worse, conspiracies in every corner, technology running amok, and apocalypse on the horizon—the dark future of science fiction films. Instead, Influentials view the future with the self-reliance, pragmatism, and optimism with which they approach the present. Building on what has been accomplished—the renewed appreciation of the balance of self and community and the integration of new technologies, for example—the society can take further steps forward, "one step at a time," and address the issues before it.

Just as they think they will reach their vision of the American Dream and the Good Life if they keep their focus, the Influentials tend to be confident that many of the problems of the society can be overcome if they are faced squarely and addressed fully. Having spent more time thinking about the future than the average person, Influentials seem to be more comfortable with the future than the average person. Having spent their lives working through problems the future holds, identifying potential solutions for those problems, and leading the way in integrating those solutions into their communities and own lives, they know that problems can be solved.

This combination of interest in the future and confidence about what it holds can be counted on to create further "spirals of influence" for the initiatives, issues, products, and services that the Influentials deem "matter" in creating a better future. It will also create interest in the future generally.

In this chapter we introduce seven trends toward which we believe the Influentials are pointing. These themes have great importance for business, government, the culture, and the society:

1. The Legacies Agenda
2. Global Connections
3. High Pace, High Peace
4. A PC-Centered World
5. Living Longer Stronger
6. No Big Brothers
7. The Limits of Convenience

The Future:
THE LEGACIES AGENDA

Every period has an issue or series of issues that defines it. In America in the 1960s, it was the rise of the civil rights movement, the sexual and cultural revolution of the Baby Boom, and the social and political disruption caused by the Vietnam War. The 1970s saw the disillusionment of Watergate, the energy crises, the Rust Bowl recession, double-digit inflation, and the Iran hostage crisis. The 1980s were marked by the Reagan agenda—"Reaganomics" and "morning in America" on the home front and "Evil Empire" Cold War gamesmanship in foreign affairs. The 1990s saw the surging stock market and economy, the self-reliance movement, and the mainstreaming of new technologies like the Internet.

More than any time since the 1950s, when Sputnik put the Soviets into space before America (spurring a broad-ranging debate over how to ensure the future for the "Baby Boom" generation), the U.S. in the first decades of the twenty-first century will consciously focus on what its *legacy* will be. This time, the focus is the *children* of the Boomers and the subsequent generations that will follow these children. This concentration on what the legacy will be for the *next* generation will be the impetus for major social and political initiatives in the coming years, including ambitious leaps forward to address major problems in the society and the world, reform movements in government and other institutions, and new monuments, public buildings, and parks. The first phase has already begun, on the global stage (in the student protests and government debate on what direction the globalization of the economy should take) and on the local level (new schools, parks, and libraries are being built at a feverish pace).

To some extent, this trend is spurred by demographics. As the U.S. has become more of a middle-aged nation, with a current median age of 35, it's logical that its thoughts are turning more to the next generation. More people are in their parenting years. In the years to come, more people will be grandparents. In addition, there is the twin force of youth. From the "birth dearth" of the early 1970s, when the number of babies born in the U.S. dropped to 3.1 million a year (actually down about 1 million from the peak years of the 1946–1964 Baby Boom), the number of babies being born per year steadily increased to nearly 4 million per year. That "echo boom" is working its way through the society, creating a demand for more schools, parks, and libraries. Among the Influentials, opinion is being set by a segment in the family years.

The nation's political agenda, in turn, has shifted in recent years. As concern about crime—a perennial worry since the 1970s and a major concern in the early to mid-1990s—has receded, the issues that Influentials care most about have been dominated by family. From 1996 to 2001, the critical period in which this new theme of the legacies agenda emerged, three issues consistently placed in the top five of the Influentials' leading concerns: "the quality of public school education," "the breakdown of the family," and the problem of "the way young people think and act," a significant pattern, given the list of two dozen issues with which these concerns compete for attention (see Figure 5-1).

Looking deeper at the data reinforces the strength of the shift. Education was twice the number one issue among the opinion-leader Influentials during this period; five times in the six-year period it was in the top five. The breakdown of the family was the number one issue once and ranked in the top three concerns five times. The behaviors of the nation's youth have been in the top five four times and twice has been among the top three concerns. The year-by-year breakdown is as follows:

1996: Crime and lawlessness, breakdown of the family, wrongdoing by elected government officials, the way young people think and act, the way the courts are run

1997: Crime and lawlessness, the rising cost of health care, the way young people think and act, the quality of public school education, the way the courts are run

1998: Quality of public school education, breakdown of the family, crime and lawlessness, the way the courts are run, the rising cost of health care

1999: Quality of public school education, wrongdoing by elected government officials, breakdown of the family, crime and lawlessness, rising cost of health care

2000: Breakdown of the family, quality of public school education, the way young people think and act, crime and lawlessness, wrongdoing by elected government officials

2001: Crime and lawlessness, quality of public school education, breakdown of the family, the way young people think and act, the rising cost of health care

Other issues beyond the agenda of family and children erupted as major issues for Influentials in this period, for example, "the rising cost of health

Figure 5-1. Trend Lines: Influentials' Leading Concerns, 1996–2001

Percentage of Influentials saying item is one of the two or three issues they personally are most concerned about. Parentheses show responses in the total public during the period

Item	1996	1997	1998	1999	2000	2001
Crime and lawlessness	44%	45%	37%	38%	40%	38%
Quality of public school education	31%	39%	46%	46%	46%	37%
	(23%)	(28%)	(30%)	(30%)	(32%)	(31%)
Breakdown of the family	42%	27%	38%	39%	49%	34%
	(28%)	(31%)	(30%)	(32%)	(35%)	(31%)
Way young people think and act	39%	41%	29%	37%	43%	33%
	(32%)	(34%)	(25%)	(31%)	(34%)	(29%)
Rising cost of health care	24%	42%	33%	38%	33%	33%
	(27%)	(29%)	(29%)	(30%)	(35%)	(31%)
Air/water pollution	17%	16%	23%	28%	22%	31%
	(12%)	(12%)	(16%)	(16%)	(17%)	(17%)
Wrongdoing by elected government officials	41%	33%	31%	44%	37%	28%
	(29%)	(30%)	(25%)	(33%)	(32%)	(28%)
Way courts are run	32%	35%	34%	26%	29%	25%
Relations between racial and ethnic groups	24%	22%	28%	26%	22%	22%
Drug abuse	21%	26%	29%	31%	27%	22%
Fuel/energy shortage	2%	4%	7%	7%	7%	29%
Having enough money to live right, pay bills	22%	27%	26%	16%	16%	17%
Inflation/high prices	16%	21%	13%	11%	13%	17%
Spread of AIDS	10%	13%	9%	18%	10%	16%
Homelessness	11%	18%	14%	12%	16%	14%
Foreign relations	15%	15%	16%	18%	15%	14%
Recession and rising unemployment	18%	8%	5%	2%	3%	12%
Terrorism	*	7%	6%	7%	15%	9%
Reducing the federal deficit	21%	19%	9%	4%	13%	7%
Getting into another war	6%	5%	8%	10%	8%	3%

Source: Roper Reports

*Not asked

care," "wrongdoing by elected government officials" (perhaps reflecting the personal scandals and impeachment process of the Clinton years), and "the way the courts are run." In addition, other issues rose in importance but did not break through to the top. For example, the environment, which has been one of the top concerns at different times in the 1970s and 1980s, grew in importance, with more citing pollution as a problem. After fuel prices jumped, there was a large increase in concern about fuel and energy shortages. After falling to an all-time low, concern about recession and rising unemployment rose as the country tilted into recession.

Meanwhile, some issues have declined in importance, creating openings for the next-generation issues to receive more attention. As the federal deficit receded, concern about the federal deficit dropped 17 percentage points, a major shift. While lunch bucket economic issues such as recession and inflation have tilted back up, they, too, are much lower than during past hard times (in 1983, 52% of Influentials cited recession and rising unemployment as a leading concern, 40 points higher than in 2001; in 1979, 59% of Influentials cited inflation and high prices as a leading concern, 42 points higher than in 2001).

As Figure 5-1 shows, education, the family, and youth have risen in the public as a whole after rising to prominence in Influentials, illustrating how the spiral of influence of the Influentials has been at work.

Having *been* at the top of the agenda for a period of time—and having the demographic momentum of a middle-aged, family-focused population behind it—the evidence points to the legacies agenda remaining the focus in the years to come. As other issues beyond those directly related to "the next generation" become part of the society's consciousness, it likely will be to the extent they are viewed through the prism of the legacies agenda. Even the war on terrorism: it seems many of the opinion leaders believe this is important not so much because it makes the world safe for them but that it makes the world safe for the next generation and those that follow. This future-oriented focus has become part of the rhetoric around the event. Terrorism *did* jump up the list of top concerns in 2002, but significantly, among Influentials, it did not crowd out everything else.

Other forces, meanwhile, will keep the society's attention on next-generation issues. Even with the echo Baby Boom, the compound annual growth rate of the U.S. labor force will be less than 1% in the 2000s and 2010s, less than half the rates of the 1970s and 1980s, reports *BusinessWeek*. With college-educated workers ever more coveted, "school reform may gain even more political currency than it has today," the magazine says.

The next-generation prism means that some initiatives will have an easier time than others in receiving attention and action. Top-to-bottom overhaul of the health care system like that attempted by the Clinton administration will probably have a hard time in this environment. A more focused program on health care for children will have greater odds of success. The same applies to Medicare and Social Security; initiatives should ensure these programs' health when today's children are old. Reform programs need to demonstrate clearly their utility to the next generation. Education, meanwhile, will likely remain an ongoing concern until there's a sense the nation has *gotten it right*.

Environmental issues are poised to receive more attention. Environmental problems rank high among the issues that Influential Americans think will be "a serious problem" that their "children or grandchildren will be facing" in 25–50 years. Of the seven issues at the top of the list that we track regularly, five relate to the environment: "starvation in many parts of the world" (cited by 83%), "congestion of cities and highways" (83%), "severe water pollution" (77%), "severe air pollution" (76%), and "overpopulation" (75%). The dark side of technology, specifically its "intentional misuse" by technological terrorists (cited by 86%) and the "lack of privacy" created by computer databases (82%), occupies the other two slots. These two concerns figure into other issues that large numbers believe will be serious problems for the next generation, including energy shortage (67%) and division between those who understand the new technologies and those who do not (61%). Education will receive continued focus: large numbers foresee illiteracy (57%) and a shortage of workers with the skills and talents demanded by a changing economy (56%) as serious problems.

Other issues can be expected to get more attention as well: 73% of Influentials believe that the spread of crime and violence to all places, a problem that probably reflects the threat of terrorism, will be a serious problem, and 72% think that "divisions between the rich and poor in this country" will be a serious problem. More than half are concerned about diseases

(57% cite AIDS and 67% the rise of a disease other than AIDS), illegal immigration (60%), and racism (56%) as well. On the other hand, only one in three foresee the rise of a new Hitler or Stalin, suggesting that, in the Influentials' view, as education standards rise and the world becomes more connected, the world will steer away from totalitarianism (see Figure 5-2).

Given the Influentials' orientation to addressing problems, it's likely these issues will receive growing attention in the years to come; however, this will probably *not* be in the business-as-usual ways of the past. Given the global mind-set of Influentials, the problems should receive an increasingly global focus. Government can be expected to play a large role; the shift *away* from government of the past two decades appears to have reversed. It's not likely the U.S. will see a return of a big government mind-set, however. Befitting the "new channels" disposition of Influentials, much of the energy and initiatives will likely be outside government, through individuals, community groups, and nonprofits. Business will have a role to play through cause-related marketing and new product development.

Science will be looked to for significant contributions. Influentials by wide majorities have for years favored "continued advances" from science and technology on medical research and environmental problems, such as alternative fuels. This disposition could mean further developments in the controversial area of genetic research, which Influentials, although with mixed feelings, have indicated a willingness to pursue if it can provide cures for otherwise intractable diseases. It's not "onward and upward" for all science and technology. Influentials have been proponents of further advances on other scientific and technological fronts—they're ardent supporters, for example, of space exploration—but they've grown skeptical since the 1970s in some areas, including nuclear power and advanced weapons systems. Still, there are few illusions that solutions will come easily. David Pendergrass, for example, thinks that the kind of catastrophic loss of life that the twentieth century saw could well recur in the new century, perhaps this time through environmental causes. "We seem to have to learn the toughest lessons the hard way," he says. *Green Gauge,* Roper's annual survey of environmental attitudes, has shown there's not a strong sense among Influentials that the society can invent its way out of environmental harm's way through the work of its scientists. With a concerted ef-

Figure 5-2. The Legacy Agenda: Problems Facing the Next Generation

Percentage of Influentials who think issue will be "a serious problem your children or grandchildren will be facing" in 25–50 years

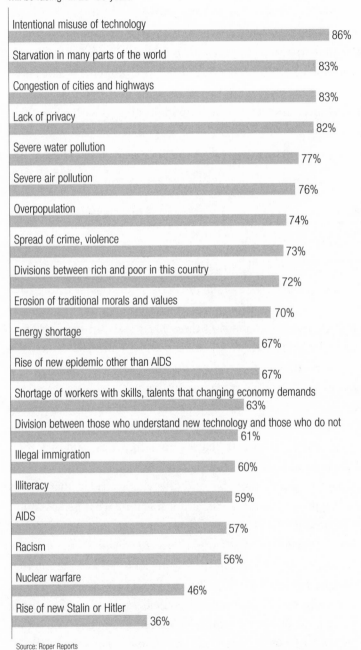

Intentional misuse of technology
86%

Starvation in many parts of the world
83%

Congestion of cities and highways
83%

Lack of privacy
82%

Severe water pollution
77%

Severe air pollution
76%

Overpopulation
74%

Spread of crime, violence
73%

Divisions between rich and poor in this country
72%

Erosion of traditional morals and values
70%

Energy shortage
67%

Rise of new epidemic other than AIDS
67%

Shortage of workers with skills, talents that changing economy demands
63%

Division between those who understand new technology and those who do not
61%

Illegal immigration
60%

Illiteracy
59%

AIDS
57%

Racism
56%

Nuclear warfare
46%

Rise of new Stalin or Hitler
36%

Source: Roper Reports

fort by the different elements of the society, however, the Influentials are confident that progress can be made.

The legacies agenda does not favor a particular party. The family agenda in some ways matches up with conservatives and environmentalism with liberals. Influentials appear to be pragmatists in their agenda for the future, though. The Influential future, like the Influential present, is not about political parties, which often as not have been the problem in recent decades, but about ideas and action—identifying problems and seeing them through to solutions.

PROFILES IN INFLUENCE

Leonard Pitt

Leonard Pitt knows what it's like to get caught up in an idea. Ideas are animating principles in his life—*Eco-Rap*, the Paris guidebook, learning Balinese mask theater, his latest performance project, and, for one several-year period, reading Greek philosophers. At times like these, Pitt says, his life is like "a tunnel" in which he lives "very joyously," with no need to "look to my left or look to my right."

"I wake up in the morning excited about what I'm going to do next. When I go to bed, I can't wait to get up in the morning. It's like discovering a clue that's so compelling, you're pushed to hunt down more." It's not uncommon in these times, he says, to "have a book in my car and pick it up and read it for 30 seconds when I come to a red light."

The best part for him, though—and the characteristic that makes Leonard a prototypical Influential—is communicating what he has found to others. In some ways, he is a twenty-first century version of the preindustrial storytellers who traveled from village to village, conveying the amazing things they have seen and heard—using jet travel and the Internet to tap wisdom and insights from other times and lands.

What Pitt uncovers in his research and travels finds its way to others. Sometimes it becomes a theater production, sometimes a book, and sometimes both. *A Walking Guide to the Transformation of Paris*, his book on how the physical layout of Paris was vastly changed in the nineteenth century, started off as a slide show that he staged for a few dozen audience members in an intimate studio space. He is currently working with the publisher, Parigramme, to turn it into a television documentary.

His passions quickly find their way to his friends as well. A self-described social being and believer in social interaction ("interacting with other human beings is what human beings do best," he avers), Pitt, like most Influentials, is very much a social creature.

He sees about 20 friends on a regular basis, for lunch, dinner, movies, theater, or coffee. Some are in theater or the arts, but many are lawyers, teachers, or businesspeople, a diversity he values. He connects to a wide circle of about 100 people, many outside the U.S., through e-mail.

Friends and acquaintances immediately know when he finds something he likes. "They cannot *not* know about it," he laughs. "I'll talk about it continuously. Or I'll make it into a show or write a book to tell them about it. When I was working on *Eco-Rap,* anybody who bumped into me knew I was doing that. People ask me what I'm doing and I tell them." Pitt's continuous communication loop extends even to small things. "I'll let people know if I've seen a movie I really like. I probably won't send out a special e-mail, but if I'm e-mailing about something else, I'll mention it."

Like many Influentials, he's wired into the era's technology. He usually makes a daily visit to the online auction site eBay. Lately he's been searching for materials for his Paris project. "I've made some fantastic finds," he says, including a two-volume history on the streets of Paris, which normally retails for $125, for $26. He's a great fan of the Web. "It's phenomenal for research. Instead of going to the library and spending hours over books, I'll do a Google search and find the information I need in a few minutes."

Causes in the community are pursued with a similar zeal. Recently Pitt launched a grassroots postcard campaign calling on friends and acquaintances to protest the razing of a downtown bank for "a horrendously ugly" office building. The effort helped secure a change in the design and an agreement to retain the "public nature" of the site by adding a restaurant. A friend once commented that Pitt has an ability to take the disparate subjects in which he is interested and "pull them all together." It's definitely a theme in his work. Many of the projects that have most engaged Pitt have involved taking something familiar and combining it with the unexpected to create a new perspective. The Paris book, for example, plays on little-known photo images of well-known locales in Paris that were taken before Baron Haussman and Napoleon III's nineteenth-century overhaul of the city's architecture. In his theater performances, Pitt often plays a Charlie Chaplin–like everyman caught up in the machinery of modern life, with influences ranging from the exaggerated frowns and smiles of Asian mask theater to contemporary music and the artifacts of modern life from wheelchairs to straitjackets.

Eco-Rap involved a similarly unlikely pairing. If large environmental organizations and communities of color in urban centers have not been exactly at odds, they have often seemed to be parallel universes. Environmental organizations in turn have received flack for being "too white" and focusing on whales, porpoises, dolphins, and redwood forests to the exclusion of inner-city concerns, like lead-based paint, chemical waste, and air pollution. The program was designed to bring the two worlds together, first through "Toxic Tour" bus trips, led by professional environmentalists, which took hundreds of kids from urban neighborhoods through pollution-tainted sites. On their return, they were assigned to create raps based on what they saw and heard. The best were selected to perform at the concerts and given prizes, including studio recording time or, one year, a trip to an international rap festival in Germany.

After all the media coverage and great statistical success, what has stayed with Pitt most are the kids themselves. One teenage girl he especially remembers was close to dropping out when she was sent on the tour to Germany. She told him when she first saw the all-white German kids she felt "so out of it." Then she heard the music come on and realized, "Man, I'm with family." After being taken in and embraced by her peers, she said she "went 5,000 miles to cross the color line." "All this heart came out," Pitt recalls.

Pitt also was changed. He'd gone into the project with an assumption that kids today have an undeservedly bad reputation. "I always believed that, if you have a kid in trouble, if you take whatever interest they have— fly-fishing, boxing, knitting, music—and immerse them in that world, that little part of themselves will lead you to the whole person." His experience bore out the belief. "You would think they would be running, screaming mad on the streets, from the conditions they grow up in, where their chances of survival to adulthood are so small, and being shunted off by the larger culture." Instead, he says, they're "like heat-seeking missiles. Point them in the right direction, and spontaneous intelligence just erupts."

The Future:
GLOBAL CONNECTIONS

For years, observers of the auto industry have said it's almost impossible to say what constitutes an "American" car. The assembly may be in Michigan or Kentucky, but the parts come from Japan, Taiwan, Mexico, Canada, and beyond.

The American lifestyle today is a lot like those cars. It's assembled from influences from around the world, and it will become more so in the future. Between travel, work, the globalization of the marketplace, and the innate curiosity of Influentials and the society beyond in the world, the *globally connected* lifestyle will accelerate at a faster pace than many people appreciate. Attitudes will likely change as well, with more Americans, like the Influentials, becoming globally minded: that is, not trying to Americanize the world but to think in new ways, piecing together *this* from one part of the world and *that* from another to create new kinds of "best of both worlds" solutions. New, global standards may emerge. So far, people in business and government have focused on the "act local" half of the modern mandate to "think global, act local." "Act local" will continue to set the agenda for business and government in their dealings around the world, but there will be more focus on what it really means to "think global."

Leonard Pitt is already thinking that way. His theater work is built on influences from cultures around the world. His travels, both real and "virtual" on the Internet, have brought inspiration for writing projects that in turn have sent him across the globe. He recently returned from a month-long teaching assignment in Stockholm. The architecture book will take him to Paris for several months, he says, especially if it becomes a documentary, "which could lead to . . . who knows?" When he left the U.S. in the 1960s to study in France and spent large chunks of his life abroad since then, it might have looked like he was breaking from the mainstream, but in fact he was leading it. Pitt regards travel as "a necessity." "The world is too big and Berkeley is too small to offer me enough. There are things I can't find here that I need in my life—art, people, lifestyles."

Influentials are pointing toward more such global interaction in the years to come. This is likely to lead to continuing cross-fertilization of ideas, tastes, fashions, reading, popular culture, home furnishings, and even beliefs (as in the recent rise in interest in Buddhism, Jewish mysticism, and Islam in the U.S.). The result will be more of a blended lifestyle and will be reflected in what Influentials think and say, where they travel, the music they listen to, how they furnish their homes, the foods they eat and restaurants they travel to, even the habits they incorporate into their daily routines.

There are many implications for business. For example, it would not surprise Influentials if someday people carried portable language translation software so that they could speak real-time with everyone, regardless of language differences. Indeed, the majority of Influentials think that within 20 years, "language translation software, built into glasses or another device, that enables you to converse with someone who speaks a different language" will be "part of everyday life" in America; 56% think so, 20 points higher than in the total public. Moreover, 41% of Influentials (16 points higher than in the total public) would like to own such a device. Language translation software is one of the technologies that Influentials would most like to have in the future.

Feel like listening to what they're listening to in Paris, London, Dakar, or Hong Kong? In another sign of increasing globalization, more than seven in ten Influentials think car satellite systems that "let you listen to any radio station in the world" will be part of everyday life as well within 20 years, about one in three saying they personally would like to have these systems.

These technologies are not so far-fetched. PC users today can tap the Web to translate letters and papers to other languages on BabelFish.com or www.freetranslation.com. They can listen to live Web feeds from across the world—for example, from African radio stations Radio Tunis, KISS 100 Nairobi Top 40, or Cape Talk radio from Johannesburg. With the wireless

Web and voice capability software, portable language translation and world radio are on track for the future.

Shorter term, there will be opportunities for business. Influentials are pointing toward more global travel by Americans. Their preferences in travel give some clues about what to expect. Experiences, enrichment, quality, and comfort—on a budget—are, in general, the formula for appealing to Influentials. More than anything else, Influentials are drawn to new experiences and activities. Seven in ten say that "eager to see new places and do different things" describes them "completely" in their approach to travel and travel planning. This doesn't mean they're going to be going off into the wilderness to the Andes, Kenya, Costa Rica, or Tibet with each vacation.

Even if it's Club Med or a domestic vacation in the U.S., Influentials tend to seek out engagement in travel. Larry Lee, Jr., for example, made a point of visiting the insurance exchange when he went to the Bahamas. More than four in ten prefer travel that can "enrich" them—as many, in fact, as cite price as a factor. More than one in three say they're "willing to rough it for an interesting trip." As Figure 5-3 shows, Influentials are substantially more likely than the public as a whole to emphasize the themes of new places and experiences (19 points), enrichment (14 points), and willingness to rough it (12 points). In terms of specific types of trips, the results suggest they like a mix: a hiking tour on one trip, and a more relaxing visit on the next trip. Following the crowds, though, is not a priority. Indeed, masses of people are a reason *not* to go to a destination. Going to the "in" places ranks last in their priorities (see Figure 5-3). But they don't give up creature comforts. About half of Influentials place a priority on "comfort and convenience." About half say they "care about quality" and are "willing to pay for it," and a fairly large number "expect good service" when they're on vacation.

They are not jet-setters, but travel abroad is a mainstream experience among Influentials. Foreign travel is worth saving up for (as the study of travel preferences notes, more than one in four Influentials are willing to make financial sacrifices to travel). The broad majority have been outside the U.S. Half have taken a trip abroad in the past three years (about twice the rate of the total public), one in four in the past year (again, about twice

Figure 5-3. Travel Priorities: What Defines Influentials

Percentage of Influentials saying phrase describes their approach to travel and travel planning "completely," with percentage point difference from total public

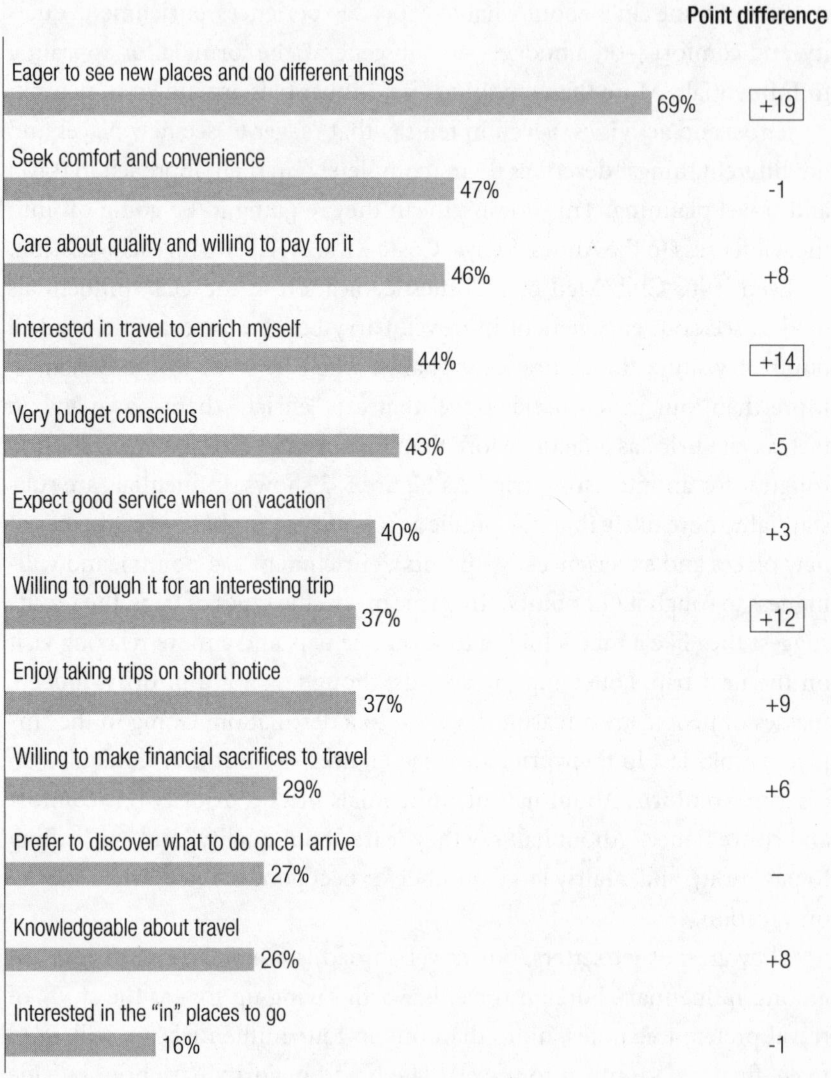

Point difference

Eager to see new places and do different things
69%   +19

Seek comfort and convenience
47%   -1

Care about quality and willing to pay for it
46%   +8

Interested in travel to enrich myself
44%   +14

Very budget conscious
43%   -5

Expect good service when on vacation
40%   +3

Willing to rough it for an interesting trip
37%   +12

Enjoy taking trips on short notice
37%   +9

Willing to make financial sacrifices to travel
29%   +6

Prefer to discover what to do once I arrive
27%   –

Knowledgeable about travel
26%   +8

Interested in the "in" places to go
16%   -1

Source: Roper Reports

the rate), with Canada, Mexico, Europe, and the Caribbean the leading destinations. An adventurous few have been to Asia, the Middle East, and Africa. Such experiences, as we've seen repeatedly, rank high among Influentials' priorities. The result makes travel one of the leading areas for Influential word-of-mouth spirals of influence. Most rate travel as an interest of theirs; 56% say "traveling to see new places" makes life richer and fuller, a response 17 points higher than in the total public—a substantial difference. "Traveling to different places around the world" is their leading daydream, exceeding even thinking about the future, and by a wide margin (67%, 25 points higher than in the total public). Fairly large numbers of Influentials, more than one in three, daydream about *living* in a different part of the world.

Influentials already lead a fairly global lifestyle. They keep up with news around the world. They communicate globally through international phone calls and e-mail. Some, like Leonard Pitt, have personal networks—and influence spirals—that transcend borders. Their taste in cuisine has become increasingly global.

Their consumer preferences reflect a global perspective as well. Influentials helped open the door to the U.S. market for a number of foreign products. They shaped opinion on foreign cars, recognizing their fuel efficiency during the 1970s energy crisis and their reliability as the quality of U.S. cars seemed to be faltering. Their opinion of U.S. cars has improved dramatically, but Influentials still give foreign nameplates the nod in terms of quality (more than seven in ten rating the quality of foreign cars as at least "good," versus two in three for U.S. cars, and one in three "excellent," versus 10% for U.S. cars). Half own a foreign car (versus about four in ten and the total public).

This increasing focus on global connections has implications in public policy as well. Influentials were among the first Americans to see the benefits of having strong connections around the world. As early as 1974, the plurality of Influentials took the position that "the more close ties we have with other countries, the stronger we will be" (46% agreeing, compared with only 11% taking the opposite position that we should "mind our own business"). In contrast, the total public was split evenly between the two positions. Influentials lined up with executives and professionals and the college-educated among the groups most likely to advocate opening up trade with other countries. Influentials were also more favorable than the average toward companies from other countries opening plants in the U.S. In 1974, years before Japanese automakers began manufacturing in the U.S., 60% of Influentials (10 points higher than in the total public) said the U.S. should encourage foreign companies to operate here rather than discourage them. Their reasoning was that foreign investment would mean more jobs for Americans.

Like other Americans, Influentials have often been critical of American business strategies. They have often been strong proponents for restricting imports, a position at variance with the prevailing theory of economists today. At the same time, Influentials saw more clearly than the public as a whole that foreign competition can make American companies sharper; in 1979, 75% of Influentials (10 points higher than in the total public) agreed that refusing to impose trade restrictions would force American manufacturers to "find better ways to make things and bring prices into line." The prescription, although tough, proved on target. American product quality improved, setting the stage for the record expansion of the U.S. economy of later years. By 1988, 75% of Influentials identified themselves as "internationalist" rather than "isolationist" (18 points higher than in the total public; Influentials were on a par with executives as the most internationally minded segment). Before the trade pacts of the 1990s, like NAFTA, Influentials in 1989 were calling for increased trade, not only with such traditional trading partners as Canada, Mexico, and Europe but with other countries as well; 48% called for more trade with the former Soviet Union (18 points higher than the total public). The idea that "the more close ties we have with other countries, the stronger we will be," with which 46% of Influentials agreed in 1973, grew to 60% among Influentials by the end of the 1980s (and, probably in part through their influence, agreement rose to 47% in the total public, up from 30% in 1974). Time will tell whether this era's preference for trade pacts proves successful; trade policy is a political thicket. Still, there is a strong sense among Influentials that economic strength is dependent on global relationships.

Influentials see global connections as key in resolving world conflict as well. The majority believe that it's better for the U.S. to police the world with other nations than to police the world alone or to take the isolationist tack of trying not to get involved at all.

In the end, being globally connected is not a rejection of America to Influentials; it's not "either/or." Nor is it a "new world order" imposed from on high but something on the human level that individuals piece together for themselves. America's ability to absorb new ideas, like its tradition as a melting pot, is seen by Influentials as a source of strength that can help create a better, more stable world—and more enriching lives.

The Future:
HIGH PACE, HIGH PEACE

Most mornings, Leonard Pitt can be found in a quiet café on Shattuck Avenue in downtown Berkeley, sipping a coffee and reading the newspaper. Sometimes a friend or acquaintance drops by and they start a conversation. Other times he just sits and watches the passing parade before he starts his day. It's a habit he picked up when he was living in France in the 1960s. He remains jealously protective of the time and believes it to be "key" to maintaining a sense of well-being through the rest of the day.

A large number of Influentials would agree. They are integrating similar periods into their own days in coffee bars, coffee shops, diners, parks, churches, and other community settings.

It's part of a trend we call High Pace/High Peace. It began in an observation that came out of our research: As the pace of life has picked up, demands for peace have accelerated. On the one hand, Americans began to work harder. More began juggling busy personal schedules and their kids, lessons, practices, and play dates. To some extent it was exhilarating.

Many Americans said their accelerated lifestyle was wearing them down, however: 49% of Americans in 2000 said they didn't have enough leisure time (up from 38% in 1975), with 22% saying they didn't have "nearly enough" leisure time. More were saying they felt stress and tension on a regular basis—half of Americans by 1999, up from four in ten in 1987.

In turn, growing numbers of Americans began carving out "high peace" from life's "high pace," havens where they could get away from it all: vacations, weekend trips, dinners out, spa days, massages, church, yoga and meditation, coffee breaks. Going back to school. All of these—and more—started to rise. Even the long vacation, something many had given up on (you *couldn't* get away from work that long . . . could you?), made a comeback. Between 1997 and 1999, the percentage of Americans saying that, given the choice, they would prefer "one long vacation" jumped 7 points to 28%.

It was like "high-tech high-touch," the observation made by John Naisbitt in his 1982 book *Megatrends* that as technology grew, there was a need for more of the personal touch of relationships. High Pace/High Peace found a similar relationship, but on the issue of *time*. By applying High-Pace/High Peace, allowing themselves to go at a high pace sometimes but stepping on the brakes for "peace" at other times, Americans could get back some control over their time. It's the self-reliant resourcefulness that has become characteristic of Americans, but in a new realm.

The trend has played out on several fronts.

People have begun to push back. It started with placing limits on technology. Americans in effect said that for all the benefits technology has wrought, technology has its limits. It's appropriate in some settings but shouldn't invade all corners of life. One of the first signs was a sea change among Influentials away from booting up their PCs on weekends and evenings to do work that spilled over from the office. The percentage of Influentials saying they used their computers to bring work home from the office peaked in 1996 at 50%. Since then it's slipped to the low to mid-40s. Attitudes have shifted even more. The proportion of Influentials citing the ability to bring home work from the office as "a major reason" to get a home computer plummeted from 68% in 1998 to only 42% in 2001.

People began saying "no" more to work generally. The proportions of Americans saying they "often" spend leisure time getting ready for work rocketed between 1991 and 1998, rising from 13 to 39%, one of the largest behavioral changes of any kind in the public during the period. Then, in 1998, it started falling, and currently it's 33%. There's growing evidence that Americans are rebalancing work and their mental health, what *The Wall Street Journal* calls "undertime," leaving the office for leisure during the day. In many offices, it's become okay to slip out to a child's Little

League game or music recital. Such activities, more workers are saying, are necessary to productivity at work. It's fine for the Internet and cable TV to work 24/7, just not people.

The tug between "speed up" and "slow down" is still strong. One of the surprising findings in our research after the 9/11 terrorist attacks was that the proportion of Americans feeling they didn't have enough time to do what they wanted to do *went up*. The pressure to slow down and appreciate life left many Americans feeling pressured to do more. "We've got to do more to get more out of life—and *now*," Americans seemed to be saying. Influentials, with their work-hard-get-stuff-done temperament and ambitious agendas, are as subject to time stress as anyone. They have been in the forefront of both the swing toward work spilling into leisure and the swing away from working 24/7 in the 1990s. They're highly susceptible to stress. Well over half of Influentials report that they feel stress at least "fairly often," placing them among the more highly stressed segments of the society.

At the same time, Influentials have been at the fore in trying to find "high peace." Influentials are significantly more likely than other Americans to say they do various things to indulge themselves, for example, taking a trip (done by 50%, 24 points higher than in the total public), making a long-distance call to friends or family (done by 48%, 18 points higher), going to an expensive restaurant (41%, 17 higher), going to a movie (40%, 14 higher), buying a book or magazine (40%, 19 higher), eating a special dessert (37%, 17 higher), getting together for a party with friends (36%, 13 higher), going to a concert or show (35%, 19 higher), taking a soak in the tub (35%, 9 higher), buying something for a hobby (30%, 14 higher), and getting a massage (18%, 10 higher).

Travel is especially important. High Pace/High Peace probably goes a long way toward explaining why travel has become so ingrained in the contemporary American lifestyle. A good vacation is a counterbalance to work, overscheduling, and stress. Despite their frustrations with the length of the workday, which sometimes never seems to end, when asked which they would rather have, a "shorter workday" or a "longer vacation," Americans choose "a longer vacation," hands down, according to one of our studies, almost the exact opposite of the response 70 years ago. Restaurants offer a similar haven. A good meal out can be like a minivacation, a chance to get a break from routine and experience something different.

Other high peace zones have begun to infiltrate the landscape. Leonard Pitt's café is one example. Pitt says that in the years he spent in France, he gained an appreciation that slowing down and spending time in cafés is what enables the French to see beauty in life. To him, more than Monet paintings, Provençal-colored linens, or French-designed cookie jars, it's what defines France. The café is a way to meet people or to keep to yourself around people. "The café is a public way of being private, and a private way of being public," he says.

That "public way of being private and private way of being public" is likely to become more integrated into the American lifestyle. There's growing appreciation of front porches and apartment stoops. Like the café, the porch and the stoop can be private or public, a place to interact with neighbors and passersby, read a book, or people-watch.

Flexibility is an important component of the High Pace/High Peace lifestyle. Some spaces, like kitchens and great rooms, already are building in flexibility, through lighting and furnishings. Consumer electronics and technology in the future may have different modes—more complex for when the user is up for the challenge, or simple modes for when the user just wants to watch a movie as quickly and easily as possible.

The flexibility in Influentials' homes—entertainment center or private retreat; learning and office center or social hub—points the way. It used to be that people went out because there wasn't much to do at home. Now, however, when asked about the main advantages of staying home for the evening, a surprisingly large number of Influentials, 31%, say there's a "large variety of entertaining things to do at home."

Some of the "pace" in Americans' lifestyle will probably ease in the years to come. Many Americans are in life's middle years, and midlife is generally the "high-stress" period of life. We typically find that people 30–44 (the median-aged 35-year-old American today is smack in the middle) are substantially more likely than older age segments to say they feel stress and tension at least "fairly often." Currently, a whopping 59% of Americans 30–44 years old tell us they feel stress and tension "fairly often, once or twice a week" or "quite often, almost every day"; the figure drops to 50% among people 45–59 years old, and falls to only 31% among people 60 and older.

Life probably won't slow down *that* much, though. Americans today have ambitious agendas, that educated, ambitious, self-reliant consciousness shift again. They like the Internet, they enjoy zipping off to some new experience, and they want to get more out of life. High pace is not likely to be retired. This tendency already is evidenced in our studies on stress. People 60 and older today may be less stressed than younger folk but they're substantially more likely to say they feel stressed than 60-year-olds 20 years ago.

The High Pace/High Peace mind-set, as it becomes more ingrained in the culture, will serve Americans well as they age, giving them more tools and ideas to shift back and forth from "active" to "relaxed" mode. High peace habits are in evidence in many of the Influentials we've profiled for this book. Isabel Milano meditates every morning. Larry Lee, Jr. makes time to work in his garden. Mike Williams spends the summer in fishing camp with his family. Shelley Miller keeps up family rituals like weekday dinners and weekend trips. Upcoming years will see more Americans developing resources to manage their stress as they try to get more out of life, and more opportunities for business to help them do so.

The Future:
A PC-CENTERED WORLD

Want to watch *Casablanca* tonight? Push a few buttons, and ask the television to retrieve it from the database of movies on the server. Not there? Tell it to go onto the Web and find it. Going to the doctor? Call up the record from last year's checkup from the desktop computer in your home office and port it onto your medical smart card.

Can't remember where the recipe is? Get on the computer and look for it. For that matter, tell the computer what you want to eat tonight. Is the kitchen cooking dinner yet? Someone at the door? Ask the robot to answer it.

Why not? For two decades, the early-majority Influentials have led the integration of new technologies like the personal computer at work and in the home. "The Jetsons"-style future with Rosie the Robot, self-cooking kitchens, home networks, and other technologies are no more unrealistic to them than, say, mobile telephones were in the 1980s.

Our studies of Influentials suggest that rather than fading into the background, the venerable PC is poised to expand its presence in the home in the coming decades. Computer closets may become as pervasive as linen closets in the coming years. With more household "systems" moving online—from kids' homework archives to the family photo collection, movie library, music collection, medical records, financial files, and utilities—it's going to make increasing sense to have a powerful, centrally located computer server that links to the various rooms around the house. Instead of losing ground to new technologies, it's likely that all the non-PC technologies in modern life (personal digital assistants, cell phones, MP3 players, and DVD players) will evolve to become more compatible with the PC, with the PC as the hub. More functions will move onto the PC as well, based on what Influentials say. The shift will, among other things, help people build more High Pace/High Peace flexibility into their lives.

The home computer network could be the starting point for a new generation of products. It already has wide acceptance among Influentials. As shown in Figure 5-4, fully 77% of Influentials expect that within two decades home computer networks will allow people to control household appliances. In addition, 44% would like to have one.

Large numbers of Influentials both expect and want other futuristic technologies as well. More than eight in ten, for example, expect information-rich medical ID cards to be part of everyday life, and 56% want one. Comparable percentages foresee—and want—tiny portable computer monitors that keep track of your health and sound alarms if something's amiss. More than three in four Influentials expect an all-in-one device incorporating the functions of PDAs, cell phones, music players, and Web access, and more than four in ten want one. Half expect computerized kitchens that can whip up meals to be part of everyday life, and about four in ten want one. Comparable percentages of Influentials expect and would like to have a household robot that could perform everyday tasks like cleaning, cooking, and answering the door, as shown in Figures 5-4 and 5-5.

All these technologies could—and should—connect to the home com-

Figure 5-4. Technologies for Everyday Life in 20 Years

Percentage of Influentials who say technology could become "part of everyday American life" in the next 20 years (first bar), and percentage of Influentials who say they personally "would like to own" the technology (second bar), with percentage point differences from the total public

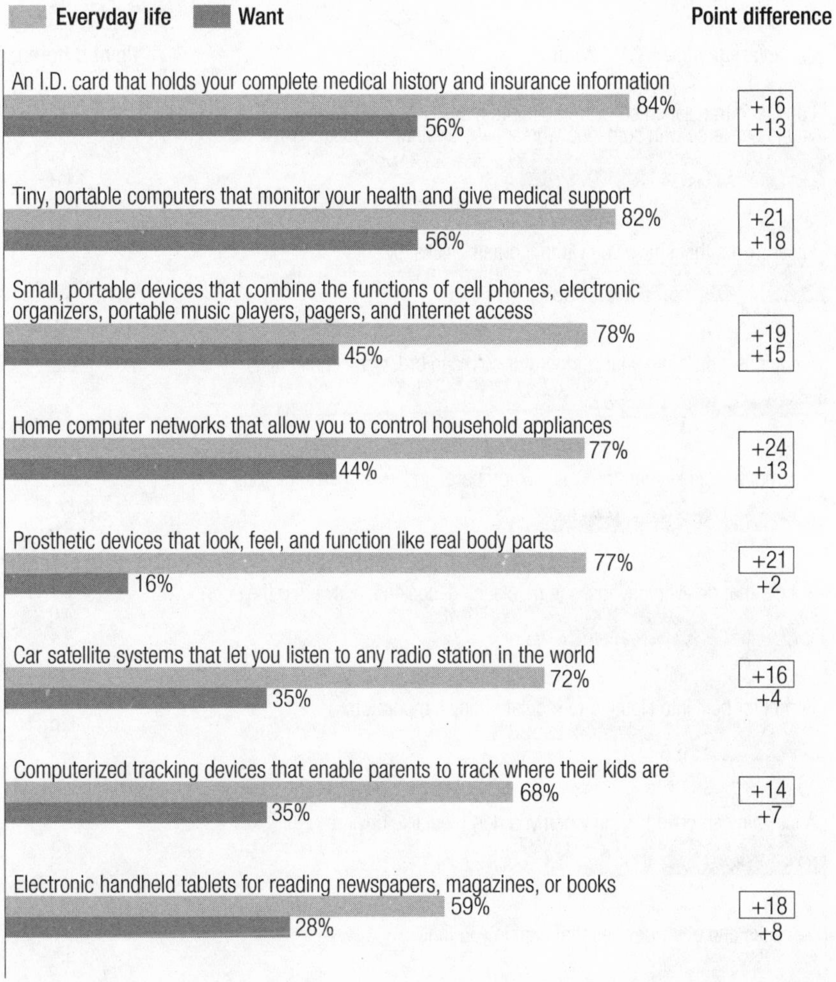

▨ **Everyday life**　▨ **Want**　　　　　　　　　　**Point difference**

An I.D. card that holds your complete medical history and insurance information
84%
56%
+16
+13

Tiny, portable computers that monitor your health and give medical support
82%
56%
+21
+18

Small, portable devices that combine the functions of cell phones, electronic organizers, portable music players, pagers, and Internet access
78%
45%
+19
+15

Home computer networks that allow you to control household appliances
77%
44%
+24
+13

Prosthetic devices that look, feel, and function like real body parts
77%
16%
+21
+2

Car satellite systems that let you listen to any radio station in the world
72%
35%
+16
+4

Computerized tracking devices that enable parents to track where their kids are
68%
35%
+14
+7

Electronic handheld tablets for reading newspapers, magazines, or books
59%
28%
+18
+8

Source: Roper Reports

Figure 5-5. Technologies for Everyday Life in 20 Years (Continued)

Percentage of Influentials who say technology could become "part of everyday American life" in the next 20 years (first bar), and percentage of Influentials who say they personally "would like to own" the technology (second bar), with percentage point differences from the total public

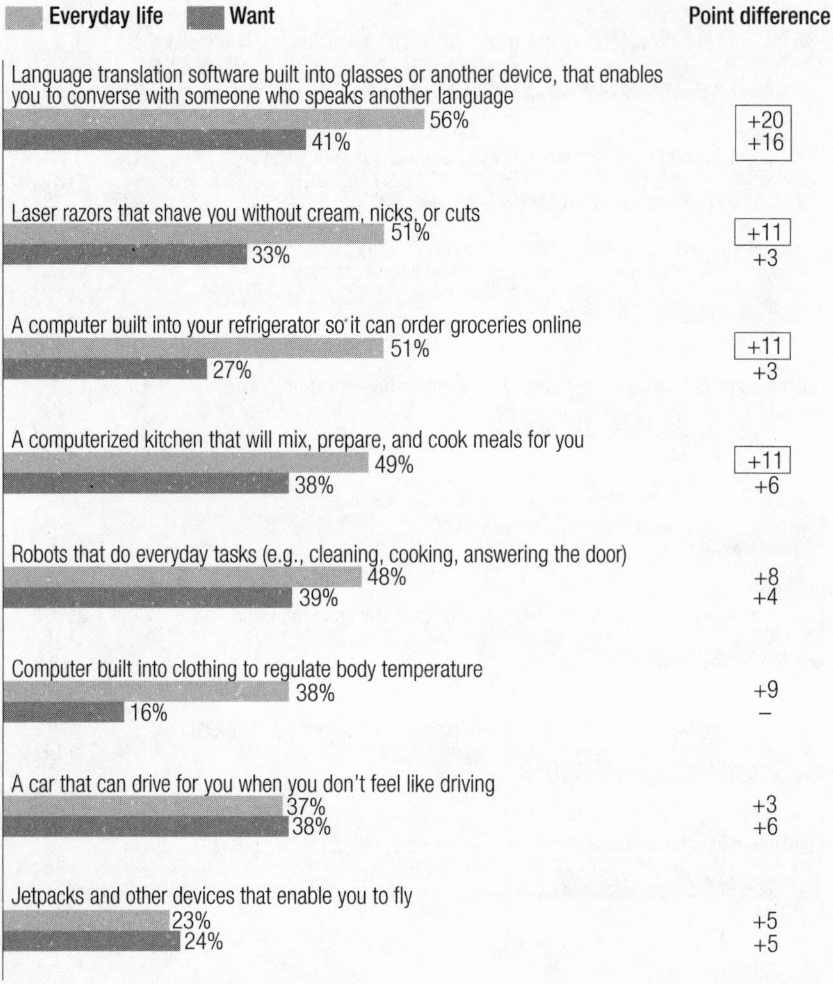

▨ Everyday life ▨ Want		Point difference

Language translation software built into glasses or another device, that enables you to converse with someone who speaks another language
- 56% → +20
- 41% → +16

Laser razors that shave you without cream, nicks, or cuts
- 51% → +11
- 33% → +3

A computer built into your refrigerator so it can order groceries online
- 51% → +11
- 27% → +3

A computerized kitchen that will mix, prepare, and cook meals for you
- 49% → +11
- 38% → +6

Robots that do everyday tasks (e.g., cleaning, cooking, answering the door)
- 48% → +8
- 39% → +4

Computer built into clothing to regulate body temperature
- 38% → +9
- 16% → –

A car that can drive for you when you don't feel like driving
- 37% → +3
- 38% → +6

Jetpacks and other devices that enable you to fly
- 23% → +5
- 24% → +5

Source: Roper Reports

puter network. The medical smart card and health monitor could use the PC to back up data and use the PC to do more complex tasks than hand-held items can handle. Ditto the all-in-one communications-music-organizer-Web device. Music files, for example, could be swapped between the portable player and the archives of the home stereo system. The computerized kitchen and household robot would probably find the home computer network a logical way to hook up, cook dinner, and make sure there are sufficient supplies for tomorrow's fare.

Other studies we have done corroborate the interest in expansion of the computers' home presence, and not just future interest. One in five Influentials say a home computer network is one of the home improvements they'd most like to make now, as many as would like a new roof, new rugs, or a home theater system, according to one study. According to another study, substantial numbers look forward to connecting the TV, stereo, and other electronics to the Internet so they can link to unlimited numbers of TV programs, musical choices, and movies (58%, 8 higher than in the overall public).

Influentials generally have a tech-oriented view of the future. They are concerned that technology will bring problems in the future, such as invasion of privacy, but the opinion leaders also believe it will bring significant advances and improve quality of life.

Even if the specific vision does not come to be, the Influentials' expectations and preferences point the direction this important segment would like technology to take, a road map for R&D for tomorrow's machines. Certain themes come through, in particular the utilitarian Influential bias toward productivity, information, and knowledge, and their desire for efficiency so they can focus on "what matters."

It should be noted that they're not into all technologies. E-books are not particularly desired. Similarly, there's only a lukewarm response to Web-linked refrigerators that order groceries for you (only 27% want them), perhaps, given the importance Influentials give food and cooking as an interest and hobby, because they prefer to shop for food themselves. Only one in four expect or want a jetpack or other device that enables them to fly.

The home network and its related technologies are another matter. This should be good news for the computer industry. The PC is poised to become the "brain" of the modern home in the Influentials' view. It's a logical position. The personal computer is the "jack-of-all-trades" medium, considered useful by large numbers of Influentials for communicating, acquiring news and information, education and training, entertainment, and buying things. It's the Swiss Army knife of media. This flexibility gives the computer room to grow and take on new functions. Computers have proven their utility to Influentials; the consensus is that computers are "a necessity" for work, and a large number feel the same about home PCs. In the end it may be consumer electronics companies that lead the way in home networking (many are already working on systems), but the research suggests that the systems that succeed with Influentials on some level will be "computer-like." With the Influentials' position as early-majority consumers, the conclusion applies to the broader market of consumers as well; they take their cues from Influentials.

Other research on Influentials suggests PCs still have room to grow. There continue to be large gaps between the number of Influentials *using* personal computers for various activities and the numbers of Influentials who say that they or someone in their household are *interested* in using computers for the task. Substantially larger numbers of Influentials express interest in using computers to consult such references as art and medical books and encyclopedias (72%) than have done so (51%), a gap of 21 percentage points or, projected nationally, about 4 million Influentials. Using computers as learning devices for kids, which has built up a sizable number of users, has a comparably large untapped audience as well, as Figure 5-6 shows.

The data suggest that some computer applications could have latent market potential. In bank transactions, there's a 23-point gap between the percentage of Influentials expressing interest (49%) and the percentage who have conducted banking transactions by PC (26%). There's a 21-point gap between the percentage of Influentials who express interest in viewing digital photos and videos (61%) and the percentage who have done so (40%). In filing income taxes, there's a 20-point gap between interest (35%) and use (15%). In personal record keeping, for example, there's an 18-point difference between interest (65%) and use (47%). Not everything

Figure 5-6. Market Gaps:
Comparing Interest and Use of PCs

Percentage of Influentials in 2002 saying they or someone in their household would be interested in using computer for activity, and percentage who do or have done it, with percentage point differences between Influentials and the total public in second column and percentage point "gaps" between Influentials expressing interest and Influentials doing the item in third column

Areas with largest gaps (of 23 items)

▨ Interest   ▧ Do/done

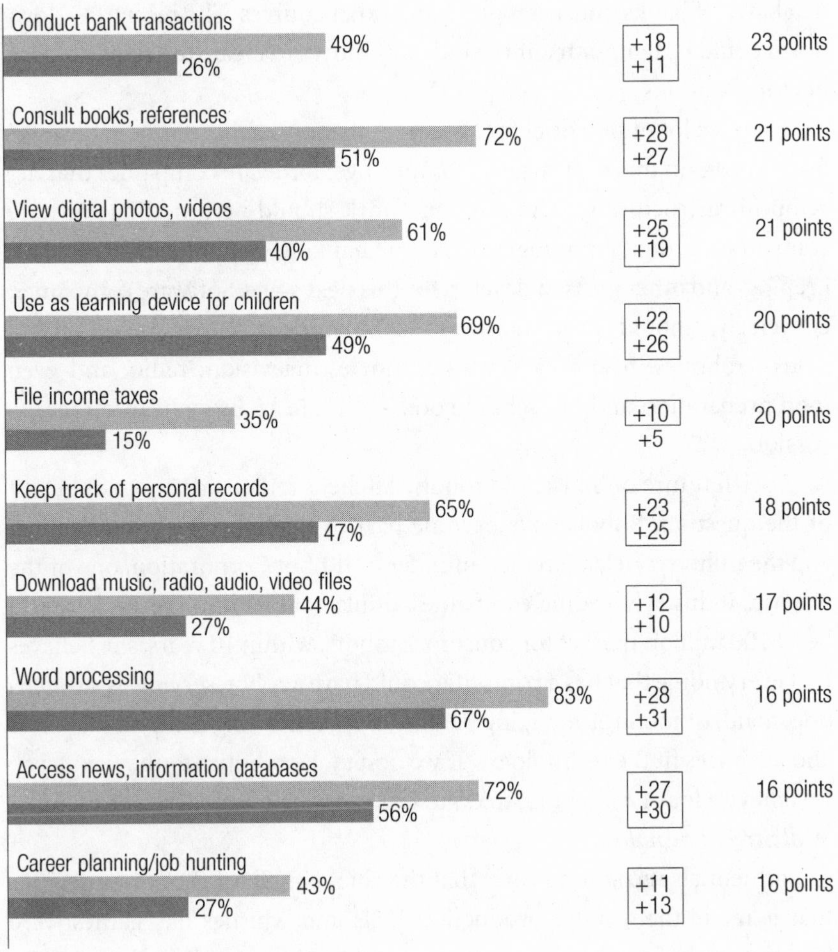

Conduct bank transactions

49%

26%

| +18 |
| +11 |

23 points

Consult books, references

72%

51%

| +28 |
| +27 |

21 points

View digital photos, videos

61%

40%

| +25 |
| +19 |

21 points

Use as learning device for children

69%

49%

| +22 |
| +26 |

20 points

File income taxes

35%

15%

| +10 |

+5

20 points

Keep track of personal records

65%

47%

| +23 |
| +25 |

18 points

Download music, radio, audio, video files

44%

27%

| +12 |
| +10 |

17 points

Word processing

83%

67%

| +28 |
| +31 |

16 points

Access news, information databases

72%

56%

| +27 |
| +30 |

16 points

Career planning/job hunting

43%

27%

| +11 |
| +13 |

16 points

Source: Roper Reports

has large untapped markets; some uses have relatively small gaps, like playing games and e-mail (already done by most Influentials). Some uses, like watching TV on the PC, generate relatively little interest at this point (15% are interested and 8% have done it).

The gaps suggest sizable numbers of Influentials are interested in these uses but have not made the plunge. These areas could be mined for new products and product upgrades, particularly as faster connection speeds make it easier to transfer large files between home PCs and the outside databases of banks, music retailers, and other sources. The recent PC slowdown could be temporary, if the industry moves to create the right kinds of new applications.

There's a lot of potential for synergy—that on-again, off-again business buzz word—in this next stage of computing. Hardware companies that develop infrastructure for the home network should be prodding software companies in digital photography, home banking, tax preparation, record keeping, and other areas to develop for this next stage. Software companies, conversely, should prod hardware companies. Companies in related fields—robotics, health care, music, movies, television, radio, and even food preparation and household goods—should be brought into the discussion.

A sci-fi future of household robotic kitchens and maids may not be out of the question. Robots have become part of manufacturing, oil drilling, and the military. Helen Greiner, founder of iRobot Corporation, one of the robotics industry's leading companies, thinks that within 5 years there will be a $100 million market for consumer robots; within 10 years, she believes that every home that has a computer could have a robot, serving as a watchdog, maid, or monitor for aging parents. Between falling component prices and advances in the technology, "if we don't take robotics to the next level, we'll have a lot of explaining to do to our grandchildren," Greiner told *The Wall Street Journal*.

Influentials recognized early that the chief benefit of the computer was that it made them more productive. Bells and whistles like games were fine, but the main attraction for them was that computers "save time" (76% agree), give them "more control" over their lives (59%), and "simplify life" (59%).

The durability of the computer may come as a surprise to some. Futurists have been predicting its imminent demise and its replacement by PDAs, supervideogame systems, "smart" appliances, and "dumb" terminals that serve primarily as Internet connections, among other things. It's possible that a new technology will rise up and sweep away everything in its path or that the industry will resolve to organize around a new standard, but consumers will have a say in what direction technology takes in the coming years. Influentials will have a *large* say in what happens—and they like the personal computer.

The Future:
LIVING LONGER STRONGER

Seventy-five-year-olds climbing Mount Everest. Seventy-year-olds running 2:40 marathons. Ninety-year-olds atop the best-seller's list. Basketball leagues for over-sixty players. Continuous education for those who want to keep going to school in their mature years. Second, third, and fourth careers for venturous souls for whom retirement is not a goal.

This may be only the beginning. Most of the U.S. population growth in the decades to come will be in its older population. According to U.S. Census Bureau population projections, 44 million of the 56 million–person growth in the U.S. population between the 2000 census and the year 2025 will be 55 years old or older—79% of the growth (see Figure 5-7). While the population refills itself at other levels, with some more growth from the echo boom, the expansion will be in the mature population.

With Americans living longer and advances in health care enabling them to live stronger, the boundaries of old age will not only expand in the next few decades, they'll be shattered, in the Influentials' view. *Carpe agem.* You may be growing older, but you don't have to stop growing.

Already, ideas about what it means to be old are being quietly overhauled. Influentials are pointing the way to four key changes.

"OLD" IS OLDER. The old thinking ("old and in the way," no one wants to see an actress over 40, the future belongs to the young) increasingly seems to be over the hill. The definition of old is already fairly advanced.

Figure 5-7. Future Growth: How the U.S. Population Will Change

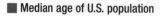

■ Median age of U.S. population

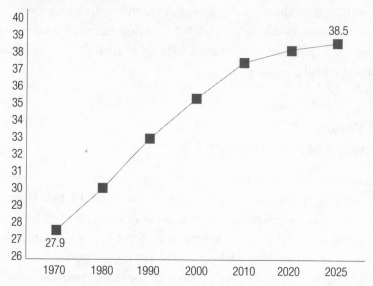

Millions of Americans 55 years and older and total U.S. population

	55+	Total population
2000	59.3	281.4
2010	75.1	299.9
2020	95.8	324.9
2025	102.8	337.8
Net change 2000-2025	+43.5	56.4

Source: U.S. Census Bureau projections

Influentials, for their part, on average think of "old" as 75.6 years, 11 years beyond the Social Security retirement age. Almost one in five Influentials think you're not old until you're 85 or older. It may not be possible to stop the clock, but the Influentials' responses suggest there's going to be more freedom for people to define their age themselves based on what they're doing and how they feel rather than social norms.

GROWING OLDER WILL BE VIEWED MORE FAVORABLY. It's already viewed, on the whole, positively by the opinion leaders. Influentials are in many ways looking forward to the coming years. They view their older years as a time when they'll be able to continue to do things they love—pursuing hobbies, learning, working, and staying connected with family, friends, and the community—while having time for new pursuits.

Influentials are substantially more likely to view aging as a positive experience than a negative one (the total public, in contrast, has mixed feelings). The ideas that Influentials most associate with growing older are "time to enjoy yourself" (65% say so, 23 points higher than in the total public) and "wisdom" (60%, 14 points higher). Large numbers of Influentials also regard it as a time for "being a good role model for young people" (52%, 24 points higher than in the public as a whole), "having time to help others" (41%, 18 points higher), and "closer ties to family" (40%, 13 points higher). Most see beauty in aging and expect to remain useful. Relatively few associate it with "no use to others" (12%) or "unattractive" per se (7%).

They don't think age will be trouble free: four in ten Influentials associate it with declining health and only one in four with financial freedom. More than four in ten are at least somewhat concerned about growing old. However, such worries could spur action to address these problems—either individual action (e.g., exercise and diet) or by business or government.

NEW TECHNOLOGIES WILL MAKE AGING EASIER. Most Influentials see continued advances in science and technology. Combined with the "why not?" mind-set, such advances will propel people to expand the impressive record of the current generation in athletics, the arts, and other endeavors. Influentials expect science to support them in various ways. More than three in four Influentials expect that within 20 years people will carry tiny, portable health monitors that track their body functions and alert them if anything's amiss, and a majority of Influentials would like to own one.

Medical information will be more accessible. More than three in four Influentials expect smart cards containing their complete medical history and insurance information to be part of everyday life in the next 20 years, and the majority would like to have one. This is logical: the technology could speed responses in the event of a medical emergency, even save a life.

THERE WILL BE MORE ACCEPTANCE OF "LOOKING YOUNGER." The old hair-coloring come-on "does she or doesn't she?" is likely to become "who cares?" or, more likely, "why *shouldn't* I?" Influentials have little problem with the idea of doing things to look younger: more than eight in ten Influentials are open to undertaking one or more practices to look younger.

Influentials particularly favor keeping up a regular exercise regimen to look younger (70% are open to it or have already tried it); indeed, more than half have already incorporated exercise into their routine to look younger. However, fairly large numbers are open to other antiaging habits as well, including hair coloring to cover gray hair (35% are open to it or have already tried it), antiaging cosmetics (25% are open to it or have tried it), or sunscreen products to avoid wrinkles (22% are open to it or have tried it). Influentials are substantially more open than the average person to some antiaging ideas, particularly exercise (19 points) and sunscreen products (10 points).

"Looking your age" may become something of a foreign concept if growing numbers follow through on their openness to looking younger. Just as people in their fifties look much younger today than a generation ago, people in their eighties may look like people in their sixties today.

But it's not everything goes. The acceptance of tweaking with appearance will probably not be the boom for cosmetic surgery that some people have predicted. Influentials aren't particularly interested in cosmetic surgery. Only 14% are open to it or have tried it (including a scant 1% who have done it), placing it far down the list of the segment's antiaging regimen.

Similarly, relatively few Influentials want to get too close to technology.

Most expect prosthetic devices that look, feel, and function like real body parts to be increasingly part of everyday life, but fewer than one in five Influentials would personally like to have them. The future of such products will be more a necessity (continued self-reliance) rather than vanity, like colored contact lenses.

SELF-RELIANCE WILL RECEIVE GROWING FOCUS. Beyond advances against the health risks associated with aging, Influentials are pointing toward self-reliance as an area of growing focus. Among Influentials, declining self-reliance is the major problem with aging, more than half citing not being able to take care of yourself (60%, 5 higher than in the total public) and not being mentally alert (56%, 11 higher) than the risk of serious disease (44%, where their level of concern is about the same as the public as a whole).

This is not an unfounded concern. AARP, the Washington-based advocacy group for people 50 and older, shows that Americans 50 and older are living longer and in many ways healthier lives than in the past. The majority of people 50 and older have at least one chronic condition, however, meaning an illness, injury, or impairment lasting three months or longer.

There's reason to want to be healthier. One of the largest breakthroughs in this century, the advance in life span that has added almost three decades to median life since 1900, has also created one of its greatest challenges: how to fill in that time. Each generation has added a little more to the answer and pushed the boundaries further.

Many labor with chronic conditions, but others have expanded the horizons on what's possible in old age. It would not be a surprise if the boundaries widened further. The examples at the top of this section are only projections of the current marks: the oldest living Everest climber was 64-year-old Sherman Bull; the record for the fastest marathon in the 70- to 74-year-old group is 3:00:24, by Ed Whitlock in the London Marathon; Helen Santmeyer, at age 88, *was* the oldest novelist to reach the best-seller list, but Jacques Barzun hit the list in 2000 at age 92 with *From Dawn to Decadence.*

Institutions will probably have to scramble to catch up if the Influentials and other like-minded Americans achieve their goal of active, ever-growing retirement. Social Security will need to undergo redefinition if many people continue to work past 65. Some workers may want new options, for example, to start drawing benefits earlier to reduce their financial risk while they start a new career and in return not draw as much per month after they turn 65.

There will be opportunities for products and services that support more vigorous, engaged lifestyles; replacing the ubiquitous TVs in assisted living centers with computers with Internet ports is a good start.

Agitation over ageism is already on the rise in the workplace. Many employers "are failing to prepare for an aging work force," says *The Wall Street Journal.*

Expect a boom in self-help books and seminars on how to get more out of the older years: "what to expect when you're expecting . . . retirement" to specifics of starting a new career, creating a family charitable foundation, different considerations for athletic training, and outdoor activities as you age.

Many Influentials already have strategies in place. Leonard Pitt, who at 60 is a paragon—performing, writing, teaching, and integrating new ideas—thinks his current lifestyle is "setting up my old age."

The conventional wisdom, like going to the gym, which he does three or four times a week, is part of the strategy. Connecting with others is also a big part. "Being connected to people is crucial to the quality of life I desire," he says. "As I get older, I've realized that, without even trying, you can become more isolated if you're not careful." The consequences, he feels, are as serious a health risk as diseases associated with aging. "Isolation is a debilitating disease that kills people."

He has a simple goal: "I want to be able to go on doing things that excite me, as I've had the good fortune to do the last 40 years." With the changes recent years have brought and that the future will bring, this is not an unreasonable ideal.

Walter Arrowsmith

At age 73, Walter Arrowsmith recently ran for City Council of Lancaster, Ohio. That the former city councilman made the decision to hurl himself back into the public arena at an age traditionally associated with shuffleboard is impressive in itself.

What is more remarkable is that it came 24 months after Arrowsmith thought his life was over. In March 1999 he was diagnosed with prostate cancer. He promptly resigned from the council and other commitments. "I quit everything," he recalls. "I thought the doctor had given me a death certificate. My father died of cancer, and I thought that's just the way it goes."

He underwent chemotherapy and 38 radiation treatments. The cancer receded. In early 2001, his doctor said he was clear to go and "do anything I want." People suggested he run for office, "so that's what I did."

The story had an even better ending: he won the election. This is a fitting second act for the outspoken septuagenarian, who in his continued activism is a model for the kinds of opportunities that will be opened to growing numbers as the population ages.

Arrowsmith's life sounds like something from the pages of a civics textbook. Before retiring, he had been elected five times to the Lancaster City Council, serving continuously since 1973, including a stint as council president. He was previously on Lancaster's school board. He held statewide office for 20 years, as deputy administrator of the Ohio Bureau of Motor Vehicles, a post appointed by the governor.

He has been an active participant in community groups as well. Involved in the Kiwanis Club for 33 years (with 7 years perfect attendance at meetings), he served for a time as lieutenant governor for the district. He has been active almost as long in the local Salvation Army (30 years), including a term as chairman of its advisory board.

He is past president of the Fairfield County Board of Junior Achievement, the national organization that encourages high school students to pursue careers in business. He also has been chairman of the administrative board of Mills Memorial United Brethren Church; first elder of Faith Memorial Church; treasurer of the board of trustees for the local YMCA; chairman of the professional division of the United Way campaign; and an active participant in the local and state Republican Party, Post 11 of the American Legion, and the Lancaster Leathernecks, a civic group made up of retired marines.

Arrowsmith's activism reflects old-fashioned conservative values, nurtured through decades of hard work. He served a tour in the Marine Corps, including time in Korea. He went to college on the GI Bill, earning a BS in engineering from Purdue University, then put in a career in management with the type of heavy industrial companies that were the backbone of the Midwest, a manufacturer of barges, locks, dams, and other gear for commerce on the nation's waterways and a maker of power transmissions.

He cites a combination of factors as influential in his life, starting with his childhood in Trenton, New Jersey and his hardworking, morally firm parents. Barry Goldwater was an early influence on his political thinking. Goldwater's book *Conscience of a Conservative* still strikes a chord, not least because of the late senator's sense of thrift. "Barry Goldwater said when he can afford a Ford, he *drives* a Ford. Not a Cadillac, even if he would rather have it." Have the things you can "afford" and "don't get into debt."

Arrowsmith is a believer in the traditional notion of service. He says he belongs to so many organizations because "I feel I have something I can bring to the organization." He finds satisfaction in "knowing I helped somebody achieve something important to them." Though he does not talk about religion a lot—preferring, in the way typical of his generation, not to wear religion on his sleeve—the idea is based in his Christian faith. He says he made a commitment to Christianity "when I was a high-schooler." For a time he considered a career in the ministry; he graduated from Moody Bible Institute. He wound up not pursuing it, but he retained Christian thinking about service, that "the Lord can use you to reach people" and that "my responsibility is to myself and my family but also to Him and other people."

Although age and cancer have slowed him, he still enjoys "the things I enjoyed 20 years ago, and I've got friends to do things with," he says. "I don't think that because I'm 73, I cease being interested in things that interested me when I was 53." A self-described "sports nut," he is a fan of Ohio State and the Cincinnati Reds, plays a little golf, and goes to high school wrestling tournaments with a friend who is a former wrestling coach.

He attributes his success with his cancer to insights from other people. "There's a great deal of communication that goes on among men about prostate cancer." As word of his diagnosis got around, "total strangers" started calling to share their experiences with different treatments; usually they'd been prompted to call by friends, who'd asked them to "call Walt and tell him how you made out." It was through one such call that Arrowsmith got the suggestion to ask his doctor about a particular drug. The social network also helped him through his radiation treatments; Arrowsmith found a friend who was also having the treatment, and they scheduled their appointments so they could go in together. It helped make the treatment routine, "like an appointment with the barber."

Later, when a family member was diagnosed with prostate cancer, Arrowsmith offered advice and insights, keeping the cycle going; "I was very pleased to share because I felt I was helped."

The Influential interest in learning is evident as well. "I'm 73 but I still need to learn a lot." It was reflected in his run for city council, in particular in his "bowling alley campaign." Like many politicians, he found the "standard technique" of going door to door and "grabbing someone by the hand" falls short in the era of two-income households. During the day, no one's at home. If you come by at night, you run into dinnertime, *Jeopardy*, the evening news, or prime-time TV; "people don't like that."

Acting on a tip he picked up, Arrowsmith decided to go into bowling alleys in his recent campaign for council. Securing permission from the operators of alleys, Arrowsmith, sometimes accompanied by his wife, went into bowling alleys on league night—when people in the bowling-crazy heartland flock to the lanes—and worked the alleys, starting on the first lane and moving down. By the time he'd finished with the forty-eighth lane, the second games were beginning, so he worked his way back down, reaching the second shift of bowlers. On a typical night he pressed the flesh with "more than a thousand" people.

"You have to understand the protocol of bowling," he says. "You don't talk to somebody who's about to pick up a split." Arrowsmith focused his energies on people away from the lanes—spouses, girlfriends, boyfriends, moms, and bowlers waiting for their game to begin. It's also important to clean up campaign brochures before you go, "so you don't leave a mess."

He has taken controversial positions. He was part of a 5:4 council majority to build a shopping mall in Lancaster that paved over cornfields. Most now agree it was worth it. The stores were "a boon" for residents who formerly had to drive 30 miles to Columbus for many shopping trips; they attract shoppers as far away as the Ohio River and have generated revenues for the city.

Like many Midwestern cities, the 40,000-person town is struggling to hang onto jobs in a competitive industrial economy marked by mergers, acquisitions, and downsizings. Arrowsmith says the city is "trying to understand what our strengths and weaknesses are" and how much it can bend on taxes to attract new companies without creating a crisis for government. The city voted a hotel tax to raise money for the chamber of commerce to promote Lancaster. Everyone is trying to "keep our ear to the ground" to hear about companies interested in relocating.

The work may lead him full circle back to schools, where he started out in politics. "A good school system is one of the ways you compete." Lancaster's schools recently produced 15 National Merit Scholarship honorees; Arrowsmith says, "we were very proud of that."

The Future:
NO BIG BROTHERS

The Influential Americans are all too aware of the possibility that the future will be like George Orwell's *1984*, with Big Brother monitoring even the minutest detail of life. They're doing their best, though, to construct a life that resounds with empowerment. Influentials are trying to point the society to a future of "no big brothers"—or at least parity between people and institutions in the currency of information.

Many are applying this mind-set in their dealings in the marketplace already and would like to see it gain further inroads. The results will pose some challenges for business. The self-reliant desire to have autonomy over one's personal information is already bumping up against the relationship marketing goal of many businesses to collect more information on consumers to serve them better.

Although privacy has become a growing agenda item for legislators, regulators, and business, the current debate is probably only the opening phase of the discussion on privacy. "Lack of privacy" is close to the top of the list of the issues that Influential Americans think will be a serious problem in the coming decades. Fully 82% of Influentials think it will be a major concern. Indeed, 77% think "increasing invasions of privacy" are "likely" to happen in the future. Of that 77%, 48% believe the increasing invasions of privacy will pose "a serious threat to our society." That Influentials are more likely than the public to feel acutely about privacy, with 10-point differences on the perception that invasions of privacy are both likely to occur and will be a serious problem in the future, suggests the Influentials are a leading indicator of growing concern in the public.

Many Influentials already see privacy as a significant concern. Almost nine in ten Influentials worry about other people accessing their personal information via the Internet. Some 83% of Influentials (18 points higher than in the total public) have heard of abuses of information, such as someone's financial history or personal history being released without their knowledge or consent. One in five Influentials says it's happened to them, that personal information has been released without their consent.

Their concerns have filtered into their consumer attitudes. Six in ten Influentials cite privacy-related issues as major disadvantages of frequent-shopper clubs, specifically that "companies might sell purchase records to other companies" (cited by 62% of Influentials, 28 points higher than in the total public) and that signing up "gives private information about you to companies" (cited by 58% of Influentials, 25 points higher). Many Influentials belong to a frequent-shopper program (in all, about half have signed up for one) and generally think such programs are a "good idea," but the depth of the privacy concerns suggests that the Influentials are not as enthusiastic about frequent-shopper programs as they would otherwise be. Privacy is a concern online as well, both in terms of possible misuse of their credit cards and companies collecting their purchase behaviors.

Influentials aren't alone in their concerns. Large majorities in the total public also think that privacy will be a serious problem in the decades to come and are worried about the Internet, for example. As early as 1998, 54% of Americans, up from 32% in 1991, said government should make "a major effort" at "seeking ways to protect the privacy of individuals in our society."

The official legislative or regulatory remedy that might come from all this concern is at this point unclear. The majority of Influentials (65%) think people should have control over their personal information and that permission to obtain information should come from individuals rather than computer database firms. This solution will not be the outcome of legislation at least in the near term. Buying and selling consumer information has become big business. The response does serve as a yardstick for the mind-set Influentials bring to the marketplace, however.

In the absence of changes in the law that give them the exclusive power they want over their information, Influentials will be hesitant to get too far into customer relationship programs. In many areas they are already reluctant to put all their eggs in one basket, particularly in terms of their financial assets. In January 2002, four in ten Influentials said they had "made it a point" in the past year to keep their investments and savings in more than one institution. Safekeeping is no doubt a major factor in their thinking. Spreading money around makes it more likely you'll be protected if an institution collapses, an event that, although unfortunate, is not out of the realm of possibility, as shown by the S&L collapse of the 1980s and the blowup of many Enron employees' 401(k)s in 2001. In addition, many Influentials are quick to sever a relationship if they see a better deal. One-third of Influentials in 2002 said that in the past year they had signed up for a new credit card offering them a better deal; slightly more than that said they canceled a credit card. One in six Influentials said they'd switched car insurers. Influentials had higher rates of switching around on these activities than the public as a whole.

The strategy of many financial services firms to become financial supermarkets, which has been driving mergers and acquisitions, including increasing cross-sector combinations that bring together banks and brokerages, for example, faces some problems from the Influentials. In addition to being reluctant to put all their eggs in one basket and being prone to shop around, Influentials also have some ingrained attitudes. For example, relatively few express openness to buying products outside of financial institutions' core product lines. Banks, to most Influentials, are for bank products—checking and savings accounts, auto and personal loans, mortgages, credit cards, CDs, and equity lines. Relatively few would consider buying products from banks outside these core areas. Similarly, relatively few are open to buying products other than mutual funds and money market funds from mutual fund firms. Relatively few would use a brokerage for products beyond stocks and bonds.

This resistance doesn't mean that financial institutions face an impossible challenge. It does, however, mean there's a pretty high bar to clear. A recent custom study by RoperASW for Peppers & Rogers Group, the customer relationship management (CRM) consultancy, on financial services customers, which focused on high-income households, is instructive. The study found that there's about a 50:50 chance of getting consumers to consolidate their assets with one institution—*if* the consumer gives the institution high marks on customer service (the basics, such as not making mistakes) *and* the consumer gives the institution high marks for CRM (being proactive and personal, giving the consumer offers that make sense for them, having a person or team the consumer can call if they have a problem, and knowing the consumer and using that knowledge in a way that serves the consumer well). If an institution clears that bar, the study suggested, the trade-off on privacy can be worth it in benefits. Unfortunately, very few institutions clear the bar. So for most the question at this point is moot. The necessary trust hasn't been established.

Being "sticky" (making it hard for the consumer to switch by building in so many benefits the consumer can't switch) certainly helps. Some financial institutions have achieved this, as have companies in other fields. America Online's primacy in instant messaging is a great example of stickiness; because so many teens were hooked on IM-ing their pals, their families were locked into AOL (there were other reasons—the ease of use of AOL and the comfort of the sheer size of AOL's user base, for example).

Stickiness is only part of the solution. As information becomes more of a currency in the society, new rules will be needed. Seth Godin's permission marketing concept is one model: companies engage the consumer first for permission, then build the relationship. Guaranteeing not to sell or swap information on consumers to other companies is probably only a first step in building trust. It would not be surprising if companies began to allow consumers to review their information, like credit agencies do (or, to use another example, the way Amazon encourages consumers to edit their recommendations in books, music, and other products). Such measures, if done well, could benefit both the company and the consumer; better information would mean more appropriate offers. It could also break down the wall between companies and consumers. In a society likely to be increasingly moving to a "no big brothers" mind-set, the best way to get more business, as our research on financial institutions shows, is to build *trust*, the sense among consumers that you look out for their best interests. Just a brother—not Big Brother.

The Future:
THE LIMITS OF CONVENIENCE

For decades, companies have preached the gospel of convenience, dedicating themselves to making everything faster and more efficient. Consumers generally welcomed it, integrating succeeding generations of products that promised to make their lives move more efficiently—supermarkets and TV dinners in the 1950s, convenience stores and fast food in the 1960s, self-serve gas stations in the 1970s, catalogs and microwaves in the 1980s, ATMs, discount store shopping, and online shopping in recent years.

Our studies of the Influentials suggest that convenience has begun to hit a wall, however. Sometimes convenience is not enough. The trade-offs that convenience demands are not worth it, especially trade-offs in "quality," a value that underlies much of the Influentials' approach to life. At times, Influentials think, it's worth it to take the time and go out to a restaurant instead of eat fast food or takeout, or take the time and go for a longer vacation, or get together in person rather than rely on electronic communication.

Ever faster, ever more efficient products and services, based on what Influentials are telling us, will not be the "automatic" sellers in the future that they often have been in the past. Instead, Influentials point to tastes becoming more selective on convenience, adopting some things, but not others, and in some cases demanding new blends of convenience *plus:* convenience plus better quality.

Such has been increasingly the case with Influentials. Despite being a group with a disproportionately ambitious to-do list, Influential Americans are not as large a market for convenience products and services as one might expect. They are not particularly enamored of fast food. Although two-thirds of Influentials say that they go to fast food restaurants at least sometimes to save time, they are not more likely to hit fast food restaurants than the public as a whole. Only 15% of Influentials do so "often," compared with 23% of the public as a whole, according to our most recent study on timesaving strategies.

Similarly, although the Influentials were among the early leaders in the trend to takeout food—in 1986, half of Influentials said they brought home takeout food at least occasionally to save time—the proportion of Influentials bringing in takeout has not budged much since then. This compares to 60%–70% or more doing home meal replacement at least sometimes in the public as a whole and other time-pressed groups, like executives, people in $75,000-plus households, families, and working women.

Food is one area in which, to Influentials, it's "worth it" to take more time, either by going out to a restaurant (something Influentials are more prone to do than the average on a given night of the week) or cooking something when you have the time. Influentials' tendency not to use eating to save time compared with the public as a whole is also evident in their behavior with microwave meals and frozen prepared foods. Influentials generally avoid eating frozen prepared meals as a time-saving strategy. Many in the group also have an aversion to microwaving their dinner to save time.

Where *do* Influentials save time? The leading response among Influentials, like Americans as a whole, is in postponing household cleaning. Apparently, a little dust is not that important in the grand scheme of things. About seven in ten people among both the opinion leaders and the total public postpone household cleaning chores at least sometimes to buy themselves time. For the majority in both groups, it's more an occasional practice than the routine, with only about one in four saying they clean often.

Influentials are also great proponents of front-loading certain activities to save time during other periods of the week. There's probably some of the High Pace/High Peace mind-set at work here: going at a faster clip sometimes to create time for "peace" in the future. Influentials are major practitioners of bulk buying. Two in three have told us on a consistent basis since the mid-1990s that they "buy in large quantities so [they] don't have to shop so often" at least occasionally to save time, with about one in four doing so often. This is about as many as, say, head to fast food eateries to save time. The strategy has made Influentials fans of discount stores and warehouse clubs.

In a similar vein, about half of Influentials use their commute and other "in-transit" times to multitask phone calls. They are significantly more likely to deploy this cell phone option to save time than the public as a whole, and indeed are among the groups most likely to do so. Some 46% of Influentials do it at least sometimes, up 15 points from 1998. As Larry Lee, Jr., our cell phone early-majority Influential, has found, being able to call from wherever you are helps you structure your day to get more done. Unlike, say, chintzing on dinner, multitasking on the commute time is not a quality of life question. The trend suggests that, as much as cell phones have been integrated into Americans' lifestyle, there's more to come. This is good news for makers of hands-free calling gear for cars—and a heads-up to restaurants and other businesses: "cell phone zones" will likely be increasingly in demand, both by callers and by folks who don't want to be bothered by ringing phones.

Nonstore shopping, which we mentioned previously in our section on e-commerce, is also poised for further integration into the American lifestyle. Influentials are significantly more likely than the average to use catalogs or online shopping to save time, about four in ten telling us since the mid-1990s that they order by phone, computer, or mail instead of going to the store at least sometimes as a timesaving strategy. Going out to stores still has appeal, but you shouldn't have to if you don't want to, in the Influentials' view.

Personal "firewalls" between people and the outside world may be more in demand as well. About four in ten Influentials say they unplug the phone or screen messages at least sometimes to avoid spending time on the phone. (Maybe the household robot will come in handy here; perhaps it can come with built-in answering machines and caller ID.) Some Influentials also hire out yardwork and housework to save time, but not in very large numbers, perhaps because of economics, lack of good services in their area to fill the need, because it's not that big a deal, or—in the case of yardwork—because they enjoy being outdoors and would rather do it themselves. High peace.

The less than uniformly enthusiastic mind-set that Influentials bring to convenience, particularly their disdain for fast food, comes through in other studies we've done. On the scale of contributions to humanity, Influentials rate fast food on a par with pesticides, genetic engineering, and television—more "bad" than "good." Even on a value for the dollar basis, fast food doesn't fare too well with Influentials; only half think it's good value for the dollar. In contrast, two-thirds of Influentials think family-style restaurants are good value for the dollar, and three-fourths say fine restaurants are good value for the dollar, despite the much higher price tags they carry than fast food. This new twist on "value" is one of the factors in "fast casual," higher quality, higher ticket fare like Britain's Pret A Manger (in which McDonald's has become a partner) becoming the growth area in the quick-serve food business.

To Influentials, saving time in the end is about creating time in the areas of life you care most about, like family, friends, food, and travel. You don't scrimp in the areas you're passionate about—like mealtime, with its opportunity to reconnect with family and enjoy fine food. The time-savers to which Influentials gravitate help them create time in the areas that matter. Multitasking phone calls while commuting, buying in bulk, screening calls, or putting off mopping the floor creates time without imposing a sacrifice in an experience they care about.

This distinction is likely to have significant implications for business in the future. The success of discount stores, which make it easy to stock up and shop less often, will continue. The same applies to online and nonstore shopping. There will be further opportunities as well for products and services that enable people to create the kind of firewalls around their time that they achieve by screening phone calls.

At the same time, there should be more opportunities for quality in some areas. Influentials point to further growth for restaurants, from casual restaurants (which 66% of Influentials have patronized in the past month, 15 points higher than in the total public), local fine-dining spots (52%, 18 higher), other locally owned restaurants (47%, 13 higher), and, yes, Starbucks and its progeny in coffee bars and other specialty stores (43% of Influentials have been to one in the past month, 18 points higher than in the total public).

Like the rest of the public, Influentials will still eat fast food; sometimes it's the best choice. They will probably be more selective, however, looking for good burgers and pizza and for more of the kind of food they get at higher-ticket restaurants (Pret A Manger and its ilk, in a sense, are offering this already), casual restaurant-quality food at lower prices and faster turnaround. The Fazoli's chain, for example, has positioned itself as offering Italian food at a quality level normally associated with more expensive eateries but with quick-serve prices and turnaround—a fairly good deal if, say, you want a quick bite before a movie. The chain also offers touches of higher-end experience, like workers coming around regularly offering freshly baked bread sticks to patrons.

There will probably be changes on the homefront as well. It's doubtful that microwave foods will recede—they serve a purpose for too many people—but cooking may work its way back into more schedules. Although cooking has become more of a leisure-time activity in recent years—something to do on weekends when friends are coming over—there are some indications it could creep back into the week with the increasing consciousness about time and the "High Peace" attitude.

Influentials like to cook (45% say it's "very much" an interest of theirs, 17 higher than in the total public); find it entertaining (37% have watched a cooking show on TV in the past month, 11 higher than in the total public); talk about it (49% are asked for advice or opinion on food, 9 higher); and go out of their way for it (more than 10% have ordered food by catalog or over the Internet, more than twice the rate of the total public). Large numbers enjoy cooking, particularly when they're having friends over (57%, 12 higher), on special occasions (56%, 10 higher), and weekend dinners (47%, 12 higher). Though they don't always have time to eat—Influentials are among the Americans most prone to skip breakfast (39% in the past 24 hours, 11 points higher than in the public overall)—they seem to compensate by making time elsewhere in the week to eat and cook well.

In some ways, the Influentials' approach to meals is very European. Perhaps it's been reinforced by the respect Influentials have seen given to mealtimes when they've traveled to Europe. Of course, they give the idea the American twist of technology. Influentials point to continued markets for new gadgets that take out the drudgery, especially outdoor gas grills (owned by 66% of Influentials, 24 points higher than in the total public), but also the occasional time-saver like a bread machine (owned by 31% of Influentials, 12 higher) or a rice cooker (owned by 24%, 10 higher).

In the end, Influentials are bringing "convenience" back to its true meaning. Look up the word in the dictionary, and you see convenience is not simply about being faster and more efficient. The first definition in the dictionary says convenience is "the quality of being suitable to one's comfort, purpose or needs." For "convenience" to continue to grow, it will have to be less about speed and efficiency and more about consumers' *comfort, purpose, and needs.* Here, as elsewhere, Influentials are pointing the way, using technologies, products, and services to get to what they love. In the end, that's what the future should be about.

CHAPTER 6

Developing an Influential Strategy

SIX RULES FOR GETTING INTO THE CONVERSATION

"WHAT'S YOUR INFLUENTIAL STRATEGY?" If you've not asked yourself this question already, you should. To succeed today, you need to connect with the people who are at the center of the conversation. Business, government, and nonprofit organizations need to have Influential strategies just as they need marketing, advertising, public relations, promotion, or Internet strategies.

Specifically, you should make sure you are reaching the decision makers who are influential in others' decisions. You should know where the opinion leaders get *their* ideas—the kinds of publications they read, the programs they watch, the radio stations they listen to, and the Web sites they go to. You should make sure you don't have the door shut when opinion leaders come to you with a complaint or question. You should be out in the community to make sure you're listening to opinion leaders' concerns. You should pay attention to what's happening in opinion leaders' lives, the issues that opinion leaders are reading up on, the problems they are focused on, their short- and long-term goals. Companies should be asking themselves if their products and services, environmental stance, and corporate practices are consonant with opinion leaders' expectations.

What the opinion leaders say and think about companies has more of an impact on what their customers are thinking and doing than companies realize. In the all-important battle for share of mind—that space in the consumer's thinking that holds opinions about products, services, companies, political candidates, solicitations from nonprofit groups, and other issues on which they make decisions—the word-of-mouth recommendations of the opinion leaders get more weight from consumers than traditional media. The opinion leaders' word-of-mouth recommendations and advice increasingly are in competition with the messages from traditional media like television, newspapers, and magazines to be the best sources of ideas and information. Word of mouth is winning.

Companies must be able to respond when they think there are errors in the public's thinking on an issue. The ads you see on the op-ed page of the newspaper on energy, the environment, health care, food safety, and other public policy issues are examples, as are the ads by nonprofit organizations that are often the flip side of the coin on these issues.

Of course, companies often are not in the vortex of a heated national debate. The more common opportunities are entering the conversation of everyday life, discovering common ground with opinion leaders and offering solutions to their problems. Toyota's sponsorship of Mike Williams's Iditarod entry, for example, which helped him solve the problem of financing the race, turned out to be a reciprocal relationship. Williams bought a Toyota truck. It was an easy call, he says. "They make good pickups." The solutions don't have to be as direct as the sponsorship of causes in which Influentials are involved, although cause-marketing campaigns *are* one of the best ways to get Influentials' attention, in the Influentials' view.

Companies can also reach Influentials by speaking to their values. David Pendergrass is also loyal to Toyota, because he has always found its cars to be reliable. As he says, "They're wonderful cars." The major reason Shelley Miller tends to be brand loyal in groceries—her tendency "to find something and stick with it"—is that it gets her in and out quickly so she can focus on more important things, like family and her responsibilities in the community.

There is clear business benefit to winning the favor of opinion leaders. Influentials are not only active in their community. They have an active approach to life. They are connected to nearly twice as many groups as the average American (seven versus four groups). The majority are intellectually engaged in a variety of topics, from news and current events to health and fitness, history, technology, different countries and peoples, art, and cooking, which means they usually have something interesting to say. Influentials are twice as likely as the average person to be turned to for advice and opinion, not only about what's going on in government and politics, but consumer and personal decisions as well, such as where to go on vacation, how to parent teenagers, ways to invest, what cars and computers to buy, and career choices.

With the multiplier effect of Influentials, the result can generate buzz far beyond their proportion in the population. Recall that 54% of Influentials recommended a travel destination in the past year, telling an average of 4.7 persons the last time they found a destination they liked enough to recommend, an aggregate of 53 million recommendations. In our experience, it's not hard for Influentials to think of things to recommend. David Pendergrass's recent recommendations, besides Toyota, range from eBay to National Public Radio's show *Talk of the Nation* to the book *Seven Habits of Highly Successful People* to using the Internet to make long-distance phone calls ("You should try it," he says of the latter. "All you need is a computer and a high-speed connection—which you have to have—a microphone and a set of headphones"). The net effect often swings others' decisions, as we found with Sophie Glovier, who wound up bringing a coterie of new customers to the local organic produce coop and the organic milk delivery service after she took an interest in organic food. Companies that don't take heed of the growing value that the public places on word of mouth risk losing more opinion leaders.

In this chapter, we lay out key points for getting into the conversation of the opinion leaders. Businesses have begun to explore numerous tools for reaching opinion leaders. We ourselves have created several different segments. In partnership with Burson-Marsteller, one of the nation's largest public relations firms, we created a segment called the "e-fluentials" to focus specifically on Internet opinion leaders. The Influential Americans are our main tool, however, with the broadest impact, the deepest archive of research, and the longest trend database.

Like consumers generally, Influentials have different criteria for different purchases. Still, certain themes run through many categories. We see six rules for those who want to listen in on Influentials' consumer decisions:

1. Be where the information is.
2. When critics come knocking, invite them in.
3. Get out into the community.
4. Make it easier—then make it easier still.
5. Know "the exceptions"—and keep up with them.
6. Be a brand, and tell the world.

"Mission Control: We've Got a Problem"

Are Influentials your competition? This is a daunting thought. After all, at 21 million, or about 10% of the adult population of the U.S., there are more Influentials than companies out there. E tu, Mr. and Mrs. America?

The fact is, business, government, and other traditional structures can't control the conversation the way they could in the past. The old command-and-control model of businesses sending out a message to consumers that built companies into huge consumer brands in the early days of television is less effective today, and not just because of the growth in media options like the World Wide Web and cable television. Increasingly, the messages from business, government, and other traditional institutions are being filtered through the word-of-mouth analyses of friends, family, and colleagues. In most categories, consumers place more weight today on what they hear from their word-of-mouth network than what they hear from business and less weight on what they hear from the traditional authority figures.

According to our research, the key period in the change was 1992–1995, the same time, not coincidentally, that people started turning inward and looking more to themselves and their personal networks for solutions to their problems. As elsewhere in American life, a transfer of power seemed to be going on. Just as "individual Americans" appeared to be gaining more power on the political front, consumers were gaining power in the marketplace. Just as government was losing some of the power it had, traditional marketing and media appeared to be losing some of the authority they held over consumers. "Increasingly, Americans say they get their best ideas and information about products and services through word of mouth while fewer turn to media sources," we wrote to clients in 1995 in our analysis of new research showing "world-of-mouth increasingly important" (as our headline put it).

The shift in the balance of power has continued in the years since. Over the following pages are a series of graphics showing the change in a market basket of 12 consumer decisions (see Figures 6-1, 6-2, and 6-3). The figures depict the long-term trend on where Americans say they get the "best" ideas and information for a decision. They point to the growing people power of consumer word of mouth. For all 12 decisions on which we have long-term trend, dating in many cases to 1975, the total percentage of Americans citing "friends," "family," or "other people" among the "two or three best sources of ideas or information" about the item is substantially higher today than at the starting point of the trend.

In most cases, the shifts have been substantial. On decisions about "improving the appearance of your home," the percentage citing word-of-mouth sources of friends, family, and other people has risen 25 points since 1977. On "the relative merits of one make of new car versus another," an integral part of the car-buying process, the percentage of the public placing friends, family, or other people among the best sources of ideas or information climbed 23 points. On travel-related decisions about "places you'd like to visit," the total citing friends, family, or other people among their best sources of ideas or information has jumped 20 percentage points since 1977. On the financial decisions about "ways of saving or investing," the total number of Americans citing friends, family, or other people has increased 17 points. There has been a 44-point increase in Americans citing their word-of-mouth sources for "new meals or dishes you'd like to try"; a 34-point gain in citing word-of-mouth sources among their best for ideas or information about "movies you'd like to see"; a 28-point increase in citing the word of mouth of people on "restaurants you'd like to try"; and a 22-point rise in citing word-of-mouth sources for "clothes you'd like to own or buy." In the four items added in 1992, there have been double-digit increases in the numbers citing word of mouth in their top tier of sources for ideas and information as well: "which brands are best" (up 16 points), "where to find the best buys" (up 19 points), "ways of improving your health" (up 28 points), and "computer equipment to buy" (up 14 points).

The Internet has garnered much attention as a disruptive force (and jus-

Figure 6-1. You Need a People Strategy Today

Percentage of Americans saying "the best sources of ideas or information" are advertising, editorial, or online/Internet sources for various purchase decisions

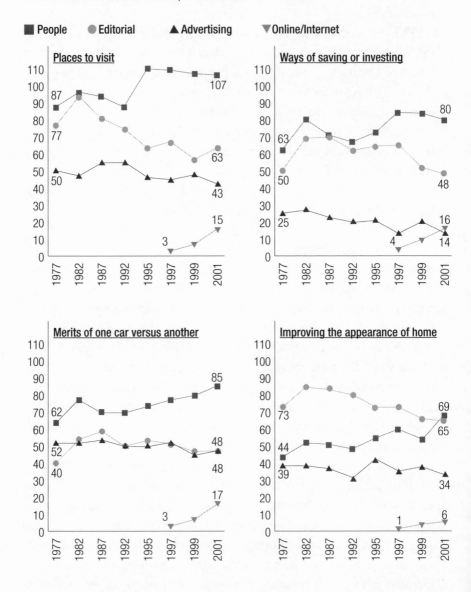

Note: "People" is the aggregate percentage for family, friends, and other people. "Editorial" is the aggregate for newspaper and magazine articles, TV and radio programs, and books. "Advertising" is the aggregate for newspaper and magazine ads and TV and radio commercials. "Online/Internet sources" is a specific item. Studies were all conducted in June or July.

Source: Roper Reports

Figure 6-2. You Need a People Strategy Today (continued)

Percentage of Americans saying "the best sources of ideas or information" are advertising, editorial, or online/Internet sources for various purchase decisions

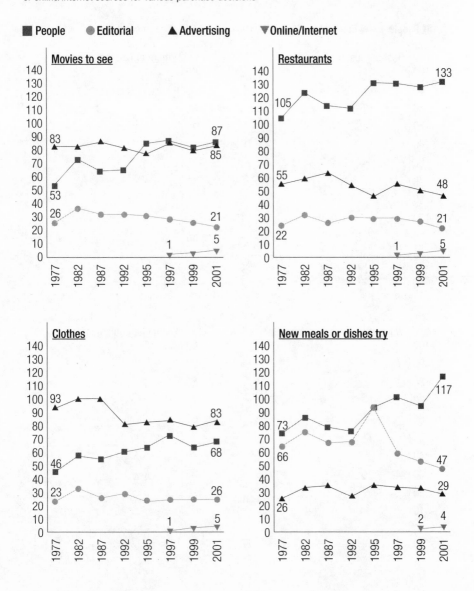

Note: "People" is the aggregate percentage for family, friends, and other people. "Editorial" is the aggregate for newspaper and magazine articles, TV and radio programs, and books. "Advertising" is the aggregate for newspaper and magazine ads and TV and radio commercials. "Online/Internet sources" is a specific item. Studies were all conducted in June or July.

Source: Roper Reports

Figure 6-3. True in Other Categories as Well

Percentage of Americans saying "the best sources of ideas or information" are advertising, editorial, or online/Internet sources for various purchase decisions

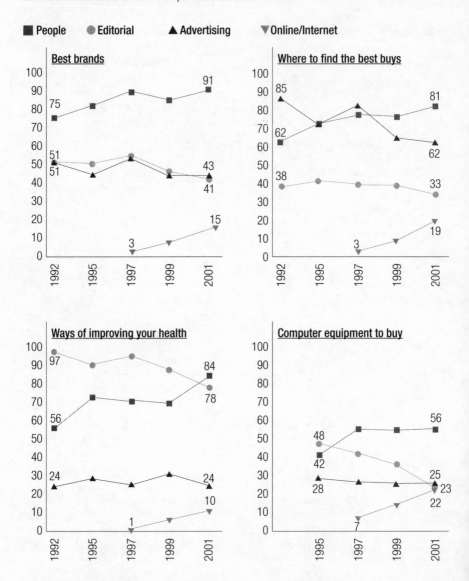

■ People   ● Editorial   ▲ Advertising   ▼ Online/Internet

Note: "People" is the aggregate percentage for family, friends, and other people. "Editorial" is the aggregate for newspaper and magazine articles, TV and radio programs, and books. "Advertising" is the aggregate for newspaper and magazine ads and TV and radio commercials. "Online/Internet sources" is a specific item. Studies were all conducted in June or July.

Source: Roper Reports

tifiably so, given the upward trend in consumers citing online and Internet sources among their best sources of ideas and information), but word of mouth has recorded greater gains. The Internet has made substantial inroads. In computer equipment, where to find the best buys, assessing the relative merits of cars, saving and investing, places to visit, and assessments of which brands are best, 15–22% of the public say online and Internet sources are among their best sources of ideas and information. In certain areas (computer equipment, for example), the Web has become one of the leading sources of ideas. But word of mouth has grown more.

In eight of the market basket of twelve consumer decisions on which we have recorded a long-term trend, consumers rate their word-of-mouth sources substantially higher than the aggregate for advertising (TV, newspaper, magazine, and radio) or editorial (TV programs, radio programs, newspaper articles, magazine articles, and books), as well as the Internet. The gap is especially large in the two food categories, restaurants (for which people have an 85-point edge over advertising, which comes in second) and new meals or dishes to try (for which people have a 70-point edge over editorial, which is rated second). When it comes to eating out or cooking, apparently, word of mouth trumps everything else. Word of mouth also has clear leadership in decisions on which brands are best (with a 48-point advantage over advertising, which edges editorial for second place), cars (with a 37-point advantage over advertising, which edges editorial for second), places to visit (with a 44-point edge over second-ranked editorial), saving and investing (with a 32-point edge over editorial), computer equipment (with a 31- to 34-point edge over advertising, editorial, and online or Internet sources), and where to find the best buys (with a 19-point advantage over number two advertising).

In only one of the twelve categories does a source that is not word of mouth continue to hold a clear advantage with consumers—fashion. Advertising continues to be the most valued source of ideas and information for what clothes Americans should buy, with an aggregate score of 83 to 68% for word of mouth.

(*Note:* We have aggregated the data because no "net" data are available from the period's early years.)

In three categories, word of mouth holds a narrow advantage. It's so close, though, with word of mouth holding a 6-point advantage over editorial sources on ways to improve your health, a 4-point edge over editorial on improving the appearance of your home, and a 2-point edge over advertising on movies, that it's probably fairest to say consumers give them equal weight. Still, that's saying a lot. Americans view their personal networks as authorities equal to magazines, newspapers, books, television, radio, and advertising.

Word of mouth did not always hold this much sway. In 1977, as the figures show, the traditional media were the most trusted source on a number of decisions. Editorial was the clear number one source for ideas and information for Americans on improving the appearance of the home, rather than having equal voice with word of mouth. Advertising ruled fashion tastes by a 2:1 margin over what friends, family, and other people said. What people said was bunched more closely together on the topic of cars with newspaper and magazine articles, broadcast programs, and advertisements. Advertising was the clear front-runner on what movies to see. In saving and investing, editorial was much closer to word of mouth. The pattern pretty much held through the 1980s. Indeed, in some categories, the traditional media outperformed word of mouth. In saving and investing, editorial was neck and neck with word of mouth in 1987.

The changes have been evident in the marketplace. The 1970s and 1980s saw an explosion of new offerings in traditional media to help consumers make decisions. In magazines, it was the era of service journalism, with features on where to find "the best" of everything, from the best buys to the best electronics to the best burgers. As Wall Street entered its first sustained bull market since the 1960s, publications and broadcast outlets expanded their coverage of investing. Many publishers and broadcasters expanded their health coverage, to help consumers weed through medical research, make smarter, more informed decisions, and lead healthier lives. Publishers poured more resources behind titles to guide consumers through decisions about how to spruce up the home and how to get the most out of their vacations. Local television news programs created consumer "action teams" to investigate rip-offs. Book publishers launched myriad new travel guidebooks, self-help health books, do-it-yourself investing guides, movie and video guides, restaurant review books, "dress for success" how-to books, computer manuals, and cookbooks for niches from 15-minute meals to vegetarian diets and ever more refined ethnic cuisine.

Many of those efforts are still being carried out, but they're less noticeable. In turn, the aggregate influence of advertising and editorial is generally down from their peak in the 1980s and early 1990s. In some cases, as the figures show, there have been sharp declines. On places to visit, for example, the aggregate of editorial sources stood at 93% in 1982; today it's down to 63%. In 1987, editorial had an aggregate score of 70% in saving and investing; it's now at 48%. In 1982, editorial had an aggregate score of 75% on new dishes to try; the rating is now 47%. In 1992, advertising scored an aggregate 85% on where to find the best buys; that's now down to 62%.

Traditional media are not down all over. In movies, advertising has remained important, particularly TV advertising (testimony to movie executives who turned Thursday night's television into a major advertising vehicle for promoting the weekend's movies). In addition, in many categories, particular shows, titles, and brands have risen during the period, regardless of the trend in the category as a whole. Oprah Winfrey creates halo effects for seemingly everything she endorses, from self-help therapies to novels. Two thumbs up from Ebert & Roeper on a video or DVD for many people means "rent this movie." A high score in *Consumer Reports* guides many big-ticket purchases. Many publications have circulations much higher today than two decades ago. The aggregate influence of traditional media is more dilute, however. The messages that the media deliver are increasingly *shared* with what people see and hear from their personal networks.

The change is visible in daily life. People don't have to wait for information to come to them. They can take out their cell phones in the aisles of the video store and call their personal experts for a review. They can call people who have gone through the medical problem they're having, swap tips online with friends when they're trying to find the best deal, or call people who have done remodeling projects they're considering. They share what they have learned—as David Pendergrass does with Toyota, *Seven Habits of Highly Effective People,* and Internet telephone calls, Sophie Glovier does with home remodeling projects, Moo Milk Express, online shopping sites, and the produce coop, or Walter Arrowsmith has done for others undergoing cancer therapy.

The key is to reach the people to whom people turn when they need ideas and information.

Six Rules:
1. BE WHERE THE INFORMATION IS

WhisperNumber.com is an example of how word of mouth has changed the flow of information. Founded in 1998 by Paul Hauck and John Scherr, a private investor and market researcher, respectively, the Hillsborough, New Jersey company operates a Web site for investors to submit their expectations for companies' earnings, revenues, and stock offerings. These estimates, along with other financial tools and research ranging from investor sentiment surveys to data mining and tracking of messages on every stock in the four leading Web message boards, often give WhisperNumber.com a more accurate read on the stock market than they could get from traditional sources.

The earnings per share estimates from the "unorthodox" service (as CBS MarketWatch called WhisperNumber.com in a 2002 article) have regularly beaten the consensus of the analysts of the big Wall Street firms. This kind of information has created a buzz for WhisperNumber.com in the financial media, where it has been called an alternative to the Street for investors "fed up with sometimes questionable relationships among analysts, companies, investment bankers, and auditors," as CBS MarketWatch put it in one story. The companies it covers have taken notice as well. PR and investor relations staffs are regularly assigned to track what the site says about their companies. Hauck and Scherr have heard from CEOs that the site's rigorous coverage of companies' stock trends has changed the earnings reporting process and has even altered the timing of executives exercising stock option plans.

For their part, WhisperNumber.com's users don't seem to mind the endorsements but don't appear to need them, either. According to the company's polls of its users, even before the credibility of Wall Street analysts was openly called into question in 2001–2002 by the Enron scandal and the New York attorney general's investigation of conflicts of interest by analysts, 96% of WhisperNumber.com users believed Wall Street analysts could be biased in their stock recommendations. Three in four investors said they thought they were better off making their own investment decisions.

WhisperNumber.com is germane to our discussion for another reason as well. It is a beehive of Influential activity. A study by Roper in partnership with WhisperNumber.com shows that 50% of 800 surveyed Whisper-Number.com members are Influentials—they have performed three or more of the eleven activities to qualify as Influentials, five times the prevalence of Influentials in the total public. WhisperNumber.com's users were particularly likely to have performed Influential activities related to getting their opinions out into the public. For example, they were seven times more likely than the public as a whole to have written an article for publication in the past year. They were six times more likely than the public as a whole to have given a speech. These findings seem to be consistent with a group of investors who believe enough in getting out their opinions on the stock market that they flock to a Web site that serves that purpose.

There's a message for all businesses in WhisperNumber.com's story. Succeeding with Influentials begins with information. A salient, meaningful piece of information is at the very least a conversation starter. It can also—if it's an important piece of information, like the consensus estimate of a company's quarterly earnings from unbiased investors—make the difference in a decision that is critical to Influentials, such as achieving financial independence, which, as we've seen, is the leading financial goal of Influentials.

Getting good information is integral to Influentials' decision process. They value information; businesses that want to get their attention should begin with offering them good, high-quality information. They should also place at least some of it in areas that are oriented to information. Influentials tend to be where the information is. They can be found in numbers disproportionate to their share of the population in media that are rich in information. We've discussed previously Influentials' love of learning (Chapter 1), high readership rates for magazines and newspapers (Chapter

3), and the priority of print sources (Chapter 3). This should be ingrained in your understanding of this segment by this time.

Probing further into the research, though, the importance of information to Influentials comes into even further relief. Although friends, family, and other people are in many categories Influentials' preferred source, information media figure heavily in their thinking on the best places to turn for ideas and information on consumer decisions, as the figures on the subsequent pages show (see Figures 6-4 and 6-5). Four of Influentials' top six sources for ideas and information about places to visit, for example, are information-oriented media: magazine articles, online or Internet sources, newspaper articles, and TV programs. For improving the appearance of the home, magazine articles are the top source of information; newspaper articles and TV programs also figure in their top six. When it comes to ideas and information on health topics, they rate magazine articles, newspaper articles, and TV programs near the top. Magazine articles, newspaper articles, online or Internet sources, and books rank high as sources of ideas and information on ways to save and invest and for retirement planning.

Among the public as a whole, advertising has the edge over editorial in many categories; among Influentials this is rare. Influentials rate TV ads as the leading source for ideas for movies to watch, and they rate TV ads third for ideas and information about videos to rent or buy. TV spots are among the top six sources of ideas and information for some other decisions as well, including Web sites, cars, restaurants, hotels, and prescription drugs. More information-oriented media score more consistently with Influentials, however. Magazine and newspaper articles rank among the top five or six sources almost across the board in our market basket of consumer decisions.

This preference for information is a major theme in Influentials' attitudes to advertising as well. If there's a secret to advertising to Influentials, it is to be creative *and* informative, which does not seem to be an insurmountable goal. Most Influentials think advertisers have a lot of work to do, however. Influentials generally think that advertising has given itself over too much to imagery and short-changes consumers on information critical to making decisions. In particular, Influentials think that advertising doesn't respect their intelligence. Only one-third of Influentials (36%)

Figure 6-4. Where Influentials Get Their *Best Ideas and Information*

Sources that Influential Americans are most likely to say give them their best ideas or information for purchase decision

Places to visit
1. Friends (49%)
2. Family (42%)
3. Magazine articles (34%)
4. Online/Internet sources (20%)
5. Newspaper articles (19%)
6. TV programs (18%)

Cars
1. Family (33%)
2. Friends (32%)
3. Magazine articles (27%)
3. Online/Internet sources (27%)
5. Other people (21%)
6. Newspaper articles (16%)
6. TV commercials (16%)

Ways of improving health
1. Other people (32%)
2. Magazine articles (31%)
3. Family (25%)
4. Newspaper articles (24%)
5. TV programs (21%)
6. Friends (18%)

Web sites
1. Online/Internet sources (34%)
2. Friends (30%)
3. Family (20%)
4. TV commercials (12%)
4. Newspaper articles (12%)
6. Other people (12%)

Saving and investing
1. Family (31%)
2. Online/Internet sources (24%)
3. Magazine articles (23%)
3. Friends (23%)
3. Other people (23%)
6. Newspaper articles (22%)

Retirement planning
1. Family (34%)
1. Other people (34%)
3. Magazine articles (24%)
4. Friends (21%)
4. Books (21%)
6. Online/Internet sources (19%)

Improving home appearance
1. Magazine articles (37%)
2. Family (34%)
3. Friends (21%)
3. Other people (21%)
5. TV programs (15%)
6. Books (14%)

Computer equipment
1. Friends (30%)
2. Online/Internet sources (25%)
3. Family (23%)
4. Magazine articles (18%)
4. Other people (18%)
6. Newspaper articles (12%)

Source: Roper Reports

Figure 6-5. Where Influentials Get Their Best Ideas and Information (continued)

Sources that Influential Americans are most likely to say give them their best ideas or information for purchase decision

Where to find best buys
1. Newspaper ads (35%)
2. Friends (34%)
3. Family (29%)
4. Online/Internet sources (24%)
5. Magazine articles (17%)
5. Newspaper articles (17%)

Which brands are best
1. Friends (36%)
2. Family (31%)
3. Magazine articles (23%)
4. Newspaper articles (20%)
5. Online/Internet sources (16%)
5. Other people (16%)

Restaurants to try
1. Friends (68%)
2. Family (43%)
3. Newspaper articles (19%)
4. Newspaper ads (18%)
5. Other people (16%)
6. TV commercials (13%)
6. Magazine articles (13%)

New meals or dishes to try
1. Friends (57%)
2. Family (44%)
3. Magazine articles (31%)
4. Newspaper articles (14%)
4. Books (14%)
6. TV programs (12%)

Movies to see
1. TV commercials (54%)
2. Friends (43%)
3. Family (37%)
4. Newspaper ads (26%)
5. Newspaper articles (13%)
6. Other people (9%)

Hotels to stay in
1. Friends (52%)
2. Family (38%)
3. Other people (24%)
4. Online/Internet sources (20%)
5. Magazine articles (16%)
6. TV commercials (10%)

Videos to rent
1. Friends (51%)
2. Family (36%)
3. TV commercials (31%)
4. Newspaper articles (15%)
5. Other people (12%)
6. Magazines (10%)

Prescription drugs to use
1. Other people (59%)
2. Family (21%)
3. Friends (11%)
4. Newspaper articles (10%)
5. Magazine articles (9%)
6. TV commercials (7%)
6. Online/Internet sources (7%)

Source: Roper Reports

think that advertising respects the public's intelligence even fairly often, and they are much more critical of advertising in this area than Americans as a whole.

They are critical about advertising's information content—and lack of it—in other ways as well. Most Influentials believe that business is misleading in its presentation of information. Almost eight in ten Influentials think advertising misleads or exaggerates the health benefits of products at least fairly often (78%). In addition, just over seven in ten think it misleads or exaggerates the environmental benefits of products (72%). Six in ten think business is guilty of making "unfair or misleading" comparisons with competing products at least fairly often. A comparable number think businesses try to use subliminal techniques to manipulate consumers. Only half credit business with making "reasonable efforts to make accurate claims" about products in its advertising (see Figure 6-6).

Influentials do give advertisers credit in some areas. They're more likely than the public as a whole to credit business with using online services and the Web to "give more information" about products (64%, 9 points higher). In addition, 63%, about the same as the public as a whole, think advertising usually gives "good, accurate information" about products. On some criticisms, Influentials are also less strong than the public as a whole, but the message that comes through is that business should work harder to give better information. Sophie Glovier seems to speak for most Influentials when she says that information makes "the most effective" advertising. It's almost time to replace her beloved Taurus, and she's finding it a problem to get good information from the ads she sees, particularly on fuel efficiency, passenger compartment size ("it has to be roomy enough for our family"), and new features, like computerized mapping, her friends are telling her about. "Ads with lots of imagery aren't helpful."

Influentials *are* impressed by advertising's creativity. About three in four Influentials think that advertising is creative and entertaining at least fairly often. The blend of ads that are creative *and* informative is rare, however.

Print is the obvious medium for communicating to Influentials, since it accommodates information better than television, but Influentials don't rule out learning something new from TV. Two in three Influentials say they occasionally learn something about products in which they're inter-

Figure 6-6. Advertising Often Falls Short of the Mark

Percentage of influential Americans who say businesses follow practice fairly often or very often in their marketing, with percentage point difference from total public

91%. . . . Set unrealistic standards of beauty through their models   +7

78%. . . . Mislead or exaggerate about health benefits of products   +6

76%. . . . Are creative and entertaining with advertising   -6

74%. . . . Exploit children by convincing them to buy things that are bad for them
or they don't need   –

73%. . . . Target women, minorities, and other groups to buy things that are bad
for them or they don't need   +2

72%. . . . Mislead or exaggerate about environmental benefits of products or packaging   +5

68%. . . . Reduce the amount of product in a package but keep same size package
and charge same price   -3

64%. . . . Use online services or Web to give more information to consumer   +9

63%. . . . Give good, accurate information about products   +1

62%. . . . Advertise in subliminal ways so people will buy products without
realizing hidden ads are affecting their behavior   +1

60%. . . . Make unfair or misleading comparisons to competing brands   -7

57%. . . . Sponsor worthwhile events and activities that benefit the public   +3

55%. . . . Make a real effort to market to minorities and represent them in advertising   -3

55%. . . . Use advertising to promote good causes and social responsibility   -3

53%. . . . Make reasonable efforts to make accurate claims about products   -3

49%. . . . Accurately represent people in my age group   –

44%. . . . Provide positive role models in advertising that portray diverse age,
racial, and lifestyle groups   -13

44%. . . . Use scare tactics to sell products   -4

36%. . . . Respect the public's intelligence   -9

31%. . . . Use advertisements to teach good values to young people and provide
them with quality role models   -11

Source: Roper Reports

ested from TV commercials, and four in ten say that, at least occasionally, they look for information about new products and services when commercials come on.

Over the years we have studied Influentials' preferences in programs and magazines. The information orientation carries over into media strategies. We see this in their own assessments. For example, 72% of Influentials, 8 points higher than in the public as a whole, say they watch "a lot" of news programs on television. In addition, 56% of Influentials say they watch informational shows on nature, history, science, and similar topics, 19 points higher than in the public as a whole. Influentials are also more likely than viewers generally to watch a significant amount of cultural programming (19%, 7 higher). Substantial numbers of Influentials say they watch many other kinds of shows as well, including movies (53%), sports (43%), dramas (39%), comedies (37%), and magazine or discussion shows (35%). But they are often less likely than the public generally to watch these kinds of shows. Thus, advertising on the top-rated comedy shows will probably sweep up a number of Influentials, similar to advertising on *I Love Lucy* or *Gunsmoke* in decades past, but advertisers will get higher concentrations of Influentials in informational programs.

Probably not surprisingly, given these preferences, public television gets high marks from Influentials. They generally describe public television with positive adjectives. Half or more of Influentials think public TV is "educational," "interesting," and "informative." Influentials are also more likely than the public as a whole to rate public TV as "generally good," "important," "stimulative," and "imaginative." Cable television, with its sheer variety of programming, captures some of those qualities as well. Influentials are substantially more likely than the public generally to consider cable as "educational." The variety is also its drawback to Influentials, however, who are also more likely to feel cable is "in bad taste" and "getting worse." Regular network TV fares worse, as a rule. Influentials are more likely than the public generally to feel it's "getting worse" and "dull," for example. Here, too, there is room to capture their interest, with more sophisticated fare, documentaries or other kinds of programs from which they can learn, or simply quality programs to relax by. After the negatives of getting worse and dull, the descriptions Influentials are most likely to use for regular TV are "educational," "relaxing," "generally good," and "interesting" (see Figure 6-7).

Particularly prized are media that are both entertaining and informative. We were tracking the trend to "infotainment" by 1994. We wrote to clients five years later that "already one of the major trends in media, the convergence of information and entertainment just keeps getting stronger," growing numbers of Americans seeking both information and entertainment in media, particularly online services and the Internet (in which 65% wanted both, up 16 points from 1997), but also television (62%, up 8), newspapers (60%, up 8), magazines (58%, up 6), books (50%, up 9), and radio (44%, up 8). Influentials' preference for information and entertainment has been, if anything, a little stronger than that of readers, viewers, and users generally.

The increased desire for both information and entertainment will probably mean growing markets for talk shows, historical programs, and documentaries that package information in engaging ways. Although "infotainment" has taken on pejorative connotations for some producers, conjuring up images of slugfest-packed talk shows, there's been a higher-end, Influential parallel. PBS, cable channels like the Discovery channel, CNBC, and the History Channel have made inroads here, segmenting off interest areas of Influentials like science and technology, investing, history, and culture and bringing higher production values and intellectual content—think Ken and Ric Burns's series on the Civil War, jazz, and New York City. Producers should be looking for new areas to mine, from unexplored topics in these interest areas to new subjects (retirement lifestyles, with the "growing longer stronger" trend, for example).

The increasing pressure to get to information quickly, long term, should lead to a rethinking of advertising. Growing impatience with advertising— for example, using the remote control to evade ads—suggests that marketers need to make sure consumers can get to information when they want it but not be waylaid when they don't want it. Single sponsorship of valuable advertising territory can achieve this end, giving more flexibility to advertisers in how and when they run their ads. As technology advances it's likely there will be opportunities to create deeper advertising resources, such as commercial channels that offer advertising but also access to Inter-

Figure 6-7. Information Ranks High in TV Preferences

Adjectives influentials most associate with public, cable, and regular television, from list of descriptive words and phrases, with percentage point difference from total public. Percentage saying they watch "a lot" of type of program, with difference from public

Cable television

65%. . . .	Lots of variety	+15
56%. . . .	Interesting	+8
52%. . . .	Educational	+22
52%. . . .	Informative	+19
43%. . . .	Generally good	+7
30%. . . .	In bad taste	+19
28%. . . .	Relaxing	+4
24%. . . .	Getting worse	+11
22%. . . .	Getting better	+5
21%. . . .	Imaginative	+5
21%. . . .	Stimulating	+5

Regular television

36%. . . .	Getting worse	+17
33%. . . .	Dull	+15
26%. . . .	Educational	+8
26%. . . .	Relaxing	+7
26%. . . .	Generally good	-4
25%. . . .	Interesting	-3
24%. . . .	All the same	+6
24%. . . .	Informative	–
24%. . . .	In bad taste	+14
22%. . . .	Uninteresting	+12
19%. . . .	Lots of variety	-2

Public television

68%. . . .	Educational	+6
51%. . . .	Interesting	+13
50%. . . .	Informative	+12
40%. . . .	Generally good	+14
33%. . . .	Important	+13
33%. . . .	Stimulating	+17
28%. . . .	Imaginative	+12
25%. . . .	Serious	+11
21%. . . .	Getting better	+3
20%. . . .	Relaxing	+7
20%. . . .	Lots of variety	+7

What they watch

72%. . . .	News programs	+8
56%. . . .	Informational shows	+19
53%. . . .	Movies	-14
43%. . . .	Sports events	-1
39%. . . .	Drama series	-1
37%. . . .	Comedy shows	-11
35%. . . .	Magazine/discussion shows	+1
32%. . . .	Game shows	-1
22%. . . .	Variety shows	-3
21%. . . .	Reality shows	–
19%. . . .	Cultural programs	+7

Source: Roper Reports

net-style databases of information for viewers who want to go further (in addition to enabling advertisers to target messages more precisely to consumers who are in the market for the product). Since the mid-1990s, we've been seeing a shift to "self-serve marketing" by consumers, with consumers actively seeking out information on products and services when they're in the market but tuning it out at other times. Technology is making it easier to make marketing self-service and should continue to create opportunities into the future.

There will be opportunities as well to make it easier for Influentials to obtain and exchange information generally. *Consumer Reports*'s most valuable property, for example, may be the online archive of its reviews, available to users when they want it. The high ratings that Influentials give to "other people" on health issues suggest that there could be a particular opportunity for bulletin boards that can connect users to professional experts, such as specialists on specific medical issues (oncology, for example), who are not normally accessible to the public.

It's key for Influentials to be in control of when and where they get information. They are easily alienated by interruptions. Fully nine in ten Influentials say that they "don't like" telemarketing calls. Indeed, 71% consider telemarketing phone calls to be "a real annoyance," even more than sitting next to a smoker (regarded as a real annoyance by 51%), neighbors not controlling their barking dogs (38%), or cell phones going off in public (19%).

The "better information" lesson applies to public policy as well. Based on what we see in Influentials, we anticipate a growing call to make it easier to get information from government—and for government to make information a greater part of policy solutions. The increasing ease with which one can get information from the Internal Revenue Service is one of the factors in its growing approval ratings. It's seems like a no-brainer to make investor education an increasing component of company 401(k) plans—especially after the debacle at Enron, where many employees bet heavily on company stock and saw their retirement funds go up in smoke. Requiring annual seminars to teach the basics of investment to employees could help prevent further such occurrences. Information, to Influentials, is the starting point for the best solutions.

Six Rules:
2. WHEN CRITICS COME KNOCKING, INVITE THEM IN

For several years now, Leonard Pitt has been waging a one-person campaign, "trying to coax, cajole and shame" the companies from which he buys products online and through catalogs "into using biodegradable material instead of repulsive plastic foam peanuts." He's written letters, banged out e-mails, and had extended phone conversations with customer service reps, and he's stopped buying from companies that don't listen. He's told all of his friends not to buy from these companies, either. With all that he has on his plate, he admits, he doesn't really have the time for this. "But after I receive a package with it, it just sticks in my craw," he says, "and I have a low-stuck-craw tolerance."

Pitt is not alone in his low-stuck-craw tolerance. At any given time, large numbers of Influentials are carrying around a complaint of some sort against a company. According to one Roper study, fully 40% of Influentials report that they had a problem with a product or service in the past three months. That's 8.4 million Influentials with a consumer complaint. The percentage is substantially higher than the percentage of the total public who have had a problem with a product or service (24%). The prevalence of complaints among Influentials means Influentials make up a disproportionate share of people with a complaint at any given time—17%, not quite double their 10% share of the population.

Influentials make up an even larger proportion of those who do something about their complaint. True to form, Influentials' activism swings into gear when they have a problem. The result suggests that when someone comes to you about a problem or service, there's a good chance he's an Influential.

Virtually all of the Influentials who have had a problem with a product or service in the past three months went on to do something about it. Most of the Influentials who had a complaint took more than one action. The recourse taken most was to complain in person to the business from which they bought the product (23% of an Influentials in the past three months). Substantial numbers of Influentials also report that they wrote or called the place from which they bought the product or service after having a problem (18%), returned the product to the place of purchase (17%), or complained to the manager of the store, restaurant, or other establishment that gave them poor service (16%). Many also told friends and relatives *not* to buy the product or service (15%). Comparable numbers stopped buying the product or service themselves (14%).

Some Influentials (between 2 and 11%) wrote or phoned the manufacturer or corporate headquarters, sent the company an e-mail or registered a complaint at the company's Web site, contacted a consumer protection agency, stopped payment on a check or refused to make payment, returned the product to the manufacturer, contacted a lawyer, or contacted the media. Further, Influentials were at least twice as likely to take each of these actions as the public generally. This adds up. Projected nationally, it means almost 5 million Influentials have recently complained at the place where they bought a product; more than 3 million have returned a product or complained about service; more than 2 million have stopped buying a product or written or called headquarters with their complaint; more than 1 million have complained electronically, contacted a consumer agency, or stopped payment; and 400,000-plus have returned the product or contacted the media or a lawyer, as shown in Figure 6-8.

When a call comes into a consumer complaint center, companies should assume it's an Influential. Influentials make up a disproportionate share of those who speak out when they have a problem, compared with their numbers in the population. Influentials accounted for more than half of the people in the study who said they'd taken their complaint to a consumer protection agency. Influentials made up more than one in three of the people who had e-mailed a company or posted their complaint on a company's Web site. They comprised about one in four of those who wrote or called the place where they acquired the product or service, wrote or called the manufacturer or headquarters, stopped payment, or stopped buying the product or service, and more than one in five of those initiating the other responses.

It's a natural, human tendency to shy away from criticism. Criticism can paralyze. It can be a tool to deflect taking responsibility. It can also be a sign of a healthy, vital society. People think a problem matters enough to air their concern. Moreover, it probably should be *expected* in a society in

Figure 6-8. More Likely to Have a Complaint— and to Do Something

40% of Influentials have had a problem with a product or service in the past 3 months, almost twice the rate in the total public (+16 points): a total of 8.4 million Influentials—or 17% of Americans with a complaint

Leading responses to the problem by Influentials, with percentage point difference from total public, national projection, and Influentials' representation among all those taking the action

Complained in person where bought product	23%	+12	4.8 million	21%
Wrote/called place from which bought product	18%	+11	3.8 million	26%
Returned product to place of purchase	17%	+10	3.6 million	24%
Complained to manager of store, restaurant, or other service establishment about poor service	16%	+8	3.4 million	20%
Told friends, relatives not to purchase product or service	15%	+8	3.2 million	21%
Stopped purchasing product or service	14%	+9	2.9 million	28%
Wrote or called manufacturer or corporate headquarters	11%	+7	2.3 million	28%
Complained about product or service via e-mail or company's Web site	7%	+5	1.5 million	35%
Contacted consumer protection agency	6%	+5	1.3 million	62%
Refused to pay or stopped payment on check	5%	+3	1.1 million	25%
Returned product to manufacturer	4%	+2	800,000	20%
Contacted lawyer	4%	+2	800,000	20%
Contacted the media	2%	*	400,000	*

Source: Roper Reports

*Public response less than 1%

which people are more self-reliant, self-confident, and informed. The task for its recipients is not to shy away from it but to engage it and assess its merits with the individual making the criticism. The example of the Influentials suggests it's worth making the effort to turn people around. The Influentials' ability to sift through information and see benefits as well as problems, and their track record of being able to revise their assessments when such is merited, and to tell others, makes them *valuable* complainers. As we've seen, they change their opinion when they see cause for change, as they did in the 1990s with the federal government, which from all-time lows of distrust in the mid-1990s, recovered a measure of goodwill with its efforts to stave off crime, reduce the deficit, reform welfare, and keep inflation in check.

Those 3.2 million Influentials who at any given time are telling friends and family not to buy a product or service after they've had a problem create a significant reservoir of negative word of mouth. Assuming that each Influential tells five people, this means that at any given time Influentials are creating 16 million negative impressions. This estimate may be low. We know from our research that Influentials often tell five people when they find a product or service they like; some studies estimate that complaints are communicated to five times the number of people as good news about a product or service.

The bottom line: Those Influentials who come forward when they have a complaint represent a vastly larger problem of potential customer dissatisfaction.

A lot of customer frustration never reaches companies. Research by TARP (the Technical Assistance Research Programs Institute) has found that one in four customers of the average American organization is upset enough at any given time to switch providers if a reasonable alternative is available. Of those upset customers, however, only 5% actually register a complaint. The Influentials registering complaints are probably the tip of the iceberg of consumer dissatisfaction.

It's probably wise to keep tabs on Influentials' criticisms. From their opinions on advertising, for example, we see not only that they want more care put into claims about health and environmental benefits, product comparisons, and product claims, and more ads that respect their intelligence, we also have learned that Influentials wish that more ads would portray people as they really look. Fully 91% of Influentials think that advertising "sets unrealistic standards of beauty." In contrast, only half of Influentials think that advertising accurately represents "people in my age group." We've learned that Influentials, more than other Americans, think that advertisers don't do enough to portray role models for the increasingly diverse society or to communicate good values to young people in their ads (fewer than half think business does this even fairly often), and that, despite the efforts some advertisers have made, 70%-plus Influentials think businesses exploit children and target women, minorities, and other groups to buy things they don't need or are bad for them.

Further, we've learned that there's growing resentment of the proliferation of advertising, 74% saying advertising "is shown in far too many places now, you can't get away from it" and large numbers saying advertising clutter has become a "nuisance" in television (62%), magazines and newspapers (46%), and the Internet (39%). These responses offer fairly clear direction—that in addition to improving its use of information, connecting better with values, and depicting people more realistically, marketers need to focus more on using advertising judiciously (see Figure 6-9).

If Leonard Pitt is an indication, Influentials will go to great lengths to fight for something they believe in. "I've told companies that for every person like me who takes the time to complain there are ten others who feel the same way," he says. In his campaign against plastic foam packing peanuts, he's told companies they've lost him as a customer until they change their policies and has even done follow-up e-mails to remind them they've lost him. He's gone as far as to e-mail information on suppliers of biodegradable packaging to the companies. He's got strong feelings on advertising, too: "stupid and wasteful." At the same time, he's an indication that there are ways out. He makes a point of buying Paul Newman products because the company donates a portion of its profits to good works. He reads labels. He goes out of his way to support products that promote environmentalism and is a loyal eBay user, as all his friends know. If Influentials represent the threat of complaining consumers, then they also hold out the promise that they will spread the word for companies that win their loyalty.

Figure 6-9. Critical of Advertising Proliferation and Clutter

Percentage of Influential Americans agreeing with statement about advertising, with percentage point difference from total public

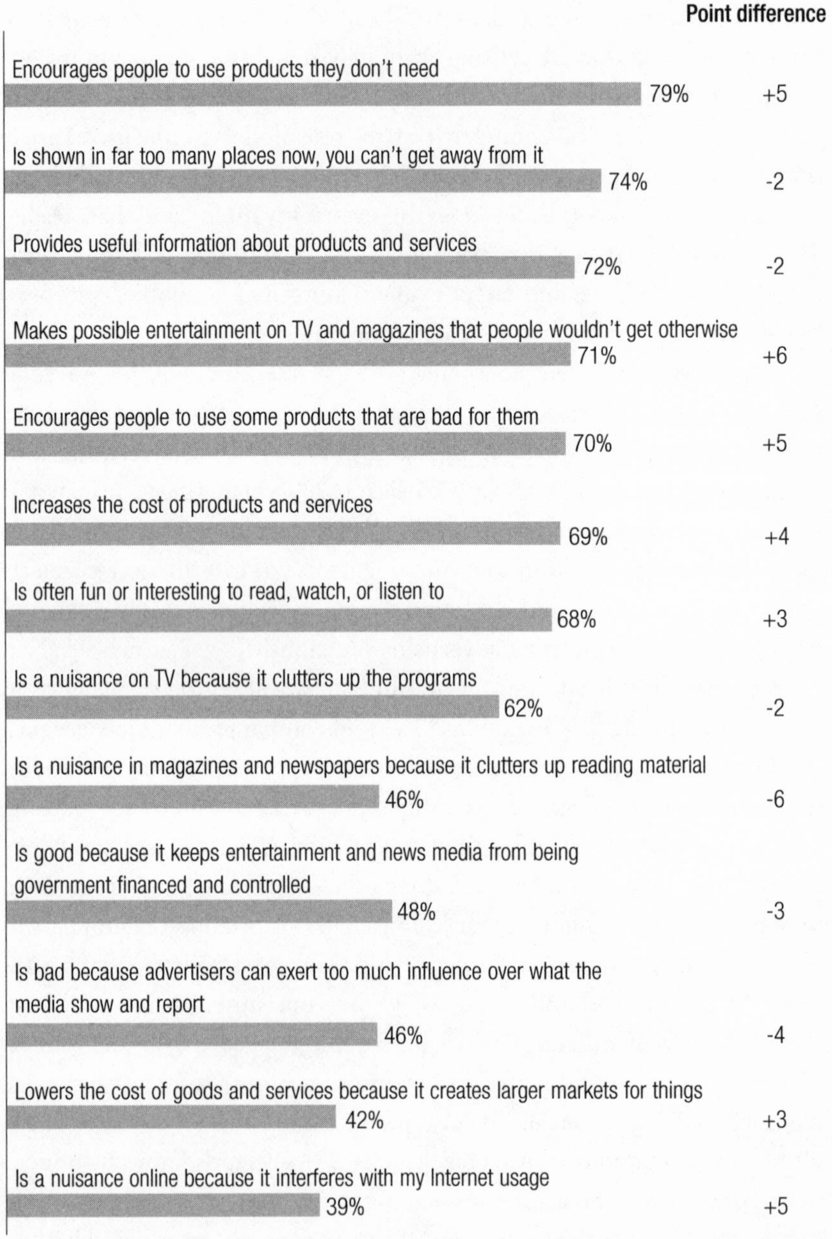

Point difference

Encourages people to use products they don't need
79%   +5

Is shown in far too many places now, you can't get away from it
74%   -2

Provides useful information about products and services
72%   -2

Makes possible entertainment on TV and magazines that people wouldn't get otherwise
71%   +6

Encourages people to use some products that are bad for them
70%   +5

Increases the cost of products and services
69%   +4

Is often fun or interesting to read, watch, or listen to
68%   +3

Is a nuisance on TV because it clutters up the programs
62%   -2

Is a nuisance in magazines and newspapers because it clutters up reading material
46%   -6

Is good because it keeps entertainment and news media from being government financed and controlled
48%   -3

Is bad because advertisers can exert too much influence over what the media show and report
46%   -4

Lowers the cost of goods and services because it creates larger markets for things
42%   +3

Is a nuisance online because it interferes with my Internet usage
39%   +5

Source: Roper Reports

Six Rules:
3. GET OUT INTO THE COMMUNITY

One of the best ways to win Influentials' favor is to become active in a cause that will produce a tangible benefit in people's lives. Says David Pendergrass, "If an advertiser wanted to reach me, I'd tell him to do something to make the world a better place." Many Influentials have benefited first-hand from corporate sponsorship—Mike Williams, for example, with Toyota's support in the Iditarod.

It may not be possible to get out to a meeting on schools or other concerns, where Influentials are probably most commonly found. Given what we have presented so far about the groups in which they're involved, though, it should not be hard to make a link to a cause Influentials care about. Building sports fields, underwriting school fund-raisers, supporting reading programs, and sponsoring Girl Scout activities are obvious places to start. Family is important to Influentials. Many are active in youth activities. More than half of Influentials report a connection to a youth-related group. Environmental efforts, such as helping to create or maintain parks, is another way to connect with a cause close to the group. As we've seen, Influentials have an abiding concern for the environment.

Becoming involved with community events generally is a third avenue. Influentials almost universally express a connection with the neighborhood or community. With almost half of Influentials participating during a typical month in a community-oriented activity (a neighborhood cleanup, food drive, or coaching youth sports), the effort would likely be noticed.

Influentials and Americans generally for some time have told us in studies that they would welcome more locally directed cause-related marketing programs. A Roper study for Cone Communications, a Boston-based cause-related marketing consultancy, has shown that, given the choice, more than half of Americans prefer companies to be active on a local (59%) rather than national (26%) or global (9%) basis. Our research has shown that, specifically, Americans support the greater involvement of companies in improving the quality of local public schools, in youth programs, and in the environment.

Other research we have done shows that programs that produce tangible results are much preferred to softer, feel-good campaigns. The public prefers specifics—college scholarships, literacy programs to teach reading skills, part-time or summer work programs, donations directly to schools for the purchase of educational materials and equipment, or sponsorship of after-school programs, arts, recreation, or mentoring programs.

Cause-marketing programs cannot make up for poor products, but they can be tiebreakers that tip the balance in a company's favor. Three in four Americans say that when price and quality are equal, they would switch to brands or stores associated with a good cause. Cause marketing can also generate word of mouth. More than seven in ten Americans have told us that they tell friends at least occasionally about companies they think are responsible, about four in ten doing so frequently. Almost eight in ten Americans have said they've tried a new product because they've heard good things about a company. On the other hand, about six in ten have refused to buy a "quality" product because they didn't like a company's practices. The Cone research has shown that Influentials are one of the groups most receptive to cause-related marketing programs. Our own research on advertising and marketing shows that, amid all the negatives, the majority of Influentials credit business for using their advertising to "promote good causes and social responsibility" (55%) and to "sponsor worthwhile events that benefit the public" (57%).

The Influentials' support of cause marketing is part of a broader set of beliefs about the responsibilities of companies to the larger society. To Influentials, the business mantra "win-win" should really be "win-win-win-win." Most Influentials think that business has obligations to four groups: customers, workers, community, and shareholders. This comes through when we ask Influentials what they consider the responsibilities of business, what they consider desirable, what they consider "nice but not expected," and what they consider "beyond what business should do." More than 70% of Influentials think businesses have definite responsibilities on fully six fronts: product safety (78% of Influentials say businesses in the U.S. have a definite responsibility of "making products that are safe to use"); worker safety (76% of Influentials say businesses have a definite responsibility of "protecting the health and safety of workers"); the environment (76% of Influentials say businesses have a definite responsibility of "cleaning up their own air and water pollution"); quality (75% of Influentials think businesses have a definite responsibility of "producing good quality products and services"); advertising honestly (74% of Influentials think it's a definite responsibility of businesses); and "paying their fair share of taxes" (72% of Influentials think businesses have a definite responsibility to do so).

In addition, substantial numbers, between 43 and 52%, think business has a definite responsibility in five other areas: charging reasonable prices, being good citizens in the communities in which they operate, paying good salaries to workers, providing health care coverage to workers, and providing jobs to people.

For decades, they have been telling us that, with due respect to shareholders, companies' responsibilities should be to their customers first, then the nation generally, then shareholders. We've seen this call for community-mindedness previously in this book, in the strong support among Influentials for the idea that business should consider "what's good for society," not just what produces profits.

Although there is more appreciation today among both Influentials and the public generally of such basic business tenets as producing profits—perhaps because more of them are investors—only one in three Influentials think business should devote itself solely to producing goods and services "at maximum profit" and limit its social contribution to generating tax dollars that others can use to deal with society's problems (32% agree). The majority of Influentials believe that businesses should "undertake to solve social problems and improve quality of life," along with producing and selling goods and services, as part of its basic mandate (59% agree). Businesses need to be part of the community. To Influentials, a better world and the bottom line—like the environment and commerce—are not mutually exclusive. They would argue that a better world is the bottom line.

Six Rules:
4. MAKE IT EASIER—THEN MAKE IT EASIER STILL

One of the reasons that David Pendergrass likes Toyota so much is that it makes his life easier. He likes to tell a story about his 1981 Toyota. He drove it for 350,000 miles, even after he'd bought two successive Toyotas—a Corolla and a RAV-4. When the vehicle's axle broke, he finally decided it was time to give it up . . . until he found out the part was covered by a recall. "They fixed it for free," Pendergrass says. "Can't beat that."

When Influentials talk about brands, they usually do so in terms of how easy the brand has made their lives. Shelley Miller's tendency "to find something and stick with it" because it makes life easier is one example, but it's far from the only one. The utilitarian approach that is part of most Influentials' personality—their emphasis on viewing useful technologies like computers as necessities more than the public as a whole, for example—generally defines their style as consumers as well.

Saving money, getting good value for the dollar, and making life easier are the main focuses of Influentials when they go into the consumer marketplace. Of 15 different statements about consumer preferences, Influentials are most likely to agree strongly that they take great satisfaction when they "get a really good deal"; on a scale of 1–10, with 10 meaning they agree completely, 74% place themselves between 8 and 10, suggesting they agree strongly. The second strongest is that "the most important thing" about a brand to them is that "it gives good value for the dollar," at 69%.

However, Influentials are willing to spend more for products and services that make life easier for their families: 53%, 9 points higher than in the public generally, say they're "willing to pay for a product or service if it will make life easier for them and their families."

They're significantly more likely than the public as a whole to try to be thrifty with credit cards: 57% say they're "trying to avoid buying things on credit cards," 9 points higher than in the total public.

The disinterest with wealth and possessions as ends in themselves that makes Influentials stand out in their vision of the American Dream and the Good Life is evident in their buying style as well. Indeed, half of Influentials (52%), 10 points higher than the public generally, are "really turned off by people's obsession with material possessions today." They're not ascetics. They're willing to spend in areas in which they're interested, such as travel, technology, and eating out. They enjoy indulging themselves as a "high peace" salve, as we saw in Chapter 5, and will pay a premium to make life easier for them and their families. Half agree, "once I find a brand that satisfies me, I usually don't experiment with new ones," a strategy that can mean spending a little more but, in their view, earning it back in efficiency. Influentials think brands are worth paying more for in a number of categories.

The message that comes through is that they're selective. (They're selective as bargain hunters as well, preferring deals and value to trying always to buy things on sale, which only about half do.) If anything, Influentials are a little *less* likely than the public as a whole to say they try to "buy only what I need" (45% agree).

Still, they're not particularly impulsive. Only one in three say they "often" come out of a store with things they didn't intend to buy. Only one in four say it makes them happy to buy things on a fancy or whim. They don't as a rule invest much of their identity in their purchases. Only one in four says the brands they buy say "a lot" about them. They don't feel particularly compelled to buy "prestigious brand names," "the newest or latest version of a product," buy brands they grew up with, or prefer "exclusive luxury brands." One in five or fewer agrees strongly with any of these sentiments.

They seem to strike a balance on researching products. On the one hand, they're not especially likely to spend "quite a lot of time" researching brands before buying (36% agree), probably because time is at a premium with them. They are even less likely to "usually just buy the same brands" because they "don't have time to investigate" (24%) (see Figure 6-10).

There are implications for business in the Influentials' utilitarian mindset. Marketing should communicate clearly the practical benefits of a product. Products should aim to offer pocketbook benefits, like value for the dollar and "a deal." New products will strike a strong chord if they make life easier for Influentials and their families (this is one area in which they're willing to trade off on getting a deal). Marketing should focus on "news" rather than being the "newest" or "latest." Appeals to status, luxury, or pres-

Figure 6-10. Influentials' Buying Style: Utilitarian

Percentages of Influentials agreeing strongly with statements related to their buying style, meaning agreement of 8 or higher on a scale of 1–10 with 10 meaning agreeing "completely," with percentage point difference from total public

74%. . . . I feel really satisfied with myself, even excited, when I get a really good deal   +5

69%. . . . The most important thing about a brand is that it gives good value for the money   +3

57%. . . . I am trying to avoid buying things on my credit cards these days   +9

53%. . . . I am willing to pay for a product or service if it will make life easier for me
and my family   +9

53%. . . . I always try to buy things on sale   -6

52%. . . . I am really turned off by people's obsession with material possessions today   +10

50%. . . . Once I find a brand that satisfies me, I usually don't experiment with new ones   +1

45%. . . . I try to buy only what I need   -6

36%. . . . I spend quite a lot of time researching brands before making a purchase   +3

32%. . . . I often come out of a store with things I did not intend to buy   -3

24%. . . . I don't have time to investigate different brands, so I usually just buy
the same brand   -7

24%. . . . The brands I buy say a lot about me   –

23%. . . . It makes me happy to buy something on a whim or fancy   -3

20%. . . . I like to buy products with prestigious brand names   -7

20%. . . . I like to buy the newest or latest version of a product   -4

19%. . . . I buy the brands I grew up with   -8

13%. . . . I generally prefer to buy exclusive luxury brands   -5

Source: Roper Reports

tige should not be expected to go far. Influentials are drawn to products and services for what they will do for them and their families rather than for any status they might confer.

Ditto nostalgia for its own sake. This is probably worth stepping back and pausing over for a moment. Appeals to nostalgia have become part of the backdrop of contemporary advertising. It's become an assumption that, whenever the nation faces a challenge, Americans want to escape to the "simpler," "safer" times of days gone by. Influentials aren't particularly susceptible to nostalgia, though. Probably because history is an interest of theirs, they know that the past isn't as great as it's often made out to be. Influentials are consistently *less* likely than other Americans to say the "good old days" of the past were "better." Indeed, they are *more* likely than the public generally to say that the past was not better than today (44% said so in 2001, 15 points higher than in the total public, as the nation was drifting into recession—as logical a time as any to wax nostalgic).

One way to demonstrate a product's utility is to get it into Influentials' hands. Marketers who try to do so will often find a receptive audience. There are many kinds of promotions they *don't* like—spam and telemarketing, for example—but Influentials are great fans of free samples. More than seven in ten like getting free samples of products in stores and through the mail. Two in three like getting free gifts with the purchase of a product. The majority like offers to try a product or service free of charge. With major purchases, such as cars, they like to get the product in their hands before making a purchase. Fully 96% of Influentials consider it essential to test-drive a car before buying. Marketers shouldn't expect to place conditions on test-drives. Half are skeptical of come-ons, for example sweepstakes that dangle big prizes in exchange for trying a product or service.

The Influentials' utilitarian consumer style comes through in our interviews. Many profess enjoyment at getting deals. Teresa Graham, for example, describes herself as "a Wal-Mart fanatic." She likes the atmosphere, she likes the variety, and she feels "comfortable" there. But mostly she likes saving money. Saving money makes life easier. Similarly, Leonard Pitt doesn't particularly care about the idea that eBay can be a virtual community where buyers and sellers meet. To him, it's a place to "buy great stuff—books, photos, postcards—that I can't get anywhere else."

A Product That Works: Debit Cards

It seems clear to us that business is not close to exhausting the possibilities for new products that mine Influentials' utilitarian interest in making life easier. Many of the new product success stories we have covered in this book are products that make life easier—cell phones (making it easier to communicate) and digital cameras (making it quicker and easier to get photos processed and distributed to friends and family), for example. Some of the products that go on to success will be fancy new technologies, but many will be basic extensions of existing products.

Debit cards, for example, don't look particularly new or different. In fact, they look just like ATM or credit cards (indeed, at this point, many ATM cards double as debit cards). They've made substantial inroads with Influentials, though, and for good reason. The cards, which automatically deduct purchases from the holder's bank account, make shopping easier. They eliminate the time hassles of writing a check or going to the bank for cash. They also eliminate the money hassles of the interest charges of credit cards, which as we've seen many Influentials are trying to use less often.

Debit cards won early awareness among Influentials. By 1995, 65% of Influentials had heard of them (versus 42% in the total public), and 14% of Influentials had one (double the 7% penetration in the total public). Many had started making purchases with a debit or ATM card (which were also beginning to be accepted by merchants). By 1999, awareness was up to 93% among Influentials (versus 70% in the total public), and 43% of Influentials had one (versus 28% of the public as a whole). Moreover, 40% of Influentials had made purchases with a debit card.

In the years since, debit cards have become more integrated into Influentials' lives. By 2000, small but growing numbers of Influentials reported they were "usually" using ATM or debit cards rather than cash, checks, or credit cards for a range of purchases, led by groceries (11%, up 6 points from 1997) and prescription drugs (11%, up 9 points), full-service restaurant meals (9%, up 7), clothing purchases (9% on purchases over $20, up 6), and gasoline (8%, up 5). In addition, some were using them for major travel expenses (6%, up 5 points from 1997), major appliances (5%, up 4 points), mail-order purchases (5%, up 4), furniture, rugs, and draperies

(4%, up 3 points), and even insurance premiums (4%) and medical and dental payments (4%), which were negligible in 1997.

By spring 2001, fully 37% of Influentials (15 points higher than in the total public) reported they had used a debit card in the past week—not as many as had used a credit card (58%), but large enough to suggest the product had begun to reach critical mass. Given the proportion of Influentials trying to avoid buying things on credit cards (57% agree strongly), there appears to be considerable room for growth.

Other research is coming to similar conclusions. A *Wall Street Journal* story in 2002 reported that one consumer payment study estimates that debit card transactions in the U.S., having doubled to 10.47 billion between 1995 and 2001, could surpass credit cards (now at 21 billion) in the next decade. The number of checks being written, meanwhile, had dropped by 1 billion to 29 billion from its 1996 peak. As the *Journal* headline said, for growing numbers, "the check isn't in the mail."

PROFILES IN INFLUENCE

Tim Draper

"Every decision you make is crucial to your success." These words of wisdom could be a Fortune 500 executive describing the high-stakes competition for consumer loyalty in the global marketplace. The speaker, however, is a bright-eyed fifth-grade boy who has just tested the market for friendship bracelets and, from the sparkle of self-confidence in his voice, found his decisions turned out fine. His class at school has just finished BizWorld, a four-day immersion in business. The curriculum involves dividing students into six-person "companies" and going through the paces of making and marketing friendship bracelets, from choosing a corporate name ("Purple Robes," "Red Inks") to designing prototypes, raising capital, devising a manufacturing process, setting prices, creating ads, and calculating profits and losses.

BizWorld is the brainchild of Tim Draper, a 43-year-old Silicon Valley venture capitalist with a blue-chip business background (Stanford undergrad, Harvard Business School, and Hewlett-Packard), an enthusiasm for new ideas ("cool" peppers his conversation), a love for his work ("our business is *fun*—we're seeing new technologies all the time"), and a passion for life, which he sees as "a great adventure." The program, which has been delivered to 25,000 schoolchildren, is part of what Draper calls his mission to spread the gospel of entrepreneurship to the world.

It's a mission that he has put into practice in his work. Draper Fisher Jurvetson, the firm in which he is a partner, has launched 150-plus companies. Draper gained star status in the tech world as the brains behind "perhaps the most influential idea in the Internet economy," according to *The Industry Standard:* the word-of-mouth "viral marketing" that propelled the free, Web-based e-mail service Hotmail to one of the greatest success stories of the turbocharged Internet economy of the late 1990s. His devotion to free markets has brought him high-profile controversy as well. In the 2000 California election, he sponsored a statewide initiative that would have given every schoolchild in the state a $4,000 voucher to attend the school of their choice—essentially turning California's public school system into a competitive market. The initiative went down to defeat after a bruising campaign.

He has since picked up and moved on, refocusing his efforts on uncovering new business opportunities amid the meltdown of dot-com stocks and the California energy crisis, which he looks at not as a failure of deregulation but as a half-hearted effort at it. He thinks there are many opportunities in alternative energy. He is an optimist. "We have investments in things that are going to be the next breakthrough." He believes technology will continue to revolutionize personal finance. He remains a believer in the Internet generally. "My guess is the biggest Internet winner has not even happened," he says. "We don't know who it is yet. It's somebody who will catch it just right."

Draper is determined to catch it right himself. He is the high-powered model for how Influentials put ideas into action. At times, his life seems like one, big information-mining venture. "It's like you have a whole bunch of tools in your shed," he says in explaining the different ways he gathers information. His best source for most needs is to talk to "all the people I know in the business." He also travels around the world to meet people and hear their ideas, from university professors to government officials. He seeks out leaders in a field in which he's interested. "After I've talked with them," Draper says, "I ask them, 'Who are the other leaders in the field?' " He reads four daily newspapers. The Net is up all day on his computer and usually gets his full focus for about three hours a day. "I tend to go to the same places, but I sometimes explore. If find a new site, I stay there awhile."

Draper is often testing ideas. He tries them out on three or four friends, or he disseminates a message through DFJ's Extranet to the company's network of contacts. When he's speaking he tries to read the faces in the crowd for reactions. The speaking engagements carry ancillary benefits: "The buzz that's created brings in entrepreneurs, and gets us talked about more."

Personal experience is probably his best source. Draper says, "If I only read about something, I don't know it as well as I should. I have to experience it to know what it's all about." He has both a professional and a personal interest in keeping up with what's new. As a result, he has a museum of personal digital assistants and handheld communications devices. His recent decision to buy a Mercedes was in part for its technology. He liked the idea of having a phone in the dashboard. He was also interested in the car's global positioning satellite (GPS) feature, which enables drivers to get directions to where they're going while they're on the road. He was pleasantly surprised by other gadgetry as well, such as a bumper warning system that sets off an alarm that becomes progressively louder as the car approaches an object (going from dee-dee-dee to DEE! DEE! DEE!). He's thinking now about buying a General Motors car to get GM's OnStar concierge technology, which connects drivers directly to customer service if they have car problems or questions.

There's a similar pattern in his personal life. He happened on Shakespeare's play *Coriolanus* last summer for the first time since college and, inspired by parallels to world events, is now immersing himself in Shakespeare's complete works. "I try to keep up on what's current, and to enhance my knowledge by studying."

He sees his career—bringing new businesses to market—as an extension of his personal philosophy. "I believe that in a free country you should be able to do whatever you want, be whatever you want, and achieve whatever you want. There should be no limitations on you. That's what I heard over and over from my parents, and from my teachers." Technology should work to enhance freedom and bring people better choices. Draper thinks technology will offer solutions to some of today's basic problems. Enabling business to direct appeals to current or prospective users should reduce ad clutter, for example. "I'm sure I've seen a thousand beer commercials in my lifetime," he says. "But I don't drink. The commercials may be nice to look at, but they're hitting the wrong person."

The different strands in his life—what he's reading, what he's buying, and so on—usually lead back to work. When he sees something new, he wonders how he could "utilize" it as a business idea. He compares the process to playing chess and thinking several moves ahead.

Viral marketing grew out of one such train of thought. Draper had always liked the Tupperware business school case study. Tupperware's direct sales system, based in the Tupperware parties women held in their homes, was built on word of mouth; by holding Tupperware parties, women gave their endorsement to the products. When Hotmail's team came to DFJ to plan the product launch, Draper thought back to Tupperware. He posed the idea to the group: You're giving away the product for free. Why not put a little marketing message in every e-mail: "P.S. Get your free e-mail at Hotmail"? With a computer click, the recipient could connect to Hotmail's Web site so they could sign up for the service, too, and after signing up, disperse the "virus" by e-mail to even more people. At first the proposal met with skepticism, but Draper kept prodding.

The imbedded Hotmail message took the concept of the implied endorsement and dispersed it across the new medium of the Internet at warp speed. It worked, and then some. In its first 18 months in business, Hotmail signed up 12 million subscribers, one of the fastest starts in history for any subscription service. By the year 2000 it had grown to 100 million subscribers. The free e-mail service had looped the globe several times over. Hotmail became the largest e-mail provider in countries like Sweden and India, where it had done no traditional marketing whatsoever. One e-mail generated 100,000 users within three weeks. In the ultimate stamp of success in the Internet gold rush of the late 1990s, Hotmail was acquired by Microsoft for $400 million.

Three lessons in particular have stayed with Draper from the Hotmail experience. First, it was cheap. Hotmail launched with an ad budget of $50,000, comparable to a couple of newspaper ads and a billboard. With one e-mail, a Silicon Valley start-up had leveled the playing field between marketing giants and entrepreneurs.

Second, Hotmail represented "perfect information." The message would not get lost in the clutter. Piggybacking an existing e-mail ensured that, unlike spam junk e-mail, it would get opened. It wouldn't be mistranslated; Hotmail controlled the medium. There wouldn't be uncertainty about impact: just measure the number of new subscribers.

Third, and perhaps most far-reaching, it brought home the global potential of the Internet. Normally, building international business is costly, painstaking work that "takes years of huge effort," with executives working diplomatic channels, building relationships, and "flying long distances again and again." Hotmail did all that in an instant. "The Internet lets capitalism fly anywhere. It really opened our minds to what can happen," Draper says.

Six Rules:
5. KNOW "THE EXCEPTIONS"—AND KEEP UP WITH THEM

Tim Draper's passion for new ideas, Leonard Pitt's integration of interesting things he has picked up in his travels, the commitment to growth and change that we have seen generally in Influentials, and the ability to drive these interests to wider audiences: these were familiar dynamics to the publishing staff of *The Atlantic Monthly*. The magazine saw them time and again in its readers. "We knew the people reading *The Atlantic* were extremely important—they would start the buzz, especially about something new or high quality or beautifully designed or technologically advanced," says Meredith Welch, the marketing director for the magazine in the early 1990s.

The challenge was to persuade advertisers, who tended to view the magazine's readers as serious, substantive—the kind of people who work at think tanks—of the breadth and depth of its readers' interests. Research documented that, true to its image as a thought-leader publication, *The Atlantic* had a high proportion of Influentials among its readers. Our portrait of Influentials as well-rounded opinion leaders and consumer bellwethers helped *The Atlantic* tell advertisers a different story about its readers. We updated and expanded our Influentials studies, taking our analysis into more areas with more detail, and produced a series of industry-specific reports with Influentials' insights on autos, health, and other areas ("The Influential Palate").

The effort produced its intended impact. *The Atlantic* won advertising contracts from makers of high-end automobiles and premium-priced consumer goods. It also became the standard for corporate-positioning advertising targeted to opinion leaders. "It was central to the success of the magazine," says Jayne Young, who as publisher of *The Atlantic* led the effort. The program showed that, more than thought leaders, the magazine's readers were fully engaged in life. They had "great brains" but also "a passion for life," says Welch. They showed it was possible to be "fun *and* substantive." The trend leaders in ideas were trendsetters across a range of attitudes and behaviors, with the result that "if you reach one Influential you sell five other people."

The Atlantic research hit upon an essential truth about Influentials as consumers. The Influentials are utilitarian in many areas, but they make *exceptions to the rule.* In these exceptions, they have a high degree of interest: they are areas that "matter." This "exceptionalism" comes through clearly when they are asked for their opinion on the subject. Influentials are more likely than the average person to express enthusiasm in the areas about which they are passionate and are more willing to pay more to get something truly special and to keep up with what's new in the field. They are also areas in which Influentials are both brand-aware and brand-loyal.

We've seen many examples in this book. The home is one. Fully 33% of Influentials, recall, say the home is one of the "one or two things" that say the most about them, only slightly behind the causes they contribute to or work for (38%) and ahead of their hobbies (28%) and jobs (25%). Home is far from the only example, however. Influentials are markedly more likely than the total public to say that the things that are "an expression" of themselves include the places where they spend vacations (62%, 15 points higher than in the total public), their cars (62%, 14 points), the magazines they read (62%, 14 points higher), and the kinds of technology they own (51%, 14 points higher), as well.

Influentials' passions can vary from person to person. They're individualistic. They like to "mix it themselves"—idiosyncrasy—rather than do merely what others are doing. Some are connoisseurs of massage (for example, the 18%, who get a massage when they want to indulge themselves, twice the rate in the total public). Some Influentials love to garden (the 44% who claim gardening as a particular hobby or interest, 15 points higher than in the total public).

There are seven key areas in which Influentials both make exceptions—with large numbers expressing the subject as something in which they are especially interested—and make substantial impact on the marketplace by being turned to for their insights and making recommendations: technology, personal finances and investing, travel, restaurants and cooking, home, health, and automobiles. Businesses should keep up in these areas. Even if they are not in those fields, they need to know what is interesting Influentials, because it may impact their business—and it gives them a more complete picture of what drives Influentials.

What does this mean, specifically?

AUTOMOBILES: In cars, they look for safety, like most Americans, but they give exceptional weight to quality. Indeed, 77% of Influentials rate "quality of workmanship" as extremely important in their car-buying decisions, 13 points higher than in the public as a whole. In addition, in what seems to be another expression of their stress on quality, 76% of Influentials say "freedom from repairs" is extremely important, 10 points higher than in the total public. Safety is the top priority for the public generally, but Influentials rate quality and freedom from repairs if anything a bit higher than safety (which is rated extremely important by 73%, the same as in the general public). Majorities also say the ease of getting the car repaired (59%), the overall cost of ownership (56%), "riding comfort" (54%), and being "enjoyable to drive" and easy to handle (53%) as extremely important—utility and pleasure. In contrast, relatively few look to their cars to confer prestige; only 11% of Influentials, 9 points lower than in the total public, rate this a key priority.

There's a distinctive, individualistic streak in the Influentials' tastes in cars. We've seen this in the Influentials we've profiled. Sophie Glovier likes not having a status car. Isabel and Bernie Milano have a passion for Jaguars. Shelley Miller has made convertibles one of her exceptions. Some Influentials (about one in ten, according to our research) place a high priority on their cars having the latest technology, as Tim Draper does. Rick White, David Pendergrass, and Mike Williams go for commonsense quality Toyotas. Larry Lee has different cars for different occasions. This individualism is reflected in our research as well. There's no one dominant style of car among Influentials. The cars in their garages run the gamut from midsize sedans (about half own one), to pickups (one in three), full-size sedans (three in ten), minivans or vans (about one in five), SUVs (one in four), and compacts (about one in five). Similarly, there's no one dream car. When asked what their *ideal* car would be, about 33% say a two- or four-door sedan; 19% an SUV; 15% a van or minivan; 12% a sports car; 11% a pickup; and 6% a convertible. Appeals to Influentials in cars need to balance their shared needs like quality and safety with idiosyncrasy.

TECHNOLOGY: Influentials are substantially more likely than the average person to say they find technology "exciting" and "use it as much as I can" (50%, 17 points higher than in the total public) or, failing that, to believe it "must be mastered to stay up to date" (31%, 6 higher). Although they sometimes become frustrated by the complexity and failings of technology, their primary attitude to it is *not* one of being cowed by it; they are significantly less likely than the public as a whole to think technology is "a bit beyond me" (10%, 12 lower) or "scares me" (6%, 3 lower). They find strong, practical benefits in technology—the ability to be more self-reliant and flexible, for example—but there's also the sheer energy of being part of something exciting or a sense of doing the right thing to "stay up to date" in Influentials' attitudes to technology. Appeals to Influentials should combine both the practical and emotional sides of their feelings about technology. That double motivation has probably contributed to Influentials being strong, consistent leaders in new technologies, from personal computers and cell phones to second- and third-wave applications and such current interests as digital photography. The flip side, of course, is that when technologies lose their edge in innovation, they lose much of their appeal. This puts pressure on technology companies. Other categories can find recourse in design (cars) or service (investing) or simply don't have technology as an element. Today's technological passion can be tomorrow's toaster (if not toast).

TRAVEL: With eight in ten Influentials interested in "different countries and people" and seven in ten Influentials describing themselves as "eager to see new places and do different things," travel may be the Influentials' leading outlet for exploration. They tend to be more interested than the norm in *most* kinds of trips, in part, for the new experiences they offer. When asked where they plan to take trips in the future, they index high virtually across the board, from the beach (54%, 13 higher than in the total public), mountains (45%, 16 higher), and trips outside the U.S. (43%, 17 higher), to weekend getaways (42%, 18 higher), cruises (42%, 16 higher), camping trips (33%, 16 higher), resort vacations (33%, 15 higher), and theme parks (32%, 9 higher), driving tours (27%, 11 higher) and train trips (21%, 11 higher), rafting trips (17%, 9 higher), ski trips (16%, 8 higher), and bicycling tours (14%, 9 higher). It shouldn't be a surprise that travel is the area in which they're most likely to say they're always looking for something new. They're budget conscious, but they "care about quality" and "are willing to pay for it"—that is, they are willing to make exceptions. Appeals to Influentials should focus on what the experience can offer them and what they can learn from it. In addition to indexing high for seeing the new and different, Influentials are substantially more likely than the norm to be drawn to trips "to enrich myself."

PERSONAL HEALTH: Self-reliance is a key theme in Influentials' approach to health care. Influentials are self-directed in their health care. They often research health questions so that they are better informed when they go into the doctor's office. They probably would appreciate quicker access to quality information: nurses, doctors, and other health care professionals available through e-mail, chats, and bulletin boards on the Web sites of hospitals, doctor groups, insurers, publications, or industry groups. Remember, "other people" beyond their immediate circle of friends and family are considered by Influentials as the best source of ideas and information on prescription drugs and ways to improve their health. Given the tendency of Influentials to air criticisms when they have them, the professionals should be especially skilled in bedside manners.

Influentials tend to take a moderate approach to personal health, steering a moderate course between laxness on the one hand and scare studies and health crazes on the other. The Influentials are more likely than the average person to watch what they eat. In early 2002, for example, 39% of Influentials said they "tend to watch" the amount and kinds of food they eat, 11 points higher than in the total public. Relatively few, though, are on a strict diet (15%, slightly above the public as a whole), either on doctors' orders or their own volition. They tend to hear first about alternative medical approaches and to be more enthusiastic than the average person when they find something they like, but the Influentials have a scale of what they consider to be really "very effective" in improving health; it ranges from prayer (56%) on the high end (testimony, it seems, to the belief that the most effective change often comes from within) to vitamins (39%), psychological counseling (32%), chiropractors (29%), massage (25%), herbal remedies (18%), yoga and meditation (16%), acupuncture or acupressure (15%), and, toward the bottom, aromatherapy (7%) and liquid protein diets (4%).

Aside from smoking, the Influentials generally view behaviors as harmful "only in excess," like eating foods high in salt or fat, drinking alcohol, being overweight, or living with tension and stress. They tend to take an organic approach to their health and well-being. Having a regular dental care routine, getting a good night's sleep, exercising regularly, and eating healthy foods, in that order, are most important to them for looking their best, far more than clothes, vitamins, supplements, hairstyle, or cosmetics. In personal health, then, Influentials are a steadying force, a good potential resource for health professionals who want the public to improve their health habits and not be rattled by scare headlines.

Influentials also make "community" exceptions. Influentials like to shop in the neighborhood. Although they're more likely than the public generally to frequent warehouse clubs and discount stores (where they like to stock up), they're less likely than the norm to shop in malls and more likely to patronize neighborhood shops and stores. This "small is beautiful" preference for neighborhood shopping may mean paying a little more, but it's worth it to them. They value the slower pace that small stores often have— "the personal touch" of being able to "get people's opinion," says Isabel Milano. Many see shopping in the neighborhood as an expression of community-mindedness, of keeping their dollars in the community. David Pendergrass also likes the chance it offers to "run into people you know." "Having grown up in a rural community, I have that rural bent," Pendergrass says. "My small shopping neighborhood exemplifies how communities should be."

Some other exceptions we covered previously. For Influentials, restaurants and cooking are occasions for connecting with family, friends, and acquaintances and opportunities for exploring new tastes and cuisine. Influentials are substantially more likely than consumers as a whole to be interested in new tastes and cuisines, to look at cooking as a hobby, and to enjoy trying new recipes, but also to see food as a source of tradition and ritual that connects them and their families with their parents, grandparents, and previous generations. In the home, Influentials' interest is still primarily family and having a private haven but increasingly expanding the home so that most things they go out for (work, library, movies and entertainment, and so on) they can have at home. In personal finances and investing, Influentials are motivated by the desire to be "set" for the future—even financially independent—and to be able to help their children, community, and broader society. Money is not so much about power or status for Influentials as security, independence, and relationships, the basis of most of their actions and beliefs.

Six Rules:
6. BE A BRAND, AND TELL THE WORLD

Teresa Graham and Wal-Mart. Leonard Pitt and eBay. David Pendergrass and Toyota. Shelley Miller and her Eclipse. It's true Influentials define themselves by their involvement in the community, work, family and personal interests rather than by the goods and services they buy, set high standards for business, and drive a hard bargain when they go shopping. They also value brands, are discerning about the benefits that brands offer, and, perhaps most important, spread the word about brands.

Most concede that brand advertising works—sometimes to their own bemusement. "I don't think I'm strongly influenced by advertising," Shelley Miller says. "But then as soon as I open my refrigerator, I realize well, of course, I am."

Influentials are skeptical of marketing and demanding of business, but they hold a high opinion of brands. Indeed, our studies reveal Influentials to be one of the strongholds of brands. They think there are meaningful differences between brands in many categories of products and services, and many think that some brands are worth a premium. Executives worried about the future of brands have a powerful potential ally in Influentials. The results suggest that the efforts that businesses have made to increase the value of their brands have been worth it and that businesses should continue to focus on brand building, by delivering what Influentials value in brands, specifically providing a positive experience and quality at a reasonable price (as in Figure 3-13).

Influentials hold brands in high regard in many areas. In durable goods, for example, more than half of Influentials think that some brands of furniture, personal computers, and compact cars are "different or better" and "worth paying more for." Large numbers, four in ten or more, think the same of refrigerators, luxury cars, washing machines, and stereo equipment. Although they're not particularly interested in fashion, just under four in ten Influentials think some brands are different or better and worth the extra money in dress clothes. In only a handful of categories do the plurality not think some brands are worth more. In these cases, Influentials generally still feel some brands are better—just not worth a higher price. In cell phones, where companies have been competing heavily on price to boost customer bases, the plurality think some brands are better, just not worth more (36%, compared with 26% who think some brands are worth more and 32% who think there's no difference between brands). Similarly, in casual clothes, Influentials' tendency is to buy brands but not pay more (given the convergence of retailers on casual clothing, probably a smart strategy). Influentials are generally more likely than the average consumer to think some brands are worth more, particularly in small cars (where there is a 21-point difference), furniture (16 points), and appliances (15 points for refrigerators and 14 points for washing machines; see Figure 6-11).

Many of these products for which Influentials have brand awareness are in areas that connect to their concerns, including career (a good computer makes you more productive), family (a solid car makes your family safe), and their hobbies and interests, such as cooking, the home, music, technology, and cars.

For similar reasons, Influentials are generally discerning in services as well. Majorities consistently say they think some brands are different and worth extra in hotels. Most think the same about health insurance and homeowner's insurance. Here again, there are compelling interests—seeing the world, staying healthy, protecting the home.

Interestingly, though, Influentials give high marks to brands in packaged goods, too, where the stakes *aren't* very high. More than half of Influentials think that some packaged goods brands are different or better and worth paying more for in a number of categories, including ground coffee, ice cream, beer and wine, cheese, and carbonated soft drinks. Substantial numbers, 40% or more, also feel so in a number of other categories, ranging from canned soup to chips, shampoo, toothpaste, breakfast cereal, orange juice, and laundry. Even in paper products or area in which only about three in ten think some brands are worth more, majorities still think some brands are at least different or better, if not worth paying more for. Only in the minority of categories do Influentials think there's little difference whatsoever, notably aspirin and bottled water. On many purchases, Influentials are substantially more willing to pay a premium than the average consumer: for cheese (17 points), coffee (12 points), potato chips (11 points), cereal (11 points), and soup (10 points) there are double-digit differences. Many Influentials also report that they have a "favorite" brand that they "usually buy" in many packaged goods categories or at least choose from a list of two or three brands; relatively few buy whatever strikes them at the moment.

The willingness to pay more shouldn't be seen as carte blanche to raise prices. The results to some extent reflect the ascent of pricey upscale fare

Figure 6-11. Brands: Real Differences in Many Categories — and Worth More

Durables: Percentage of Influentials saying some brands are "different or better and worth paying more for," with point difference from total public

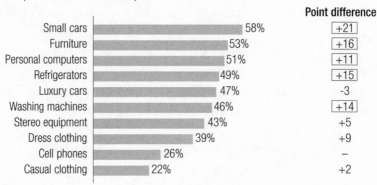

		Point difference
Small cars	58%	+21
Furniture	53%	+16
Personal computers	51%	+11
Refrigerators	49%	+15
Luxury cars	47%	-3
Washing machines	46%	+14
Stereo equipment	43%	+5
Dress clothing	39%	+9
Cell phones	26%	–
Casual clothing	22%	+2

Packaged goods: Percentage of Influentials saying some brands are "different or better and worth paying more for," with point difference from total public

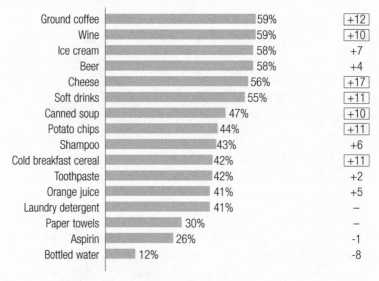

Ground coffee	59%	+12
Wine	59%	+10
Ice cream	58%	+7
Beer	58%	+4
Cheese	56%	+17
Soft drinks	55%	+11
Canned soup	47%	+10
Potato chips	44%	+11
Shampoo	43%	+6
Cold breakfast cereal	42%	+11
Toothpaste	42%	+2
Orange juice	41%	+5
Laundry detergent	41%	–
Paper towels	30%	–
Aspirin	26%	-1
Bottled water	12%	-8

Percentage of Influentials who think there is "a great deal of difference" between well-known brands, with point difference from total public

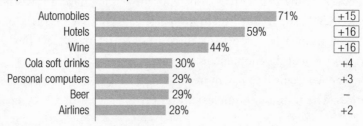

Automobiles	71%	+15
Hotels	59%	+16
Wine	44%	+16
Cola soft drinks	30%	+4
Personal computers	29%	+3
Beer	29%	–
Airlines	28%	+2

Source: Roper Reports

like Starbucks coffee, Häagen-Dazs or Ben & Jerry's ice cream, and European kitchen appliances, but it's likely that a major factor is the utilitarianism that we see in Influentials' buying style, and in specific Influentials like Shelley Miller. To Influentials, it's worth paying a *little* more for the peace of mind associated with a brand and be done with it, so they can get on to more important things. They seem to prefer to save their time and brainpower for areas that are most important to them, like their careers, community work, family, and personal interests. It's that Influential ability to discern "what matters" that we see as a mark of their personalities generally.

Tim Draper is a case in point. One might think that being a tech highflier, he'd be most brand loyal in categories like computers or cars. Draper says he's most brand loyal in mundane products, however. "A brand will not mean much to me in cars," he says, "but in toothpaste it might." He's been a loyal Crest user since he was a kid. "I don't want the hassles of deciding on a new toothpaste." On the other hand, the time and effort that he spends, say, on cars—he has recently been investing his resources to learn more about OnStar and other new car technologies—can open windows of business opportunity for him in his work as a venture capitalist. Similarly, he's thinking about buying an Apple Computer (to go along with his Windows-based machines) to keep up with the Macintosh system.

Draper has company. Some of the categories in which Influentials are most brand loyal are not categories in which they perceive much difference between brands. Only 29% of Influentials think there's really a "great deal of difference" between different brands of coffee, for example, but 59% think some brands of coffee are different *enough* to be worth paying more for—one of the highest scores for *any* product or service—and 50% have a favorite brand that they usually buy. Similarly, only 30% of Influentials think there's a great deal of difference between brands of soft drinks, but 55% think some brands are different *enough* to be worth paying more for—again, a very high score. More than two-thirds have one favorite or a list of two or three brands. Look into the refrigerator of an Influential in a year, and you'll probably see the same brand of soft drink. A car, cell phone or computer might be a different story, though.

Note to political candidates: the trend toward treating candidates as "brands" has some merits (for example, forcing them to focus their message), but Influentials' view on brands suggests that the metaphor can be taken too far. Candidates, especially challengers, should be where people's *passions* are, not in the "dependable" utilitarian position that brands generally hold for Influentials. Ronald Reagan may have jokingly admitted to being sold like soap, but he will be remembered more for the passions he stirred ("Mr. Gorbachev, tear down that wall"). The same could be said for John F. Kennedy ("Think not what your country can do for you but what you can do for your country"), Franklin Delano Roosevelt ("We have nothing to fear but fear itself"), and third-party challengers from Ralph Nader in 2000 to Ross Perot in 1992 and back through the nation's history.

This disconnection between brands and passions may be why the politicians-as-brand concept rubs many Americans the wrong way. Brands are great for what they are, but to Influentials, they're not what most defines life. Brands are not bought to create self-image. Influentials have enough other things to define themselves, including family, work, interests, and community involvement. Brands help them save time for more important things . . . like political involvement.

PROFILES IN INFLUENCE

Sarah Vokes

On the face of it, Sarah Vokes is probably the Influential that CEOs would least like to see on their way to the office. Chances are, she'd be on the other side of a picket line, protesting the company's policies. The 22-year-old Vokes has no qualms about questioning the status quo. As an undergraduate at Carthage College, a small, liberal arts school in Kenosha, Wisconsin, she posted critiques of fashion advertising on campus bulletin boards to provoke a discussion on the message Madison Avenue sends young people through its use of waif-like models and the constant push to consume. She organized events on such sensitive subjects as date rape, domestic violence, and discrimination against gays and lesbians. She was active in Stingray, a campus feminist study and activist group, and cofounded ALLY (for people of ALL sexual orientations), for straight students to show support for gays and lesbians. She was one of the protesters at the inauguration of President George W. Bush in 2000.

"The greatest value in my life, in the world, is social justice," says the Duluth, Minnesota native, who plans to go to law school and, eventually, to teach college and do nonprofit work. "Whatever job I have, whatever work I am doing, I want to be working for social justice. I want to be making a difference. Money isn't as important to me."

Business will have to find common ground with Sarah Vokes in the years to come. She is not alone. Various surveys show this generation is more progressive than students a decade ago, more globally focused, and more oriented to community service, but less committed to the traditional political process.

Sarah Vokes knows that what she does sometimes gets under people's skin. "I think that learning a lot of times comes from tension," she says. She holds the Influential beliefs that "people make a difference," "it's important to be involved," and "if there are things you don't like, you should step up and do something to make a difference," be it "voting for the candidate you support," "volunteering for the party you believe in," or "volunteering in a soup kitchen or shelter."

Vokes tries to live out her beliefs in her purchase decisions. She buys long-distance phone service through Working Assets, a San Francisco–based firm that donates a percentage of its profits to nonprofits. She "loves everything" about Working Assets. She generally researches a company's social policies and weighs them in her decisions. Sometimes, she opts out. She drives a 1990 Nissan Sentra inherited from her parents, who themselves bought it used. She bought her laptop computer used, trading in her family's old computer. It works fine for her needs: word processing, e-mail, and online access. She talks with her husband, Ryan, and her circle of friends about the materialism of the society "and how we can confront that." She generally thinks she has "too much stuff as is." "Our culture conditions us to be consumers, that it's our job and our duty as Americans to buy things."

At the same time, she selectively lets in technology. The Internet is integrated into her life. One of her first efforts for ALLY was creating a list.serv. She uses the Web "all the time" for consumer decisions. "I wholeheartedly believe I can find anything online," Vokes says. She recently signed up for a health insurance plan in part because of its Web site, particularly a feature that allows users to find providers wherever they are simply by entering a current address on the insurer's Web site.

In addition to her main causes, she does a lot of what she calls "random volunteering." After college she spent a year in Washington, D.C. on a fellowship to study rural poverty. She helped update the League of Women Voter's Web site on local election issues around the country and volunteered for the D.C. Rape Crisis and the Democratic Party (working the phone bank). In college, she participated in the campus Youth Ministry Group and Amnesty International.

Vokes says she had good volunteering role models while growing up. Her father was active in United Way, Lighthouse for the Blind, and their church. At 13, Sarah was asked to join the staff of a magazine by a neighbor who was frustrated with traditional girls' magazines. The publication, *New Moon*, written by and for girls, went on to build a circulation of 30,000 and win a clutch of awards. It was "a great example, if you don't like what you're reading go out and start a magazine."

That theme remains very much part of her life. Vokes and her husband are trying to bring their beliefs into their marriage now. They decided to have a "union ceremony" rather than a traditional marriage with its requisite marriage license as an act of conscience because current law does not allow homosexuals to marry. "There are so many instances in which I enjoy privileges that I haven't done anything to deserve, due to my upbringing, education, middle-class status, and race," she says. "This struck me as a situation where I could do something, and reject a privilege." They created their own ceremony involving family and friends. Says Vokes, "We didn't want our marriage to be something someone did to us, but something we were doing to ourselves."

Vokes says it was not hard to tell her Mom. "I think she was, like, OK, Sarah, whatever," she laughs. "I'm a stubborn, strong-willed person; I'm always telling her new things I'm going to do or not going to do. My parents are pretty supportive. They're used to me standing up for what I believe in."

The Good News—and Your Challenge

Of all the surprising findings revealed in our research on American reactions after the September 11, 2001 terrorist attacks on New York and Washington—the surge in optimism in the future, the sense of resilience, the spirit of unity—one of the most intriguing concerned advertising.

When asked how business should respond in those very uncertain times, three in four Influentials (and comparable numbers in the total public) said that in addition to beefing up security, contributing to worthy causes, and creating public service ads to rally the country, business should "advertise as usual." Their responses brought home an important lesson. Like factories running at full shift, airplanes filled with business travelers, and delivery trucks streaming across the interstates, advertising is for many Americans the background hum of a healthy economy. "Companies have to advertise," Tim Draper says. "It's critical. They need to capture customers and keep them happy. Advertising is a huge part of that."

The good news for business is that, for all of the criticism that Influentials have of business, they are often advocates for business. Influentials may be constantly prodding business to do better, but they also recognize the areas in which business meets its objectives. Influentials see value in business. Across the years, they've been significantly more likely to believe that "what's good for business is good for the average person" (usually 50%-plus) rather than "what's good for business is bad for the average person" (usually below 20%). This ability to see both the accomplishments and failings of business—rather than being an unabashed booster, rose-colored glasses optimist, or unvarnished cynic—probably makes it more effective when they make an endorsement.

Influentials have high standards for business—seeing many tasks as a "definite responsibility" of business, in numbers often larger than in the public as a whole—but Influentials also think it is meeting its obligations in a number of key areas. The Influentials give business particularly good marks in product quality, one of the core functions of business. In late 2000, with the stock market down sharply and the economy gearing down to recession levels (conditions far from ideal for business), almost nine in ten Influentials (86%) said they thought business was fulfilling its responsibilities at least fairly well at making good-quality products and services. This was up 25 points from the responses of Influentials in 1980, when the quality of American goods was openly disparaged—a noteworthy change.

Influentials saw product quality as strong in a number of specific industries as well: 85% of Influentials rated product quality good or excellent in home electronics; 83% in home computers; 82% in home appliances; 76% in the lodging industry; 73% in the food industry; 72% in foreign automobiles; and 65% in domestic automobiles.

Large numbers thought business was meeting its obligations in other ways as well. Just over nine in ten Influentials (91%) said business was fulfilling its responsibilities at least fairly well in developing new products and services. Wide majorities of Influentials credited businesses with doing a good job on making products that are safe to use (84%), protecting workers' health and safety (83%), being good citizens in their communities (77%), and creating jobs (73%). On certain key issues there was impressive improvement. Perceptions on product quality, for example, rose 15 points from 1980. Although prices remained a sore point—only 45% of Influentials thought business did a good job of charging reasonable prices for products and services—there was improvement here as well (up 10 points from 1980; see Figure 6-12).

Does this mean business can relax? No, far from it. There were still a number of areas in which majorities *don't* think business is living up to its obligation. Besides delivering on reasonable prices, fewer than half of Influentials think business is meeting its obligations to advertise honestly (26%), take care of its pollution (34%), pay its fair share of taxes (44%), or provide health care coverage to its workers (47%). The percentage believing that business meets its obligations to "pay good salaries and benefits" to its workers *fell* 22 points to 53% between 1980 and 2000. Influentials are markedly more critical in many areas than the public as a whole—far less likely to approve of business performance on advertising honestly (by 22 points), cleaning up its pollution (15 points), paying its share of taxes (12 points), providing health care coverage (12 points), and charging reasonable prices (10 points). There's a key message here for companies: business executives who look only at the top-line response of the total public will

Figure 6-12. Business' Responsibilities and How Well It's Fulfilling Them

Percentage of Influential Americans saying item is "a definite responsibility" of business and percentage who think business is fulfilling its responsibility "fairly well" or "fully," with point difference from public

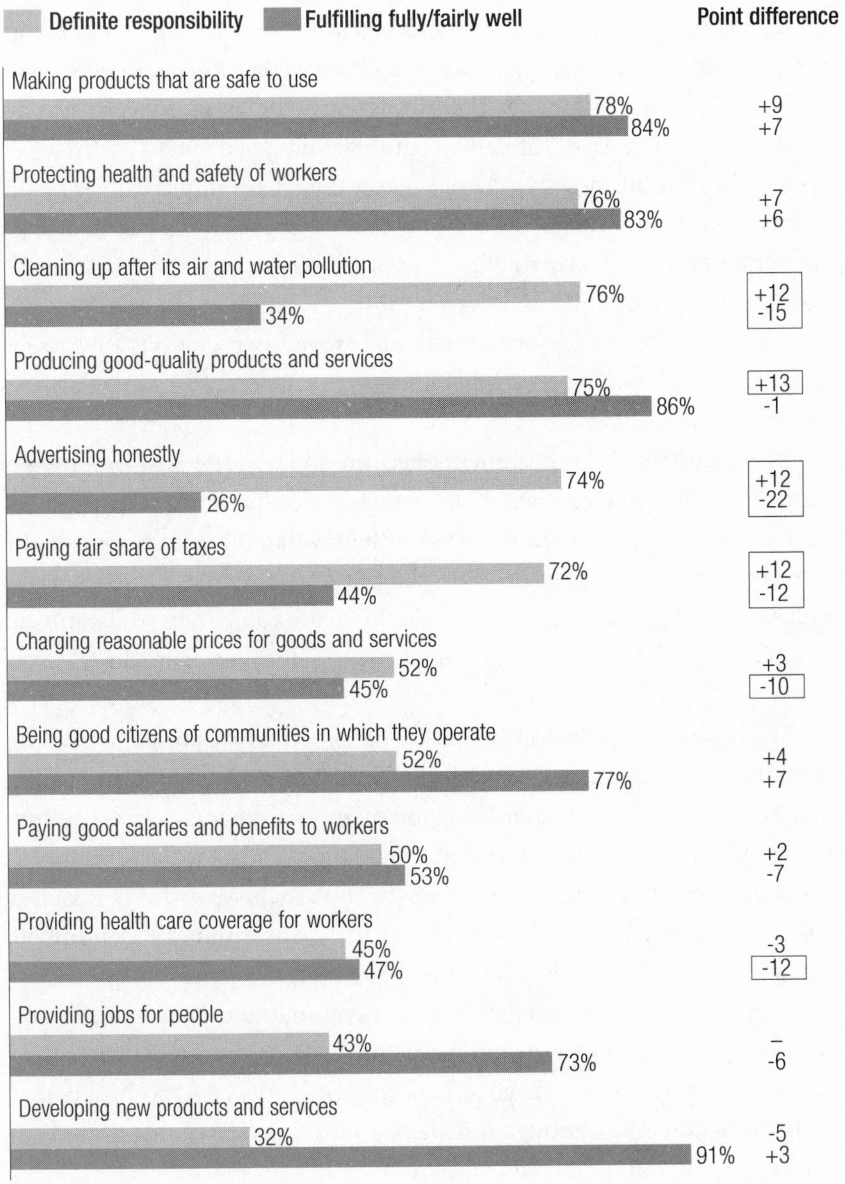

▓ Definite responsibility ▓ Fulfilling fully/fairly well   **Point difference**

Making products that are safe to use

78%   +9
84%   +7

Protecting health and safety of workers

76%   +7
83%   +6

Cleaning up after its air and water pollution

76%   +12
34%   -15

Producing good-quality products and services

75%   +13
86%   -1

Advertising honestly

74%   +12
26%   -22

Paying fair share of taxes

72%   +12
44%   -12

Charging reasonable prices for goods and services

52%   +3
45%   -10

Being good citizens of communities in which they operate

52%   +4
77%   +7

Paying good salaries and benefits to workers

50%   +2
53%   -7

Providing health care coverage for workers

45%   -3
47%   -12

Providing jobs for people

43%   –
73%   -6

Developing new products and services

32%   -5
91%   +3

Source: Roper Reports

miss a strong undercurrent of discontent among the opinion leader Influentials.

To be sure, the improved performance has a flip side. As business has done better in such areas as product quality, the Influentials have focused more attention on other problems, like executive pay, customer service, and the environment. Business *accomplishments* have become *assumptions*. In 1980, for example, product quality was almost a universal concern among Influentials; fully 97% of Influentials in 1980 said quality was a "definite responsibility" of business. As quality perceptions have improved, rising 25 points since 1980, though, it's become less of a priority: the percentage of Influentials rating quality a definite responsibility of business has *fallen* 22 points since 1980. Influentials haven't stopped caring about quality, pricing, or innovation. As performance has improved, expectations have risen. Business is *supposed* to do *better.* "I know you can do this," Influentials say, "now what about *this?*"

As yesterday's accomplishments become today's new baseline, there's greater risk of disillusion when business does not live up to consumer expectations. This lies behind the sense of betrayal in the 2002 implosion of Enron and the wipeout of many of the 401(k) accounts of its employees, accusations of accounting irregularities by many companies, and conflicts of ethics on Wall Street. It's becoming a mantra: business is supposed to do *better.*

The business agenda is growing. Global practices are poised to become more of a concern. Large numbers of Influentials say they're personally concerned about businesses making too many investments overseas simply to benefit from lower wages and less regulation. At home, large numbers think businesses pay senior executives far too much. Many think business still doesn't give enough attention to customer satisfaction. Large numbers believe business doesn't do enough to help workers balance work and family. Many think business pays too much attention to short-term profits and not enough to the long term, and pays more attention to stock prices than to its consumers. Corporate governance is also a concern, specifically that companies don't have enough outsiders on their boards of directors. That message again: *business should do better.*

Business is not going to be able to solve the problems facing it quickly or easily. It's going to take effort, probably comparable to the effort that executives in the 1980s put into turning around the decline in the quality of American goods. Moreover, business is not going to be able to do it alone. In this era when decisions are conversations and when people place more weight on the word-of-mouth insights of the opinion leaders in their circle of friends and relatives than what they hear on TV and read in the paper, business needs the influence of the society's opinion leaders. Companies need to know who these opinion leaders are and need to know what they're thinking, what they're doing, where their "water stations" are, how the opinion leaders create "spirals of influence," and how to work with them and for them.

In this book, you've met an important group of opinion leaders who fit this description. They may not be the first names that come to mind when you think about the people with influence in this country, the leaders of government, CEOs of large corporations, or the wealthy. Rather, they're the people in cities and towns across the country who are active in their community. People who are highly engaged in their workplace and personal life. People who are interested in many subjects and connected to many groups. People who know how to express themselves—and do so. People whose opinions, because of their position in the community, workplace, and society, are heard by many others and influence decisions in others' lives. People who can propel your next new business idea to great height, or doom it to failure. People who you need to know and understand in today's fragmented, competitive marketplace. People who give you a window on the future. The Influential Americans.

Most of the research in this book is drawn from Roper Reports, the consumer trends service of RoperASW. Started in 1973, Roper Reports regularly surveys Americans' attitudes and behaviors on a variety of topics, ranging from their values and aspirations to their thinking on issues facing their communities and the nation; consumer and investor confidence; attitudes about advertising, brands, and marketing; and purchases, planned purchases, and purchase influences in categories from financial services to computers and technology, autos, personal health, food and dining, media, the home, leisure and entertainment, travel, consumer electronics, and apparel and personal appearance.

Our data, insights, and the advice we offer based on our research are used by hundreds of leading companies and ad agencies to understand better consumer decision making, identify opportunities for new products and services, position products and services more effectively, develop marketing strategies, and anticipate and respond to change in the consumer marketplace and the society.

The quantitative research we conduct for Roper Reports is based on two interviewing methods: face-to-face and telephone. The bulk of research reported in this book is from the in-person surveys. Our face-to-face, at-home surveys for Roper Reports are based on interviews of a cross section of 2,000 adult Americans, 18 years old and older, representative of the population of the United States.

The content of the surveys is a combination of trended questions (many dating to the 1970s) and new questions that are generated to respond to changing marketplace dynamics, events in the world, and client requests.

Influential Americans are drawn from the surveys through a question (described in the Introduction) that asks respondents which, if any, from a list of activities gauging involvement in community, social, and political activism they have performed in the past year. Influentials typically range from 8 to 14% of survey respondents and about 10% over the course of a year (in seven 2001 in-person surveys, for example, Influentials constituted 9.8% of respondents).

The margin of error is generally plus or minus 7 percentage points at a 95% confidence level on comparisons between Influential Americans and the total public.

On aggregate, full-year data, such as the demographic data presented in Chapter 1 (age, gender, income, occupation, and others), and the "Influential" social and political activism data presented in Chapters 1 and 4 (attending a meeting, giving a speech, running for or holding political office, for example), the margin of error is generally plus or minus 3 percentage points.

The telephone surveys for Roper Reports began in late 2001 to allow us to survey Americans on a more frequent basis than is possible in face-to-face research and to turn around the results much more quickly. We believed this was essential as America was entering a particularly volatile period following September 11, 2001. In each of the telephone surveys a representative cross sample of 1,000 Americans 18 and older were interviewed.

Beyond these two quantitative methods, further insights have been drawn from Roper Reports TrendWhys focus groups with Influentials and from one-on-one interviews with Influential Americans drawn from the Roper Reports database and other sources.

It is our intent to continue the conversations we are starting in this book through our client research and consulting services, as well as through research and perspectives that we post on our Web site. For more information or for recent insights and findings from RoperASW on the leading trends and values of Influential Americans or Americans in general, as well as global insights from our worldwide consumer trend services, please visit us at www.roperasw.com.

THERE ARE TWO AUTHORS whose names appear on the front cover of this book, but the research, analysis, and insights about the Influential Americans is the product of the talents of literally hundreds of people who have worked for RoperASW and its predecessor companies over the past 80 years. Some of these individuals are contemporaries of ours and people we are proud to call our colleagues; others worked at Roper well before our time. Roper was founded by Elmo Roper, and although neither of us ever met him he was by all accounts a pioneer who saw the need for the public to have its voice heard by government officials and corporations. He is one of the founding fathers of the public opinion and marketing research industry. His son Burns ("Bud") Roper was Chairman of Roper when we both joined the firm and helped to continue the proud tradition of his father. Bud taught us both to respect and admire the collective wisdom of the American people, a lesson we try never to forget.

Bud Roper and his partner at the time, Shirley Wilkens, had the foresight in 1973 to begin Roper Reports, providing an ongoing monitor of what the American people were doing, thinking, and buying. By including the battery used to define the Influential Americans in each wave of Roper Reports, they created an unparalled database on which we could draw, tracking the ways in which the Influentials have helped to lead trends in public opinion, consumer behavior, and lifestyles over the past 30 years. Joining Bud and Shirley in the ongoing development of Roper Reports over all these years has been a long list of colleagues—too many, unfortunately, for us to list here. In particular, we would like to thank the individuals who have helped to oversee the Roper Reports service over the span of many years, including Tom Miller (who developed the first in-depth report on the Influentials and coined the term "Influential Americans" to describe a group that was hitherto known as the "political/social actives"), Brad Fay, Holly Heline, Carolyn Setlow, and Cary Silvers. We would also like to thank our colleagues Paul Leinberger, Diane Crispell, and Judy Langer, who constantly provide us with insight into the trends that drive the American consumer marketplace. Jay Wilson, who was the CEO of the Roper firm before Ed, was a constant source of encouragement for us to develop and market our consumer trends expertise.

We would also like to thank the many people who work behind the scenes in the data collection and processing of market research studies, including our sampling department, field department, coding and editing department, data processors, word processors, print shop, and certainly neither last nor least, the thousands of interviewers who have worked on our behalf over the years and who agree to go door to door during all seasons of the year to interview Americans in their homes. These intrepid interviewers provide us with data so that what we write is more than merely our own opinions. More recently, we have also begun to include telephone interviews as part of the Roper Reports program. We thank all those involved in our telephone interviewing operations, as well.

The Roper Reports analytical team, living up to its promise of "turning data into intelligence," made thoughtful suggestions and ensured our facts were accurate: Drashti Bhatia, Jennifer Cain, Debbie Gailliard, Ferdinand Giese, Phil Lutz, Andrea Newman, Edwin Roman, Kathy Sheehan, Ashley Steinmetz, Liz Vazquez, and Jared Weiner. Carol Albert and Eleanor Kung turned the data into the handsome figures that illustrate this book.

Leo Bogart was Roper's client at Standard Oil of New Jersey when the study of opinion leaders that led to the development of the Influentials battery was started. Leo went on to have a long—and still active—career in our industry, and we thank him for the time he spent recounting the early days of the research into influence in America.

Many thanks to the team at Lark Productions, Robin Dellabough, Lisa DiMona, and Karen Watts. Without their hard work, considerable skill, and belief in our idea about the power of the Influentials we would still have only a concept but no book in print. Lark's Bram Alden contributed far above and beyond the usual summer internship.

Bill Rosen at The Free Press was more our intellectual collaborator than editor. From our first meeting he pushed us to think harder and go further. He engaged us in creative dialogue to produce results we are prouder of—and managed to make the process enjoyable rather than arduous.

Publisher Martha Levin made extra time to lobby enthusiastically for the book. Andrea Au and Michele Jacob were always efficient and smart in their handling of both our book and us.

On a personal level, Ed wishes to thank four individuals who were instrumental in his career development at critical stages: George Gerbner, Madelyn Hochstein, and the aforementioned Jay Wilson and Bud Roper. He is indebted to the four of them for the faith they had in him and all they taught him. And the love of his family—his wife Karen and children Isabel and Meredith—lifts him up and inspires him day in and day out.

Jon would like to add thanks to his family, Robin, Joel, and Flynn, for keeping him on course and keeping faith; his brother, Steve, and extended Berry and Ramey families, his first and in many ways most important teachers after his parents; his mentors, starting with Richard Reynolds and Jerry Woodring; and his alma mater, Earlham College, for offering him a haven to write.

Finally, we thank most especially the twelve individuals who shared their stories with us so graciously to help bring our research findings to life: Walter Arrowsmith, Tim Draper, Sophie Glovier, Teresa Graham, Larry Lee, Jr., Isabel Milano, Shelley Miller, Dave Pendergrass, Leonard Pitt, Sarah Vokes, Rick White, and Mike Williams. Their generosity, insights, and active engagement in their communities make *The Influentials* a better book, living proof of what makes America a fascinating unfolding story.

Ed Keller is the CEO of RoperASW. A global marketing research and consulting firm, RoperASW serves many of the world's leading companies in the areas of brand strategy, customer loyalty management, corporate reputation, and communications effectiveness. A nationally recognized expert on marketing and consumer trends, Keller serves on the board of directors of the Advertising Research Foundation and is a member of the Market Research Council.

Jon Berry is a vice president with RoperASW and senior research director of Roper Reports, which for 30 years has been tracking consumer trends for many Fortune 500 companies and leading brands acrosss multiple industries. Berry is a former marketing editor of *BusinessWeek,* features editor and columnist for *Brandweek,* and San Francisco bureau manager for *Adweek.*